For Dad

Media Control

Media Control

News as an Institution of Power
and Social Control

ROBERT E. GUTSCHE, JR.

Bloomsbury Academic
An imprint of Bloomsbury Publishing Inc

B L O O M S B U R Y

NEW YORK • LONDON • OXFORD • NEW DELHI • SYDNEY

Bloomsbury Academic

An imprint of Bloomsbury Publishing Inc

1385 Broadway	50 Bedford Square
New York	London
NY 10018	WC1B 3DP
USA	UK

www.bloomsbury.com

BLOOMSBURY and the Diana logo are trademarks of Bloomsbury Publishing Plc

First published 2015
Paperback edition first published 2017

Library of Congress Cataloging-in-Publication Data
Gutsche, Robert E., 1980-
Media control : news as an institution of power and
social control / Robert E. Gutsche, Jr.
pages cm '
Includes bibliographical referecens and index.
ISBN 978-1-62892-296-7 (hardback)
1. Mass media–Political aspects–United States–History–20th century.
2. Mass media–Political aspects–United States–History–21st century.
3. Journalism–Political aspects–United States–History–20th century.
4. Journalism–Political aspects–United States–History–21st century.
5. Press and politics–United States. 6. Social control–United States. I. Title.
P95.82.U6G88 2015
302.23'0973–dc23
2015015866

ISBN: HB: 978-1-6289-2296-7
PB: 978-1-5013-2013-2
ePub: 978-1-6289-2295-0
ePDF: 978-1-6289-2294-3

Typeset by Integra Software Services Pvt. Ltd.

Contents

Preface

This book is just as much a "come to Jesus" for me in terms of my relationship to journalism, education, scholarship, and the daily fight for equal treatment in our media, as it is commentary on media. To set a tone for my purpose, then, I share the following statements that motivate and shape me more than I could ever say in a preface made of my own words. I have cited the origins of the statements to the best of my knowledge.

About Journalism

I may be rancid butter, but I'm on your side of the bread.

– E. K. HORNBECK, A NEWSPAPER COLUMNIST SAID TO BE BASED ON H. L. MENCKEN IN THE PLAY AND FILM INHERIT THE WIND

Newspapers aren't always on the side of liberty. Not everyone agrees on what liberty means. Some struggles never end. And it's not the newspaper that's forever at risk of dying and needing to be raised from the grave. It's the freedom of the press.

– JILL LEPORE, "THE DAY THE NEWSPAPER DIED," THE NEW YORKER, JANUARY 26, 2009

Prior review by administrators undermines critical thinking, encourages students to dismiss the role of a free press in society and provides no greater likelihood of increased quality of student media.

– JOURNALISM EDUCATION ASSOCIATION'S ADVISERS CODE OF ETHICS

About Life & Learning

You are what you think.
The better the writer is, the more the writer appreciates
the editing. The worse the writer is, the more the writer
complains.

– *MATTHEW ROTHSCHILD, EDITOR OF* PROGRESSIVE MAGAZINE,
IN ISTHMUS, *MAY 1, 2009*

Life is not a race.
I'm sorry for talking while you were interrupting me.
Brick walls are there for a reason.
They let us prove how badly we want things.

– *AUTHOR RANDY PAUSCH IN* THE LAST LECTURE, *2007*

About Books

Books are notes from the field, bound and domesticated, life
brought into narrow focus. Get rid of a book? No way. Everyone
is a brick keeping the building standing. Books are my life. I leave
and come back, and the books I find there tell me I'm home.

– *NOVELIST JOSHUA FERRIS, IN* THE NEW YORK TIMES
ROOM FOR DEBATE BLOG, DECEMBER 27, 2009

These scattered thoughts coalesce, for me anyway, in a way of thinking that questions everything, that demands interrogation, and that, with a tone of urgency, stands for social justice, yet it is with these thoughts in mind that I wish for the reader to begin this project.

Robert E. Gutsche, Jr.
May 2015
Miami, Florida

Acknowledgments

I am thankful to a host of people who have contributed to this book. I first wish to thank my editor, Katie Gallof, and the reviewers who all helped strengthen the book's purpose and approach. I also thank Bianca Morrison, who worked as a research assistant for the first stages of this project and continued to supply vital insights, criticism, and solutions to make the writing clear and concrete. Special thanks go to Andre Brock and Scott McKenzie who have been mainstays of support nearly every day as writing partners. Others who have provided insight upon what appear in the following pages include Dušan Bjelić, Kristy Hess, Jack Lule, Bob Franklin, Annie Franklin, Judy Polumbaum, LaTasha DeLoach, and Karina Blanco.

Without Frank Durham giving me the knowledge and the sense of power to embark on a life of scholarship, this project and most of my scholarship would never have emerged. I have also benefited from the support and conversations with Mary Fisher, Dan Berkowitz, Erica Salkin, and the staff and faculty at Florida International University's School of Journalism and Mass Communications, including Juliet Pinto, who continues to provide much support for my work. Teresa Ponte and Maria Elena Villar have also been guiding lights, as has Dave Park, who was always available with a boost of deep thoughts. Special thanks go also to Moses Shumow for his collaborations and his comments on early versions of this project.

Without doubt, I am also indebted to my many semesters of students who have all challenged and shaped the messages I present here. At the risk of excluding names, I wish to thank students who contributed directly to this project: Alicia Sandino, Stephanie Mason, Charnele Michel, and students in my Fall 2014 Digital Theories course and my Fall 2014 and Spring 2015 Theories of Mass Communications courses for their inspiration and comments.

Introduction

Chapter Purpose

This introduction presents the book's overarching purposes and approach. It introduces the reader to my own experiences with media—and in media—in an effort to ground the project not only in a theoretical framework, but also to validate the ideas presented throughout the book as being a personal and scholarly examination of the role of media in everyday life. The second part of the introduction places this project in today's landscape of increasingly overt forms of surveillance and social control on the part of world governments and news outlets. The chapter ends with an outline of the book.

Guiding Questions

1. What's the definition of "news"?
2. How might one measure the potential influence of news in terms of how we interpret everyday ideas and activities?

Key Terms

Ideology: Explanations of and meanings assigned to everyday life that serve the powerful and are evidenced by socially acceptable and unquestioned data

Media Control: The common practices of news construction, institutions, and representations that occur across media outlets and mediums as a means to justify and enforce elements of social control

Power: A fluid and inherent ability to influence individuals and social situations through force, ideology, and/or information

---

THE EXPERIENCE OF EXPERIENCING POWER: A BEGINNING

We each wield power. Most of the time we do so without applying physical force. Efforts to employ power in everyday life are a bit hard to identify. It takes power for me to convince you to do something or for me to do something you suggest. It takes power to wake up in the morning, to decide to purchase one thing over another, or whether to purchase anything at all. Our power is at the center of what we create and what we destroy. Power operates through the choices we make about where to go, who to talk to, and how to respond to our surroundings. Power is in our language and in our interactions with each other, with things, and with ideas. And that power is exerted to control.

We use our power to control—or to attempt to control—an outcome of a conversation between friends or enemies. Sometimes, we wish to control the actions of others. Yet, in many ways, each of these types of power-control scenarios relies on power that most of the time is absent of fists and weapons. In fact, physical force is rarely the best indicator of power's presence. Force is, in and of itself, a moment of power being exerted, yet within and behind the physicality of force steeps the power of veiled or unspoken relationships related to pressures and complexities of contested meanings of language, rhetoric, and rationales for our actions. It is that type of power, particularly related to the press, that this book explores. For this project, I define *power* as a fluid and inherent ability to influence individuals and social situations through force, ideology, and/or information—and control.

My hope for this project, first, is to successfully argue for an approach that recognizes power as force in which it is seen as a verb as much as a noun, revealing the *act of power* in how it appears and is applied in and through our social activity. Power lives in ideology and in the ability we each have to interpret, to accept, or to diminish dominant interpretations of life, and my focus on *this power*, for the purpose of this project, operates around actions, interpretations, and indoctrinations of and through the press. Therefore, my arguments throughout these pages revolve around the claim that the press, too, is an *ideological act of power*. I make these arguments as a means to assist in the radicalization of the field of Journalism Studies.

My second hope for this project is to challenge normative—and maybe also other cultural—interpretations of the press as being merely representatives of or observers of power systems. Rather, I contend that the press should be viewed *as its own* power system and one that is *of* dominant power systems that are focused on control. This is not the way the press is normally discussed in journalism scholarship. I do not ignore, then, the many other scholars in this field who acknowledge elements of power within journalistic decision-making, within journalistic organizations, within relationships of sourcing, ownership, and in terms of how power may be identified within dominant press explanations. However, many of these scholars release the institution and individuals of the press—and those who argue that the press serve the public—from any sense of responsibility for social policies and conditions within which the media orchestrate on behalf of the power elite. Certainly, debate related to the media in the United States surrounds several popular themes:

- The degree to which the press is politically liberal or conservative
- The ways in which the press may influence public discourse and individual thought on social and cultural issues
- The financial and political benefits to corporate owners of media monopolies
- How effective individuals can be both inside and outside of media outlets to create "change" and challenge the status quo
- The possible function of social media to diminish the voice of dominant, mainstream press

These, however, are not the debates I wish to have in this project. Instead, I am interested in making direct connections between the control function of the power elite (see Chapter 1), which is rooted in physical force and threats of physical force, and that appears in indoctrination tactics, including the farce of a publically invested news media. I am not fully alone in this critique, though many of the voices, including for instance, Robert McChesney, who contributes to a similar discussion through a framework of political economy, skirt the issues of culture that inform control systems inherent within the mediated elements of daily life. Even Edward Herman and Noam Chomsky[1]—those who might first come to mind as arguing for media as a tool for propaganda (see Chapter 1)—do not, to my satisfaction, apply control as a mainstay function of the press.

Rather, media scholars tend to showcase the interactions between the press and other institutions in ways that shape society in sociological terms. Missing is the critical analysis that connects media to the power elite in ideological terms that results in moments of force upon the subjugated, of oppression in the silencing of the alternative, and in the purposeful distraction of the public from intentional collaborations between the press and the power elite. Feminist scholars are likely the most aligned with the approach I am describing, though little critical, feminist work appears in Journalism Studies itself in ways that implicate the press as benefiting dominant cultures of control and as obfuscating the histories of today and yesterday for future dissemination that maintains the status quo (see Chapter 4).

As political economists and radical scholars, Herman and Chomsky—and those influenced by their work—address the function of the press to indoctrinate the public to the wishes and aims of the power elite, including corporations, governments, and demagogues. Still, much of this work is based on a national and international level of media creation and dissemination in ways that discuss the function of the high levels of government and business in ideological collaboration with elite and establishment press. Ignoring the local level of the press as they do—the hometown paper and regional news outlets that broadcast to localized audiences and function as a level of our media system that reaches the widest audiences—limits the public's ability to deeply interrogate the ideological control that the press push upon our ranks of society closer to home. As I discuss in Chapter 2, scholars attempt to explain this local effect of the press through agenda-setting—the idea that dominant media outlets influence the newsworthiness and meanings of particular issues that then seep through the media ecosystem. But, this still is not what I am attempting to discuss in *Media Control*.

Our society's dedication to Western, hegemonic control in every facet of our lives—reinforced, if necessary, by force—contributes to local manifestations of such force and control in our neighborhood schools, in the back yards of our friends and neighbors, on our main streets, in the suburbs, and in inner-cities, in a city's outer rings, and in local city council chambers and voting booths that is rationalized, normalized, and even celebrated by the press.

The degree to which local control is critical to the success of a larger power elite is why much of this book discusses national or international issues through the lens of local coverage from second- and third-tier cities in the United States. So, while *The New York Times* and CNN are mentioned and analyzed in this book, there is a shared commitment to places and news outlets that rarely appear in journalism research, though their contribution to local community identity and the application of power elite ideologies are forefront in the outlets' operations. Explicating the operation of "media control" at the local level—which in this case I am considering of a geographic region and space within a larger sphere of nationhood—is vital for understanding the degree to which news media focus on ideological indoctrination to dominant cultural norms and on the assimilation of the public to desires of the power elite.

Processes of control that exist within the work of media do not rely solely on individual extensions of power, on the role of a viewer to influence another, nor on the hope that groups will influence other groups. Members of media and representations of dominant culture within media must function in tandem with each other, to be pushed from one level to another, reified, and challenged in ways that result in the maintenance of dominant ideology. In this, I am describing a process of culture constructed by interactions of normative and ideological functions of the press, and I am calling for an examination of what I refer to as *media control*—the common practices of news construction, institutions, and representations that occur across media outlets and mediums as a means to justify and enforce elements of social control. Through this exercise and a rearticulation of the functions and processes of the press discussed elsewhere in several scholarly and professional disciplines, my final hope for this project is for it to help us better understand the close connections the press make between news of the day and the dominant meanings of our daily lives.

There is no need to rebuild the wheel of understanding related to the workings of media in order to build a concept of "media control." The parts are already there. For instance, interpreting communication as culture, as James Carey does,[2] with its cultural rituals, myths, narratives, and meanings—elements beyond the purview of scholars identified earlier in this introduction—complicates even the most banal of news. We need not to rehash the value or virtue of this approach. We need only to further complicate what has been complicated. In other words, "media control" is something that has existed since communication/media was formed.

This project, however, presents approaches and analysis that raise the application of radical interpretations of media to make it more likely for members of society to see elements of control within things such as local coverage of high school proms, car crashes, house fires, graduations and retirements—even obituaries. Each of these types of stories holds cultural meaning and is designed and replicated across society to align local communities with interests of a larger power elite. Take a simple example: News coverage of local parades, for example, embeds into narratives of the event "traditional American values" that are reinforced by stories of "the hometown" in which photojournalism features flags of the United States and scenes of children interacting with members of the Armed Forces and local police during a welcome "invasion" of military and police activity; overarching narratives of explanation and personification within these stories themselves tend to promote a single community identity that elevates uniformity.

In these ways, a simple parade story creates an "us/them" dynamic within a single geographic area that present dominant stories of desirable community activities, behaviors, and people and exclude counter-narratives that confuse clean articulations of what the community "is." My own early—and some of my late—days of reporting focused on creating and re-creating these senses of the "hometown," particularly during US holidays. It is hard for a news outlet to ignore big community events, but it is even more unheard of for local news outlets to diminish the local patriotism of our communities in our coverage. Parade coverage, then, provides an opportunity not only to "cover" events of the day but also to "cover" the dominant ideological position of American Exceptionalism that connects our local communities to larger notions of nation.

On July 4, 2001, for instance, I wrote about the holiday's "meanings" for the local community of La Crosse, Wisconsin, for its newspaper, the *Tribune*. In that piece, I positioned the article around the people at a large river-front celebration:

> If Bill Budd and Sharon De Blieck dress up as George Washington and Thomas Jefferson next Fourth of July, they can count De Blieck's daughter out.
>
> Heidi Wiebke, 17, stood along the Mississippi River in Riverside Park on Wednesday, while the older couple talked about patriotism. She was embarrassed by their idea of perhaps coming back next July 4, dressed as two of America's Founding Fathers. All three live in La Crescent, Minn.
>
> Thousands came to the first day of the Riverfest celebration, in the park where the river overflowed only a few months ago. Crowds cheered as water-skiers flipped and jumped on the river. Others sunbathed on the grass.
>
> Some people came to the park with lawn chairs, some bearing U.S. flag designs. But that symbol of patriotism didn't satisfy Budd and De Blieck.
>
> "I would hope," Budd said, "that today would be more about the Fourth of July" than the start of Riverfest, which continues through Sunday.

After introducing the story's characters (also known as sources), the story focused on the "meanings" of the day, their activities, and of the news article itself:

> On the far south end of the park, Budd, De Blieck and Wiebke set up their lawn chairs. They talked about the sacrifices of people like Washington, Jefferson and John Adams in the fight for American independence. "Those people lost their homes and a lot of their lives," Budd said of some early American patriots. "But the people here celebrate the fireworks instead of the meanings of today."

De Blieck said the Founding Fathers sacrificed family life because of the fight for independence. "They must have spent so much time away from their families," she said. "And their families probably didn't want to go to Pennsylvania with them and probably did not understand what they were doing. That must have been hard."

The couple wish there was an authentic re-creation of the signing of the Declaration of Independence in La Crosse. They said they may try to organize one for next year, so people can have a better understanding of the holiday.[3]

By the end of the tale, the dominant, "normal" behavior and ideologies have become quite clear, so much so that there is little room to interpret the story's—and the newspaper's—position on US history, the importance of celebrating the nation's "birth," and the rewards that are assigned to those who exude proper Americanism.

One might expect such patriotic coverage about such a patriotic event, yet the type of media control that this book discusses is of a more embedded nature in which events and issues of the day are not presented in specific and overt frames of meaning—such as in the example above—that benefits dominant structures of patriotism, exceptionalism, and racial superiority. The overt stories of American Exceptionalism, like what I have shared, formulate the dominant meanings of acceptable identities approved by the power elite that guide what is later pronounced through language, embedded more subtly within larger familiar storylines of explanation and consistent messages over time that appear in everyday news across mediums, news outlets, political lines, and generations of journalists and audiences. In other words, there are hints as to the meanings that the audience is to understand in everyday news that are reinforced by the occasional overt lesson on "American values," many of which are connected to recognizing and maintaining the authority and virtue of institutions of dominance and authority, particularly the authority of institutions of discipline and punishment with which news media are direct collaborators.

Below, I provide a brief example of how the press formulate constructs of power messaging that may help the reader understand how I am approaching the news as acts of control.

The article that appears at left is one I wrote in the *Wisconsin State Journal* in Madison, Wisconsin, in 2002. Headlined, "Man is shot in parking lot" and carrying a subhead of "Victim was behind a Town of Madison apartment building when he was hit in right arm, abdomen," the article provides a subtle, but clear, reinforcement of the status quo in terms of providing "acceptable" forms of evidence for understanding daily news events. At the right column,

Original text	Explanation of text
A man was shot in the right arm and abdomen behind an apartment building Sunday night.	The story begins by focusing on the most significant information—someone was shot—while the headline contributed the location and other details. Already, we "know" what the story is.
The man, who was in surgery at an unidentified Madison hospital Sunday night, was shot about 8:45 p.m. when he was in the back parking lot of the apartment building at 2717 Pheasant Ridge Trail, off East Badger Road.	In the second paragraph, the reader is told details of when and where the event occurred, the geographic element of which provides meaning by tapping into any dominant ideologies of particular neighborhoods or addresses. Further, meaning is assigned to the event if audiences see the geography as a "bad side of town." If so, the crime is awarded even more drama and surprise.
Police said the injuries were nonlife-threatening. No arrests had been made by late Sunday. Two men have been interviewed as witnesses to the shooting, said Scott Gregory, acting town of Madison police chief. He said police are looking for an older, white four-door car seen leaving after the shooting. Gregory said the shooting victim wasn't from the Madison area.	In the third through fifth graphs, "the police" appear as a source, that stand alone from other sources. Thus, the reader is left to insinuate that the "facts" presented above were provided by police and are of absolute authority.
Victor Dixon, 23, of Madison said he knew the man who had been shot and was visiting with him at the apartment building before the shooting.	By the sixth graph, the story has established its "truth" to the degree that any witnesses—even if counter to the dominant "truth" of the story—can appear to further drama through personification, in which the story becomes about human lives rather than sterile information.

Dixon said he left for about thirty minutes. When he returned, he saw people surrounding the man, bloodied by the gunshot wounds and lying in a hallway inside the building.

"I don't know why someone would do this," Dixon said. "He don't know nobody here."

The last two graphs characterize the case at hand, the location of where the event occurred, and the people involved in the story. The police source is presented as an institution with a minor acknowledgment of the human element besides the police chief's name. Further, that the article stated the victim "wasn't from the Madison area" and presented the witness's comments in "improper grammar," the reader is left to interpret meanings associated with just what type of person was involved in the shooting—and possibly why.

I present a short structural analysis of the elements of power and control that build throughout the article.[4]

The above analysis is meant to be generalizable only to the degree that it helps to present the particular patterns of storytelling that journalists are trained to follow that meet the needs of both journalistic production and of explaining social conditions that appear in the news. More specifically, I used the above example because it represents everyday news storytelling in that it:

- Is focused, at the time, on a recent event of supposed interest to the perceived audience

- Includes local geographies as being settings within which the meanings of the story are played out

- Presents local institutions, such as the police, as a single source of explanation and authority with which an individual's interpretations of the news event are to be aligned

I do not remember the night I wrote that brief story, but after years of examining the journalistic form and processes—including my own experiences within social and cultural environments of journalism—I can determine, with some certainty, the degree to which I was "aware" in the crafting of this story and hundreds of others like it of the embedded cultural meanings—a process Stuart Hall refers to as a stage of "encoding"—that would then be "decoded" by the reader.

Turning to the shooting story above, for example, I obviously interviewed someone related to the event other than police sources, but in terms of presenting the "facts" of the story, the article was still single-sourced in that it relied only on the police as an institution from which to gain information and "facts." Dixon, the victim's friend I had talked to and quoted, for instance, did not serve as providing "facts" of the case for the story; he was instead at the end of the story to provide what we call "color," a term used to refer to action, environment, and detail. It was only the police official who was considered worthy enough for me to break a journalistic cardinal rule that mandates journalists verify and triangulate information that they present in the news through multiple sources.

In each hard news story ever written, the structure of the story, unless given adequate space and relevance that would alter normal circumstances—all of which would be determined by a host of factors within the newsroom that day—begins with "just the facts," specifically facts coming from police sources, the theory being that the police are a universal, trustworthy, and authoritative source. Furthermore, the argument goes that police information goes through a process of filtering and verification of its own within the police organization so that when it is funneled to the reporter, she can take it as verified "fact." So while some of the structuring of the news story depends on the resources available to report the news and on the access to space to publish the news, the journalist also relies on the validity of sources necessary to maintain a sense of journalistic "objectivity." In this case, the assumption is that the police themselves, are "objective" sources of information that could not possibly bias press articulations of the "truth." Such an assumption allows us to begin to argue for more radical understandings of media control by identifying the control mechanism that exists between police and press in terms of shaping the information released to the public.[5]

But to argue as journalists and scholars interested in normative and social scientific explanations of the news often do that I as the reporter and my editors did not operate with knowledge of how to craft news as a consumer product by using stories of shootings, poor grammar, and police information, would be misleading. Just as journalists are socialized to journalistic norms and values (see Chapter 2), they are trained in storytelling and ways of explaining the world that empower them to:

- Select "newsworthy" stories that will be viewed as favorable and meaningful items for audiences so as not to disrupt the flow of capital to news creation by publishing something that would be counter to audience tastes

- Provide, when applicable, dramatic storytelling in which sources are characters and environments are settings within which the characters play out the events of the day and reveal common and shared social conflicts and power relations that reflect a "reality" recognized by audiences

- Present the news with moral meanings for interpretation within a collective (i.e., the news audience) in ways that reify dominant cultural and social norms and that punish members of society who operate outside of these norms

- Maintain the social and cultural authority of the press itself and of fellow social institutions for even further legitimization in future times of social and ideological crises

- Require the power messages to be interpreted by the audiences in ways that distance journalists from fellow institutions and claims of explanation that run counter to their proposed purpose of serving the public with objective information

Indeed, in the police story above—which, admittedly in some communities would be considered banal, while in others it would serve as an example of "big news"—the text relies on the reader to make meaning and to ascribe relevance on her own. In 2002, the City of Madison (not the Town of Madison, which was landlocked by the city) saw three murders, for instance, compared to eight the year prior and six in 2003. In other words, for a region of some 500,000 people, the murder rate was quite low, as were other forms of violence, including shootings at the time. Without an everyday narrative of what violence existed and what it meant, journalists and their audiences were left to imagine the details of the crime and to construct meanings to what was considered in the press as counter to the "norm."[6]

The role of news myth (see Chapter 2), then, becomes vital to explaining the world through stories and narratives grounded in the power of dominant ideology that is told and retold through authoritative means. The "imaginative power" of news storytelling via myth and its tool of verisimilitude allows journalists and audiences to interpret and tell meaningful tales about the everyday in ways that equate "facts" to "truth" and the omnipresence of journalism and its sources as an authoritative and objective narration that can be cast as only "reporting the news" in service to the public. The authority and power ascribed to journalism veils the process of manipulation of information that is conducted through journalistic processes and production.

Beyond subscribing to the sense of authority that is assigned to media messages, audiences (which include sources, officials, the traditional media consumer, and journalists themselves) validate explanations of and solutions for issues of the day, which often relate to the use of (or threat of) authorized force and discipline. Naturalized manifestations of force or discipline and the threats of such action are as imagined as the tales within news stories. As Christopher Hedges writes in his book focused on violence, "When we allow mythical reality to rule, as it almost always does in war, then there is only one solution—force."[7] Elsewhere, he states:

Every society, ethnic group or religion nurtures certain myths, often centered around the creation of the nation or the movement itself. These myths lie unseen beneath the surface, waiting for the moment to rise ascendant, to define and glorify followers or members in times of crisis.[8]

It is these notions of war and of myth as applied in the press that I wish to address throughout this work. I will be complicating the notion of "war" and violence later but insist on expressing here first that I approach our society as one in which we live a perpetual war of ideology and power (see Chapter 4) through which we not only apply violence in terms of fighting physical battles with physical weapons, but with immaterial ones, as well. Our emotional and cognitive battles are the ones in which dominant articulations of gender, masculinity, nationalism, virtue, ethnicity, and race play a formative role in the emergence or maintenance of control and power, elements which play out through the following pages.[9]

In the end, analysis of local news through a lens of power and control, which has often been more acceptable in examining the embedding of dominant ideologies of the nation's power elite on national and international stages,[10] reveals power as inherent in all aspects of knowledge and understanding and in the processes of interpretations of the everyday that, in order to maintain one's legitimacy in society, meet the standards and norms of the safe and popular, that are then used to justify harm through police and military action, harm through ideological social control of what is "good" and "acceptable" in social interactions of youth, and harm in the support of police brutality that penetrates our schools and communities with the support of citizens who sit idly or by the press that propagandize the benefits of violence. "The news media and law," write the authors of *Representing Order*, "also (share) an affinity in claiming that their policing is in the public interest." Indeed, they write that:

[t]he basis of this claim is the appearance of neutrality. The consequence of this claim is that the news media and law are able to accomplish a degree of legitimacy and authority for their own institutions, while also

selectively underpinning or undercutting legitimacy and authority of other social institutions.[11]

The authors might be correct in their assessment of selective, institutional conflict as a core feature of media power and control, but as I argue in this work, the "underpinning or undercutting" of institutions is a *performance* to suggest a distance between the institutions and an independence of thought and is an *act* to counter any potential claims from the public of institutional collaboration that would threaten the sanctity of journalistic objectivity (see discussion of "flak" in Chapter 1). Throughout the rest of this chapter, I place myself further into the creation of this project by explicating not only my ideological positions related to media and control but also to examine the role my own experiences with media that have contributed to the construction of these beliefs.

Clarifying constructs and characterizations

The reader should note that by this point I use the terms "the press," "news," "journalism," and even "the media" interchangeably. While I acknowledge the potential complications in applying these terms so widely, I do so because I reject that each term in today's press/news/journalism/media landscape holds fast its own clear and common definition. At a time when "infotainment" has become "news," political and news satire serves as "journalism," and corporate conglomeration has blurred the lines between concepts of "the media" as being news, as being "news-as-entertainment," and as being "media-as-entertainment," a single term in this conversation about news and power provides little clarity.

   I will, however, throughout this project define the specifics related to the "news" of which I will be examining, yet even those specifics should not determine for the reader the degree to which news *is or is not* entertainment, for instance. Still, by leaving these definitions fluid, the reader is able to add her own interpretation to the arguments being made and to focus on the ideological acts of media rather than to focus on a specific field or sector that might mire critical analysis of communication as action.

   As I discuss in greater detail in Chapter 4 and again in the Conclusion, debate about terminology and conceptualizations often serves not to provide nuance and to empower but to distract us (1) from maintaining a sense of clarity about how power systems operate and (2) from examining the potential surrounding the roles we may hold in our social systems as consumers, journalists, scholars, students, and citizens.[12]

It is my hope, then, that by blending and blurring terminology, we can confuse the conceptualizations of exactly what media and medium is at play—and in what ways—in the cases this book discusses. Throughout the confusion of examining what we believe is "so," but with parameters that I hope to form for the purposes of these discussions, we may be able to come to new and advanced interpretations of modern messaging that some of us have never imagined. I also recognize that this project joins a large library of work on journalism, Journalism Studies, and perspectives on power, control, and social order. Yet, what appears in the following pages, much of it built upon the work I have been doing in Journalism Studies over the past several years, is meant to identify the press as an act of power at multiple levels of social performance and cultural meaning. Specifically, and as I have discussed earlier, I am interested in how such power is enacted in everyday, daily journalism—particularly journalism that occurs locally. And, it is more on this point I wish to discuss before moving forward.[13]

As I briefly touched upon above and discuss in more detail in Chapter 3, news media are as much a product of geographic markets as they are of economic markets of capitalism, which is an important perspective to understand when dealing with the ideological meanings assigned to local news media messaging. Whereas in capitalism the market provides the financial systems for survival, the news medias' connection to geographies and related ideologies of the geographic collectives provides the authority and legitimacy upon which the press act to enforce dominant power dynamics. In other words, the press function as a force of power and control by telling stories and providing explanations of specific regions and areas of their audiences *to their audiences*. News organizations define the meanings of world events and events from other geographies through the lens of the local news audience in an attempt to always connect news of the day to local lives and local ideologies that, in turn, reinforce the legitimacy of the local journalists who are telling the stories.

The connection of geographies to the lives and times of local audiences explains the rationale for journalistic localization and specific pages within local publications that discuss "World News," "Regional News," and the very use of the dateline—the words that appear at the beginning of news articles that place the story within a specific space. These words, OFTEN WRITTEN IN ALL-CAPS, either indicate where the journalist was when reporting the story, or as has become the norm throughout the news industry, merely serve as a marketing tool for showing audiences the wide reach of the news organization, even if the reporter wrote the piece from behind her desk in the newsroom. Datelines, therefore, represent how locality functions as both ideological and financial constructs through which the press operate to reify the power positions of fellow institutions and cultural positions.

In building an argument for expanding the contribution of local media messaging to the studies of media power and control, I have tried, when appropriate, to analyze local news coverage in places where I have either lived or worked as a journalist—places where I might be able to interpret local social and cultural spheres as presented by the press because of my interactions with those environments and, in some cases, involvement through those media outlets. All of this is to explain why readers will be introduced to some places within the United States of which they may never have heard—from small-town Tomah, Wisconsin, where I spent much of my childhood, to Milwaukee, Wisconsin; Omaha, Nebraska; Iowa City, Iowa; and Miami Gardens, Florida.

While scholars can certainly write about places they have never been, for this project I wanted to focus, largely, on places I may know a little more about to help place the analysis of media control in each situation to some of the specific cultural and social environments occurring at the time of news events. In the spirit of qualitative cultural examinations of communication and culture, I subscribe to the validity of one's ability to blend personal experiences expressed within a reflexive framework of language and *ideology*—explanations of and meanings assigned to everyday life that serve the powerful, what Thompson defines as "meaning in the service of power."[14]

This is not to say that I am an expert on the complexities within each of these locations, but such context helps when making deeper, ideological connections as a way to express my meanings of "media control." Another reason for examining the local effect of media control in the local media of these places is to challenge whatever public imagination might exist about these locations. Iowa, for instance—often confused with Idaho and other Midwestern and Plains states that look and sound similar—is a space of great migration of inner-city blacks over the past thirty years that has created challenges in terms of how long-time Iowans welcome and interpret newcomers.

The Midwest, in general, continues to be a growing hotbed of racial tension that has occurred in discriminatory educational treatment and an over-criminalization of blacks. The murder of a young black man by a white police officer in Ferguson, Missouri, in 2014, for instance, attracted national attention in discussions about racialized policing and militarization of local police forces (see Chapter 4). Another murder of a young black man by a white police officer occurred in early 2015 in Madison, Wisconsin, a city steeped in local public imaginations as a liberal bastion, but that has an unspoken history of racialized educational and policing institutions.[15]

The Midwest does not escape its own horrors of police conduct that is representative of the acts of police murder that occur across the United States. Just as *The New York Times* reported in February 2015 about years of brutal treatment of inmates in an Attica prison, *The Guardian* released a report that Chicago police used a Homan Square warehouse codenamed "black site" to abuse minority suspects and others who protested against police activity since at least 2011. In March 2015, National Public Radio reported (1) that in Milwaukee, public schools were found to be suspending "black high school students at a rate nearly double the national average," (2) that the state "incarcerates the most black men in the country," and (3) that such efforts may be aligned with "sentencing and policing policies that disproportionately affect African-Americans."[16]

Examining local media messaging of spaces throughout the Midwest not only challenges any imaginations of these as being "fly-over states" that grow corn and churn cheese but that hold meaningful moments of power and control that shape the lives of people living there. Furthermore, I wish to use examples from these places to articulate the problems associated with today's post-race ideologies and ignorance related to racial and ethnic identities that have been frequently shared with me in the past few years, particularly the racist comments that also come from black social activists, such as, "I didn't know there were black people in Iowa."

South Florida, another location where much of this book is focused, is equally as mired in public imaginations of itself—particularly of Miami of the 1980s, the *Miami Vice* days of drug-running and bank robbery shootouts. Even locally, South Florida's communities are cast in a bright light of imagination of Miami and its highlife, including the spaces of South Beach, the luxury of Lincoln Road, and the fashion and entertainment industries that cast the region in a limelight of flash and flair. Miami-Dade County alone, however, has more than thirty incorporated cities, and more people living in unincorporated Miami-Dade County than in incorporated areas. The complexities of these dozens of governments, of identities formed so much around recent immigrants and the Cuban influx of the twentieth century, and of fractured geographies based on economic inequality create a complex cultural sphere.

But even South Florida is not aware of its own competing "geographic imaginaries." Hispanics and Latinos make up a supermajority of Miami-Dade County with those categories being further split based upon what Latin, South American, and even Caribbean influences have emerged each decade of the region's development. US blacks, then, living in South Florida become merged in the public image with Haitians, dark-skinned Latin and South Americans, Cubans and Dominicans.

In early 2015, for example, local public radio in Miami reported that, according to recent studies on segregation in the United States, "four of the ten metro areas with the lowest levels of poverty segregation are in Florida—Orlando, Tampa, Miami and Jacksonville." Overall, the study from the

University of Toronto's Martin Prosperity Institute, ranked South Florida "in the top 10 percent most segregated metro areas in the United States."[17]

That white folk (i.e., Anglos who do not identify as Hispanic or Latino) only make up some 15 percent of Miami-Dade's 2.6 million people provides a sense to the population here that this is a "diverse" region. But, as the news messages from South Florida that I focus upon in this project reveal, traditional White Supremacy upon which dominant US ideology is based is not absent. And, it is for this reason that I have selected two vastly different regions of the United States to focus most of my analysis of news coverage, save for the moments of analysis elsewhere. Again, my hope is to challenge dominant place-meanings of US geographies through which one can examine the ideological acts of media messaging without being mired in the safety of "knowing" what one thinks she knows about a particular place or people.

Explicating media experiences

This project has its roots in my own early interactions with power—and with the control associated with it—which were often connected with the press, not to mention, of course, the many moments of punishment and influence of childhood that just come from other avenues of control. My early connection between power and control and this thing called "the news" began on weekend mornings when I would sit with my parents in a coffee shop in small-town Tomah, Wisconsin.

Together, we would spend at least an hour each of these mornings flipping through the pages of the *Milwaukee Journal* and the *Milwaukee Sentinel*—and then what became the *Milwaukee Journal Sentinel*. On those mornings, my parents would order a second (or third) pot of coffee, and we would not leave until every drop was finished.

They read the *La Crosse* (Wisconsin) *Tribune*, the local *Tomah Journal* and *Tomah Monitor-Herald*, and the *Wisconsin State Journal*, published in Madison. My parents would grab sections of the *Chicago Tribune*, if available in the free pile of papers at the cash register, and we would pass them around the table, the pile of print at its center in constant movement. I would go on to write for each of these newspapers as a young adult, the experiences of which taught me the tools and rules of the trade and led to me teaching for an industry that I now both love and hate.

I know now that I was lucky then. My family did not have much money, but we had enough for these weekly breakfasts, and my parents had the time to spend in such leisure to read editorials about current events and to discuss news stories about local issues and people. I would listen as they would debate the issues that appeared on the pages. And, while I do not pretend that I understood exactly what they were talking about, I was able to pick up on the trends of what was important to them—crime, taxes, governance, and economics.

What I found was that my family and their friends focused much of their daily conversations about concerns and worries, joys and interests, on what they had seen or heard in the news. It is not that these folks were not able to create or tell their own stories outside of the news, but there was something about having the "most information" about a topic to carry on conversation, to become civically "invested" through voting on these issues and people, by attending town hall and union meetings as my father did, and ultimately by recognizing a power system in which decisions that we may make as individuals may not be our own and that our efforts at employing agency can come with consequences.

At home, my parents would religiously watch the *CBS Evening News*, and it was there where the discussions I was exposed to by my parents at the coffee shop, in my school classrooms and textbooks, and in entertainment were reified and justified by talking heads on the nightly news. I found that the news was where consequences for individual actions and collective decisions played out in war and social unrest and where the world was explained. I remember my interactions with TV news as occurring as early as the Challenger space shuttle explosion in 1986 (I was five) and in news coverage of the Ross Perot presidential campaign in 1992. I was twelve at the time of Perot's run, and I remember forcing my parents to stop the car at a crowded intersection in Milwaukee just so I could get a Perot yard sign. I remember that I was a fan of his ears and his pitchy voice; I did not know his politics, I just thought he was funny to watch. By the age of seven, I knew all of the names of the reporters on *60 Minutes* and would recite them at the start of each broadcast—or even just on a whim.

The news has always been there and has always been of a great importance to me. But, just as much as the news was part of my life from the earliest I can remember, so were memories of being afraid and alone when faced with even the most distant media representations of life and death. I remember always worrying a tornado would come and rip apart our house like what I had seen on the news. I remember not being able to sleep because of fears that I would not remember to breath; I think I had seen a story about that on TV once.

While some of my childhood fears were just part of childhood worry, I suppose, I found myself intrigued by media representations of these fears, and I struggled with the ability of drama to capture representations of reality. The first time I saw a dead body, for instance, was in the movie *Stand By Me*. Alongside railroad tracks in a wooded stretch of land that resembled the deep brush surrounding my home, the boy's body quite simply freaked me out one

Saturday afternoon on TV when my parents were away for the day. Making matters worse, the movie aired amid live news alerts and coverage of air raids and the launching of anti-aircraft weapons during what would later be referred to as the *First* Gulf War.

War footage glowed green on the screen as TV cameras captured the night air raids. Street and building lights reflected white and yellow fog in the lens. Sirens filled the airwaves. Just as when I was watching *Stand By Me*, scared of the scene as the characters who appeared to be my age discussed death, I watched what appeared to be the end of the world in TV montages of war on the ground and from the sky via video feeds as US missiles plowed into concrete barracks "somewhere else." That, too, must have been death, I thought, watching the destruction on the TV news alerts but not seeing the bodies blown apart on the ground.

Even when my parents were around, the scenes and sounds of war via media scared me. Specifically, I recall one cold winter's night drive to my Cub Scouts meeting when our headlights lit only a few feet of the darkness around us and the radio station transmitted news coverage of the war. Long pauses between the reporter's voice let air-raid sirens sing. My father and I rode in silence. I imagined what the scenes of war might be like and wondered if anyone else listening to this broadcast was also afraid about how what was happening "there" in this place called "The Persian Gulf" might affect us "here" at home.

Our house sat a mile or so East of Fort McCoy in Western Wisconsin, an Army base that served as a staging ground for the First Gulf War, and a place from which a good number of my elementary school classmates and family friends worried that someone they loved would be deployed. The real fear, of course, is that those loved ones would not return. Our proximity to the US Army base brought a reality of war home in other ways, too: our house would shake daily as military personnel tested munitions—sometimes in a fury of four or five booms in a row that would knock pictures from the wall and wake us from our sleep; overhead, Army choppers buzzed our tree-tops, flying so low over a field in front of our house that I could see through the open side doors and make out the facial features of its passengers; higher-up, fighter jets would rocket across the sky, roaring as they rolled, pitched, and darted in their daily exercises; even the occasional trip that would take us on the Interstate through Wisconsin would be clogged with miles-long lines of military convoys heading to the Army base.[18]

Thankfully, I have never personally experienced what may be considered our dominant understandings of physical warfare, but the degree to which the *First* Gulf War—not to mention the *Second*—became a normal part of my life via TV and radio when I was a child reflects the layered interaction of and with war, particularly in terms of the indoctrination to dominant ideologies associated with it.

In my hometown, American Patriotism was a common demand in our classrooms, in our churches, and in our idle conversation at the local Pamida. Signs of war were all around us: tanks and fighter jets announced the entrance to the local Veteran's Administration hospital where my father worked; at Fort McCoy, acres and acres of camouflaged trucks and tanks were repainted from greens and browns and blacks to tan to make them easier to hide in the desert, and they were parked behind a chain-linked fence on Highway 21, in plain view by the public passing by. Our daily lives continued almost undisturbed by the war; we merely incorporated it into our normalcy.

Throughout high school, I followed a sense of nationalism that ignored the critical functions of our military—and of our media—that I had normalized throughout my childhood. I wrote patriotic essays for local American Legions to help pay for college, knowing the end product that the judges wanted to see in which the United States was presented as The First Free World. Now, I can see that in the back of my head at the time, I was storing stories of the soldiers from World War II, Korea, and Vietnam whom I had met—their tales of harrowing feats and bravery balancing between celebratory nostalgia and sadness.

With me in their living rooms, these veterans shared stories of loss with gain. There was a complexity in their experiences and stories that I failed to capture at the time, forcing their thoughts into a common narrative of sacrifice and prosperity. And, even though each war has its own narrative of context and conflict—the World Wars presented through a lens of altruism, the other two I mentioned mired in confusion and controversy—it was not until I left for college that I was able to reflect upon both the blatant and latent role that the US government and its press had played in my early years and through which I ultimately have come to question the stories I had been told and retold.

Back then, I was never critical of the stories from the veterans themselves and I dare not, even now, attempt to reposition their comments then into my frame of mind today. I did, however, as I began to move throughout the journalism field, start to critically evaluate the "same old stories" of war I had written about in which American heroes sacrificed so much for so many. The narratives of US Exceptionalism that appeared in each of these tales lost its thrust the more I was able to reflect on my growing-up around veterans at the VA where my father had worked and on the experiences shared with me by homeless veterans I would meet as a reporter.

Again, it was these interactions in which my commitments to rhetoric of the Free World were carved away, beginning slowly and becoming elevated as I entered the media world myself, crafting stories that attempted to explain social deviance from the position of a select few institutions, stories that maintained the legitimacy of police and military violence, stories that separated the media and its power and control from "unpopular" moments of disorder by fellow institutions, and stories that would again align ourselves with institutional triumphs.

My father had spent twenty-one years in the US Navy before he left to earn a master's degree in Social Work from the University of Connecticut. This led to us moving from Maine to Wisconsin a year before I watched the Challenger explode. My father took a job at the Tomah Veterans Administration Medical Center where he conducted group therapy and completed another twenty-some years of service. His work focused on helping vets address the many issues that they tend to carry with them following their time in the military—regardless of whether or not they "saw action." My early, patriotic indoctrination had trained me to interpret these men's problems—including daily confusion about their surroundings, physical struggles due to a worn-out body, emotional loss that shown in their eyes, and in even the simplest of behaviors that cast them as operating outside of "the norm"—as having been "sacrifices" for their "service" to their country.[19]

My skepticism about this explanation for such pain, however, grew as I began to really listen to my father's experiences working in the VA system. Exhausted at the end of each day, he would discuss the bureaucratic explanations for why his patients were not getting what they needed. Coupled with my own fears and concerns about war, my albeit limited exposure to sites and sounds of warfare, and the cynicism of TV sitcoms that I grew up on such as *Murphy Brown* and *The Golden Girls*—shows that questioned the status quo through humor and current events—I came to recognize the power of dominant explanations of the world that often go unquestioned by the citizenry and that, in fact, are maintained by the very people who suffer from such explanations.

One of the moments that really changed how I view the work of our military, in particular, and what ultimately has led to the perspectives and the interests of media messaging that I address in this book, happened around Christmas 2003.

I was flying from Washington, DC, to Wisconsin, sitting on a flight next to a man, who like me was in his early 20s. He had a crew cut. He sat erect in his seat. On his lap, he held a stack of papers stuffed in at least three separate manila folders.[20]

"You're in the military," I said to him. It was not a question.
"Yeah," he replied. "How'd you know?"

"Because you guys are the only people in the world who have to travel with a stack of documents on your lap that prove your existence."

He chuckled.

"I'm heading back from Iraq," he said, and he began to tell me about his time fighting Saddam Hussein's forces.

The man told me that his Hummer had been flipped by an exploding IED and that he had just been released from a US military hospital in Germany. Once he landed in Wisconsin, he would be taken to the same Fort McCoy that I had been familiar with, where I had spent Saturdays shopping at the Exchange, where I had watched my military train during public events to celebrate the nation's holidays. I cannot quite remember what the soldier said would happen to him after he checked-in there and after he delivered his papers—our conversation only lasted a few minutes and we finished the flight in silence—but at the airport after I gathered my bags and headed to the parking lot, I saw him sitting on the floor, leaning against the wall, waiting for a ride.

Wishing him the best, I asked how long he had for his ride to arrive.

"Tomorrow," he told me. "They said they couldn't send anyone today, so I could wait or take a taxi."

I was appalled. The Army base was about forty minutes away, a straight shot up the Interstate, and the US military could not find someone to get this guy? A soldier who had just "sacrificed" for our "freedoms?" It did not matter that it was also Christmas time? Where was the "Christmas spirit"?

Without pause, he accepted a ride to the base—specifically to the Army barracks where he was to report; I was going that way anyway. Once we arrived, I walked him in to find his commanding officer, shared my disdain for the treatment of this soldier and bid them farewell. It was hard for me at that time to accept that this treatment of our soldiers was so commonplace—and so true—that a civilian would be responsible for transporting troops during a time of war. More troubling was the thought that if our Armed Forces treat our own soldiers this way—and the ways I had seen throughout my childhood that had led so many to experience homelessness and chemical dependency—we really must treat humans from other nations, our enemies, and people who operate within our own society outside of the norm like pure shit. It was then when I began to question my role as a citizen in our Great And Only Democracy. What was it I was upholding as a citizen—and as a journalist?

By this point, I had been a journalist for going on ten years and had reported for local and national newspapers, relying on the sources of our police and military officials, our business leaders, our elected politicians, and our like-minded celebrities—all who seemed to provide the same explanations for daily life, all who seemed to support the same kind of capitalism, and all who seemed to just sound scripted in their explanations of the world. At the time, their consistency seemed to support the "truth" of what they spoke, but something just did not seem right. My reality was not lining-up with theirs.

I had started reporting when I was fifteen, having first written editorials for the local *Tomah Journal* and *Tomah Monitor-Herald* about the need for compassion for understanding the changing faces of those dealing with AIDS and, in other pieces, for the need to maintain our community's patriotism on specific holidays.

My first opinion piece had really appeared in the mid-1980s when I dictated to my mother my praise for a local fireworks display. I had seen my father craft his own letters to the editor about local and national issues (and I still have a scrapbook where some of his work appears).

Not absent of mistakes and challenges of learning the trade, I worked for those same local papers throughout high school, moving to regional, state, and national newspapers as either a freelance writer or staff member throughout college. My journalism focused on business, local and state news, and contemporary US culture. I moved from journalism to journalism education in the mid-2000s, graduating from the University of Wisconsin-Madison's journalism school and entering graduate school to understand the cognitive process of learning and socialization. Along the way, I also helped launch the online nonprofit Wisconsin Center for Investigative Journalism at the University of Wisconsin-Madison in 2009 and later that year cofounded another online nonprofit news outlet, The Iowa Center for Public Affairs Journalism with Pulitzer Prize winner, Stephen Berry, at the University of Iowa. Since then, my journalism has been blended into my teaching and research, with activism as its main focus.

During my nearly twenty years working in and around the journalism field, it has only been in the last few, though, that I have come to understand the social experiences and cultural meanings of working in a newsroom—the ideological function of accuracy and sourcing to maintain "legitimacy," the dance of love and hate with police to represent "objectivity," the dedication to politicians and businesses who provide access to what becomes news content, the false expectation that elected officials should uphold some oath to serve the public that maintains the presentation of the press as a watchful "Estate."

Though critiques of journalism abound, I have come to believe that there is no such thing as "good journalism," and that journalism is a cultural construct upon which values can be ascribed only when discussing the news as a social process. At the cultural level, news is an ideological function that acts toward maintaining popular rhetoric.

The act of news, in and of itself, holds particular meanings related to the construction of ideology, which may in effect be hegemonic in that it places the good of the few over the good of the many, but as an act is neither "good" nor "bad." The value of outcomes of the news, which this book articulates are manifested in violence, are open to interpretation in that what may be "good" for some is not for others. Those values, then, apply not to the act of a cultural function but to the relationship of dominant ideology to social action. Put simply, there are normative means by which to judge the "quality" of news, but journalism holds its particular cultural functions that can be neither "good" nor "bad"; it operates with particular goals in mind—the least of which is to provide objective meanings for what appears on the news or occurs in life.

Meanwhile, I find myself as a journalism professor, training future communications professionals with the same-old techniques of covering public meetings, highlighting the views of official sources and the value of official data that advances the needs and interests of the power elite while we refuse to consider forms of advocacy journalism that is focused on dismantling power structures. Hence, this project comes at a time of increased public awareness—and normalization—of government and corporate tracking and surveillance that is celebrated by mainstream press, which ultimately provides a moment in which we can radicalize the field of Journalism Studies in ways that can best examine the Orwellian nature of government-led control that is no longer alive only in fiction. Indeed, we are living in Huxley's *Brave New World*, and it is time to explore it with the radical tools required to push past the mire of US hegemony.

In the end, I like to tease my father that I became a reporter and then a professor who attempts to undermine most of what I learned in my youth because of his influence. We may not share the same politics, but I would like to think that I try to apply the same zealousness I saw in him those times he spoke with passion against government-induced homelessness that came about due to inadequate funding and intentional, politicized bureaucracy. It is the same zeal that carried him into work each day that carries me through these pages.

PURPOSE OF THE BOOK

This book maintains two themes. The first builds upon recent debates about surveillance conducted by world governments and corporations and a recognition of the hyper-militarization of local law enforcement agencies in the United States as an opportunity to articulate the role of the press in furthering and instituting this watching and punishment through the daily activities of maintaining the ideologies of the power elite. The second theme deals with the ways in which the press indoctrinate members of their own ideological communities and the public to veil the violence inherent in news storytelling and to distance the press from the everyday collaborations with some of the same institutions the press mandates it is to hold accountable.

Both elements of this book require critical/cultural approaches that continue to be under attack by a growing, neoliberal and anti-intellectual system of higher education in the United States that is focused on professionalization and conformity (see Conclusion), and it is against this hostility that the book attacks with a specific tone and argument. Below, however, let me first discuss these themes in greater detail.

Theme 1: Press surveillance and protecting the power elite

My interest in the control function of media doubled in 2010 when twenty-five-year-old Chelsea (formerly Bradley) Manning, an intelligence analyst for the US Army, leaked more than 700,000 "sensitive" government documents and videos related to the illegal war in Iraq and Afghanistan to WikiLeaks—a whistle-blower website organized by Julian Assange, among others. One of the videos was of a 2007 air attack of a Baghdad neighborhood that killed seven innocents, including a Reuters news photographer. The video footage, which WikiLeaks edited and released under the title "Collateral Murder," shows grainy shots of military personnel flying in a helicopter above the neighborhood as they determined among themselves and over radio with military leaders off-site if and how to engage with persons on the ground who appeared to be terrorists.[21]

The video includes an audio track of Army personnel issuing the orders to "fire" and discussing the "good shots." On the ground, men scurry to safety as bullets burrow into the ground and into concrete walls of nearby buildings. Dust clouds the street as the assault rifle pounds away and the viewer sees the men, riddled with bullets, falling to the ground. Some crawl to help another. Some do not move at all. The firing continues as a van comes to rescue the men, and as the helicopter gunfire roars, it pushes metal into a van that was carrying children.

An investigation by the US government, while incomplete in the minds of many touched by the violence and the deaths related to our nation's invasion into Afghanistan and Iraq, indicates that military personnel had mistaken one of the man's camera bags for a surface-to-air weapon that could take down the helicopter. The soldiers were found to have acted properly given what they knew about Iraqi insurgent threats in the area of New Baghdad.

And, while the footage shows a rarely seen and gruesome side to war in which all enemies of the state look the same, little public discussion was had about how our nation's military engages with the "enemy." With a slight hint of caution in momentary skepticism of "official" reports about progress in the war in Iraq, the press returned to its cheerleading on behalf of US interests: The deaths were cast as merely unfortunate as WikiLeaks and Assange and Manning became the story, which focused (1) on the role an "open" internet plays in "leaks" of "secrets," (2) the ability of the US government to control its own information, and (3) the professionalism of mainstream media that covered "Collateral Murder."

Furthermore, news reports of Manning's July 2013 conviction of several charges, including espionage, were overshadowed by his statement that he identified more as a woman than as a man, and that Bradley was now openly known as Chelsea. Debate about the degree to which the Army would supply hormone therapy for Manning's transition overtook other news angles, including (1) the types of information released in the files she leaked, (2) her motivations for leaking such information, and (3) the many questionable international actions of the US government that appeared in the files, including confidential information on US military efforts and embarrassing State Department documents, many of which included US officials' disparaging comments about heads of state around the globe.

After Manning's sentencing in which she was to be placed in military custody for thirty-five years, her personal life was used in the press to mark her as "crazy" and to remove any power she might have held as a member of the military to discuss with any authority the dealings of US forces. Indeed, photographs of Manning in her uniform soon became replaced in the press with a selfie that she had taken—her long, blonde hair and lipstick the focus of public discussion surrounding the pic. At the same time, Assange was portrayed as a recluse who, as of early 2015, was holed up in the Ecuadorian Embassy in London to avoid prosecution in several countries for an alleged sexual assault and for his role in releasing classified documents to the world. Assange claims the sex charges were made as a way to shame and delegitimize him and the website with the single aim of distracting the public from information about worldwide, US-led collaboration and collusion against the interests of private citizens.[22]

Releasing the secrets

Manning's stories took a serious backseat in 2013 when lawyer and journalist Glenn Greenwald, who at the time was a reporter at the United Kingdom's *The Guardian*, released reports about the US government's spy network that was leaked to him and a team of confidants by Edward Snowden, a twenty-something who worked both for the US Central Intelligence Agency (CIA) and National Security Agency (NSA). Overnight, words such as PRISM—a data-mining system operated by the NSA—appeared in mainstream press as journalists hurried to report on the reporting, relying on Greenwald as Snowden's front-man and on canned responses from the US government about the tens of thousands of "top secret" documents Snowden initially released.

Among his many other findings, Greenwald reported that during one month in 2013, the NSA's Boundless Informant program, through the agency's Global Access Operations, had gathered data related to phone calls and emails that numbered in the billions and that had been funneled through US telecomm infrastructure. Worldwide, the agency during that time had collected 124 billion phone calls and 97 billion emails. In short, the reporting found that the US government was spying on US citizens through their own telecommunications infrastructure while also prying into the private worlds of global leaders, suspected terrorists, and business executives.[23]

Over the next year, Greenwald's reporting revealed that the NSA had been growing its surveillance on US citizens' emails, phone calls, metadata, and social media since the early 2000s. Even since revelations came to light in 2005 that the Bush Administration had concocted a legal argument that the president could order mass surveillance on citizens via government and military resources in order to fight "terrorism," little could have prepared even the most cynical for the amount of energy being used to capture the movements of those living in The Free World. (In May 2015, a US federal appeals court ruled that the NSA programs were illegal and not covered by any mandates of the Patriot Act.)[24]

The NSA's acts, Snowden's materials confirmed, were not just limited to the efforts of the public spy agency, but relied on governmental collaboration with the private sector. For example, both Verizon and AT&T were found to be complying with (and providing little fight against) orders from the US government to release private communication information. These findings provided further evidence that the public-private surveillance net that has been cast over the United States—and much of the world—depends just as much on private industry as it does on public efforts supported by the nation's citizenry.

That the efforts stretched so far and were so deeply embedded in the everyday practices of public and private entities revealed the power behind the belief that the more eyes we have watching, the safer we all are. Furthermore, tricked through "thought control" designed to convince us that the altruism of securitization appears in the normalization of security, even the most local of entities had come to adopt hyper-securitization as a natural fit for our American Way of Life (Figure I.1).

FIGURE I.1 *A sign on the back of a Starbucks in Fort Lauderdale, Florida in November 2013. It reads, "THIS PROPERTY IS PROTECTED BY VIDEO SURVEILLANCE," anthropomorphizing ideas such as "surveillance" and reflecting a normalized belief that technology has an inherent ability to take action, in this case to "protect." Photograph by author.*

Snowden's files also revealed that much of the private-public intelligence collaboration is based on independent contract work. Greenwald's reporting— and the re-reporting from other news organizations that came late to the game—showed a direct connection between corporate elites, educational institutions, media conglomerates, and the US military and spying agencies. "The NSA itself," Greenwald writes, "employs roughly thirty thousand people, but the agency also has contracts for some sixty thousand employees of private corporations, who often provide essential services." Indeed, Greenwald continues, Snowden himself "was actually employed not by the NSA but by the Dell Corporation and the large defense contractor Booz Allen Hamilton."[25]

International mainstream/elite press published Snowden's leaked information, initially in Germany's *Der Spiegel*, the United Kingdom's *The Guardian*, and *The New York Times*. Other news outlets picked up the publishing pace, including *The Washington Post, Le Monde*, and wire services. But that these media outlets began to regularly report about the shocking information within Snowden's data—including US spying through video games, the capturing of individuals' keyboard strokes, and mobile phone metadata of US citizens and a handful of world leaders—was of no consequence. Even the most direct lead in a December 2013 *New York Times* article, "N.S.A. Dragnet Included Allies, Aid Groups and Business Elite,"[26] which stated quite clearly that US spying was extended over some sixty countries and equally focused on citizens and government and business leaders, led to little change in everyday press collaborations with other power groups, as this book will discuss in Chapter 5.

Journalistic narratives applied to interpret the level of governmental surveillance at this time merely allowed the press to present itself as a "watchdog" institution as journalists appeared shocked and awed by the revelations of government spying. Hacking and surveillance for the purposes of control and order—often through the threat and use of violence by the US government and its corporate and global government allies—was presented in US news media as "facts," with very little independent journalistic verification or even reporting that would balance such arguments against the nation's normative dedication to "independence," "privacy," and "freedom."

In fact, the press did very little to complicate the news of the day by investigating power systems with their own efforts and maintaining the status quo by marginalizing "radical" positions of criticism against such surveillance. Yet, this initial analysis of how media covered the release of these secrets begs the question of what role the media *really* holds in global collaborations of militaries and corporations that represent the purest form of US imperialism.

Subjugation through fear

Throughout this book, I present arguments for particular understandings of "media control" that answer the question of just how news media operate within the construction of our daily lives—and in the interpretations of those lives. I first build upon the assumption that subjugation is not a media outcome; it is media's core purpose. In other words, the purpose of media is to maintain social divides that support the supposition that in our capitalism-democracy "there must be losers for there to be winners." Part of this subjugation occurs through the application of dominant ideologies in media rhetoric.

Take, for instance, the notion of "martial law," the ability of the government and its military to maintain local police control and to demand the order of people and spaces normally under civilian rule. As William Arkin writes in *American Coup: How a Terrified Government is Destroying the Constitution*, hints of possible "martial law" in the US post-Vietnam "lingered as a consequence of nuclear war or foreign attack, civic cheerleading promising that civil authority would be rapidly restored." Similar arguments have been made even recently in the local police takeover of the streets in and around Boston following the Boston Marathon Bombings in 2013 (see Chapter 2), and in the police-press control over people and information following the 2014 shooting of a black young man by a white police officer in Ferguson, Missouri, and after the grand jury's decision there not to indict the officer who had been accused of shooting without justification (see Chapter 4).[27]

While martial law was not claimed by law enforcement and military officials in these instances—despite the degree to which it was occurring—press attention to the swarms of police in riot gear and their explanations for and of disorder that ensued (racialized in both instances) mirrored responses to police violence in New Orleans following the 2005 Hurricane Katrina, which displaced a majority of the city's blacks and sent police barreling into the streets with weapons rather than with food and blankets.

That martial law can occur without someone saying it is occurring (indeed, the claim of instituting martial law would be far too devastating to the legitimacy of police forces than merely executing it) speaks to the power of rhetoric in times of crisis. As Arkin argues, martial law is an "oxymoron" in that "it is as much about what does not exist as what does." In other words, martial law and its myths of a calm, orderly, and fair/just civilization that is to be returned to the citizens from moments of chaos through the intervention of government/military intervention suggests that the civilization was truly those things of fairness, equality, and safety before the "disorder."

But, that myth is based on a fallacy that this previous/natural "order" was of a civilian mandate, with a focus on the interests of the public and absent of an always-looming military threat. Furthermore, rhetoric of protectionism via a government/military and even a local/civilian police force maintains that the aims of these institutions include peace—a peace demanded by and for the public for a negotiation of shared outcomes absent of threats of force and all to stave off pending doom of which we all fear (Figure I.2).

Control through violence

Notions of social distress—of which martial law should really be considered— are frequently calmed and solved through the solution of force. How these solutions flow to the public through press explanations is what this book attempts to decipher. News media operate as more than messengers in particular moments of ideological crisis, when the public needs to be aligned with solutions to problems from the power elite—especially when those solutions include force against the public itself.

FIGURE I.2 *In this age of normalized securitization, even universities have armed themselves with military grade weaponry, as represented by this military issued response truck that was part of Florida International University's arsenal in August 2014. Photograph by Donny Boulanger. Used with permission.*

Journalism provides a ritualistic function that extends beyond providing information; the press provide explanation, and these explanations for everyday events, social issues, and individual actions that appear as "news" revolve around larger, dominant cultural norms within a given society that lead to control. In recent US history, ideologies of increased surveillance, control, order, and protection shared among the government's military, local police forces, schools, private enterprise, and the press have surrounded fear appeals that bank on confusion and distress similar to that experienced by a child watching war on TV, listening to it in the dead of night, and trying to understand its human toll.

Fear demands a story in which someone needs protection and a hero to do the protecting. Perhaps the most common of myths, the hero almost always comes to the rescue or identifies within the victim a sense of power and control so that, even indirectly, the hero saves the day even if it is through the actions of the victim. Just as centuries before, today the hero still wields a weapon to fight the demons; the hero leads a people to victory; and, the hero knows best what ails and what heals (see Chapter 2).

The cultural norms and historic tales we tell within our own communities are not necessarily our own, however. Yet, each of us holds the power to interrogate these norms and stories, not with the expressed intent to undermine what we believe to be "true" but to examine the degree to which these truths can handle the pressure of being "false."

Understanding that dominant explanations of the world spread through storytelling (i.e., literature, music, dance, official histories, law, journalism), which emerges from positions of power and holds types of power of themselves to shape individual interpretations and actions in the world, though, also means that what we find in our investigations of our truths must be addressed. Therefore, I am particularly interested in the role of the news media in such cultural storytelling and view news media as collaborators within systems of power and culpable for social and cultural environments.

For example, in his book, *The Watchdog That Didn't Bark*, which examines press coverage—or lack thereof—of the financial crisis of 2007/2008, Dean Starkman writes that the "failure" of journalism to address the pending doom of the collapse as early as the 1990s "was not of the industry, but of the imagination."[28] Put another way, the norms that led to the subprime bubble and the loss of financial solvency of some of the nation's largest financial institutions were not enough to provide a sense that a problem was brewing and that this problem was economic genocide. The cheating and overlending, the completion of ill-advised mergers and investments was merely commonplace to business reporters, so much so that such behavior and processes were not enough to call attention. It was only when reporters were faced with the notion that there was "scandal" at the center of the collapse, Starkman argues, that journalists responded as "watchdogs" over the financial sector.

Clearly caught in the public limelight as "missing the story" in the decades of profiteering that led to the bust, journalists attempted to maintain the public's trust, apologizing for their mistake but never admitting, of course, that press-business partnerships (what could be considered an element of Starkman's concept of CNBC-ization) were intentional collaborations that fit within a media system that relies on waiting for a story to break, watching those who are breaking—or could break—a story, and punishing those participants through media shaming (see Chapter 5). As Chapter 2 discusses in greater detail, these processes of the press—processes of normalizing fear and supporting securitization *vis-à-vis* media propaganda—require machines that work through various forms of indoctrination to spread conservative political and social thought about everyday life.

Media control also revolves around justifications of and for violence or justifications of threats of and for violence (including economic violence), whether that violence emerges within language, through a bank account and bad mortgage, or at the end of a gun that is embossed with explanations of normative notions of normalcy and virtue of natural social roles of the press. As journalist James Fallows writes:

> Reporters and pundits hold no elected office, but they are obviously public figures. The most prominent TV talk show personalities are better known than all but a handful of congressmen. When politicians and pundits sit alongside each other and trade opinions on Washington talk shows, they underscore the essential similarity of their political roles.[29]

White supremacy in news storytelling

The shared political roles that Fallows mentions surround the function of White Supremacy, which is the cause for violence that emerges from the power elite's military and police force. In the next chapter, for instance, I make such an argument by identifying elements of today's power elite within a racialized lens. While there's more than enough research about how media messages contribute to social conditions through racialized stereotyping and marginalization, which leads to the subjugation of particular sets of citizens, this project focuses on the ways in which racial subjugation serves as a primary effort of the media in terms of the intentionality of messaging through dominant cultural lenses that do not allow for legitimate and authoritative explanations that may be counter to those of "The Fourth Estate."

In this sense, the press operate as an institution of white domination that recalls histories and explanations of the world that come from Western/Anglo/white perspectives with the intention of maintaining a status quo that benefits future generations of white folk, which involves the function and act of violence to enforce submission. As I further clarify in Chapter 3, another way to consider what I mean by "white" is to consider the term as corresponding with "non-black," those of skin color and tone, heritage and self-identification that may not be distinctly "black," "American-black," or "African American," but who do not benefit from dominant society in ways similar to those of lighter skin colors.

This distinction becomes important as more and more citizens in the United States consider us to be living in a post-race society, but where in reality those with darker skins and those considered "black" are oppressed at greater rates and in greater ways (see Chapter 3).[30] Even more will be discussed in Chapter 5 and in the book's Conclusion about how mainstream news media continue to maintain relevance of racialized force for order and control by adopting social media as a tool for public participation. For instance, new media technologies turn the public to viewing media on-demand, on tablets, on mobile phones, and away from a passive interaction with TV screens, cable boxes, wires, and confined spaces of living rooms in ways that tighten ideological relationships between race, the citizen and journalism, which enhances the public's involvement with the interactivity of media and its meanings. In this way, the public becomes an active member of the media's policing force, which is examined in this book's second theme, discussed below.

Theme 2: Media, indoctrination and control

Another main theme of this book is to identify the ways in which news media maintain a list of approved behaviors for society and present those lists through coverage that is designed to maintain order. News that dictates compliance to dominant ideology polices society and its members as a means to record patterns of misbehavior and ideological mismanagement for the sole purpose of instituting discipline that will bring society back in-line with the status quo. US citizens—and viewers of US media—are indoctrinated to follow the flag into wars, into big box stores (think, George W. Bush's infamous statement to spend, spend, spend following the 9/11 attacks), and to adopt governmental use of technology as a primary tool for protection.

Consider, for a moment, the hyper-militarization of local law enforcement and the confusion surrounding the US government's use of drones and surveillance on its own citizens, which has done nothing more than increase during the Obama Administration.[31]

Because individuals are under constant threat of personal attack by political and media institutions if they present radical claims counter to governmental and media expectations of behavior and beliefs, news media become anything but complicit in the application of thought control. In the end, our public hears only the comments and critiques of government and media via mainstream news because, simply, safe and approved opinions are the only ones that news outlets are willing to air. And, because the powerful—those with money, weapons, and the ear of the media—so benefit from cultural calm and social order, which is only in the interest of the protection and prosperity of the Free World, I argue throughout this book that such media-sponsored democracy is too often a veil for ideological oppression.

Up until immediately following the 9/11 attacks at the World Trade Center in New York, the idea that US officials would surveil their own citizens may have seemed strange—maybe even anti-American. Our government, we said then, would only monitor those suspected of terrorism, those who deserved to be watched, and those who had previously been shown to try to harm American interests. Few realized—or wanted to realize—that their government was already watching us and had always been in partnerships with private business, public ideologues, and members of the "free press" to surveil and influence its citizens, as have governments and merchants from even the earliest of societies.[32]

Now, surveillance is synonymous with democracy. Order is patriotism. Hidden within cynical language that stretches the country (and polls that support it) that Congress is "untrustworthy"—as is the press—are generations of critical histories that when applied to today's news reveal that neither has the US government nor has its press been interested in resolving issues of and for the people. Governments are designed with the press in mind, as the media hold stakes in private financing that allows government-press partnerships to produce messages that serve and protect elites, traditional histories of society, and shared traditions that maintain dominant social roles and cultural values. Through such means, the media institute order.

This book, therefore, challenges initial assumptions that the press merely are left to cover only what they are told by officials, only what reporters have seen and have been able to verify themselves, or only what eyewitnesses report. The arguments I make throughout this project build upon notions that have been presented before—that the press operate within a system of social and cultural pressures but that members of the press also have choices about what becomes news and how it is interpreted. It is within these choices, driven by ideologies shared with fellow power institutions, that journalists operate within a larger system of control and power. They are not observers looking in on a system, because they are within that system.

The press, in fact, serve as a lynchpin of power and the application of force applied by governments, their militaries and local police in order to maintain that power. Throughout the following chapters, I make what may be read as causal claims about power, about the role of media in society, and about the use of force against citizens. I understand that these ideas may be met with rigorous skepticism, if not outright disbelief. In fact, my arguments may even be categorized as "conspiracy theory" (see Chapter 3). Yet, there is something here to be examined, something in terms of power and news, journalists and police, citizens and democracy, and the role of force and threats of force within and of the news at the local level.

PLAN OF THE BOOK

Because of the aims I wish to meet, this book has several audiences. For scholars, I wish to contribute to a radicalization of Journalism Studies that provides value to increased critical analyses of the news, particularly local news, in ways that question the violent power of media and control. From this project, journalists would benefit from related discussions about the *cultural* influence of their work. I emphasize the word "cultural," because the journalistic trade boasts dozens of websites, magazines, and news columns that examine the degree to which the press function as a democratic tool, but very few—if any—assess the ways in which the press embed moral lessons and question the degree to which news practices and products support power systems.

Students—a term I use to include more than those organized in a classroom—are an obvious audience for such an academic approach to a professional field, and I discuss below ways in which this project is designed to help integrate the ideological analyses of these pages into daily life and work. I also have a desire for the average reader who may be interested in journalism, culture, power, and control to apply this book in their challenges of traditional modes of interacting with the news—and even popular critiques of the news (see discussion of news literacy in Conclusion).

The audience should note that *Media Control* is, in many ways, a continuation of work I have conducted in journal articles and in my first book, *A Transplanted Chicago: Race, Place & Press in Iowa City*, published in 2014. In these works, I have attempted to explicate issues of media power and control at the local level, and I return to those pieces throughout this project to reveal the press' role in a culture of White Supremacy that, despite any discourse of living in a "post-race" society, divides US society with a black-white dynamic. Indeed, it is this dynamic that fuels the root of increased militarization of police forces and the basis for control and surveillance.

To guide readers through these arguments and cases, this book presents several features in each chapter, including:

- A Chapter Purpose, which serves as an overview to introduce the reader to those pages' main arguments and approaches, as well to map the chapter itself

- Key Terms, which are also listed in a glossary at the end of the book, at the top of each chapter focus the reader's interpretation of the subsequent discussions through a particular conceptual framework; the terms cross between chapters but are highlighted in those where the terms are best examined

- Guiding Questions that appear at the beginning of each chapter help frame the subsequent analyses with approaches that may help the reader come to interpolations that connect the concepts to practice and to further questions about news and ideology

- Discussion Questions appear at the end of each chapter to create a fluid discussion from the beginning of an argument and analysis to its end; the questions are designed more to guide discussion than to lead to specific answers

- Chapter References appear throughout each chapter that suggest the reader can go to previous pages or to future sections within the book for more on specific examples or for further examination of a particular concept; the intention is for the reader to use this book not necessarily in a chronological manner, but in their own way

- Notes at the end of each chapter continue the main narrative of this text, providing depth in some cases, evidence in others, and context that helps the reader continue to examine the terms applied throughout this project and the cases examined

- Original Artwork by Jared Rodriguez, who has supplied images for websites such as truth-out.org, appear at the beginning of each chapter; such visual communication and expression is meant to influence and to inspire a broader audience and to complicate the modes of language that can be used to discuss issues of communication and control

With these additives, *Media Control* may appear to be a textbook—and it may be used as such—but it is not one. This project revolves around original arguments and evidence and is rooted very much in my own experiences as a journalist and as a media scholar. *Media Control* is, therefore, a manifesto of sorts that is meant for journalists, scholars, students, and citizens to provide a foundation upon which radical assessments of the power acts of media messaging can be applied.

Lastly, even though this book focuses on the role of the press in US society, some of this work is also dependent on conceptualizations related to the press, police, and social control in the United Kingdom, largely because of the nature of the two geographies' ideological foundations and relationships. Indeed, much communication scholarship in the United Kingdom provides a more critical perspective than in the United States and provides a much needed and valued approach to media operations in this country.

The book unfolds as follows:

Chapter 1, "Power, Propaganda and the Purpose of News," places the reader in a setting of increasing worldwide militarization and social control through the lens of media control. The chapter begins by arguing that news coverage of mass-closings of US embassies in 2013 under the fear of international terrorism is representative of work journalists perform as a collective and moral force in collaboration with powerful political and corporate leaders. This chapter focuses on explicating power and propaganda that will be extended throughout the book in ways that suggest journalistic "objectivity" and "watchdogging" veil the inherent—and intentional—power functions of the Fourth Estate. The idea of "information" in this project, therefore, is provided within a framework of power, the assessment of which depends on relationships between the messenger(s), the audience(s), and the cultural context(s) surrounding communication. Throughout this discussion of how the press, in this case, worked to maintain popular, public agendas of the power elite, I build connections between Journalism Studies, cultural theory, and critical perspectives of race—including whiteness—to reveal how news media operate in relationship with private business, law enforcement, and governments (the power elite) to exclude news explanations that threaten the likelihood of the public to accept dominant interpretations of justice.

Chapter 2, "Making News: Purposes, Practices and Pandering," explains how, as an institution, news socializes its own and indoctrinates the public to the power of the press through fear appeals that are intended to shape social behaviors. The chapter begins with an analysis of how US press covered the 2013 Boston Bombings through narratives of terrorism and protectionism with which the press institute ideological control. At the core of my argument and analysis of news in this case is that journalistic interpretive communities in the United States do not operate independent of naturalized democratic values absent of human interaction, desires, and power. In other words, it is here where I place the press as a human construction, a constant struggle between individual agency and the ability of dominant culture to incorporate alternative perspectives to maintain dominant power systems, explicating the role of the press as a paternalistic and propagandistic power force to support US plutocracy. By introducing the reader to methods by which journalists boost local, dominant ideologies and banish alternatives through the application of myth, this chapter sets a foundation of sociological and cultural understandings of how the press deepen cultural meanings of everyday events for the benefit of the power elite. In turn, this chapter begins the larger argument of the book—that acts of mainstream journalism-as-ideology, press practices, and methods of press socialization weaken the purpose of the press as serving the public good.

Chapter 3, "Displacement and Punishment: The Press as Place-makers"—a play off of Michel Foucault's *Discipline & Punish*—argues for a concept of "news place-making" as a power function of news media that is applied through press demarcations and characterizations of space and place. Building upon previous work in human geography, journalism sociology, and critical spatial studies, this chapter connects the physicality of journalism—a field focused as much on the "where" as on the journalistic traits of explaining "who, what, why, and how," particularly in an age of mobile media and geotechnologies—to a rich history of rhetoric within news coverage of urban and rural displacement and disorder. More specifically, with the intent of placing these perspectives more purposefully within the field of Journalism Studies, particularly in terms of news coverage at the local level, I discuss the seemingly more covert ideological applications of place in journalistic storytelling, what I call "news place-making." I also further operationalize a concept that I began to examine in some of my previous work—the idea that "journalistic boosterism," that which maintains and empowers dominant cultural positions of collective identities that then deploy messages of approved behaviors, including consumption and patriotism, serves as a form of "social banishment," a forced marginalization and removal of undesirables from society.

To do so, I first turn to an analysis of juxtaposed local coverage of rural poverty and urban disorder through a lens of patriotic martyrdom and a rise of "nuisance" properties as a reflection of urban and black "disorder" in Des Moines, Iowa in 2014. This analysis examines an element of how (1) the press cover what has become a decades-long forced black migration in the Midwestern United States and (2) how news representations normalize protectionism of white space, an analysis which identifies place and White Supremacy as critical elements of US journalistic ideology. The chapter further examines news place-making through the participatory methodology of mental mapping in Iowa City, Iowa, to present a new way of viewing the power of the journalistic interpretive community and the racialized role of place-making in the press—particularly through storytelling of neighborhood schools as representative of neighborhoods and their residents.

Chapter 4, "News as Cultural Distraction: Controversy, Conspiracy and Collective Forgetting," argues that "the news" is meant to pit the press and its messages against the public by marginalizing those who provide alternative explanations for news events in moments of cultural trauma when the press provide an "offensive line" for the power elite in order to justify the messages and meanings of dominant groups. This chapter focuses on the ideological role of press conflict, controversy, and conspiracy at the center of media messages surrounding two cases in which the media focused on explanations of "conspiracy theory" and of "collective forgetting." Specifically, the chapter examines the role of "conspiracy coverage" to marginalize the role of gun violence in US society and to ignore inadequate gun policies that allow for rampant civilian onslaughts of each other and that fuel the militarization of US public schools that contribute to the "school-to-prison pipeline."[33]

In this chapter, therefore, I examine news related to the 2012 Sandy Hook Elementary School shooting in Newtown, Connecticut, in which twenty children were killed and in which news media focused on "conspiracy theories" of a Florida communications professor that the event was a hoax rather than discussed the issues of gun culture maintained by local police agencies and the nation's entertainment complex. I also examine how the use of "conspiracy theory," "confusion," and "controversy" in news contributes to the justification of violence by the power elite and serves to support acts of press violence against individuals and communities considered a "threat" to the power elite.

This argument is tied to an analysis of news coverage out of Ferguson, Missouri, in 2014 surrounding the killing of a young black man in the St. Louis suburb by a white police officer. The shooting—and the later decision by a grand jury not to indict the police officer—led to rioting and to a national discussion on race and militarized local police forces. In the end, I am not interested in presenting a single explanation for either of these news events. Rather, I turn to the first to explicate the ideological purposes of casting "conspiracy theory"; the second provides an opportunity to argue for a notion of "collective forgetting" that, in the case of Ferguson, was informed by the country's racist history and the normalization of neoliberal principles and "urban memory," which contribute to the maintenance of a race-based future.

Chapter 5, "Normalizing Media Surveillance: Media Waiting, Watching and Shaming," dissects direct collaborations between the press and other power structures by discussing how news contributes to a surveillance and control state. The chapter includes an analysis of how journalists, public officials, and business leaders in 2013 discussed the expected onslaught of black tourists to Miami Beach, Florida, as part of the city's Urban Beach Week in ways that cast the partiers as threats to local "community" and non-black "identities" of South Beach. Building upon work related to surveillance and sousveillance, I explicate three elements of press surveillance—waiting, watching, and shaming—to showcase how such coverage normalizes a war mentality and industry reinforced through racialized national press rhetoric and the "localization" of economic and security benefits. Furthermore, I present press surveillance as an act of power and force rather than an idle process of sitting back and recording society by identifying press "waiting" and "watching" as ideological acts that build a foundation for more overt forms of press power, including "media shaming" as punishment in a moment of a rising police state in the United States and the militarization of the country's local police forces.

In Chapter 6, "The Violence of Media Sousveillance: Identifying the Press as Police," I examine how explanations of police activity and authority operate within a realm of press legitimacy that shapes dominant interpretations of how police should deal with perceived public disorder. My analysis of news coverage of press and public calls for an increased police presence police disorder in Miami Gardens, Florida, during a time of increased "black-on-black" violence—even when the police were secretly recorded snooping through a private business and harassing its patrons—explicates the ideological function of "police myth" that maintains police have natural authority to institute and maintain order. By examining how the press explained the legitimate authority of police in the community prior to and following the camera footage, this chapter implicates the press as a member of a larger police force, extending the traditionally reductive notion of the journalistic community as being only among those considered journalists to include "outsiders" through the press adoption of "police myth."

In the book's Conclusion, "The Myth of Being 'Post-Media' and Why Americans Will Always be Media Illiterate," I summarize the main elements of media control articulated in this book and move into a discussion that implicates journalism education, journalistic socialization, and public efforts at creating a sense of "media literacy" as means to distract both the public and the press from discussing the issues of today that would challenge— and possibly cripple a portion of—the power elite's media control. I examine previous media literacy movements to explain that by incorporating business, military, and governmental interests, mainstream news outlets and educators, together, indoctrinate current and future generations to understand that news media must make profit and limit public involvement to maintain the status quo. At the core of this effort, I argue, is a socialization and pacification of journalism students through constant collaboration with corporate and private interests, including an infatuation with "digital media" and the promise of "digital democracy" in which students are driven by educational institutions to jobs in private industries that serve the power elite—not the public. This conclusion also implicates areas of journalism research, such as news myth and the structure of the journalistic interpretive community, as being rooted in White Supremacy that is often used to justify physical violence and threats against citizens by military and local police forces.

Discussion Questions

1. What complexities exist in defining "the news," and how do they complicate conversations about the role of media in everyday life?

2. What might we suspect are initial reactions by the public at large (and of journalists, for that matter) to statements that news media hold a power of social control, and what must one do in order to approach and/or counter those initial reactions?

Notes

1   Edward S. Herman and Noam Chomsky, *Manufacturing Consent: The Political Economy of the Mass Media* (New York: Pantheon Books, 2002).

2   James W. Carey, *Communication as Culture* (New York and London: Routledge, 2009).

3   Bob Gutsche, Jr., "For some, holiday is about independence," *La Crosse Tribune*, July 5, 2001.

4   Robert E. Gutsche, Jr., "Man is shot in parking lot," *Wisconsin State Journal*, November 25, 2002.

5   For more on how meanings are embedded into text, see Stuart Hall, "Encoding/decoding," in: Hall, et al., ed. *Culture, Media, Language* (London: Hutchinson, 1980), 128–138.

6   City of Madison Police Department Annual Reports (2000–2001; 2002–2003; 2003–2004).

7   Christopher Hedges, *War Is a Force That Gives Us Meaning* (New York: Public Affairs, 2002), 22.

8   Ibid., 46.

9   See, Eric Duggans, *Race-baiter: How the Media Wields Dangerous Words to Divide a Nation* (New York: Palgrave MacMillan, 2012).

10 George Lakoff and Mark Johnson, *Metaphors We Live By* (Chicago and London: University of Chicago Press, 1980); Richard V. Ericson, Patricia M. Baranek, and Janet B.L. Chan, *Representing Order: Crime, Law, and Justice in the News Media* (Toronto, Buffalo and London: University of Toronto Press, 1991).

11 Ericson, Baranek, and Janet B.L. Chan, *Representing Order*, 7. Other works of note by these authors related to media power and control include *Negotiating Control* and *Visualizing Deviance*.

12 For example, see Robert E. Gutsche, Jr., Consuelo Naranjo, and Lilliam Martínez-Bustos, "'Now we can talk': The role of culture in journalistic boundary work during the boycott of Puerto Rico's *La Comay*," *Journalism Practice* 9, no. 3 (2015): 298–313, doi: 10.1080/17512786.2014.963358; Dan Berkowitz and David Asa Schwartz, "Miley, CNN and *The Onion:* When fake news becomes realer than real," *Journalism Practice* (2015), doi: 10.1080/17512786.2015.1006933.

13 Robert McChesney makes a similar case in terms of addressing issues of democracy in the uses of new technologies in *Blowing the Roof off the Twenty-First Century: Media, Politics, and the Struggle for Post-Capitalist Democracy* (New York: Monthly Review Press, 2014).

14 John B. Thompson, *Ideology and Modern Culture* (Stanford, CA: Stanford University Press, 1990), 20.

15 For more, see "Shooting of Tony Robinson," wikipedia.org, http://en.wikipedia.org/wiki/Shooting_of_Tony_Robinson. Since the initial drafting of this book, several more black men died at the hands of police that then became national news. These men included Walter Scott, 50, who was shot in the back by a police officer in North Charleston, South Carolina, in April 2015. Video of this shooting spread across the internet and led to the indictment of the officer. Also in April 2015, Freddie Gray, 25, died while in police custody in Baltimore, Maryland. His death led to protests and "riots" in that city for several days. In early May 2015, six police officers were charged with his death.

16 Tim Robbins, "A brutal beating wakes Attica's ghosts," *The New York Times*, February 28, 2015; Spencer Ackerman, "'I sat in that place for three days, man': Chicagoans detail abusive confinement inside police 'black site,'" *The Guardian*, February 27, 2015; Kenya Downs, "Why is Milwaukee so bad for black people?," *National Public Radio*, March 5, 2015, http://www.npr.org/blogs/codeswitch/2015/03/05/390723644/why-is-milwaukee-so-bad-for-black-people.

17 For more, see WRLN, "Income is only one of the ways South Florida is segregated," wrln.com, March 3, 2015, http://wlrn.org/post/incomeonly-one-ways-south-florida-segregated; Moses Shumow and Robert E. Gutsche, Jr, *News, Neoliberalism and Miami's Fragmented Urban Space* (Lanham, MA: Lexington, forthcoming); Robert E. Gutsche, Jr. and Moses Shumow, "'NO OUTLET': A critical visual analysis of neoliberal narratives in mediated geographies," *Visual Communication*, forthcoming; Moses Shumow and Robert E. Gutsche, Jr., "Urban policy, press & place: City-making in Florida's Miami-Dade County," *Journal of Urban Affairs*, forthcoming.

18 I should note that my home was also some twenty miles West of Volk Field, an Air Force base. Though I never had much personal experiences on that installation, the base was also actively used during both Gulf Wars.

19 To be clear, I do not intend to represent all veterans—even those I met in my life—as mentally deranged, always-depressed, or in-need of medical or financial assistance. The range of outcomes that come from war is as diverse as the individuals themselves who deal with those outcomes. In these stories of "sadness," I saw an equal number of interactions of joy. I heard laughter more than I heard cries of pain. I saw men—and women— who had made lasting friendships, who were married, who were happy to be single. It was, however, the degree of need that I saw and the stories of abandonment by their government and the public at times of need told by "America's heroes" that influenced me the most.

20 The story that follows is presented to the best of my memory.

21 View "Collateral Murder" here: http://www.collateralmurder.com.

22 Manning released her statement to the TODAY show on NBC. The statement can be read here: http://www.today.com/news/i-am-chelsea-read-mannings-full-statement-6C10974052; See also, Julie Tate and Ernesto Londoño, "Manning found not guilty of aiding the enemy, guilty of espionage," *The Washington Post*, July 30, 2013. About the media shaming of Manning and the process of criminalization by news, see Josh Stearns, "Criminalizing journalism: Manning, media and you," August 6, 2013, http://truth-out.org/opinion/item/18009-criminalizing-journalism-manning-media-and-you; Julian Barnes, "What Bradley Manning leaked," *The Wall Street Journal*, August 21, 2013, http://blogs.wsj.com/washwire/2013/08/21/what-bradley-manning-leaked; Charlie Beckett and James Ball, *WikiLeaks: News in the Networked Era* (Cambridge and Malden, MA: Polity, 2012).

23 Glenn Greenwald, *No Place to Hide: Edward Snowden, the NSA, and the US Surveillance State* (New York: Metropolitan Books, 2014).

24 To be clear, the US government and corporations have had the abilities—and have employed these abilities—since the nation was formed.

25 Greenwald, 101. Also, in 2010, *The Washington Post* published "Top Secret America," a project that focused on the public-private intelligence network, which can be read here: http://projects.washingtonpost.com/top-secret-america. See also Chapters 4 through 6 of this book for discussion on power collaborations.

26 James Glanz and Andrew W. Lehren, "N.S.A. Dragnet Included Allies, Aid Groups and Business Elite," *The New York Times*, December 20, 2013.

27 William Arkin, *American Coup: How a Terrified Government is Destroying the Constitution* (New York, Boston and London: Little, Brown and Company, 2013), 34.

28 Dean Starkman, *The Watchdog That Didn't Bark: The Financial Crisis and the Disappearance of Investigative Journalism* (New York: Columbia University Press, 2014), 287.

29 James Fallows, *Breaking the News: How the Media Undermine American Democracy* (New York: Vintage, 1997), 36.

30 Robert E. Gutsche, Jr., *A Transplanted Chicago: Race, Place and the Press in Iowa City* (Jefferson, NC: McFarland, 2014); See also, Christopher P. Campbell, *Race, Myth and the News* (Thousand Oaks, CA: Sage, 1995); Teun A. van Dijk, *Racism and the Press* (London and New York: Routledge, 1991); Michael Kimmel, *Angry White Men: American Masculinity at the End of an Era* (New York: Nation Books, 2013); Michael Omi and Howard Winant, *Racial Formation in the United States: From the 1960s to the 1990s* (New York and London: Routledge, 1994).

31 Associated Press, "Report: Secret drone memo to be disclosed by Obama administration," *The Guardian*, May 20, 2014.

32 For history, see Andrew Pettegree, *The Invention of News: How the World Came to Know About Itself* (New Haven, CT and London: Yale University Press, 2014).

33 Catherine Y. Kim, Daniel J. Losen, and Damon T. Hewitt, *The School-to-Prison Pipeline: Structuring Legal Reform* (New York and London: New York University Press, 2010).

1

Power, Propaganda and the Purpose of News

Chapter Purpose

This chapter examines news as both a social and cultural construction. It begins by visiting news coverage of terrorist threats in 2013 that US officials said were collected through government surveillance programs and which led to the closing of US embassies across the globe. Press coverage suggested the threats were further evidence for expanding government spying, which at the time was under debate in Congress. Through the case, the chapter builds a foundation for understanding power, propaganda, and the role of the press in propagating dominant ideology.

Guiding Questions

1. What are some of the major ways to define power, and how does one identify and measure those definitions?
2. What role does the press play in either supporting or refuting popular definitions of power, and what are some examples of such coverage?

Key Terms

Information: Expressed knowledge shaped by cultural and social forces
The power elite: A collective of individuals and institutions that control a society's economy, political order, and military with interests of maintaining order
Propaganda: A pejorative representation of information used as a means by which to marginalize and distract from realities counter to dominant ideology
Whiteness: Ideology of racial superiority by people considered to be white, which appears pervasive in dominant US cultural distinctions of class, language, race, and social norms

---

EXPLICATING THE EMBASSY EVACUATIONS: THE PURPOSE OF BANAL NEWS

On August 4, 2013, international press reported that the United States would close eighteen to twenty-two of its embassies (the numbers changed over the course of the coverage) for as long as a month following ominous "ongoing concerns about a threat stream indicating the potential for terrorist attacks emanating from al-Qaida in the Arabian Peninsula [AQAP]."[1] Speaking on behalf of the government's terror gurus, President Barack Obama spoke on NBC's *Tonight Show* two days after the embassies were closed, saying:

> ... it's entirely consistent to say that this tightly organized and relatively centralized al-Qaida that attacked us on 9/11 has been broken apart and is very weak and does not have a lot of operational capacity, and to say we still have these regionalized organizations like AQAP that can post a threat, that can drive potentially a truck bomb into an embassy wall and can kill some people.[2]

While it was not the president's most articulate statement, his comments—and, maybe more than anything else, his appearance on the popular late-night comedy and entertainment show—revealed the normalcy of talking about "terrorism" in US society. We have become so accustomed to such discourse that it seems to make its way into nearly every setting for conversation. We worry about the threats to our lives by outside forces so much so that even the most obscure of movie theaters in US cities refused to show the 2014 comedy *The Interview* in which amateur hit men (their real jobs in the movie are as entertainment journalists) were selected by the CIA to assassinate North Korea's Kim Jong-un, an alleged dictator.

In June of that year, North Korean officials threatened forceful action against the United States and its interests if the film was released—just one of the many instances of rabble-rousing by members of the North Korean government over the past decade. In December, Columbia Pictures, which distributed the film directed by Seth Rogan and Evan Goldberg, initially refused to release the film, citing concerns about terrorism and possibly even danger to members of the studio and moviegoers if the film ticked off North Korean leaders. Studio executives also said their decision to halt the release was related to a major hack to their parent company, Sony, which the FBI somehow blamed on the North Korean government through the hack group Guardians of Peace.

Only after Obama spoke out against the decisions to can the film by Columbia and Sony, saying the companies had succumbed to terrorism and that their decision suggested a chilling effect on the use of the First Amendment (remember, however, that Sony is a Japanese company and the First Amendment and "freedom of speech" are mainstays of US ideology), did Columbia Pictures release the film in select theaters. The viewers who braved the threat of violence (some cited the Colorado theater shooting during a showing of *Batman* in 2012 as reasons for not wanting to attend a controversial showing)[3] were characterized as patriots—even if a bit worried for their safety.

ABC News, for instance, covered a showing in New Jersey—at one of the obscure theaters that had decided to show the film—this way:

Everyone knew what was coming—the controversial death scene in the movie about a fictitious assassination plot against North Korean leader Kim Jong-un—but then the lights cut out.

One packed movie theater was left bewildered when a sudden power outage struck 1,300 customers in Clifton, New Jersey, including Allwood Cinemas at a critical moment towards the final moments during a screening of "The Interview."

Barry Cohen, who attended the 1:30 p.m. screening with his wife and grown son, said they "had no idea" what was going on.

"When it lasted more than five seconds, we though that maybe it was part of the movie and then we realized that it wasn't," Cohen told ABC News.

Even though a power outage would have caused confusion in any circumstance, the threat issued by a hacking group that it would attack theaters screening "The Interview" led to understandably hyped tensions, moviegoers said.

Some people ran out of the theater," Cohen said. "There was another couple near us, the woman turned to her husband and said, 'Let's get out of here!' She didn't even wait for a refund or anything."[4]

Mediatized integration of fear and rhetoric into even the most obscure of news events throughout the country contribute to an incessant need for public protection by US forces and local police. Over the past twenty years in this nation, driven by rhetoric surrounding 9/11 fears that "everyone is out to get us," authorized violence, sometimes against our own people, has been set as a new kind of normalcy that has only been made overtly clear by reactions of corporations and citizens to threats of foreign force, such as the possibility that the North Korean military could possibly care enough to bomb a movie theater in Clifton, New Jersey.

Even the most bizarre fears—some of which are discussed later in this chapter—are treated with such legitimacy in the press that news coverage about terror attacks on US property and people blend with larger concerns about "attacks" on a US-style of life. Issues such as the alarming rates of autism among our youth, the mass murder of dark-skinned citizens at the hands of police, the threats to our environment from pollutants, increasing heat, rising sea levels, and diminishing access to clean water, are marginalized, in part because the sources of these threats are not so clear and the solutions for these issues are too costly to the power elite's financial and cultural caches. "Terrorism," on the other hand, holds more salience than climate change for news audiences and is something that can be addressed through violence, added "protection," surveillance, and the arming of local police forces—the effects of which are showcased in the continued slaughter of young, black men (see Chapters 5 and 6).

Indeed, Obama's involvement in discourse surrounding *The Interview* and in commenting about the pending doom under which the United States should live during his *Tonight Show* appearance reveals that media producers and politicians have an expectation that audiences have enough familiarity with unified, singular meanings of North Korea, al-Qaida, 9/11, and maybe even the president's reference to the ominous acronym AQAP ("Al-Qaeda in the Arabian Peninsula") that the entertainment venue was a perfect place for Obama to make his rationalization for closing US embassies. It is not even clear that members of the US Congress have these terms down, let alone that they have a complex understanding of these intricacies and the rhetoric being spilled to justify increased intrusion into any sense of privacy and independence from fear of our own government.

But, the terrorist threats—and who might have made them—were not what was really at issue during the *Tonight Show* talk. The session was just another moment in which media and fellow members of the power elite were able to set the stage for deepening the fears of the US public to support violent intervention into our lives.[5]

Terrorism as scapegoat

To further complicate things related to coverage of the embassy closings in 2013, US journalists speculated that the government's spying, which had revealed the threats, came from powers awarded to US officials under the Foreign Surveillance Act—not the information gathered from Edward Snowden and the subsequent release of information related to mass NSA surveillance (see Introduction). With this speculation, the spy information was characterized as legitimate and not to be confused with any suspected government-led mass surveillance efforts under "scrutiny" by Congress that same month. Not surprisingly, press coverage further marginalized the NSA measures by treating debate over spying as a game of political Ping-Pong rather than a reality that may have been counter to traditional values of US democracy.

Political parties vied for TV attention rather than led a public movement to challenge the validity of spying powers that members of Congress had seemingly supplied themselves and that they employed in passing legislation that attempted to legalize such efforts or that set standards for oversight. *The New York Times*, for instance, described the political conflict as a "subject of a fiercely partisan debate, with Republicans accusing Obama administration officials of making misleading statements about connections between the attackers and Al Qaeda." Additionally, the *Times* used the threats as a means by which to revive debate about a 2012 embassy attack in Benghazi, Libya, from which US Secretary of State Hillary Clinton suffered a political punch for somehow being solely responsible for an apparent lack of adequate security that contributed to the carnage; the attack had led to the death of the US ambassador to Libya, J. Christopher Stevens and at least two others. What has become referenced in the press since then only as "Benghazi" also became a key challenge against Clinton in the 2016 presidential election.[6]

Furthermore, just as officials and journalists cast nearly every "threat" to US interests and lives as imminent if without superior military protection and action, the 2013 embassy threats were an opportunity, via the press, to establish the authority of government officials who were there to save the day through increased militarization and surveillance programs. "To the members of Congress who want to reform the NSA program, great," the press quoted US Sen. Lindsey Graham as saying, for example:

> If you want to gut current legislation, you make us much less safe, and you're putting our nation at risk. We need to have policies in place than can deal with the threats that exist, and they are real, and they are growing.[7]

Even press from the United Kingdom, a US ally, relayed a message from US Sen. Saxby Chambliss that he made on NBC's *Meet the Press* the morning the closures were announced. His comments struck at yet another fear in the United States at the time—Muslims:

> There has been an awful lot of [terror] chatter, which is very reminiscent of what we saw pre-9/11 … As we come to the end of Ramadan, which

is always an interesting time for terrorists, and the upcoming 9/11 anniversary, this is the most serious threat that I have seen in the last several years.[8]

Few members of the mainstream US press called the announcement of these international threats for what they were—a point of distraction from US government spying. The United Kingdom's *Guardian*, however, did not let the moment slip. One of their headlines told the story directly: "US embassy closures used to bolster case for NSA surveillance programs." In the story, *Guardian* journalists wrote:

> Privacy campaigners criticized the widespread linking of the latest terror alerts with the debate over the domestic powers of the NSA. Amie Stepanovich, a lawyer with the Electronic Privacy Information Center, said: "The NSA's choice to publish these threats at this time perpetuates a culture of fear and unquestioning deference to surveillance in the United States."[9]

In the United States, Patrick Smith, on the website Salon, touched upon this sentiment when he wrote several days after the embassy closings that:

> the silence among our newspapers and broadcasters ... confirms only how dangerously circumscribed Americans political discourse has become. It is all text and subtext now, and the subtext, by definition, is known but never allowed to pierce the surface of silence.[10]

Still, mainstream news coverage in the United States survived criticism of hyping news of the 2013 embassy threats, because journalists harkened to the Benghazi attack from nearly an entire year before as a way to justify assigning fear in the most recent case. 2013 coverage operated with a banality in which government officials and members of the press provided fodder for politicians and corporate weapons experts to attack opponents of a national spying effort. Little of the news about the 2013 threats was dramatic enough to remove it from the everyday notions of living in a "War on Terror" so much so that officials appeared as polished experts on the issues at hand, a sense of authority the press used to explain the need for added public surveillance and violence.[11]

Even the most basic reference to the potential for failed protectionism that had allegedly led to the Benghazi attack made the notion of spying a necessary practice of and for "national security." Indeed, relating the threats to the Benghazi attack and the subsequent uses of the attack to justify international military responses for future protection represent the most blatant of ideological work conducted by news media at the time, even if the use of evidentiary news events is banal. The ability to present a news narrative with unquestioned validity when it is based merely upon a single source (i.e., the government), as it did in this case, hinged on the fact that the political debate about the threats was so boring that no one was really paying attention.

Covering terror news as part of the "public service"

As I will discuss throughout this chapter, a collective and single-minded moral charge to "serve the public" allows journalists to collaborate with powerful political and corporate leaders under the guise that their shared efforts will maintain public agendas. Conversely, however, journalistic collaboration with fellow social and cultural institutions only deepens meanings of everyday events in ways that benefit *the power elite* —what I define as a collective of individuals and institutions that control a society's economy, political order, and military with interests of maintaining order. In the case of the embassy closings, as well as in the case of the indoctrination of fear and nationalistic unity spread by discourse surrounding *The Interview* release, press reliance on information from public officials that go uncorroborated provides a moment in time for the press to reify their position as liaising between the public that is in need of "protection" and the virtuous representatives of our nation and local communities that appear in the news to gain added recognition of their importance. At the center of these ideological acts, the press operate to assist fellow members of the power elites to call for expensive military action and for economic investment to support US paternalism through policies of isolationism and violence. These collaborative calls for action are also used to distract the public from other issues in a way that narrows what becomes public discourse to topics only of interest to and of benefit to the powerful.

Undoubtedly, many who are reading this book are too young to have experienced the immediate rhetorical aftermath to 9/11, clearly one of the most pivotal moments in modern history that has shaped how US publics experience and explain everyday life. Missing from the collective consciousness of this newer generation is the hyper-Americanized movement away from political xenophobia that led to criticism of the Clinton Administration's investment in the global community to rallying of the US people to become the world's police force. Nonetheless, these same readers have had the opportunity for a decade now to watch the attacks on television, the images burning into their memories by repeated viewings.

And almost as surely, these readers today likely experience a comfortable life in which they can go shopping, eat at restaurants, buy cars, and travel the world without much concern besides a layered sense of alertness (i.e., the motto of "See Something, Say Something") that our government and media have indicated is appropriate and necessary for the continued safety of us all. Spoken within the naturalized discussion of US-led international war is our collective thanks to the Armed Forces and our vigilant politicians for providing our safety. But, the benefits of "freedom" as we know it today come instead from an indoctrination of the public by the press to obey and to conform in ways that these acts themselves contribute to a response to terrorism. This mindset allows us to feel as though we are participating in our own protection, under the tutelage of our authorities. Yet, we increasingly live in an age of mediated fear, inundated with messages of danger that reinforces the elite's interest in ideological isolationism and rampant international terrorism of our own creation.

I do not mean for such statements to be read through a lens of simple determinism. Rather, I mean to say the forces of fear, capitalism, and US Exceptionalism have become so embedded within media communication that "everyday news" (in which terror news has become incorporated) plays an active role in training a citizenry to be involved in their own sense of exceptionalism. Missing from much US press coverage about the embassy closings, for instance, were outcomes of US military stationed throughout the world already in problematic, "proactive" movements to "protect and serve" US interests: Our nation's surveillance planes soared over Yemen and much of the Middle East, our drone striking against "suspected" terrorists in those areas that have led to the killing of thousands. Instead of providing these "facts" as such and in ways that help to explain hostilities toward Westernized nations, US press released scenes of military disembarking US citizens from embassies as threats increased, scenes that showed dramatic evacuations via C-17 transport planes that removed US personnel across the globe, an exodus, in my reading, away from the "tribesman" of the East to the "civilized" New World and without any clear context as to why we were in these locations in the first place.[12]

The public, then, was intentionally left with a lack of context—in this case, the reason for such spread of US military across the world and the potential conflicts inherent in our nation's involvement in the daily lives of other places— which left room for distraction caused by immense consumerism and anti-intellectualism upon which our valued corporate (and media) enterprises are based and maintained. The power elite and its media indoctrinate the citizenry well and to the degree that arguments made thus far in this book have more than likely already been read as counter to notions of "common sense." In turn, the possible meanings opposite of dominant ideology that have been made—and that will be applied throughout this work—are dismissed as nonsense, as "liberal" propaganda, as "socialism," as "unpatriotic," and even as "inaccurate" or "unsubstantiated."

With little surprise, then, US-led war-mongering—which includes the use of flag-waving citizens as much as the action of profit-hungry politicians, corporate partners, and a prize-hungry press—drives the military-industrial complexes to new levels of open and excusable extremes. Mediatized sinister applications of threats associated to US interests and lives return world leaders and citizens to cries of fear—even if such threats last only for a couple of days—supported by popular racialized sentiments of "the other" and justified needs for military (and press) readiness to mobilize and enforce its hegemony at a moment's notice.

David Unger further explicates dominant fear ideologies discussed thus far in his book, *The Emergency State*. He writes that these ideologies:

> ... blind ourselves to the lessons of the irregular wars that have bloodied us in Vietnam, Iraq, and Afghanistan, imagining that they are somehow exceptions and that our military failures on these typical modern battlefields should not challenge our notions of unchallengeable American military power.[13]

In this way, the press serve as a dictator-machine of ideologies and actions rather than a messenger of information. Moreover, the press operate in these ways to promote the indoctrination of the public and resulting oppression as a natural outcome—and function—of a "free" and "democratic" society under the value-laden veil of "freedom," "law and order," and logical repression.

Fundamental to these functions and acts of the press are the ideas of power and the power elite, which is further examined below. Beyond contributing to notions of the power elite as merely being constructed of and by individuals, however, I am interested in applying more radical positions of power application among and via the press that move our interpretations of even the most dull news to tools of indoctrination that operate in a sense of normalcy per the direction of the power elite's ideological constructs. Therefore, the remainder of this chapter sets a stage for examining local applications of power acts by the press in the news of everyday life. In other words, I mean to implicate the press as being of and for the power elite and begin that conversation by explicating the very notion of power itself.[14]

POWER: A BRIEFING ON NEWS
AS COMMODITY

Power as examined in this project revolves around that of *information*, which I define as expressed knowledge shaped by cultural and social forces, and which often holds embedded, dominant meanings that guide the like-minded to proper interpretations. The idea of information, in this project, consists of constructs such as facts, ideas, and language that are assigned to explicate expressed knowledge. When discussing how knowledge is formed and distributed *as information*, one must consider several factors by asking:

- Who has access to shape information?

- Who and how was the information distributed?

- Who benefits from the information?

- Who and how will this information maintain the ability of an individual or of collectives to shape future perceptions of issues, events, and people?

Identifying processes of information-creation allows us to recognize a level of power within the content and contexts available that are serviced by a palette of ideologies tapped in times of meaning-making. Information about geographies, commerce, personalities, and meanings of literature and of war, for instance, holds particular benefits to dominant meanings that last through public discourse and uphold the authority of the select few who work to shape and maintain meanings. For example, there is little wonder, then, why dominant imaginations of Disney World, Las Vegas, and Mount Rushmore hold similar place-meanings that situate capitalism, modernity, and US Exceptionalism in favorable positions.

If only one of the three held these meanings, that single location would stand out as a delinquent, its motives questioned. In other words, each holds their own meanings of what it means to be "American." Yet, because enough geographies, these ones included, share in the same goals of patriotic capitalism, there is little notice that Disney is a private, profit-driven corporation, that Las Vegas banks on contemporary tales of personal freedom via "sin" and "vice," and that Mount Rushmore is built on sacred land and supports a paternalistic reading of the past as a means to support the "rights" of future US expansionism through violence, a method of development upon which the country was founded. Still, the questions listed above and the corresponding articulations of "Americanization" through rhetoric of built environment seem similar to movements of "media literacy" that have swept through US society over the past several decades.

However, as discussed in this book's Conclusion, the popular answers given by those who strive for such literacy are rooted in the same capitalistic and "Americanized" ideologies that put the interests of the power elite—and its politics and corporations—at the forefront of interpolation that does nothing more than to further indoctrinate news users to be news consumers. Therefore, while much of this book deals with a form of power and violence being exerted through and by the military, economic forces, police and the press, also common to each of the cases examined here is the rhetorical recognition of power inherent within meaning-making assigned to actions and actors that appear in the news through collaboration between dominant ideologies, ideological power brokers, and the press. Therefore, please consider the following discussion to be an argument not just to define "the power elite," but as one to help explain the notion of *power* and what it means to be *elite*.

Defining power

Power holds multiple definitions that align with an equal number of diverse approaches to examining just exactly what power is. One approach to understanding power defines the concept "as the production of causal effects" that focuses on an "agent's intentional use of causal powers to affect the conduct of other agents." In this sense, power operates amid interactions between a "principal" agent and an agent of the subaltern or of the subjugated. In other words, this approach sees power as a moment when an individual or collective directly influences the activities or actions of another. Another approach to understanding power focuses on how power is constructed, maintained, and executed through rhetoric and—at times—with the help of supplementary physical manifestations.[15]

In many ways, both of these major approaches to understanding power examine the concept through a lens of social structures and institutions and argue that power's resulting outcome of social control manifests itself in the implementation of desires maintained by dominant power structures. Yet, within these two approaches, power appears in different and meaningful ways that further challenge the creation of any singular interpretation of the concept. John Scott outlines two major forms of power—elementary forms and developed forms—that are helpful for initial discussions about power studies (Figure 1.1).[16]

Map of Power Relations

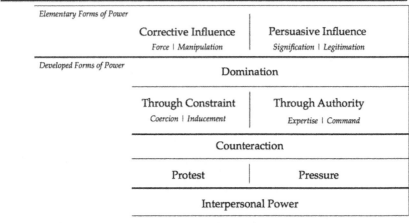

Elementary Forms of Power		
	Corrective Influence *Force	Manipulation*	**Persuasive Influence** *Signification	Legitimation*
Developed Forms of Power	**Domination**	
	Through Constraint *Coercion	Inducement*	**Through Authority** *Expertise	Command*
	Counteraction	
	Protest	Pressure
	Interpersonal Power	

FIGURE 1.1 *Scott's articulations of power.*

Elementary forms of power include corrective influences and persuasive influences, both of which rely on force/manipulation and signification/legitimacy. From the establishments of power, such as police forces and governmental and legal rhetoric, social structures and modes of power maintenance are enforced through indoctrination and communication. Messages in and of themselves inherently carry a form of persuasion designed to manufacture authority and legitimacy for both the communication and the communicator, but the function of power operates in the ways in which threats to society are presented as "real," costs associated with a product are "just" and "fair," proposed actions of an institution are altruistic and rooted in the "interest" of the nation or its people. The power is in the persuasion.

Furthermore, Scott argues, messages presented to the audience as "truthful" and "objective," coming from legal and religious institutions and institutions of force (both public and private military and police), for instance, function to implement direct action in their maintenance of power establishments. And, the more a form of power is established, the more forms of developed power emerge, which can appear in several forms, including:

- Domination instituted by constraint or authority, which contributes legitimacy to the rationales of life, including the ability to attain prosperity, reified through the authority and command of social actors

- Counteraction in forms of protest or pressure against social leaders
- Interpersonal power, the use of individual agency, and collaboration with fellow individuals in means to operate against a power system

At their core, each of these levels of power rely on a society with consistent social order, one that holds legitimacy based upon its long-standing existence, but which also operates a veil of "shared governance" and "opportunity." As cultural commentator Christopher Hayes writes:

The legitimacy of a hypercompetitive social order such as our own derives from a shared sense that everyone is playing by the same rules, that there is an inherent fairness to the terms of the social contract, and that the system basically manages to confer the benefits on the most deserving.[17]

Hayes, again, writes that:

the appeal of such a system extends far beyond the relatively small number of the poor and the working class who are able to actually capture the brass ring at the top. Like the lottery, the meritocracy allows everyone to imagine the possibility of deliverance, to readily conjure the image of a lavish and widely successful future.[18]

Overt levels and layers of power that appear in news stories related to public efforts at enacting power tend to be characterized as specific "movements," whether or not the movements are representative of power as discussed here. These popular definitions of power fall into their own category of interpretation in which the power being enacted is done with the intention of benefiting the masses but actually continues subjugation through confusion and distraction (see Chapter 4). Much public and scholarly discourse has been dedicated to the "counter action" of the Arab Spring "movement," which lasted from 2010 to 2012 during which thousands throughout Arab countries rioted against their political leaders, turning to social media as an organizing tool. Scholars and social mediates alike argued the Arab Spring represented "the power of the internet" and the ability of individuals to use social media to change the world.

Rightfully, however, some scholars and journalists have considered the Arab Spring to be a Western-influenced effort to reveal the potential of an "American democracy." The "movement" was, in this argument, an effort to institute US-based rhetoric of revolution and individualism. These scholars and social commentators have tempered rhetoric to understand that social movements take time, involve much cultural conflict, and are often unrecognizable in the moment. Calls for viewing the Arab Spring/social media as power that can overthrow "the system" are premature, in this line of thinking, and wishful thinking on part of technological determinists. I happen to agree, in large part, with these critiques of congratulatory discourse of the Arab Spring, because while this criticism of the rhetoric surrounding the "movement" does not attempt to diminish the "power" of individuals to create change, it better articulates power relationships between social media and users and forces through a more nuanced focus on how power is easily misconstrued, in this case as a co-option of tyrannical governments for the benefit of media-technology fields of profit.[19]

When discussing power and social movements, one might also consider the political rise of lesbian and gay communities of the late twentieth century in the United States as an example of an interpersonal form of power in that not only as a moment in which protest occurred but as one in which a shared sense of power among a people led to social action. These might be more accurate representations of power/social movements, though even with the political success as of 2015 with the US Supreme Court deciding to decide on the "rights" associated with gay marriage, it is up for debate the degree to which "rights" being recognized in these cases is really a form of incorporation in which alternative perspectives are brought into dominant ideology as a way to pacify subordinate groups (see Conclusion).[20]

Amid this conversation of power, it is easy to become confused by the notion that power is a commodity that we hold. This project approaches power as something that is not a commodity, something that cannot be awarded, given, or taken away. Power is expressed. In the quest to characterize and code those who are "in power" and operate in and with power within social institutions, though, the very idea of "the power elite," which is discussed later in this chapter, suggests that power is "earned" and can be "shared." Even the above articulations provide a similar structured paradigm of power as a commodity. Allow, however, this confusion about power to remain for a bit longer so as to build a gap between what we "know to be true" and what is being argued here about power. This confusion will help later when we piece apart the power within the power elite in ways that challenge the concepts of "power," "the elite," and "the press" by separating them from one another and then gluing them back together.

To further examine power as an expression, Michel Foucault addresses power as not-a-commodity when he writes:

Do not regard power as a phenomenon of mass and homogeneous domination—the domination of one individual over others, of one group over others, or of one class over others; keep it clearly in mind that unless we are looking at it from a great height and from a very great distance, power is not something that is divided between those who have it and hold it exclusively, and those who do not have it and are subject to it.

His next statements are especially crucial in understanding that power must:

> ... be analyzed as something that circulates, or rather as something that functions only when it is part of a chain. It is never localized here or there, it is never in the hands of some, and it is never appropriated in the ways that wealth or a commodity can be appropriated. Power functions.[21]

It is here where Foucault's articulation of power operates against dominant notions that the power elite is rooted in a US meritocracy that can best be explained through neoliberal principles and social policies alone. Certainly, Foucault is not suggesting that there are no categorizations of social structures that operate to oppress. Instead, he is arguing—as do I—that power is one thing and the way we tend to discuss power and the powerful is another. It is, therefore, in the construction of communication and the means of culture that power operates as neither a backdrop, nor as a result, nor as an outcome of social action or communication of what is natural or acceptable. Power is at the forefront, operating as it does through its own means, counter to the ways in which we are taught and the ways in which we tell others that power works. Foucault writes:

> Power is exercised through networks, and individuals do not simply circulate in those networks; they are in a position to both submit to and exercise this power ... In other words, power passes through individuals. It is not applied to them.[22]

Such an approach is especially helpful when talking about culture and communication, in part because, as according to Marshall McLuhan—and supported by others, including James Carey—communication that is placed in front of us is not always recognized for its many parts. As with fish in water, the water is not apparent until tainted; in this case, US ideology of purity poisoned by appearance of power and control is what this project attempts. And, it is with this approach we move closer to a discussion of "the power elite" as a concept that is to be challenged to include the press. We are also approaching a construction of the press that includes within its ranks aims of the power elite. This discussion, though, must begin with understanding a direct connection between the development of information, its transformation into news, and the power inherent in the product that is news.[23]

The power of information: The early days

Today's US power systems are based, in large part, upon power structures of government, commerce, and information-creation/sharing within Britain at the time of colonialism in the New World. "The Founding Fathers" of the US were interested, or so we are told, in breaking from the rule of a king, a singular ruler that enforced a singular economic and religious system with only the power awarded by God as rationale and with physical and economic violence as the key tools of power-maintenance. Popular histories leave out the clear economic and physical violence rooted in the "Fathers'" similar commitments to dogma that rationalized and legitimatized threats and uses of force in early efforts of The Great Rebellion, and histories also ignore that not all "Fathers wished for complete distance from the power of the crown."[24]

What popular histories of this nation's birth seem to agree upon, however, is the role of communication in its expansion, the destruction of the "uncivilized," and the unending possibilities for prosperity that emerged. Mass development via mass destruction had been realized for centuries prior to Anglo settlements in North America and both inside and outside of Western Europe to which early settlers here were indoctrinated. At the center of this most recent expansionism was—as it continues to be today—access to information and the rhetorical and physical expressions of that access.

In Medieval times, for instance, governors quickly built a list of challenges related to "limitations in the information at the disposal of government" with expressed intent to solve the problems and maintain their upper hand. These limitations included:

- The speed with which information flowed in a time of complex and expensive means by which to travel

- The accuracy of that information in the initial stages of creation

- The financial costs of transporting information across often vast and treacherous landscapes while protecting that information from theft or alteration

- The selection of those deemed worthy to provide information to leaders of large geographies, who could be trusted with advising the ruling classes through an interpretation of information that best articulated means of establishing power

- The appointment of those who could successfully institute authority of high-level leaders at the local level, thereby securing how information was distributed and maintained within the interests of the powerful

As a result, information between audiences and governments—their institutions being the single influence on the establishment of business and social affairs of the time—relied upon a trained system of information flow placed at a premium in which "cooperation with those who wielded social power and with the institutions of local authority," included constables, priests, and what we may envision as the more traditional herald in the town square.[25]

Throughout history, such individuals and institutions of information obtained and shared what could be considered early forms of "news" through merchants, those with the ability and interests in crossing geographies, peddling and packaging information about battles between nations, of expansive expeditions conducted by governments, and of environmental challenges to crops and, therefore, the possible effects on production of goods and the vitality of the marketplace. Such information was often shared (and continues to be) in private correspondence between knowers; indeed, trade secrets, economic forecasts, battle plans, and local gossip each maintain the most value when kept hidden, highly managed, and shared systematically and only when necessary.

The commercialization of information, however, further complicated the notion of power, veiling the influence of who could afford to create, sell, move, and purchase information. Early shipments of information among world societies operated amid mixtures of oral, visual, and written forms and appeared in varieties of outlets including churches, individual interactions in coffee shops or living spaces, postings of information in the town square, discourse in the market, and the distribution of printed leaflets. The commodification of information as news occurred as information was interrogated based upon its:

- Timeliness
- Ability to clarify or complicate previous understandings of particular people, places, events, and ideas
- Value in terms of power-positive outcomes related to its application

This increased value of "new information" provided those who shared and received information-as-news not only with financial profit, but also with public recognition for their role in having and sharing information.

But the power of news had a price. The day's newsmen, as they were, were the ones taking the risk for which they should be compensated, the theory went, and compensated they were, because news sold. "News about faraway events was precious," writes Andrew Pettegree in *The Invention of News*, "but [it was] difficult [and expensive] to verify." He continues:

The quantity of rumour, travellers' tales and eyewitness accounts available in the marketplace therefore played a crucial role in making sense of what might be received in confidential letters. It was valuable to be ahead of the crowd, to buy up grain before it shot up in price on report of an impending dearth. But to act on a report that turned out to be false, or exaggerated, could be more disastrous than not to have acted at all.[26]

But, the news was not just information to be bought and sold. By definition, this information, this news, also held cultural meanings and significance in terms of power. Just as she who holds information about advancing or fallen troops in a time of war or news of a drought's effect on crops that can contribute to future actions of military and the market, those who present information to the public or to business sectors, to warlords or to rebels, shape interpretations of that information's social and cultural meanings. And, it is this process of meaning-making that makes news the most profitable in terms of financial and cultural power. The value of information can be thrice fold when it is packaged in rhetoric—and that is just what the power elite do through news.

INCORPORATING THE NEWS: JOINING "THE POWER ELITE"

Ten years after World War II and following decades of watching tyrannical rule spread throughout Europe, US government and corporate exploitation of corresponding public fear of war led to continued, rampant industrialization and the need of politicians and advertisers to understand just how human needs and desires for safety and prosperity could be fed through commerce and militarization. In 1956, C. Wright Mills identified meanings behind these movements for interpreting human behavior as an effect of "the power elite," those who "transcend the ordinary environments of ordinary men and women [and who] are in positions to make decisions having major consequences." Through his work, Mills presented to the public a social hierarchy, or caste system, if you will, that revealed the inner-workings of commerce and governance to the general public. Much of Mills's work focuses as much on the construction and establishment of the power elite as on the outcomes of their rule and decisions in terms of economic and social policies. Mills clarifies that:

[w]hether [members of the elite] do or do not make such decisions is less important than the fact that they do occupy such pivotal positions: their failure to act, their failure to make decisions, is itself an act that is often of greater consequence than the decisions they do not make.[27]

At a time when the United States had joined with world allies against the Nazi bloc, blasted nuclear weapons in Japan to showcase the power of US forces, led efforts to identify and punish the era's warlords, and issued efforts such as the Marshall Plan to build growth throughout Europe and orders to dictate the reconstruction of a "democratic" Japan, the United States was at the peak of applying its modern hegemony through policy, politics, and economic forces across the globe. Still, Mills writes that the United States could hardly escape its origins in Old World Order (European fiefdom from which the United States emerged) and continued to operate with overt forms of power and a clear designation of who was elite both inside and outside US society.

Even today, while historians write of Medieval castles as not merely temporary places for villagers' refuge but instead as established signs of feudalism, of power and ownership, of a down-upon looking, we fail to recognize the physical identification of the US elite within corporate high towers, schools without windows, and concrete strip malls of commerce, their meanings embedded into brands, logo-fied, traded in on the stock exchange, and present in high school one-upmanship.

The rise of subtle signs of US hegemony that show themselves in moments of individual cost-benefit analyses of what to purchase at the grocery store, of which level of education or how much education is affordable, of which of the dozens of cereals, jeans, tennis shoes, and flat screen televisions one should buy has transformed the covert into the overt. We speak plainly about what we can afford and what we cannot. We proudly wear—or embarrassingly hide—our brands of clothes, the types of places we live, even where we went to school, if we did at all. These personal choices (though one could argue some of these decisions are not based on choices but on the circumstances in which we find ourselves) and outcomes, however, are not absent of decisions being made outside of the self.

These outcomes are directly connected to a consumer society created by US businesses and politicians postwar in ways that helped to rebound a failing US economy and placed, through the establishment of the United Nations and the World Bank, the United States at the center of globalization efforts to dominate the political-economic spheres of civilization. As I discuss in Chapter 3, US suburbs emerged following the war as new and formally educated homeowners, benefiting from the GI Bill and other forms of educational and lending programs through the US government, create cookie-cutter neighborhoods with white picket fences, white heads of household, and US flags flying over manicured front lawns.

In theory, the ranks of the power elite may no longer be limited to white, male landowners who operate within a constructed meritocracy meant to subdue hopelessness among the masses. Certainly, these characteristics would have helped one track down many members of the power elite, but in a globalized world, power elites who influence US society and set and maintain dominant ideologies are geographically spread far and wide. There are now questions about just who fit into the notion of the power elite, who dictate the marketplace and media spheres designed to define the norms of the day—important questions with answers that, if at the very least, can help in an argument that the press is the keystone to the power elite's purposes and practices.

Who's in the power elite?

On its face, the power elite may still appear a very simple notion: They are the people in charge—the rich, the powerful. More importantly, however, the power elite should be understood in terms of whom it includes and whom it does not. And, while we may be able to identify and argue for particular people and positions within the system as being in or out of the elite—maybe those who vacation to the Hamptons, the United Arab Emeritus, and places the rest of us have not even heard of, those who attend Ivy League schools or who are members of closed or secret societies, such as Skull and Bones—the power elite is perhaps better identified in terms of the power abilities of those individuals who, according to Mills:

- "are in command of the major hierarchies and organizations of modern society"
- "rule the big corporations"
- "run the machinery of the state and claim its prerogatives"
- "direct the military establishment"
- "occupy the strategic command posts of the social structure"[28]

These categories, which maintain their virtue today, position us to explore the ability of a few to make decisions that affect so many in so many aspects of our lives. This small circle of select individuals operate within a tiered system of advisors, and it is *these individuals* that we are more likely able to identify, who we may even know or be able to talk to. Two groups of lower-level elements of the power elite with whom we may have daily exposure in particular are of specific interest to identify.

Professionalized politicians

Professional politicians contribute to a middle level of elite power structures. These are people we may see on the TV, who represent our national, state, and city legislative and governing bodies. These long-term and widely known names direct the interests and values of the elites through national, regional, state, and local governments, in part because of their public popularity. But, these women and men also gain popularity or notoriety because of the very nature of how they have professionalized politics as spaces of organized, systematic languages and norms to which one can be trained.

Despite their popularity with the public—or at least their recognizability sometimes as lifelong politicians—these professionals operate within a particular rhetoric designed to rebuke any suggestion that the politicians are in politics for themselves. "No American runs for office in order to rule or even govern, but only to serve," Mills writes, identifying the use of political rhetoric that is expressed to the public. "[H]e does not become a bureaucrat or even an official, but a public servant."[29] And, the public, by and large, buys what the pols are selling. Even in times of political elections when the press address the spending habits and power of politicians' campaigns, report on politicians' tax records (if and when individual politicians release them to the press), the public finds it within themselves to forgive any overspending or indiscretions.

And, because the US political system has become so professionalized, as Mills writes, even the press have been trained to comply with—and to benefit from—the system: For example, local and regional television stations make a killing on the rates they sell to campaigns to air the very same commercials that the media rerun during newscasts to critique. Never have I seen, anyway, transparency in terms of the profits that local TV markets make off of selling airtime to candidates, even when the press—as I did for several election cycles in Wisconsin—hound the TV stations to see their books. The data I was reporting for the *Milwaukee Journal Sentinel*, for instance, only dealt with how much each campaign spent during a specific time period in a specific market; we never asked about how much of that revenue, which easily reached into the hundreds of thousands of dollars in some regions, was pure media profit created by the political process.

Celebrities as cultural leaders

Another category of the power elite infrastructure that Mills addresses and that is of interest to this project includes the ideological construct of celebrity. Alongside politicians, Mills writes, celebrities fill a gap within the political structure of relaying information, values, and explanations to the citizenry through entertainment, political stages, and news media. Such individuals are closer to "us" than to the "them" of the hidden elite: Movie stars sign their autographs—in-person; *New York Times* best sellers appear on the Wendy Williams Show; the affairs of sports stars are plastered on grocery store tabloids.

But beyond just entertaining us, Mills argues, they serve as a daily reminder that *anyone* can be an *American Idol* with the potential for access to the benefits of an elite class. He explains:

> In America, this system is carried to the point where a man who can knock a small white ball into a series of holes in the ground with more efficiency and skill than anyone else thereby gains social access to the President of the United States.[30]

The celebrity-politician dynamic in recent memory has become so overt that making lists of connections between politicians, power structures, and super stars would take up an entire book of its own: action movie star Steven Seagal has become a reserve sheriff's deputy; Bruce Springsteen opened for presidential candidate Barack Obama; George Clooney has worked for the United Nations. Even Elvis went to see Nixon. More important to understanding power and the elite than identifying just whom it includes, however, is in identifying "the power elite" *as a function* rather than a description.

Mills argues that the power elite (as a process) operate within three institutionalized units: the economy, the political order, and the military order. These relationships have amazing media connections in that journalists from major news and entertainment outlets cover the same stories of celebrity endorsements, discussions between politicians and celebs, and turn to celebrities over politicians to explain the needs and interests associated with particular social and political issues and policies. A select group of trained and socialized "representatives" functions to flow communication from elites to the citizenry, using common language and shared explanations for the world that veil power structures. That these representatives appear in entertainment and in "everyday situations" such as on the covers of grocery store magazines, on news websites and social media feeds, and on evening newscasts normalizes a system in which the rich and famous set public policy.[31]

Units of the power elite

To further examine the power elite, it is helpful to understand the units of structure within which the characters and members of the elite operate. Again, Mills identifies three sectors that have been carried throughout scholarship on elite theory: the economy, the political order, and the military order.

The economy

The first unit Mills identifies, the economy, is a force the power elite applies through rhetoric similar to that of the politician and of the celebrity—that capitalistic corporations, celebrities, politicians, and public institutions provide a "good" or a "service" via consumption and neoliberal principles. Little press coverage, outside of specialized media such as CNBC or *The Wall Street Journal*, speak directly to the system's hunger for immense profits. Instead, mainstream journalism, which itself strictly benefits from capitalism, ignores and diminishes issues of labor, maintaining a single narrative about only the business owner, the value of the stock owner, and the politicians who are either helping or hurting business with financial policies.

Patriotism via capitalism is embedded within everyday news, presented by the press as of utmost importance for furthering collective and individual prosperity. Indeed, news media barely wagged a finger when the US Supreme Court upheld the "public service" role of corporations in 2005, for instance, by allowing private business to benefit from eminent domain, the process of taking one's private property for public use. Whether eminent domain was a virtuous act in its original conceptions aside, the Supreme Court's decisions altered how even the most local of communities can be transformed by legal and financial arguments made by major corporations to take private land for whatever they can argue serves the masses.

Neoliberal movements that call for private enterprise to replace defunded public services make room for a government-backed removal of what seems to be one of the most precious "American" values—private ownership and control, particularly of land, capital, and ideology. Still, the privatization of eminent domain is a perfect example of how the power elite work in terms of process: A select few, with private profit in mind, remove with force ownership from another private owner through a governmental stamp of approval that is based in rhetoric of "economic good" for all. In turn, the news media—either ignorant or intentionally unavailable—report on the outcome of public policies and financial transactions that are, even if at first questioned by a portion of the population, normalized as approved and natural signs of progress. The outcomes that emerge days or years later—such as the removal of old businesses for new ones, old homes for new homes, and the public destruction of entire neighborhoods for new, private development simply because the neighborhood and/or its residents are undesirable to community leaders—are presented as merely news of the day.[32]

The political order

The political order, a second unit of the power elite's machine identified by Mills, consists of a centralized network of governments, private enterprise, and decision-makers (including the courts) that are funneled to local levels of social institutions through actions of "democracy." Spending on the military, health care, education, and day-to-day resources to run the government and its ventures contributes to tight-knit relationships between politicians and private dollars. Author and social commentator Thom Hartmann, for instance, writes that our corporate-political-ideological government is further influenced in more overt means than just operating within corrupt capitalism.

For instance, organizations such as the American Legislative Exchange Council (ALEC), which at the time of Hartmann's writing in 2013 boasted some 2,000 members who were elected officials and operate as a "shadow government," create public legislation that makes its way—often verbatim—into actual law and carries with it the private interests of the legislation's authors. The group, which counts among its major funders corporations such as ExxonMobil, Wal-Mart, Koch Industries, and BO (also known as British Petroleum), regularly presents to state legislators some 1,000 bills; the organization estimates 20 percent of these are turned into law. Among their many efforts to influence US democracy is ALEC's authoring of legislation requiring voter ID cards, a move progressives say is racially driven to keep particular sets of voters from the polls.

The fairly ominous ALEC defines its mission as one to:

> advance the Jeffersonian principles of free markets, limited government, federalism, and individual liberty, through a nonpartisan public-private partnership of America's state legislators, members of the private sector, the federal government, and general public.[33]

Even with ALEC's missions and actions out and open in the public, politicians and members of the press escape unharmed for their complacency and collaboration in allowing such partnerships to go unchallenged. Though if media did challenge such collaboration, corporations that own and operate the press might have to address how their own acts contribute to public expectations and pressures for the average US resident to obtain a sense of "The American Dream" through mass (and media) consumption, consumer and educational debt, and gendered and racialized notions of an American Life built, in large part, on the imaginations of the democratic process and a "free market."

With the protection of the business sector, which funds media production through advertising, the power elite and its press are further sheltered from criticism in their ignoring of intersections of social and cultural institutions in the creation of "reality" by stacking the deck of media rhetoric in times of economic and social crisis with layers of arguments that turn audiences away from placing blame on main characters of the political/economic system. If and when the media distraction through professionalized and celebrity rhetoric that puts traditional ideology above counter-narratives from alternative publics does not work (see Chapter 4), the power elite turns to its third unit to enforce order.

The military order

Mills examines a third unit of the power elite's system, that of military order, as being a direct branch of the government and of the economic model of capitalism. The military (and I consider local police as part of this sector, as discussed in Chapter 6) functions among the power elite's toolkit to influence the citizenry's compliance with political and economic decisions. For many nations, war has long been a means of expansion, commerce, industrialization, profits, and nation-building. As mentioned previously and discussed in greater detail in Chapter 2, US involvement in World War II served more as an ideological and economic safety net for the nation to recover from the Great Depression than it did in maintaining democracy and ending a Holocaust.[34]

The operation of the power elite's "inner circles" of the professional politicians, celebrities, and their units of force maintains a US democracy that is a direct product of and for plutocracy. Ours is a government of the wealthy and of the few, a system that has existed in the country since its birth but that in the last century or so has seen its ability to deepen and share in profit and power with an increasingly collaborative and profitable news media as a means to maintain public fear of threats that bolsters a militant society run by war profiteers and maintained by powerful global and local forces of control.[35]

News coverage of today's politics-as-usual in which military strength and the war economy are front and center often reads like a list of high school yearbook superlatives. For example, in December 2013, *The New York Times* announced an addition to President Obama's Administration in ways that buried the addition's private, economic interests by presenting his economic connections in a normal and almost expected light. The article, "New Obama

Adviser Brings Corporate Ties," heralded the naming of John Podesta, a former chief of staff to President Clinton and aide to former Senate majority leader Tom Daschle, as an Obama "senior advisor." And it reads as a laundry list of Podesta's connections as an advisor or investor to corporate America.[36] These corporations included:

- Northrop Grumman, a defense contractor
- Pacific Gas and Electric
- Eli Lilly, a pharmaceutical company
- Equilibrium Capital and Joule, "clean energy" companies
- Gryphon Technologies, a Department of Defense and Department of Homeland Security contractor

Additionally, the article states, Podesta had either sat on the board of directors of or had negotiated other financial ties with the Center for American Progress or had lobbied for Capital Hill policy changes that would benefit the interests of his friends in big business. That the establishment press would cover such an appointment and its close connections between corporations, military, and governance serves less as a watchdog role than it does a legitimization of the power system. In fact, the *Times* relied on a solid source to verify Podesta's appointment—a White House spokesman, who was quoted as saying:

> [Podesta's] appointment and background is completely consistent with the administration's ethics pledge [to distance corporate lobbyists from presidential decision-making], which was never intended to ban anyone who works in the public policy space from joining government service. To the contrary, he is exactly the kind of person you hope to attract to public service.

The post-9/11 climate of fear has funded a fear economy in which "public service" has become an expectation of the corporate sector in ways that lead to companies partnering with government and military interests, directed by public monies, to manage billions of dollars that enhance the war-making power of national militaries and local police departments. A focus of the federal government since 2002, grants awarded to local and regional police units have bolstered commerce between governments and private war corporations.

Indeed, the local citizenry, from urban centers to rural countryside, has become so familiar with military grade weapons, armor, and vehicles (including drones, tanks, and surveillance trucks) being purchased by (or being awarded to) local governments that the appearance of this equipment seems a natural progression of technological perfection (see Introduction). Between

2002 and 2009, for instance, the Los Angeles Police Department's budget used to reinforce an already violent and well-equipped police force grew from $840 million to $1.32 billion. The private sector boomed amid that growth; Motorola, for instance, received some $16 million in contracts and did another $37 million in contracts with the city in that timeframe.[37]

The three units of the power elite discussed here—the economy, the political order, and the military—converge and reveal themselves best in today's militarized society in which schools, designed to educate our future about business, "democracy," and "history," are grounds for police and power battles designed to stall independent thought and undesirable behavior. Critics of elite theory, however, argue that the structure of the economy and of governance as presented by Mills and in work on elite studies since function within a deterministic and simplistic approach and ignore the individual citizen's role in self and social governance. These critics suggest that, instead, those interested in identifying a system of the power elite are not presenting critical analyses of society but instead fueling discontent among a select and naïve few who are ripe with panic.[38]

Still, this project calls for investigations to implicate collectives of individuals—not merely structures and institutions—as operating within a powerful elite in order to articulate the means by which power is executed via media processes, actions, and meanings. And, while all of this might be hard to muster, Hayes writes that:

> So long as the franchise is granted to a small enough group of people, or the layers of representation between the masses and political leaders are sufficiently attenuated and mediated by powerful interests, a democracy in name can still feature rule by the few over the many.[39]

The remainder of this chapter—and some of the next—provides a foundation related to notions of the press and the field of Journalism Studies, upon which the rest of this project builds arguments for seeing daily news as power elite propaganda.

CONCLUSION: INTERPRETING NEWS AS PROPAGANDA

Upon hearing the word propaganda, one might easily think of tales of strategic communication or of disinformation in World War II or of the Cold

War, Communist-style posters of workers, of labor, and of the myths related to the Red Scare. Popular imaginations upon which we form our immediate impressions of everyday life tend to rely on overt and popular representations, however, that lack both context and a commitment to challenging the status quo through new and complicated ideas. "Propaganda," then, has become a term that means we are tricked or forced into believing a certain something that, in the end, is "wrong" and harmful to our existence. But this is not how the term is expressed in this project.

This section will argue that news is propaganda, attempting to revive within the field of Journalism Studies an awareness of the intentionality within media messaging that is often cast aside. In the sections below, I provide a brief analysis of how Propaganda Studies have been approached—or dismissed—within Journalism Studies. From there, my analysis of media control throughout the rest of this project operates under the premise that news is and operates as propaganda of and for the power elite.

The problems with propaganda

Because of the stigma and misunderstandings associated with popular notions of propaganda, even by John Nichols and Robert McChesney, who have together produced volumes on US hegemony through critiques of the country's mainstream media system, scholars argue for a more compassionate view on the media's role in expanding the nation's plutocracy. Theirs, for example, avoids the fact that our propagandistic media is rooted within the most idealist construction of US democracy. They write:

> In a nation where repeated waves of media consolidation have made a handful of multinational corporations the arbiters of public discourse, a culture of bigness has contributed to the creation of a lumbering and lazy media ... The pathologies of unchecked deceit, injected into the body politic by the conflict-shy media, have so infected the body politic that for many Americans there no longer is information or the means of acquiring it.[40]

In effect, such statements remove responsibility from news media as being a power institution, relying on passive constructions of laziness and wariness and the ill intentions of individuals and systems outside of media to explain the nation's current state of "democracy." Mills, on the other hand, takes a much more media-centric approach in his explication of indoctrination processes in the US when he writes about the effects of middle-class rhetoric (i.e., an expectation that each citizen demands "individual success") and the role of "the propagandist" who works "alongside or just below the elite." This propagandist uses the media effectively enough to "control the very formation of public opinion in order to be able to include it as one more pacified item in calculations of effective power, increased prestige, [and] more secure wealth."[41]

Of course, Mills goes on to destroy any idealistic approach that the media have the power to change the world merely through words. Countering any sense of determinism on the part of media power and ability, he writes that early forms of Mass Communications held the public's trust to the degree that communication—and communicators—did hold a dominant sway over citizens. An expanded media system, he argues, has diluted some of that trust. But, because even the widest media system maintains a dominant ideology of nation, economy, individual value and roles, and threats to society, I argue, one should not be distracted because Mills focuses his interpretations of media propaganda as being that which comes from the advertiser.

In all fairness, advertising and the construction of the public's political mind was the burgeoning medium at the time he wrote *The Power Elite*. Mills's work still provides a wide opening for interpreting propaganda as a cultural—not merely a social—effect of media power and control. In *White Collar*, for instance, Mills examines the propagandistic function of popular culture. He writes:

[P]opular culture is not tagged as "propaganda" but as entertainment. People are often exposed to it when most relaxed of mind and tired of body; and its characters offer easy targets of identification, easy answers to stereotyped personal problems.[42]

Still, the seminal works on the power elite and much of the work that has emerged since still do not, to my satisfaction, relate the role and function of (cultural) propaganda to everyday journalism. In this project, therefore, I identify popular uses of the term propaganda as a pejorative representation of information used as a means by which to marginalize and distract from realities counter to dominant ideology.

Put simply, the notion of propaganda upon which this book is based recognizes how the term's popular meaning marginalizes unpopular discourse and ideology. As a consequence, this approach also interprets information traditionally not assigned a propagandistic title such as police blotter, military and other "official" reports, and corporate financial releases—messages that have been designed to direct appropriate social behavior and cultural explanations of life—as a form of "thought control" that perform enhanced functions when they appear in the news media, often verbatim or elevated in importance, which ultimately leads to my definition of "media control."

In 1997, and then again in 2002, Noam Chomsky released a small monograph titled *Media Control: The Spectacular Achievements of Propaganda*. Emerging from the neoliberal Reaganomics of the late 1980s and the first US-led military action against Iraq in the 1990s, there was little wide acceptance of Chomsky's critique of democracy and his explication of thought control. Still, he—and others since—have tried to expose the role of the press as an active tool for spreading oppression, for formulating ideological dominance, and for serving profit-driven rhetoric through both straight news, advertisements, and business news that is all too often mired in notions of the press as a pivotal cornerstone of nationalism and individual sovereignty. Again, however, Chomsky focuses on national and international press reports and leaves little room in his own work for a critical examination of the ideological functions of the press at local levels.

Yet, one of Chomsky's many reads on how media promote the needs and orders of the powerful, eliding those the press are said to protect, his *Media Control* furthers the concepts of what Edward Herman and he released in their late 1980s book, *Manufacturing Consent: The Political Economy of Mass Media*. Throughout much of his work over the past decades, Chomsky mirrors a clear articulation of how democratic societies operate behind a veil of citizen participation, representation, and access to both the work and benefits of private business, while promoting and protecting the values and interests of the few. The work you are reading today, then, is rooted in what is considered Propaganda Studies, revolving around articulations of Herman and Chomsky's Propaganda Model, which I examine below.[43]

Defining the Propaganda Model

While Chapter 2 examines news construction from a perspective of Journalism Studies, within which very few scholars acknowledge the legitimacy of the propagandistic approach, I present the Propaganda Model first with the intent of charging the conversation throughout the following chapters with a perspective more radical and critical of power relationships. To begin, the Propaganda Model is based on five "filters":

- Media ownership, which dictates the economic value of media and directs the approval of expenditures and acceptable costs to consumers that provide the most profit possible from each element of a media product[44]

- Media funding, such as advertising, which not only influences the financial abilities of the press to operate, but also introduces social pressures in terms of publishing advertising—and news—as content that "builds community" and is of an appropriate cultural meaning (see Chapter 5)[45]

- Sourcing—the lifeblood of news; where and from whom the press get information, commentary, "evidence," and credibility in terms of what journalists cover—and how (see Chapter 2)

- Flak, the manifestations of tensions between the media, audiences, and fellow power institutions that provide a moment of boundary maintenance in terms of what is adequate journalism; this filter provides a veil to suggest media operate separately from the power system by working "against" other institutions (see Chapter 4)

- Anti-Communism or an "Us-Them" dichotomy; initially presented during the Cold War, this filter has been reframed by scholars to better represent its ideological purpose, which is to create divides between dominant and subordinate communities and audiences (see Chapter 5)

In order to identify and to measure these filters, the Propaganda Model relies on several "predications":

- That mainstream news media will rely on official sources to present ideologies that reify power positions, such as notions of nation and of capitalism; relatedly, collective histories of a dominant community will be sanitized to protect its current ideologies

- That media scholarship that applies the Propaganda Model and reveals corporate-source-ideological connections within the news will be marginalized in scholarly arenas

- That such media scholarship threatens normative assessments of the news and power structures and, therefore, will not only be marginalized by professionals and scholars alike but will be removed and undermined despite any validity or academic rigor because of its ability to adequately attack power structures[46]

Scholars turn to Chomsky's methodological recommendations to address the above predictions and to identify media filters that I employ throughout this project. These approaches include (1) comparing moments in history for comparisons in coverage to reveal ideological positions of power and

(2) examining media sources, content, and discourse to reveal embedded meanings of culture and power.[47]

Still, I am aware that I will have to contend with critics in my own field of Journalism Studies who view examinations of news-as-propaganda as being without merit. In his book *Sociology of News*, Michael Schudson, for instance, presents a critical discussion of propaganda or "thought control" studies that are indicative of most popular types of criticism. In that discussion, Schudson attempts to explain the difficulty in defining "media effects" in terms of both research aims and in practicality from which he expands into a discussion on the values of examining news through a lens of propaganda. In short, he states that explanations of propaganda result in a deterministic "effects" approach to media, which he states is troublesome:

> One reason it is difficult to establish media effects is that we operate with oversimplified models of how the media affect society. We ask simplistic questions. We fail to separate out the different questions that address media effects.[48]

While I question the virtue of discussing Propaganda Studies within the subfield of media effects research, it is still important to address how Schudson continues by defining propaganda as an unnecessary and somehow-zany construct to begin with. He writes that those invested in Propaganda Studies somehow wish to lead the public to believe that:

> [t]here is a dictator or a Machiavellian publisher or an elite of self-serving journalists who campaign for an idea or program, insinuate it between the lines, repeat it ad nauseam until at last it sinks in and the public follows along despite its own best instincts. According to this model, the media are a weapon of psychological warfare.[49]

What Schudson writes-off as a "conspiracy theory" (see Chapter 4) or as a fallacy, however, this project heralds as a truism that does, indeed, operate with intentionality to obfuscate and oppress. Especially ironic is Schudson's reference in his sentences above to war, weaponry, and psychology as tools to undermine the possibility of a propagandistic element of journalism (an argument left open to interpretation), in part because much of the early work in Mass Communications relied on forms of psychology and today borrows from Literary Theory and Rhetoric Studies to make claims about media messaging.[50]

Schudson continues by arguing media operate in terms of symbols and mythical stories (a topic he writes about widely) that put mainstream media on par with other "important influences on the fabric of society," such as faith and religion. Still, he claims that "the media offer only words and images, not love or hate, nothing but symbols, not aid, not notice, not attention, not sentience."[51] His point that "culture is the language in which action is constituted, rather than the cause that generates action"[52] is well taken, but one must not get lost in the incessant need to balance notions of power between an individual and a cultural artifact without taking a risk in placing too critical of a lens on any one influence that operates—in Schudson's words—within a "web of meanings, and therefore a web of presuppositions, in relation to which people live their lives."[53]

That said, Schudson does help this project by identifying press functions within a collaborative power system, which he identifies as "facets of news influence" with which my arguments of news-as-propaganda are aligned. These facets consist of:

- Information upon which audiences can act, which he calls "Information as Cause," and with which citizen awareness of criminal behavior and actors can help solve crime, or with which information of possible medical conditions may help influence a person to seek medical care

- Information that has been provided through methods of "public legitimacy" and/or public interest. Schudson considers such information "News as Amplifier." In this category, journalists are said to publish a particular story stamped as "newsworthy" based upon criteria that the information is simply of interest to large audiences

- Information placed within a moral or political "slant" or "bias" represents what can be referred to as "News as casual Agent"[54]

Therefore, if news can be all of these things (and, as Chapter 2 suggests, even more complicated), why are approaches such as the Propaganda Model considered so radical? As the remainder of this book will suggest—and which seems a logical connection that anyone could make—no one likes to have their power questioned, including journalists, politicians, business owners, and, most certainly, academics. Maybe notions of propaganda challenge all of our senses of authority, and that is why it is avoided.

In the end, this chapter has attempted to build a connection between the role and purpose of the press and the interests and actions of the power elite, incorporating the two concepts to be aligned as one through the concept of propaganda. I have argued that this project capitalizes on the power of propaganda, of "thought control," and of "conspiracy theory" in order to rescue any radical leanings to understanding media messaging through the notion of "media control."[55] In future chapters, I examine the power structures of journalistic institutions and outcomes to further argue that news-as-propaganda operates to maintain publics' commitment to systems of *whiteness*, an ideology of racial superiority by people considered to be white, which appears pervasive in dominant US cultural distinctions of class, language, race, and social norms.[56]

Discussion Questions

1. To what degree do histories of news creation and information-sharing in the US coincide with notions of propaganda?
2. To what degree is today's news aligned with propagandistic motives?
3. How does scholarship operate to obfuscate critical examinations of media?

Notes

1　Matthew Lee, "US to reopen 18 diplomatic missions after threat," bigstory. ap.org, August 9, 2013, http://bigstory.ap.org/article/us-reopen-18-diplomatic-missions-after-threat.

2　Matthew Lee, "U.S. embassies and consulates to reopen after terror threat," *The Huffington Post,* August 9, 2013, http://www.huffingtonpost.com/2013/08/10/embassy-closure_n_3736288.html.

3　2012 Aurora shooting, Wikipedia, http://en.wikipedia.org/wiki/2012_Aurora_shooting.

4　Meghan Keneally, "Power outage during final moments of 'The Interview' startles audience," ABC News, December 26, 2014, http://abcnews.go.com/US/power-outage-final-moments-interview-startles-audience/story?id=27842958.

5　As a note of clarity, I use the term "United States" rather than "America" to identify the country and "US citizens" or "residents" rather than "Americans" for two reasons. First, the term "America" has come to singularly represent the United States of America, which is in North America, and ignores other locations and cultural constructs by the same name, such as Central America, Latin America, and South America. Second, "America" also connotes a level of patriotism with which I am not comfortable and which relies upon imaginaries constructed in values inherent to efforts of nationalism. The United States, or the US, on the other hand, recognizes the construct of a governed body, led not merely by culture but by social and economic politics of a government and its military—not necessarily its people.

6　Associated Press, "'CIA officials' testimony sheds light on Benghazi consulate attack," *The Guardian*, December 14, 2013; Mark Mazzetti, Eric Schmidt, and David K. Kirkpatrick, "Benghazi attack called avoidable in

Senate report," *The New York Times*, January 15, 2014. For more about the role of "terror" as an ideograph for creating American isolationism and maintaining its empire, see Glenn Greenwald, "The same motive for anti-US 'terrorism' is cited over and over," *The Guardian*, April 24, 2013.

7 "US embassies to reopen in Middle East and Africa after terror threat," *The Guardian*, August 10, 2013.

8 Dan Roberts and Robert Booth, "NSA defenders: embassy closures followed pre-9/11 levels of 'chatter,'" *The Guardian*, August 4, 2013.

9 Spencer Ackerman and Dan Roberts, "US embassy closures used to bolster case for NSA surveillance programs," *The Guardian*, August 5, 2013. Commentary related to the rhetorical action of the threats in relationship to the surveillance hearings did appear in some web journalism, yet was not presented as a valid position in explaining the coverage in mainstream news coverage in the US. For example of commentary that appeared, Josh Voorhees, "Did a conference call involving Al-Qaida's 'Legion of Doom' prompt all those embassy closures?," Slate.com, August 7, 2013, http://www.slate.com/blogs/the_slatest/2013/08/07/al_qaida_conference_call_daily_beast_reports_the_u_s_listened_in_on_a_global.html.

10 Patrick L. Smith, "There is no terrorist threat: The feds want you to think there is, compliant media goes along," Salon.com, August 9, 2013, http://www.salon.com/2013/08/09/there_is_no_terrorist_threat_the_feds_want_you_to_think_there_is_compliant_media_goes_along.

11 For an interesting discussion on what it takes to be considered an "expert" on "terrorism," see "Glenn Greenwald on how to be a terror 'expert': Ignore facts, blame Muslins, trumpet U.S. propaganda," DemocracyNow!, January 13, 2015, http://www.democracynow.org/2015/1/13/glenn_greenwald_on_how_to_be.

12 "Yemen security alert: US and British citizens told to leave—as it happened," *The Guardian*, August 6, 2013.

13 David C. Unger, *The Emergency State: America's Pursuit of Absolute Security at All Costs* (New York: Penguin, 2012), 9.

14 Aeron Davis, "Whither mass media and power? Evidence for a critical elite theory alternative," *Media, Culture & Society* 25 (2003): 669–690; Sharon Meraz, "Is there an elite hold? Traditional media to social media agenda setting influence in blog networks," *Computer-Mediated Communication*, 14 (2009): 682–707.

15 John Scott, "Modes of power and the re-conceptualization of elites," *The Sociological Review* 56 (2008), 29.

16 Ibid.

17 Christopher Hayes, *Twilight of the Elites: America after Meritocracy* (New York: Crown Publishers, 2012), 69.

18 Ibid., 47.

19 Douglas Kellner, *Media Spectacle and Insurrection 2011* (New York and London: Bloomsbury, 2012); See also, Joseph Massad, "The 'Arab Spring' and other American seasons," aljazeera.com, August 29, 2012, http://www.aljazeera.com/indepth/opinion/2012/08/201282972539153865.html.

20 David G. Savage, "On gay marriage, Supreme Court to weigh equal rights and states' rights," *Los Angeles Times*, January 19, 2015.

21 Michel Foucault, *Society Must Be Defended* (New York: Picador, 1997), 29.

22 Ibid., 29.

23 See G. Stuart Adam's comments in the Forward to James W. Carey's *Communication as Culture*, and Carey's own comments within the book; see also, Marshall McLuhan, *Understanding Media: The Extensions of Man* (Cambridge, MA and London: MIT Press, 1994).

24 For a telling of US historic figures that identifies their commitment to power, see Harold Holzer, *Lincoln and the Power of the Press: The War for Public Opinion* (New York: Simon and Schuster, 2014); Howard Zinn, *A People's History of the United States* (New York: HarperCollins, 2003).

25 Jeremy Black, *The Power of Knowledge: How Information and Technology Made the Modern World* (New Haven, CT and London: Yale University Press, 2014), 129; Additionally, these communicators were not actually what we would consider "newsmen," because news was not their sole commodity. The news would often share a ride with crops, with passengers, with produce and spices. Shipping the news with other products made the movement of information affordable—and profitable.

26 Andrew Pettegree, *The Invention of News: How the World Came to Know About Itself* (New Haven, CT and London: Yale University Press, 2014), 49; For function of news and communication, see Bruno Bettelheim, *The Uses of Enchantment: The Meaning and Importance of Fairy Tales* (New York: Vintage Books, 2010); Dan Berkowitz and Robert E. Gutsche, Jr., "Drawing lines in the journalistic sand: Jon Stewart, Edward R. Murrow, and memory of news gone by," *Journalism and Mass Communication Quarterly* 89, no. 4 (2012): 63–656; Susan Jacobson, Jacqueline Marino and Robert E. Gutsche, Jr., The digital animation of literary journalism," *Journalism* (2015), doi: 10.1177/1464884914568079.

27 C. Wright Mills, *The Power Elite* (Oxford and New York: Oxford University Press, 2000), 4.

28 Ibid., Chapter 1; To review Mills's progression of the power elite, see also, Edward Barratt, "C. Wright Mills, power and The Power Elites—a reappraisal," *Management & Organizational History* 9, no. 1 (2014): 92–106, doi: 10.1080/17449359.2013.853619.

29 Mills, 17; The 2012 presidential election showed a connection between the power elite and professional politicians when presidential candidate Mitt Romney was taped at a private party speaking about the US class system, in which he said: "There are 47 percent of the people who will vote for the president no matter what. All right, there are 47 percent who are with him, who are dependent upon government, who believe that they are victims, who believe the government has a responsibility to care for them, who believe that they are entitled to health care, to food, to housing, to you-name-it. That's an entitlement. The government should give it to them. And they will vote for this president no matter what. And I mean the president starts off with 48, 49 … he starts off with a huge number. These are people who pay no income tax. Forty-seven percent of Americans pay no income tax. So our message of low taxes doesn't connect. So he'll be out there talking about tax cuts for the rich … My job is not to worry about those people. I'll never convince them they should take personal responsibility and care for their lives. What I have to do is convince the 5–10 percent in the center that are independents, that are thoughtful, that look at voting one way or the other depending upon in some cases emotion, whether they like the guy or not." (See, http://en.wikipedia.org/wiki/Mitt_Romney_presidential_campaign,_2012.) Here, we see the identification of what Mills refers to as *crowds* and *cliques*. These higher-level social groups overlap and intersect, with many in these groups having been educated in the same places and continue to operate with shared missions and member's lists.

30 Mills, 74.

31 For popular politicians and entertainment connections, see http://en.wikipedia.org/wiki/List_of_actor-politicians; for notions of "truthiness," see Priscilla M. Meddaugh, "Bakhtin, Colbert, and the center of discourse: Is there no 'truthiness' in humor?," *Critical Studies in Media Communication* 27, no. 4 (2010): 376–390.

32 See, http://en.wikipedia.org/wiki/Kelo_v._City_of_New_London. To be fair, private enterprise has always been at the winning end of public removal of private land, yet political and press rhetoric was applied to veil forceful nature of land removal for profitability. "Public good" rhetoric, as discussed throughout this book, is a favorite of press discussions related to violence by militaries and local police agencies; for more on cases related to eminent domain, visit the Institute for Justice at https://www.ij.org/cases/privateproperty.

33 See Thom Hartmann's description of ALEC in *The Crash of 2016: The Plot to Destroy America—and What We Can Do to Stop It* (New York and Boston: Twelve, 2013), 168–173; Also, only a few mainstream news outlets covered the failures of legislation designed to reign in corporate corruption and to maintain a sense of social responsibility among housing lenders, for instance, which led to the 2007/2008 financial crisis, which, by the way, followed decades of moments in which corporations (i.e., AOL Time Warner and Enron) were found to be running rampant in their profit-making. One exception to coverage that merely reported on the events of the crash includes a *New York* magazine cover story on March 2, 2009 upon which fraudulent financier-turned-convict Bernie Madoff was mocked-up on the magazine's first page to appear as Batman's Joker under the headline, "Bernie Madoff, Monster. And the people who enabled him."

34 Also remember that America's own Holocaust—the slaughtering of American Indians as the country expanded in the 1800s—was authorized by the US Congress, implemented by the US military, and both funded by and helped to fund private, American enterprise and Exceptionalism. For more, see Ward Churchill, *A Little Matter of Genocide: Holocaust and Denial in the Americas* (San Francisco, CA: City Lights Publishers, 2001).

35 For a clear argument, see Bill Moyers's "The Great American Class War: Plutocracy vs. Democracy," truth-out.org, December 12, 2013, http://truth-out.org/opinion/item/20583-the-great-american-class-war-plutocracy-vs-democracy.

36 Eric Lipton, "New Obama advisor brings corporate ties," *The New York Times*, December 12, 2013; The *Times* is careful to note that Podesta was no longer working as a lobbyist when assigned the Obama post "and therefore does not have to worry about the Obama administration's self-imposed ban on hiring lobbyists to administration jobs."

37 Darwin BondGraham provides a much more detailed report on force spending by the LAPD and the specifics of a former police chief's public–private business connections in "From top cop to the corporate boardroom: Ex-police chiefs spin through revolving doors into the private sector," truth-out.org, December 11, 2013, http://www.truth-out.org/news/item/20554-from-top-cop-to-the-corporate-boardroom-ex-police-chiefs-spin-through-revolving-doors-into-the-private-sector.

38 See critique of the power elite in G. William Domhoff, "C. Wright Mills, Floyd Hunter, and 50 years of power structure research," *Michigan Sociological Review* 21 (2007): 1–54.

39 Hayes, 139.

40 John Nichols and Robert W. McChesney, *Tragedy & Farce: How the American Media Sell Wars, Spin Elections, and Destroy Democracy* (New York and London: The New Press, 2005), 4.

41 Mills, *The Power Elite*, 315.

42 C. Wright Mills, *White Collar: The American Middle Class* (Oxford and New York: Oxford University Press, 2002), 336.

43 See discussion of "post-capitalist democracy" in *Blowing the Roof off the Twenty-First Century: Media, Politics, and the Struggle for Post-Capitalist Democracy* (New York: Monthly Review Press, 2014); Additionally, I have been influenced heavily by the debates surrounding Capitalism, Socialism, Marxism, and the media. For more, see discussion in Yanis Varoufakis, "How I became an erratic Marxist," *The Guardian*, February 18, 2015, http://www.theguardian.com/news/2015/feb/18/yanis-varoufakis-how-i-became-an-erratic-marxist; For more on the Propaganda Model, see Brian Michael Goss, *Rebooting the Herman & Chomsky Propaganda Model in the Twenty-first Century* (New York: Peter Lang, 2013); Jeffery Klaehn, *Filtering the News: Essays on Herman and Chomsky's Propaganda Model* (Montreal, New York and London: Black Rose Books, 2005).

44 This project does not focus much on media ownership; however, readers can learn more from storied scholars such as Robert G. Picard at www.robertpicard.net.

45 Even the most alternative of media sources—designed to counter the hegemony of concentrated, ideological chains of the mainstream—must turn a profit in order to exist (see discussion of nonprofit news in the book's Conclusion).

46 For such a discussion, see the introduction to Ellen Lewin, *Feminist Anthropology* (Malden, MA, Oxford, UK and Victoria, Australia: Blackwell, 2006).

47 Klaehn, Chapter 1.

48 Michael Schudson, *The Sociology of News* (New York and London: W. W. Norton and Company, 2003), 23.

49 Ibid., 23.

50 It is both unfair and inaccurate to judge a scholar as one thing or another simply by a few sentences of their work, particularly in the case of Schudson, a preeminent scholar who often does write about the cultural and complex nature of journalism, so I do not wish to do so. That said, this writing is especially telling in how easily critical assessments of media (and its scholarly validity) can be marginalized and discarded.

51 Ibid., 24.

52 Ibid., 25.

53 Ibid., 26.

54 For the first two categories, see Schudson's discussion on pages 29–32. To be clear, Schudson does not add a term to his description of this moral "slant" or "bias," though to maintain a clear categorization, in this discussion I refer to this as "Causal Agent."

55 Oliver Boyd-Barrett, "Judith Miller, *The New York Times*, and the Propaganda Model," *Journalism Studies* 5, no. 4 (2004): 435–449; Peter A. Thompson, "Market manipulation? Applying the propaganda model to financial media reporting," *Westminster Papers in Communication and Culture* 6, no. 2 (2009): 73–96; Andrew Mullen, "Twenty years on: The second-order predication of the Herman-Chomsky Propaganda Model," *Media, Culture & Society* 32, no. 4 (2010): 673–690; Simon Cottle and Julian Matthews, "US TV news and communicative architecture: Between manufacturing consent and manufacturing democracy," *Journal of Broadcasting & Electronic Media* 57, no. 4 (2013): 562–578.

56 Just as I have argued in my previous scholarship, there is no such thing as identifying a racist ideology within US society, because US ideology is inherently racist in that the categorization of society is based on interpretations of race.

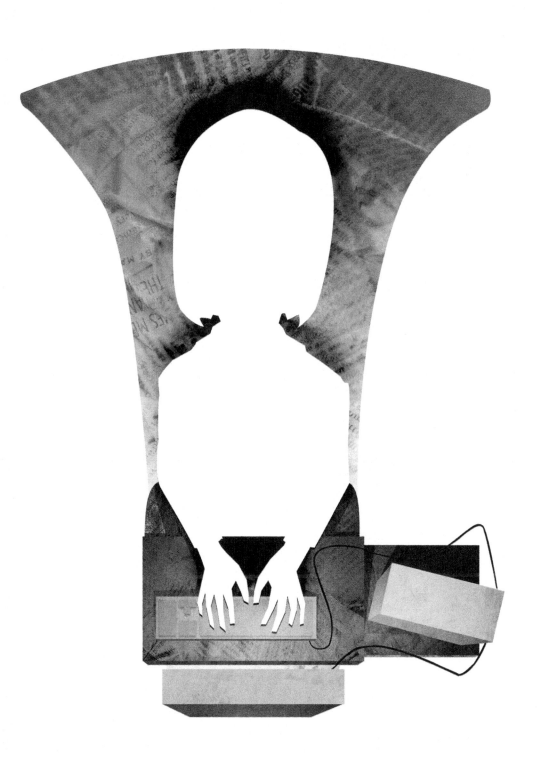

2

Making News: Purposes, Practices, and Pandering

Chapter Purpose

This chapter provides a foundation related to social and cultural meanings of news. It begins with an analysis of how US press covered the 2013 Boston Bombings, an example that positions the press as key to presenting dominant ideologies of the power elite. Moreover, this case is representative of how the press indoctrinate the public to elite "thought" while playing the part of "The Fourth Estate." Furthermore, the chapter discusses about how press "make news," particularly at a time of growing state and private surveillance, in which the media participate to grow a weaponized society that protects the interests of the press and fellow institutions of the power elite.

Guiding Questions

1. What purpose(s) does "the news" provide to citizens and fellow institutions?
2. How do we know what we know about "the news," and how do citizens award the press its legitimacy and authority?

Key Terms

Cultural Text: A source/symbol; a cultural manifestation that can be "read" for meaning

Journalistic Interpretive Community: A collective that shares dominant ideologies of their shared identities, purposes, and explanations of the world

Mythical News Narrative: Long-standing cross-cultural storylines and characterizations of people, places, and events told by news media to apply dominant explanations approved and maintained through power

READING NEWS AS NATIONAL RHETORIC: THE BOSTON BOMBINGS

April 15, 2013 started like any good day for a terrorist attack: crisp, collected, and with the joy that comes in Boston with Patriots Day, which remembers colonists' victory over British oppression. Reds, whites, and blues pepper the area, mixed amid flags from across the world that line city streets. It is also the day of The Boston Marathon, and spectators gather at coffee shops along Boylston Street within blocks of the finish line. There is the usual hustle and bustle, spots of cheers from the sidelines, runners grunting, and the sound of sneakers hitting the pavement. A good day for a run. But the perfect day is ready to be broken. At 2:49 p.m., a pressure cooker packed with nails explodes and pushes smoke into the air. The street shakes. Twelve seconds later—another explosion. Screams. The sirens start.

Later referred to in the press as "twin" explosions—no doubt a direct reference to the fireballs at the Twin Towers on 9/11—they send shockwaves that toss people aside and shoot shrapnel that take off limbs and which, in the end, kill three people and injure more than 260. Video footage catches scenes of runners falling to the ground. Above them, police, security forces, and spectators scurry to their aid. The explosions play over and over on YouTube and on cable news channels—the puffs of smoke captured by private and public cameras.

Some of the images from that morning are gruesome: One of the most popular photographs captures a runner, seemingly conscious and alert, being pushed in a wheelchair. His leg is severed. Immediately, these scenes are entered into media memory and labeled "The Boston Marathon Bombings." The name is later renamed into something easier for newscasters to call it: The Boston Bombings. And, it is then when, with very little evidence and without context and insight into what had happened that morning and why, the explosions are hyper-Americanized and used in the press to position the events over the next few days—including the execution of military-police activity on Boston streets equal to that of martial law—as legitimate, necessary, and in the name of "American" peace and justice. Immediate press coverage of these events—and the rationalization of such police and power activities—would prove just how far the War on Terror had taken US citizens in accepting violence (and the threat of violence) against those suspected of "harming" "us."

This chapter begins with a reading of news coverage of The Boston Bombings to further identify how local news indoctrinates local audiences with nationalistic ideologies, particularly at a time of crisis. For the purposes of showing how nationalistic demands of the press and the power elite played out at the local level of the nation's media system, I first turn to the front page of *The Birmingham News* in Birmingham, Alabama, as what I consider to be representative of the local, ideological agenda-setting performed in the days following the bombings. Following this discussion, I then examine how narratives of securitization as a national and patriotic priority appeared in national and local press to normalize military–police action in and around Boston following the explosions, which turned the city and its suburbs into a warzone.

Explicating news coverage of a single event sets the scene for this project that is designed around a recent movement in US society and culture to demand unquestioned forms of force in the nation's cities to protect what the press consider "the lives of Americans," while what is really being protected is the business and moral interests of our elites. It is this take on the news that appears in further discussions about the field of Journalism Studies, some of its seminal works and approaches that will help define "media control" throughout this book.[1]

Before the bombings

No news event occurs within a vacuum. By this I mean that what becomes the news does so because of an event's relationship to current contexts. Since the 9/11 attacks, the US press have taken on a self-imposed duty of placing US security and exceptionalism at the forefront of nearly all major crises in the world. The press have done so to the degree that fears of anti-US "terrorism" have normalized fears of how "anti-Americanism" and threats of violence against the United States are connected to the potential for another Great Recession—the worst-case scenario for a capitalistic democracy.

Appearing amid these emerging cultural norms and press explanations for international disorder, much of which has been caused by the United States itself, news coverage of The Boston Bombings began with the simplest of explanations: it must have been international terrorism. Casts of "authorized knowers"—those whom journalists turn to as official and virtuous sources who present ideologically adequate explanations for social issues examined in the news—had already been set, and they were ready to work.

Relying on "knowers" to present dominant and unquestionable explanations via news coverage causes the audiences' imagination, through verisimilitude, to take over in terms of connecting "the facts" of "the story" to an event's relationship to everyday life. Based upon a media system revolving around "authorized knowers" and prearranged narratives of explanation that are established even before any event is identified for its "newsworthiness" and covered in the press, journalists and their audiences have been primed through multiple levels of cultural indoctrination to employ their imaginations in ways that assign authority to particular media messages and sources. Only the imagination relishes *The New York Times*, for instance, as being worthy of a public following that is then further conditioned by social systems surrounding its financial, political, and cultural weight.

News items themselves operate within a similar sphere of audience verisimilitude, a process similar to what James Ettema has identified as a resonance of meaning and the "imaginative power" of news. I build upon Ettema's argument that resonance of news meanings "elevates news to myth and deepens it into ritual" to the degree that the imagined is real and the explanations from imagined authorities are authoritative. By examining in what ways news relates "to our imaginations that build upon a society's fears, collective memories, and shared wishes for the future," so much so that "issues of today become 'normalized' to fit into a world of imagined realities that relate to dominant moral narratives and that connect to our own lived experiences," we understand that what is not embedded into ritual and that which is not resonant also matters in examining the power of media control in the construction of culture.[2]

The "imaginative power" of the media is so central to my articulation of "media control" that in 2013, for instance, I applied articulations of the news imaginary to news coverage of "the Miami Zombie," a dark-skinned man who had attacked a light-skinned homeless man near the *Miami Herald*'s former downtown location the year before. In that case, cars zipped past on the city's MacArthur Causeway while Rudy Eugene, naked, bit into Ronald Poppo, ultimately destroying some 70 percent of his face.

Curious about how quickly the press were able in that case to inject into the news overarching narratives of meaning from which the audience is expected to interpret the event, I looked at breaking news coverage from the *Miami Herald*, the *Sun Sentinel* in Fort Lauderdale, Florida, and Florida's *Orlando Sentinel* for roughly the first month. What I found was that each newspaper, independently, turned to the same explanations for Eugene's behavior.[3] They included that he:

- Was on synthetic drugs at the time of the attack
- Had practiced Voodoo, which spurred the violence
- Had smoked marijuana before the attack
- Was a zombie

- Was a cannibal, an explanation that, when coupled with notions of Voodoo, held racial connotations in characterizations of Eugene, Voodoo, and cannibalism of a dark-skinned "savage"

- Was merely a by-product of a strange Miami culture

However, each time the press presented a potential cause for the attack, each explanation was derailed by official reports related to the case, including that:

- No evidence of synthetic drugs was found in Eugene's body during an autopsy

- Eugene's family insisted he was a Christian and did not practice Voodoo

- No evidence suggested Eugene had consumed marijuana prior to the attack

- Through statements made to the public from scientists at the US Centers for Disease Control and Prevention, the medical community knows of no virus that can turn someone into a zombie

- No human remains were found within Eugene's stomach

- The last explanation—that Miami made him do it—just flittered away without much analysis to indicate if there was something in the water or culture that could lead to such behavior

What I found surprising from this examination was the lack of any suggestion throughout the coverage that Eugene might have suffered from some kind of psychological break. Again, while I was not interested in what exactly caused Eugene to act as he did, I wondered why the press all but ignored the potential that mental health or mental illness could have been as possible an explanation as him being a zombie. To address why this explanation might be missing, I argued that news coverage represented a moment to examine the "imaginative power" of the news that ultimately "cast Eugene—and thereby others with aberrant behavior—as being cursed by otherwise unexplainable craziness or weirdness" and that explanations absent of mental or emotional discussion "somehow seem[ed] to be more acceptable than a medical discussion about mental health as a possible explanation." Additionally, I argued that:

the appeal of zombies through popular culture and the resonance of racialized discourse that involved Voodoo and foreign cannibalism overpowered the cultural familiarity of mental illness—a stigmatized explanation—as a legitimate and accepted medical explanation for behavior.[4]

In other words, I suggest that because press coverage of mental health and mental illness has been so ripe with stigma in the United States so few members of media audiences—and so few "authorized knowers"— were likely to understand the complexities and legitimacy of that explanation well enough to present it to audiences. Explaining that Eugene's actions were possibly a result of a psychological issue would force a complicated conversation about stigma related to mental health and mental illness and may, in fact, attack the power elite in the sense that public institutions are increasingly defunded and marginalized because they only deal with the few "insane" citizens. It was much easier, then, for the press to pick up novel ideas about the attack than to spend time and resources mired in a conversation about structural and economic inequalities in terms of the nation's mental health industry.

My reading of "The Boston Bombing" coverage below is situated in a similar ideological analysis in that it applies a dominant lens of journalistic "imaginative power" in ways that are critical of the potential meanings of texts that appear via news myth and narrative. Through my reading, I argue that the press covering the bombings operated quickly to institute immediate explanations for the event by turning to what would hold the most resonance with audiences—that the event was caused by foreign terrorists. In turn, the initial coverage began an immediate process of marginalizing alternative explanations—or ignoring those explanations—as the story progressed and allowed dominant articulations of what caused the bombings to filter to the local press level for further indoctrination of US Exceptionalism.[5]

The breaking news

In breaking coverage of The Boston Bombings, terrorism quickly appeared as the single, clear cause. "It's not clear whether (the bombings) might have been carried out by foreign or domestic terrorists," CNN's Wolf Blitzer told audiences shortly after the explosions. However, Blitzer was clear enough to say that the explosions were "carried out by a sophisticated group or an unsophisticated group" and "could have been just a lone-wolf type terrorist." Citing "federal authorities," the channel's Breaking News ticker echoed his statement as fact: "TERROR ATTACK AT BOSTON MARATHON." As he continued his coverage, however, Blitzer, breaking-down a speech made by President Barack Obama earlier in the day, points out with a smack of scrutiny and disappointment that Obama "never used the word terror or terrorist." Right on cue, CNN's ticker scolded: "OBAMA STATEMENT DOESN'T SAY 'TERROR.'"[6]

By this point, however, it did not matter whether Obama characterized the explosions as "terrorism" or not. The press already had. Throughout the first days of coverage, newscasters continued to relate the morning's explosions to past "terror attacks" against the US public: Oklahoma City; the first and second World Trade Center attacks; Columbine; the Sandy Hook Elementary School shooting in Newtown, Connecticut (see Chapter 4). Each of these place names has come to hold a natural spot in the narrative of US Exceptionalism over the past two decades, casting the nation and its citizens as victims at the center of harm caused by foreign terrorists, of wayward domestics, of the misled and the mentally ill, with little attention given to the complexities of the country's foreign policies, of those slighted, ignored, oppressed, and controlled within its borders.

Coverage of The Boston Bombings would end up looking no different. Within minutes, the explosions had already been assigned a name by the press—and an explanation—and one that would ignore that some of the very same attacks remembered by the press in initial coverage had been conducted by US citizens. From the outset, The Boston Bombings would be explained through a simple story of US citizens under attack, even though it would take weeks—and even months—for the most basic, confirmed facts to emerge about exactly what might have happened and who may have been behind the event. Throughout the first week in newspapers across the country, headlines carried a common and shared explanation for what became a "three-day manhunt" as federal, state, and local law enforcement in and around Boston effectively instituted martial law in the city and its suburbs, looking for those suspected of planting the bombs and setting them off remotely.

The role of local press across the country became clear in the search as scenes of urban and suburban disorder emerged on all mediums, threating a national calm. Through press coverage journalists:

- Justified the need for added surveillance and vigilance to maintain our safe streets

- Rationalized the use of force against the suspects so as to deter future acts of disorder

- Unified citizens against the common enemy in an act of retaliation even at the local level of society

In Birmingham, Alabama, on April 17, for example, the front page of *The Birmingham News* carried four headlines related to the bombings, which together built a storyline indicative of national and local press coverage in the United States in those first days (Figure 2.1). The paper's first headline, "**A NATION MOURNS**: 'YOU CAN'T JUST STOP LIVING,'" lined the top of

FIGURE 2.1 The Birmingham News, *April 17, 2013. Courtesy of Alabama Media Group and newseum.org. Used with permission.*

a photograph of a lit vigil candle, a statement of national resiliency and of an entire nation having been attacked and having experienced loss. The partial quote about "living" during a time of disaster came from a Boston Marathon runner who appeared in the corresponding news column. Humanization of the national crisis through the lens of a marathon participant placed the press—and the reader—amid a collective of shared experiences and meaning, positioning each of us as the victim, as a collective, and with a call to action that would right this wrong, making the paper's other headlines read as instructions on how to handle the crisis.

The newspaper's second headline, "**ON HIGH ALERT**: '(WE) REFUSE TO BE TERRORIZED,'" sits above a photograph of a member of law enforcement, standing on the balcony of a regal government building. He holds an assault rifle, his finger ready at the trigger, a US flag lowered in the background. The headline itself serves as a directive that "WE"—all of us within the nation who have been identified in the news headline above as being affected by this attack—should maintain our vigilance against those out to get "us." The danger might not yet be over, the headline suggests, and we must be on the watch for this thing called terrorism that is cast as unnatural for those in the United States to experience.

From this language, the reader is to understand that "normal war" happens in countries and terrains where the lives of those whose homes have been burnt or demolished under a tyrannical government and that we in the United States are (and should be) spared such tragedy. From this message that all in the United States—the "we"—should "refuse to be terrorized" positions the reader to accept that the citizens of this "nation" share a single identity and should react in the same way to the explosions, while also recognizing the bombings as especially rare and devastating *only because* it happened on US soil.

A third headline running down the paper's front page, "**THE INVESTIGATION**: '... BRING THEM TO JUSTICE,'" provides a call to action from the press to continue the investigation with the intent of setting a scene for retaliation. This headline is indicative of how the press identify expectations for how news events should be resolved. In this example, the press provide guidance to the citizens of the United States in how they should respond. The photograph depicts investigators, dressed in white frocks, gloves, and boots at the scene of The Boston Bombings. One man appears to be inspecting debris; another man stands, supervising with a look of authority. Inherent in the headline and photograph is the message that those who would "bring" those "responsible" to "justice" are in and of themselves "just" and hold a natural authority to collect evidence as they see fit, to examine evidence through a single—even sterile—approved lens of interpretation.

These men, the photograph suggests, have the authority and legitimacy to dictate the meanings of the evidence and, perhaps, the outcome of the punishment. Indeed, solutions, explanations, and responses to crises that appear in the press must always match dominant cultural and social norms and expectations if journalists are to maintain their legitimacy with audiences and keep their positions of power. Placing men of war, of government, and of authority at the center of the hard decision-making fits with a commitment of US society to hegemonic masculinity. Based on such a gendered-structure, *News* headlines relayed clear propositions surrounding the events of that day:

- What happened: Foreign terrorists attacked the United States (yet again), striking at the center of the nation's historic quest for liberty—Boston

- Who did it, and why: "Anti-American" terrorists sought to destroy the values and prosperity of the Free World

- What should be done: US citizens should unite to identify terrorists and bring them to justice by all means necessary to secure US freedoms

- Why vigilance matters: We are at war, as a fourth headline in the *News* informs, in bold text: **"Emergency chief: 'This is what we expect from war'"**[7]

In covering The Boston Bombings, the US press—from the national to the local levels—performed functions that reified dominant cultural interpretations of the explosions and the immense police-military. The press committed this act by:

- Placing themselves within the story as civic leaders; reporters are ready and willing to cover the "truth" of the story's causes and consequences

- Relying on dominant race narratives in the United States to characterize terrorists as dark-skinned "others" that supported arguments to attack those who threat US ideologies and interests

- Identifying and marginalizing the suspects as "foreigners" so as to strengthen the public's resolve for authorizing violence in seeking "justice" for the attack

- Celebrating law and order through harrowing stories of increased, local militarization that was necessary to "get the enemy"

I discuss each of these elements below in greater detail to reveal the ideological acts of violence and imperialism within press discourse.

Presenting the press as cultural, civic heroes

News images from the day of the attack held meanings designed to drive viewers and readers to recognize a call for national unity against "terrorists:" photographs and video stills were peppered with US flags, vigils, and police-to-the-rescue that appeared in newspapers from the *Los Angeles Times* in California and *The Pantagraph* in Bloomington, Ohio, to *The Tribune-Star* in Terre Haute, Indiana, the *Herald-Leader* in Lexington, Kentucky, *The News-Star* in Monroe, Louisiana, and *El Nuevo Herald*, a Spanish-language newspaper in Miami.[8] Through design and language, each of these newspapers told the same story as *The Birmingham News* and CNN—someone was out to get "us," that the United States had been struck at its very core, and that the center of the solutions and challenges to this threat was an informed and responsive media. Indeed, US press took the bombings personally and covered it in ways that led to a national cry for solidarity, US-led justice, and nationalism.

Furthermore, at the root of explaining The Boston Bombings, even the most local of journalists questioned the ability of their own towns and cities to protect themselves from terrorists and to catch suspected villains—especially international ones. Local press did well to hold a watchful (or "watchdog") eye over the abilities of the police and public leaders to maintain individual security (for more on media waiting and watching, see Chapter 5). In one case, *The Sun* in San Bernardino, California, posed a "watchdog" question of local police preparedness while also reassuring readers of their safety, as one article exemplifies:

> If terrorists ever strike Southern California, police and federal agents here will immediately ask the same question those in Boston did Monday: Where are the cameras? The answer: almost everywhere.[9]

The news story continues with what was a common vein of protectionism that celebrates the spread of security and surveillance cameras as a form of protection, suggesting that private and police cameras in Boston would "help find answers to the bombings" and could help stop crime elsewhere, too. Furthermore, by relaying and interpreting information to the public about how average citizens could hunt-down the suspects, the press positioned themselves, too, as helping to catch the suspected criminals.

Racializing the story

US news media can go little distance in a news event before applying racialized discourse, and The Boston Bombings coverage did not escape this trend. On April 17—two days after the bombings—CNN's calm and collected John King provided a description of a suspect for which authorities and vigilant US citizens should have been looking. "I want to be very careful about this, because people get very sensitive when you say these things," King told viewers. "I was told by one of these sources who is a law enforcement official that this is a dark-skinned male." Despite his hedging and his subsequent statement—that "[t]here are some people who will take offense for even saying that"—King provided the single description of a familiar terror suspect: "A dark-skinned male."[10]

King's colleague, Wolf Blitzer—seemingly from nowhere—chimed in to clarify. "We can't say whether the person spoke with a foreign accent, or an American accent," he said. "That would be premature." Yet, by this point, it had not been too premature to suggest, as they already had, (1) that this was indeed a "terrorist attack," (2) that we were "at war," and (3) that the suspect or suspects more than likely had dark skin and identified as male. To be fair, King later Tweeted that *he* did not characterize the suspect as a "dark-skinned male," but that the "[s]ource of that description was a senior government official. And I asked, are you sure? But I'm responsible. What I am not is racist."

The need for King and Blitzer to identify the villains—including in terms of race—fits within the normative duties of the press to provide any information that they have—and fast; usually, the journalistic standard is to provide verifiable—and verified—information, though journalists tend to get some leeway when it comes to moments of breaking news. Thus far in the initial coverage of The Boston Bombings, however, the press had served another role than just to provide verified information; they provided the meanings associated with the bombings to local and national audiences through a lens of individualism, particularly in ways that express what the bombings should mean to each person. Put another way, the news about the bombings in Boston was presented as being a local issue anywhere in the United States, that the "terrorist attack" represented immediate threats and danger to audiences—and audience members—throughout the nation.

Expression of individualism, though, did not occur without a larger association with a collective—the United States as a "nation." Providing explanations to the collective, then, required both an identification of the individual in the news—achieved through the humanization of coverage—and the immediate connection to the single collective that each person could possibly be associated with—the United States. This collective, however, needed to be identified and maintained well beyond the characterization of a foreign enemy that had been trained to terrorize streets of the United States. The collective needed elements of domestic fear associated with the potential villain that reified the need for constant concern that terror may lurk around any corner, possibly (however unlikely) from someone with the domestic scene.

To be sure, the press has long identified domestic "others" and "threats" as having "dark skin," associated even through generations of distance to primitive and savage "dark skinned" folk elsewhere in the world. Racialized history in the United States pits light-skinned, suburban heroes against dark-skinned, inner-city savages, including in the presentation of American blacks in entertainment and news media (see discussions of race in Chapters 3 and 4).[11] Furthermore, by legitimizing a characterization of possible suspects of The Boston Bombings as "dark-skinned" simply because it was an "official" description—and, therefore, also characterizing it as "newsworthy" without any other identifiable information or verification—CNN (and the multiple news sources that carried this news) further justified the need for blatant discourse of "the other," of "the threat" as being non-white, a seemingly normal and safe color.

Building upon centuries of racialized discourse, official and authorized murder, segregation, and legalized hatred for "dark-skinned" blacks in the United States, news about who might have been out to bomb Boston became cast as a case for justifiable and historically sound responses to address racialized disorder. Such a *mythical news narrative*—what I define as long-standing cross-cultural storylines and characterizations of people, places, and events told by news media to apply dominant explanations approved and maintained through power—helps media demonize US blacks (and other dark-skinned folk) for their association by skin color and destroys any subordinate efforts to challenge dominant racialized ideologies.

It is that reliance on the imagination of racial difference that reifies social acts and public discourse related to race—especially when that discourse appears in the approved pages of the news. In the case of the bombings, news audiences would soon have images of the suspects that would reinforce an "us/them" dynamic that is based on categorizations of race and "othering" based on geographic explanations of difference.[12]

Using images to identify and ostracize the protagonist

By April 18—three days after the bombings—US news audiences finally received images of The Boston Bombings suspects, which had been captured by a private department store's surveillance video aimed at public space. Later that day, and into the early morning hours of April 19, a military-grade mass shutdown of Boston and its surrounding areas was in place as police searched for two brothers who would later be identified as Tamerlan and Dzhokhar Tsarnaev.

Local police said that the pair had, in the days following the explosions, murdered a police officer who worked for the Massachusetts Institute of Technology, carjacked an SUV, kidnaped its driver, and sped off into Watertown, Massachusetts, where they initiated a shootout with police. There, Tamerlan was said to have been shot by police, run over by his brother, and died. Dzhokhar escaped deeper into Watertown, later to be captured from his hiding place inside a boat in someone's backyard as thousands of law enforcement officials searched the city and forced residents to stay inside.[13]

Just as the press shared police images of the brothers as having already been convicted of committing a crime and labeled as terrorists, news coverage painted a picture of the police as the sole answer to creating calm, to protecting the public, and to instituting justice. Police were cast as heroes in a real-life action and adventure movie: Officials provided news photographers access to capture images of herds of police and military as they tromped through the suburbs, dressed in SWAT gear, some with video cameras on their helmets, all with combat boots, Kevlar vests, and assault rifles at the ready. Men and women in FBI, State Police, and ATF fatigues, with guns drawn, driving military green Hummers, trucks, and tanks, made the "man-hunt," for all intents and purposes, a moment of entertaining martial law.

These scenes were presented in tight photos of police-in-action and starry-eyed night-shots of action under street lights. While these were not perhaps natural and normal scenes in the United States (though as this book later argues, military scenes of US suburbs have become increasingly naturalized), at the very least they were welcome ones to a nation fraught with fear.[14] To tie the press images together in a single, consistent meaning, news media across the country relayed language fed to them by law enforcement and government officials to diligently describe Boston as being "on lockdown" or as being "shut down," while other places, including Fenway Park and major intersections, were cast as "deserted" while "a suspect was hunted." Such passive language about the role of the military and US law enforcement stood out as a means of approving the acts. Indeed, few media outlets covered the situation thusly, for instance:

BOSTON UNDER SEIGE: City under "unofficial" martial law

Militarized local police pound through city for possible bombing suspects; action unquestioned by government officials

Passive language that the press did use—that a suspect "was hunted" and that the space "was on lockdown" or was simply "shut down" reified the pacification that was expected of the public that their cities were, without permission, designated battle zones.[15] Pacification of the press and of the public, though, never proved to be a problem, as the US public replayed reactions to police and military activity following the destruction of New Orleans during Hurricane Katrina in 2005 and the hyper-militarization that followed. In the case of The Boston Bombings, the enemies were made just as clear as those cast as "refugees" from their homes in NOLA, their potential to destroy the United States designed by the press and politicians, the radical police reaction and protest that they, in fact, were not instituting "martial law" made legitimate.[16] Most concerning about the pacification of the US public— and its press—was their unquestioned dedication to authority based upon a national ideology of racialized hatred of the domestic other and national xenophobia that equates to isolationism and the acts of violence required for isolation to security.

Celebrating control

Once news of Dzhokhar Tsarnaev's capture appeared across local news outlets in Boston, the press stayed in the streets to make photographs of celebration (Figure 2.2). News videos showed crowds cheering throughout Boston-area neighborhoods as police marched in parade-fashion. One video shared on the *Wall Street Journal* website showed college-age women dressed in pajamas cheering the capture, surrounded by a crowd and washed in the glare of police lights; men carrying a US flag down the street, yelling "Boston, baby. Boston strong. Nothing can tear us down." Over the following weeks, "Boston Strong" became the mantra for local recovery and took stage alongside "Never Forget," "Let's Roll," and "Ground Zero" as idioms applied in the press to route public discourse to the victimization of the United States as a "pure nation" absent of critical discussion about US-led hostility and intervention in social and cultural affairs abroad—and at home—that could help explain news events assigned to terrorism.[17]

Breaking news of The Boston Bombings—and the press celebration of its resolution—fueled dominant narratives of explanation about the continued War on Terror in which

> the American press has been schizophrenically immersed within a culture of fear and cruelty punctuated by law-and-order driven promise for personal safety, certainty, and collective protection…[18]

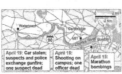

FIGURE 2.2 Journal & Courier, *Lafayette, Indiana. Courtesy of newseum.org. Used with permission.*

Nearly a week after the bombings (April 21), for example, famed—and semi-retired—journalist Tom Brokaw spoke on NBC's *Meet the Press* along with a star-studded cast of experts and officials to dissect days of political and press speech that had assigned an international identity to the brothers, presenting them as foreign—and Muslim—terrorists.

"With the death of Osama bin Laden, Islamic rage did not go away," said Brokaw, apparently an expert on Islamic rage. "In fact, in some ways, it's more dangerous. This is a perfect example." He continued:

> There's a lot we still need to know about what motivated (Dzhokhar Tsarnvaev), obviously. He's a Chechen, but their beef is with Russia, not with us. But, he's also a Muslim. And the fact is that Islamic rage is still out there. We saw it in Times Square. We were very, very fortunate under those circumstances. So there has to be more vigilance, obviously.[19]

Brokaw's comments—which really were the most mild of the unmeasured assertions made about Islamic and radical connections to global anti-Americanism during that morning's show—fit the tone of the overarching media discourse about The Boston Bombings. The rhetoric gained greater power through legitimation of such celebrated "experts" and "officials," many who held personal investments in the social and economic structures surrounding US aggression and violence. In fact, others who appeared on that morning's show to discuss The Boston Bombings included:

- Deval Patrick, the Governor of Massachusetts, who has held positions with Texaco, Coca-Cola and with ACC Capital Holdings, which owned AmeriQuest and Argent Mortgage—lenders involved in public debate about subprime mortgages in the mid-2000s

- Pete Williams, a US Justice Department correspondent for NBC who served as Assistant Secretary of Defense for Public Affairs under Dick Cheney

- Mike Rogers, a Michigan Congressman who served as Chairman of the House Intelligence Committee and had worked as an FBI agent

- Michael Chertoff, chairman and cofounder of the Chertoff Group—a "Global Security Services" company—and a former Homeland Security Secretary

- Michael Liter, a former director of the National Counterterrorism Center—a government intelligence agency—and an NBC national security analyst

- Dick Durbin, at the time Assistant US Senate Majority Leader and a lifelong politician

- Doris Kearns Goodwin, a Pulitzer Prize-winning historian and author who holds a Harvard Ph.D. and who helped President Lyndon B. Johnson draft his memoirs

- Peggy Noonan, a columnist for the *Wall Street Journal*, who had once worked as a speech writer and an assistant to President Ronald Reagan

- Jeffrey Goldberg, a hawkish author and writer for Bloomberg View and *The Atlantic*, who has also written for leading, elite publications, including *The New Yorker*

Celebrity-insider media performances such as *Meet the Press* and its heavily "officialized" news reports from authorities who have hands dipped in government-corporate collaborations are used to frame public consciousness to reflect the activities and appearances of the power elite. Henry Giroux refers to news shows like *Meet the Press* as evidence of a:

link between the media and corporate power [that] becomes more integrated into audio-visual spectacles that shock and massage the mind and emotions with a theatricality of power and a steady regimen of fear, violence and vengeance.[20]

Militant rhetoric from a journalist of Brokaw's stature among such a crowd of government and corporate leaders not only so very easily assigns power to such political and ideological positions but provides a sense of authority to journalists-as-experts and increases calls within the journalistic community for increased watchfulness and action—including strong collaborations with government, business, and police forces (see Chapter 6). Calls from the press to maintain a popular sense of order and control, such as in coverage of The Boston Bombings was focused on "getting the enemy" and relied on the voices of social authorities, members of the power elite and its media partners, and did so particularly because the "terrorism" of this case lacked a specific nation-state or organized militant group having had claimed responsibility for The Boston Bombings.

Without video footage of further threats from such a group and with no immediate threats from the Obama Administration to retaliate against a particular group of people, thereby pitting our military against another, journalists became responsible for explaining causes for the violence through media-state sponsored rhetoric that drives a "spectacle of terror and fear

[that] has become America's chief source of entertainment." In this way, the voices of authorities took the place of an identified enemy, filling the gap of the unknown with ideologies that constructed the enemy from our minds and collective memories.[21]

Beyond the bombings

Today, The Boston Bombings have either left much of the publics' collective memory or have been marked down as yet another sign of war against the United States. There is even a chance that it has been replaced by yet another equally or more destructive nationalized news event to reassure US citizens that the War on Terror continues and, honestly, may never end. And so in that way, perhaps, The Boston Bombings was not a special instance, a spectacular example of terrorism, of a battle in the War on Terror, or of hyper-Americanized news coverage. But, The Boston Bombings coverage does provide insight into exercises of a dominant media function—urging, celebrating, and performing social control—and that it may not be special in any other way as far as news events go and reinforces just how everyday news coverage (and its narratives) maintains US hegemony. The following section provides a background on Journalism Studies and on the approaches and processes for critical and cultural examinations such as the one above. In so doing, this chapter concludes with an analysis of current interpretations of how journalists work as a collective to tell common tales of explanation for everyday life that serves as social control.

Narratives of Journalism Studies:
Politics, profits and media-making

The Boston Bombings can be read as yet another moment in time when journalists across the political spectrum and the mainstream media sphere constructed supposed attackers as nothing other than non-American. From the get-go, the story *was not just* about the explosions; it was a chance to reify US Exceptionalism. From constant use of photographs of US flags to talking heads spewing suggestions that Muslims wish to harm patriotic US citizens, journalists presented the bombings as an attack on US ideals and values rather than, as one might assume, provided the "facts" as they came and—as "objectivity" would require—removed emotional appeals for increased nationalism during a time of crisis.

Press "bias" for constructing and claiming national identity is often confused as being a sociopolitical one rooted in the largely two-party political system of the United States, benefiting one party over another. Still, none of this serves as evidence against notions of journalistic objectivity among audiences. Press "bias" that presents victims and villains within "objective" rhetoric of sourcing, verification, and accuracy is instead viewed as the representation of one source over another within overt tales of tragedy and victory. Media scholars John Nichols and Robert McChesney (who were mentioned in Chapter 1) were close to capturing the type of "bias" I examine in this book, though in their work they, too, become distracted by political-economic debates about the function of the press in a democracy. "If professional journalism has a clear ideological bias, it is toward those in power," they write, in ways that make journalists "flat-footed and playing defense, obsessed with not appearing unfair to conservatives, and having far fewer qualms about sticking it to wimpy liberals."[22]

However, unlike media critics—and perhaps even some media scholars—I very rarely argue that the media is or has been "duped" or "tricked," act as "complacent," or are even politically "biased" in presenting the news. As a reminder to the reader, I am not interested in making a critique of "good" or "bad" journalism, or even questioning the guilt or innocence of the press in providing a watchdog estate for the purposes of providing the public with a voice in their governance. In these ways, then, I approach journalism not as an outcome of social and cultural forces that then appear online, in print, or on cable news, but as a process and as a function. In other words: News is an act. But what does this look like in practice?

By examining modern US press history in its relationship to war—at home and abroad—we are able to validate critiques that the press function under the guise of keeping us safe and under the watchful eye of "objective" and "verified" information about what may harm us, to show support for broadening US military and local police surveillance and violence in a country constantly under threat of (ideological) attack.[23]

Embedded into the banality of the daily news and into coverage that proposes a familiar narrative and explanation for events and issues, boosteristic news (see Chapter 3) serves as an act of communication-as-power to further "weaponize" the media and their ability to manage their "thought control" throughout its iterations of everyday life.[24] While there are many other books that discuss the origins of Mass Communications and Journalism Studies, few seem to identify what I consider, at least, direct connections between popular philosophies on media systems and practice and critical perspectives inherent in the act of scholarship.

As briefly mentioned in Chapter 1, what has become Journalism Studies, particularly in the United States, emerged from decades of research influenced by the threats of global Nazification and government propaganda surrounding World War II and American expansionism, the hyper-militarization and industrialization of which both corporations and politicians were desperate to understand in terms of the possibilities of influencing via consumer and voting behavior.

Mass Communications scholarship initially focused on how advertising, political beliefs, and individual actions interacted with media messages and social conditions of the day. One of those main conditions was some citizens' increased access to postwar wealth. Returning US soldiers and a society high on its renewed exceptionalism were quick to jump at low-cost but modest homes in new suburbs, personal automobiles, and white-collar work that provided a disposable income. Expanding US suburbs also paved the way for economic and political advertising, a significant boost for media companies to expand entertainment and news. The political rise also provided an opportunity for the press to expand their "public service" function and open new venues for advertising their authority.

Simultaneously, scholars became interested in media messaging and found their ability to conduct market research that was valued by private entities. To suggest that the beginnings of Mass Communications research in the United States operated solely within a realm of scholarly inquiry, then, would be inaccurate; early efforts were directly connected to industry and government—how to sell products and politics—with very little focus on the power dynamics involved in the communication under study and the ability of individuals to make choices. Put another way, early media research in the United States taught us how to hack the pocketbook and the voting booth. Still, some of the original understandings of how media operate have maintained their relevance and are of particular importance to this project.

Below, I discuss the role of two major concepts that help us examine the power functions of media that contribute to the institution's ability to control the masses—gatekeeping and agenda-setting. More than anything, this discussion is a critique of how these ideas fit into the project at hand and is by no means a complete history of the richness of scholarship in the fields of Mass Communications and Journalism Studies; instead, the notions of "gatekeeping" and "agenda-setting" are two of the most likely well-established candidates for explaining my explanations of "media control," though I argue both of these approaches still lack the ability to adequately identify the clear power dynamics of the press and its relationship to the power elite.

Gatekeeping: What passes—and what does not?

The concept of gatekeeping is a mainstay of approaches that complicate the process of news-making, which this project uses to whittle-away at normative explanations of media intentionality, socialization, and control. The idea is that information interacts with social forces and individuals who operate as "gates," either allowing information to flow further through news production or setting it aside and excluding it from the final product. Gatekeeping helps establish an understanding of how audiences (or journalists' perceptions of audiences) and other social pressures influence what becomes "the news." Kurt Lewin is often cited as the theorist behind modern-day gatekeeping. He describes the function as a process similar to how food moves from the seed to the field—hence his application of "Field Theory."

Lewin argues the seed turns into a commodity that is harvested from the plant itself, processed and sent to the marketplace, selected by the user and placed in the shopping cart, then put into the pantry, prepared in the cooking pot, and ultimately delivered to the plate. Information, Lewin argues, undergoes a similar process of growth, harvesting, manufacturing, selection, delivery, and consumption. Just as food moves through gates of pressures (sun, water, weeding, purchasing, production, and consumption), news passes through gates in a process that is influenced by cultural, economic, and human interactions.

A seminal study on gatekeeping—The Mr. Gates Study in 1950—explored how a single newspaper editor identified, selected, and discarded potential news items based upon his perception of how the audience would respond and by following newspaper policies of what type of information appeared where, what the newspaper traditionally would and would not publish, and what types of news received what kind of attention.[25]

Since then, scholars have been better able to describe how news is commoditized based on the costs of identifying it, capturing it, producing it, and releasing it to the public. Its value is determined by the public reaction— will people buy it, watch it, or talk about it? Is there potential for advertising surrounding it? Will people pay to sell their goods in news mediums generally?

In 2009, Pamela Shoemaker and Tim Vos published an updated articulation of gatekeeping. In that work, they argue that in an environment of increasing globalization and digital communication, gatekeeping and field theory can be key to understanding the ways humans communicate by expanding our examination of the social processes involved in our evolving societies.[26] Around the same time, Leo Bowman suggested that even in a digital age, with its multitude of online media sources that serve as publication venues, traditional gatekeeping processes continue to operate amid spheres of power. For instance, journalists make choices related to the degree to which they question sources early in the process of information-gathering and that this functions as a means by which information is filtered to pass through a journalistic gate—or is stopped at the gate as the journalist relies on her ideas on how the information will be received or how it interacts with her own personal and professional values.[27]

Gatekeeping studies contribute to the argument that traditional (old-school) journalism defers to the authority of sources rather than questions the merit or accuracy of a source's information, suggesting the journalist herself is a primary gate at the initial stage of information-gathering. However, unabated acceptance of "official" sources—even the notion that journalists themselves should be experts on the stories they cover—reveals within the gatekeeping process a weakening of the journalistic Fourth Estate, its "objectivity," and its ability to "watch out" for "the public good" that is constrained to a select few.[28] Still, the expansion of gatekeeping as a means to understand both the social *and the cultural* elements of news is challenged by scholars who argue digital news outlets across the internet provide out-of-the-institution perspectives that create new gates of critical analysis.[29]

Perspectives among many gatekeeping approaches limit the mode of media to traditional views of sender-receiver that have long been replaced by more complete cultural interpretations of how information is recognized, assembled, distributed, interpreted, appropriated—and reappropriated—among audiences. To journalists and to their corporate-political backers, "the news" has never been a priority in and of itself; at its most basic level, news is power construction that follows methods of cultural indoctrination—even in a digital age—that since its earliest forms shapes how information is gathered and assessed in the journalistic community while creating space for advertisers to peddle their products and for politicians to air remedies for public grievances.

Journalism has always walked a fine line of being a voice for the public good that can expose corruption, as a product to inform citizens about the workings of their governments, and as a means to maintain a sense of cultural coherence as societies morph and as alternative explanations for daily life that challenge dominant thought grow in volume and authority. And, as I discuss in the book's Conclusion, Journalism Studies continues to struggle with a clear and consistent understanding of the role digital forms of communication play in such perspectives as gatekeeping, especially in the digital age where audiences-as-users interact with journalists on Twitter, news corporations track and monitor news audiences through the clicks they make, what they search for, and what they share.

To fully address issues of power within media practices and processes, more work must be done from within the newsroom or from the perspective of newsworkers to address just how—and why—the press operate as it does and select its messages for public consumption.

Agenda-setting: News as public schema

As journalism has morphed over time into new mediums that, on the surface, present the news as this mythical watchdog and objective service, approaches to Journalism Studies have attempted to identify a purpose, or set of purposes, behind media beyond that of economic interest.[30] The concept of agenda-setting explores meanings behind what media cover, how, and what publics should think about the news by analyzing patterns of news coverage to measure how the news "agenda" is funneled from businesses, politicians, police, and journalists across media outlets and from dominant media outlets (i.e., *The New York Times* and CNN) to regional and local media.

As agenda-setting has evolved, scholars have moved away from using the concept to solely explore correlations between sets of news coverage and the possible influence on audiences to attempt to understand how media messages set what we think and talk about (the agenda), and how we should think about that agenda. At least one comment about the aims of agenda-setting research in the 1960s still rings true today: "the press may not be successful much of the time in telling people what to think, but it is stunningly successful in telling readers what to think about."[31]

Agenda-setting relies, largely, on two levels of operation. First-level agenda-setting examines the potential for messages to hold a salience—or recognizability—of messages across coverage of particular issues or events. Second-level agenda-setting deconstructs media messaging for ways in which messaging embeds meaning. Here, as David Weaver writes, agenda-setting—which is often at this stage confused with the many definitions of "framing"—examines the role of messaging in terms of its resonance, or its ability to shape meaning-making in terms of a culture's most inherent values. It is at this second-level, then, where agenda-setting scholars hope to express how media messages move beyond telling us what to think, but *how to think*.[32]

Today, agenda-setting includes a more coherent look at how audiences participate in media agendas through social media, moving us from understanding the potential of user-generated content to user-mediated content, content which is not only offered by users to users, but which often goes through a process manipulation and direction beyond the initial creation in order to contribute to networked, social discourse.[33] Susan Jacobson, for example, attempts to break into understanding what she calls "the press" monopoly on "agenda-setting" by examining the role of audience commenting on the Facebook page of MSNBC's *The Rachel Maddow Show* and the possible influence of those comments upon what content was then aired on the show.

In short, Jacobson argues that audiences may have a direct influence on the tones, topics, and types of coverage that appears in some aspects of the news, having examined three-weeks worth of the show's Facebook conversations and the topics addressed in the broadcasts. Jacobson is careful in her assertions, identifying that those who watch *The Rachel Maddow Show* and who feel compelled to comment on the show's Facebook page may have similar interests or social capital, which allows them to engage in debate and discussion. But, she also notes that the show's Facebook page functioned as a two-way street in that producers sought story ideas from the Facebook audience.[34]

User-generated material, which also reflects changes to understandings of news gatekeeping, has emerged as a means by which the news agenda is influenced directly by user participation and the developed thought of who sets the agenda—and how. Home footage of the Rodney King beating in 1991 in Los Angeles and media use of the images of white officers beating King, who was black, was rerun across the country during subsequent rioting in 1992. This was, perhaps, one of the first user-participatory moments in recent media history to gain such attention among such wide audiences.

In that case, news media released, played and replayed the grainy images from a personal video camera. Such participatory measures, however, have expanded, as have the media's interest in the financial value of involving citizens in setting the agenda and extending, to some degree, the ability of the press to comment on the meanings within the news.[35]

Still, applying agenda-setting—or even framing—concepts alone do little to examine the power intentions behind the construction of particular media. These approaches ignore more obvious reasons for the interest and access to the core of journalistic efforts by both users and news outlets. First, user-generated information is usually free. More than that, its potential for profitability is immediate. With little to no investment by media outlets in the creation of audience media, what makes its way to the web or hyperlink allows for a lofty return. Second, user-generated information is bound to be released (and usually, ultimately is anyway) elsewhere other than on a news site or from within the journalistic community. Therefore, not publishing such information as news would risk threatening the relevance, authority, and legitimacy of journalistic institutions.[36]

Dan Berkowitz and I made the argument in 2012, for instance, that the role of journalistic authority in terms of the press' ability to influence public thought and policy was being tested by the rise of satire journalism—so much so that *The New York Times* included news satirist Jon Stewart in the definition of "who's a journalist," in part to maintain the cultural legitimacy and authority of the *Times* at a moment when popular discourse would have us believe more people were getting their news from cable comedy journalism than from traditional outlets.[37]

In late 2010, Stewart had lambasted members of the US Congress for not approving health-care relief for rescue workers who had become sick from their time working at Ground Zero following the 9/11 attack. Right before the end of the year, Congress reversed its approach and pushed the legislation through. On December 26, media reporters Bill Carter and Brian Stelter at the *Times* referred to Stewart's presentation earlier in the winter—and its correlation to a Congressional shift—as representative of famed TV journalist Edward R. Murrow, who, too, had been influential through his journalism to create political change.

Specifically, Carter and Stelter asked in their piece, "[a]nd does that make that comedian, Jon Stewart—despite all his protestations that what he does has nothing to do with journalism—the modern-day equivalent of Edward R. Murrow?"[38] In our analysis of coverage about the *Times* article on blogs and online versions of legacy media, we argued that the popularity of satire journalists, such as Stewart, had forced discussion of journalistic boundaries to the degree that the *Times* needed to bring the Comedy Central star into the journalistic community not to provide Stewart with credibility but to further legitimize legacy media, which includes traditional sources of journalism, such as the *Times*. We also argued that the use of collective memory (see Chapter 4) in this case was not only employed to provide identification of journalistic boundaries to news users but to the journalistic community, as well. We wrote that:

> Most simply, the initial endorsement became a direct form of boundary adjustment to recapture ownership of a lost journalistic opportunity. As the endorsement became more controversial, it served as a broader institutional moment for a variety of mainstream organizations and blogs to engage in boundary work that addressed a broader media spectrum.[39]

As that case suggests, then, media agenda-setting is not just about setting the aims for what journalists cover—and how to cover it—but also holds within the agenda-setting process itself social and cultural influences of power and control used to shape the news, including for those making it, particularly in a time of massive threats to the journalistic institution's popularity and overt ideological solvency through expanded media outlets and social networks.

The scholarly field of Journalism Studies will continue to turn to approaches discussed above to help explain decision-making related to what is determined (by both journalists and audiences) as being newsworthy. At the center of the analyses that appear in this book, however, is the human condition—the selection and rejection of what may or may not make sense to journalists' understandings of audiences. It is this connection of the journalist and the user to the ultimate potential influence on human life and the potential for security and prosperity that drives the purpose of the news, I argue, such as in the case of The Boston Bombings that is built around intentionality within the journalistic community. This idea is discussed next in an analysis of "media power."

FROM SOCIAL POWER TO "MEDIA POWER"

In 2013, Sarah Stonbely argued that early sociological studies of newsrooms focused more on organizational elements, such as routines, deadlines, economic forces, and social roles of journalists, rather than on the construction of journalistic values and ideologies. Such studies, which included the one involving Mr. Gates, set the stage for the rise of ethnography and social theory within a field interested in news as a social commodity. Indeed, Stonbely writes:

> Discussions about values often took a functionalist stance, asking not how those values came to be present in news but showing how values that were present were in harmony with the [news] organization's imperatives.[40]

And, because little of the early work on news-making identified clearly the power of a journalist's personal value system, neither did the work discuss the influence of her *agency*, the ability to act otherwise to evoke social change. The reporter's ability to choose what she considered news from a line of various options was acknowledged, though the true force of the journalist's role of self was rarely expressed.

In the beginning, scholars were mostly interested in setting a stage of news as an organizational process that challenged traditional, normative explanations of newswork. But, as with all things, scholarship evolved, and some of the seminal work in this field, including by Gaye Tuchman and Herbert Gans, was soon problematized with the introduction of Cultural Studies in the United States, which built upon earlier work dedicated to Social Science.[41] Stonbely, for instance, writes that "to newsworkers [professionalism] meant autonomy and objectivity; to the sociologists it meant internalizing organizational imperatives in service of established power."[42] Soon enough, journalists found their notions of "professionalism" further complicated by notions of postmodernism and critical/cultural approaches that were seeping into US institutions from Europe.[43]

By examining these transformations of journalistic theory and the field's "professionalization," Simon Cottle argues that the major Social Science approaches of newsroom studies of the past continue to hold a grasp on how we examine news today.[44] He argues that early scholars' interest in journalistic routines still complicates the sense and role of journalistic agency in newswork, having incorporated journalists so much into a system of decision-making that the norms of the institution overshadow the abilities—and certain influences—of the self. As individuals, then, we are left with a diminished sense of power to operate as we may wish and, in turn, scholarship that attempts to examine deeper social and cultural connections between media and users removes a notice of power that individual journalists hold—or have the potential to hold—in what and how they report the news.

Nick Couldry and James Curran analyze media as operating within power structures in several ways. First, they argue that power is expressed *through* media messaging in that institutions use the media to direct power to audiences. Here, the media serve as a platform for distribution. In a second examination of media-power interactions, the press apply their own power to messaging in terms of how they decide to cover institutional messages and affairs of the day. In this sense, journalists are seen as operating within an institutional collective through which they process their power in decision-making.

Couldry and Curran present a third way of understanding media power by expressing how power operates in and through the press by using an analogy in which power is water cascading over a waterfall, creating hydrological energy as it passes through a power plant and then sent back out to stream. In this analogy, the media is viewed in terms of its "intensity, size, and impact on the ground below (whose 'power,' in a word) depend almost entirely on the weight and direction of water collected on the land behind the waterfall." The power of the water in this scene occurs throughout the ability and potential for its movement over the rocks of the waterfall, creating directions and pathways of pressure and volume.[45]

Still, Couldry and Curran see "media power" in the analogy working yet another way in which media is the hydrologic power plant, accepting the water after it pushes over the shapes of rocks at the top and bottom of the waterfall, touches the hydroelectric machinery, and flows into a body of water, having expressed its energy, transforming itself from water to energy and back into the stream. In this sense, then, the power plant needs to be examined for its interactions with the water, the ways in which the water is altered in terms of its purpose, and how it is transformed through the process into water being sent back into the stream. In other words, "media power" functions as a constant flow, very much like as Michel Foucault describes it (see Chapter 1).

In the above analogy, the power of media operates in a larger system in which multiple "power plants" might be developed to compete for water-power, to hold and share information, to challenge the upstream power plant, and it is these elements of power—its movements and manipulations—that need to be examined. Even though "alternative media" sources through the internet, like underground Vietnam newspapers of the day, challenge traditional constructions of mainstream media construction, I argue that media power should be viewed in yet another way so as to formulate what I mean in *this project* as media control.

In my view, the waterfall itself is not merely just water and rocks and barriers and boundaries of the shoreline that interact with the flow of information, that alter the direction and energy of the water. Instead, the waterfall operates upon the structure of the cliff, the rocks, and boulders that make its shape, the role of gravity that causes the water to flow in the first place, that captures and shapes cascades, its ripples, drops, and cuts that the water pushes through.

These elements cannot be ignored or cast aside, as Couldry and Curran suggest they should, stating that "no one would say that the waterfall itself has 'power,' properly speaking, even though the particular configuration of rocks at the waterfall's edge would have a minor influence on the way water falls below."[46] To remove the rocks and shoreline from the discussion to focus only on the power plant, however, would be to remove the notion of the waterfall itself. In other words, while there are interactions that must be examined in terms of media power, it is important not to view the waterfall, in this discussion, as operating upon or merely with the rocks of the natural formation in which the water flows. The waterfall is ideology and culture, the rocks and its height, pitch, age, and width the lens through which communication flows. The only difficulty in this interpretation of the analogy is that, to most readers, most likely, the waterfall is viewed as something that can't actually be removed, and the construction of which is a natural feature. In other words, my analogy wishes to examine the role of what is considered "natural" in terms of our ideologies with which media function.

To be clear, I am presenting a construction of "media control" that might build upon structures that are counter to those articulated by Curran and Couldry. In *Media and Power*, for instance, Curran seems to align himself with a major critique of Herman and Chomsky's Propaganda Model (see Chapter 1), that "all *important* influences to which the media are exposed flow in one direction—in support of the *status quo*."[47] He writes that media operate with social actions of forces outside—and inside—their organizations that allow the press to operate against influences that push the press to representations that support the status quo. Curran goes on to present these influences as being:

- State censorship of private journalism

- High entry costs to produce media

- Media concentration that wields economic and political power

- Corporate ownership that may influence ideological functions of the press

- Mass market pressures that may sensationalize the news to reach wider audiences

- Consumer inequalities that place some niche media products above others

- Advertising influence that shapes coverage toward an elite readership

- The rise of public relations

- News routines, practices, and values

- Exploited cultural and social capital

- Dominant discourse and ideologies

Each of these is a valid influence and, as this book will address, is inherent to the propagandistic approach to media messaging that appears in this work, just as much as they are central to the arguments of the Propaganda Model itself. Still, within dominant presentations of media-power relations, scholarship ignores the intentional and hegemonic responsibility and connections inherent in the acts of journalists and users and the power-act of ideology, journalistic and otherwise. In the final section below, therefore, I present levels of analysis that can be applied to interpret media-as-text and as-process that will help us to piece apart the role of ideology—particularly the role of journalistic ideologies—in ways that undermine the normalization of the "Fourth Estate" and social functions said to function on behalf of the citizenry and to identify deeper and contentious relationships between the press and the people.

CONCLUSION: INTERPRETING JOURNALISM THROUGH LEVELS OF ANALYSIS

Decades of scholarship and practice focused on interpreting journalism as an act and a process rather than merely an outcome has led to shared levels of analysis that allow one to explicate the embedding of cultural meanings into

Approaches to Media Messaging

			Hierarchy of Influences Model (Shoemaker & Reese, 2014)	
Individuals	Routine Practices	Media Organizations	Social Institutions	Social Systems
Content is influenced by journalists' personal and professional values	Micro-organizational routines shape journalistic function that influence content	Macro-organizational norms and values influence the micro-level journalistic work and content	Journalism joins other social structures as an institution of social norms, values, and relationships	Ideological forces operate via institutional relationships to maintain media's social legitimacy
			Levels of Journalistic Analysis (Berkowitz, 2011)	
Individual	Organizational	Professional	Institutional	Cultural
Journalists enter field with values that are molded to meet needs of the news institutions; worker agency/ autonomy debated	Journalists interact with news norms and values to shape news production	Journalists become homogenized by social and cultural structures and expectations; workers penalized for breaking mold	Ownership, press "freedoms" and an outlet's mission is measured in relationship to fellow social institutions	Meanings of news are viewed as "common sense," unquestioned, or framed by insider-outsider perspective

FIGURE 2.3 *Models of explaining social and cultural influences upon newswork.*

news and that turns news itself into text (Figure 2.3). In this section, I introduce levels of analysis and end the chapter with two final concepts central to this project—the role of news myth and conceptualizations of the journalistic interpretive community—through introductions of the concepts that later in the book are enhanced through an explication of their inherent power and control functions. First, however, let us examine the role of journalist as an individual agent of change and how she operates within social and cultural norms to construct and characterize the news.

The "journalistic self": The appearance of agency

Journalists enter the field with predetermined values and perspectives that are hard to shake while on the job. These values function to assist reporters and editors in making decisions about the potential value of a news item and help determine what approaches to use in covering the news. I have referred to this in previous work as the *journalistic self*—"a compilation of a journalist's personal values, experiences, and biases that shape her view of the world and of what is and what isn't news."[48]

Furthermore, this recognition of the self within one's journalistic identity acknowledges that journalists have an ultimate right and responsibility to examine their agency in making choices that may be counter to societal and organizational expectations. These personal views interact with needs and expectations of the newsroom, including organizational roles, deadlines, and expectations related to workload, productivity, and adherence to journalistic standards, and make it so that operating outside of journalistic norms can result in significant negative outcomes for the journalist, including a constant threat of dismissal from the workplace.

News as organization: Order and punishment

Journalism is viewed as operating within two realms of organization, one which enforces a dominant characterization of the field as a whole and another that sets standards for the journalist in terms of conducting her work within proper structures and procedures.

Characterization and cohesion

The first realm of organization that journalists work within is focused on efforts of professionalization in terms of operating within daily routines, during moments of breaking news, and on the whole, operating as a cohesive collective. These standards maintain consistency in what is considered news, what sources are appropriate for comment, what professional courtesies to fellow social leaders are acceptable, and what explanations can appear in the news that maintain a society's values. Initial socialization to journalistic norms—either through formal education or through the first days and years on the job—forces the journalistic self to develop a sense of identity within the field that is further developed within a second level of journalistic organization.[49]

Journalistic routines and practices

It is not enough for journalism-as-organization to hold particular norms and standards of operation. Journalists, it is argued, must police themselves in order to ensure adherence to the rules, routines, and practices. Warren Breed introduced the notion of "social control" in the newsroom as a means by which to regulate appropriate behaviors and adherence to journalistic norms. Threats of punishment for operating outside the norms—what are also referred to as the "journalistic paradigm"—almost always include the termination of employment and loss of livelihood for the journalist, and the threat of such measures is the mandate for compliance.[50]

Journalistic "boundary work" functions in other ways, as well, including embarrassing a journalist who strays from the norms, conducting journalism that debunks unacceptable reporting, and other forms of organizational ostracization if a journalist does not comply (see further discussion below). Here, the journalist must decide the degree to which her own values of "self" fit with the field's and to determine her ability to operate within the expectations of "doing good journalism" within institutional structures.

Institutional rule: Money and politics

The risks to journalism organizations are great if they do not operate within larger institutional norms that are set beyond the organization of the news outlet itself. At this level of news-as-institution, journalists must manage their social relevance and legitimacy with audiences and other social institutions in order to maintain access to potential news and to be respected within society as a voice of authority. At this level, issues of ownership and political economy also operate as a major influence upon the news and the standards that are applied to journalists. For example, as an institution, journalism must maintain a shared, collective history and interpretations of press "freedoms," rights, and responsibilities to the public, such as building a sense of nation and community through approved types of sources.[51]

News as text cultural text

Perhaps the most vital element of understanding levels useful for examining news—and which certainly is of most importance to this project—is the level of interpreting news as a form of and artifact of culture.[52] Explanations of journalism that rely on notions of professionalism, objectivity and bias "[mask]" understanding by making normative judgments about what is good and bad about journalism," writes Dan Berkowitz in *Cultural Meanings of News*, thereby also masking power dynamics inherent in the types, styles, and causes of journalism in society and elements of culture.[53]

Journalists must be able to tap into the dynamics of an audiences' culture(s) in order to maintain authority with audiences related to representing the foundations of cultural norms. As do most scholars who argue for an understanding of communication as a ritual of culture, Berkowitz wishes to examine the following elements of cultural characteristics of news to reveal:

- Anthropological positions of lived cultures within newswork

- Forces influenced by increasingly global societies

- A means by which society maintains dominant power structures[54]

In order to examine the degree to which journalists present news in ways that recognize dominant culture and the function of power and control in that presentation, questions of a text that can be asked are:

- What is the main thrust and meaning of the text?

- How did the text appear? Did the story air before a commercial break? After a weather segment? On Page One or in the business section?

- Who and what were the sources of the text?

- How was the text reTweeted or disseminated beyond the media outlet, and by whom? What did they have to say about the text?

- In what ways did images and language reify the text's main messages?

- What meanings exist—or need to be created—within scholarship to help explain ideologies that appear in the text?

The cultural level of analysis is where we see how news brings people together as a form of community building and provides collective identity and cultural cohesion through common and shared narratives and mythical explanations, which is a core purpose of this book's radicalization of Journalism Studies. In the next chapter, I begin to apply the concepts and approaches discussed in Chapters 1 and 2 in ways that challenge the characterization of journalists as storytellers to include the direct influence of welcomed, social and cultural collaborators, such as private business leaders, government officials, and police.

More specifically, I challenge traditional notions of news myth that apply dominant explanations for daily events and social issues through common narratives of everyday life, but in ways that examines the intentional application of power and control of the press in commonplace tales and characters. Throughout the work that comes, therefore, I apply notions of news myth as an act—not an outcome. These articulations will further provide a foundation for the application of media control in the rest of these pages and ultimately explicated in the book's conclusion.

Discussion Questions

1. What connections can be made between influences identified within the levels of analysis presented in this chapter and elements of the Propaganda Model discussed in Chapter 1?

2. How do descriptions of myth in this chapter incorporate elements of power as defined in this book thus far?

Notes

1 For instance, see Gaye Tuchman, "Making news by doing work: Routinizing the unexpected," *American Journal of Sociology* 79, no. 1 (1973): 110–113.

2 James S. Ettema, "Crafting cultural resonance: Imaginative power in everyday journalism," *Journalism* 6, no. 2 (2005): 131–152.

3 Robert E. Gutsche, Jr., "Zombies, drugs, and Florida weirdness: 'Imaginative power' and resonance in coverage of Miami's 'Causeway Cannibal,'" *Journalism Studies* 12, no. 4 (2013): 555–567.

4 Ibid., 564.

5 For related conceptual background, see Robert E. Gutsche, Jr., "Boosterism as banishment: Identifying the power function of local business news and coverage of city spaces," *Journalism Studies* (2014), doi: 10.1080/1461670X.2014.924730; and, Richard V. Ericson, Patricia M. Baranek, and Janet B. L. Chan. *Representing Order: Crime, Law, and Justice in the News Media* (Toronto: University of Toronto Press, 1991); See Chapter 1 for discussion of "terrorism experts" as well as "Glenn Greenwald on how to be a terror 'expert': Ignore facts, blame Muslims, trumpet U.S. propaganda," *DemocracyNow!*, January 13, 2015, http://www.democracynow.org/2015/1/13/glenn_greenwald_on_how_to_be. For more on the role of verisimilitude in news coverage, see Michael Bourke and Robert E. Gutsche, Jr., "News-masking: A theoretical perspective on the rituals and artifacts of news-making" (working paper); P. Theunissen and G. Mersham, "'New Zealand's darkest day': The representation of national grief in the media: The case of the Christchurch earthquake," *Journal for the Study of the Arts and Humanities in Southern Africa* 18, no. 2 (2011): 386–403.

6 View some of the coverage here: https://www.youtube.com/watch?v=GS_93kQRpqk.

7 To discuss gendered coverage of government, press coverage of politicians, see Robert E. Gutsche, Jr., James Carviou, and Rauf Arif, "Change that couldn't happen: News media's commitment to hegemonic masculinity through collective memory in the 2008 presidential election," In *The Iconic Obama, 2007–2009: Essays on Media Representations of the Candidate and New President*, edited by Nicholas A. Yanes and Derrias Carter (Jefferson, NC: McFarland, 2012).

8 View front pages of US newspaper coverage described here in the Newseum's Front Pages section: http://www.newseum.org/todaysfrontpages/archive.asp.

9 Eric Hartley and Sandra Mazza, "After Boston: In a California terrorist attack, cameras would be watching," *San Bernardino Sun*, April 14, 2013, http://www.sbsun.com/general-news/20130416/after-boston-in-a-california-terrorist-attack-cameras-would-be-watching.

10 I watched this report, and others like it, with a bit of disappointment. At the time of the event, I wondered, for once could not the suspect just

be a white, fourteen-year-old girl from the suburbs who, angry that her parents grounded her for skateboarding on the sidewalk, sought retribution? In all honesty, that explanation likely rings as far too unbelievable; of course, we should have been looking for a "dark-skinned man." But could it have been a dark "American?" I do not know if anyone would have believed that, either, though; view video of the bombing here: http://www.huffingtonpost.com/2013/04/17/john-king-boston-bombing-dark-skinned-male-ifill_n_3102195.html?utm_hp_ref=media.

11 For immediate sources on issues of race in US dominant ideology, see Kimberle Crenshaw, Neil Gotanda, Gary Peller, and Kendall Thomas, *Critical Race Theory: The Key Writings that Formed the Movement* (New York: The New Press, 1996); Becky Pettit, *Invisible Men: Mass Incarceration and the Myth of Black Progress* (New York: Russell Sage Foundation, 2012); George Lipsitz, *How Racism Takes Place* (Philadelphia, PA: Temple University Press, 2011). For discussion on entertainment representations of police, see Aaron Cantu, "'Do what you gotta do': Cop shows bolster idea that police violence works," *truth-out.org*, March 16, 2014, http://www.truth-out.org/news/item/22433-do-what-you-gotta-do-cop-shows-bolster-idea-that-police-violence-works.

12 Robert E. Gutsche, Jr., "'Life beyond fingers': A response to news photography of an 'urban ghetto,'" *Visual Communication Quarterly* 21 (2014): 14–23.

13 For a timeline of events, see http://www.huffingtonpost.com/2014/04/14/boston-marathon-timeline_n_5145615.html.

14 For photographs, see http://www.cbsnews.com/pictures/boston-on-lockdown/1/.

15 For more on the role of passive language in press storytelling, see Robert E. Gutsche, Jr. and Erica Salkin, "'It's better than blaming a dead young man': Creating mythical archetypes in local coverage of the Mississippi River drownings," *Journalism: Theory, Practice, and Criticism* 14, no. 1 (2013): 61–77.

16 For discussion on "refugees," see Hemant Shah, "Legitimizing neglect: Race and rationality in conservative news commentary about Hurricane Katrina," *Howard Journal of Communication* 20, no. 1 (2009): 1–17.

17 Ina Rae Hark, "'Today is the Longest Day of my life': *24* as mirror narrative of 9/11," In *Film and Television After 9/11*, edited by Wheeler W. Dixon (Carbondale, IL: Southern Illinois Press, 2004): 121–141; Inderpal Grewal, *Transnational America: Feminisms, Diasporas, Neoliberalisms* (Durham, NC: Duke University Press, 2005); Barbie Zelizer and Stuart Allen, *Journalism After September 11* (London and New York: Routledge, 2002).

18 Henry A. Giroux, "Lockdown, USA: Lessons from the Boston Marathon Manhunt," truth-out.org, May 6, 2013, http://truth-out.org/opinion/item/16175-lockdown-usa-lessons-from-the-boston-marathon-manhunt.

19 Watch the video here http://www.nbcnews.com/id/51611247.

20 Henry A. Giroux, "States of paralysis: America's surrender to the spectacle of terror," truth-out.org, August 17, 2010, http://www.truth-out.org/archive/item/91312:states-of-paralysis-americas-surrender-to-the-spectacle-of-terror.

21 Ibid.; see also Bethami A. Dobkin, *Tales of Terror: Television News and the Construction of the Terrorist Threat* (New York, Westport, CN, and London: Praeger, 1992).

22 John Nichols and Robert W. McChesney, *Tragedy & Farce: How the American Media Sell Wars, Spin Elections, and Destroy Democracy* (New York and London: The New Press, 2005), 33.

23 By providing very little critical analysis of federal efforts to institute the military as a common-sense institution, efforts to militarize our youth include replacing traditional high school graduation assessments with a passing grade on the military's aptitude test. See, Pat Elder, "Minnesota law substitutes military test for graduation requirement," truth-out.org, February 2, 2014, http://www.truth-out.org/opinion/item/21503-minnesota-law-substitutes-military-test-for-graduation-requirement.

24 For review, see Steve Powers, "Weaponized media, legitimacy and the Fourth Estate: A comment," *Ethnopolitics* 9, no. 2 (2010): 255–258. I do not intend for this brief commentary to be representative of Powers's positions but use it as an example of clear language that states a dominant position of connecting issues of media control to technology.

25 The Mr. Gates study is still quite relevant today in that it provides a clear and concise ethnographic approach to newswork. Even in times of changing media and production, the decision-making process by Mr. Gates resembles how journalists decide what is newsworthy today. See, David Manning White, "The 'gate keeper': A case study in the selection of news," *Journalism Quarterly* 27 (1950): 383–390.

26 Pamela J. Shoemaker and Timothy Vos, *Gatekeeping Theory* (New York and London: Routledge, 2009). See also Tim P. Vos and François Heinderyckx, *Gatekeeping in Transition*, (New York: Routledge, 2015).

27 Leo Bowman, "Re-examining 'gatekeeping': How journalists communicate the truth about power to the public," *Journalism Practice* 2, no. 1 (2008): 99–112; Robert E. Gutsche, Jr. and Erica R. Salkin, "News stories: An exploration of independence within post-secondary journalism," *Journalism Practice* 5, no. 2 (2011): 193–209.

28 See further debate and discussion in Barbie Zelizer, *Taking Journalism Seriously: News and the Academy* (Thousand Oaks, CA, London and New Dehli: Sage, 2004).

29 For more, see Axel Bruns, *Gatekeeping: Collaborative Online News Production* (New York: Peter Lang, 2005).

30 For overarching discussions on the state of intersections between journalism practice and journalism studies, see Karin Wahl-Jorgensen and Thomas Hanitzsch, *The Handbook of Journalism Studies* (New York and London: Routledge, 2009); James W. Carey, *Communication as Culture* (New York and London, 2009); Daniel A. Berkowitz, *Cultural Meanings of*

News (Thousand Oaks, CA: Sage, 2011); Jason Salzman, *Making the News: A Guide for Activists and Nonprofits* (Boulder, CO: Westview Press, 2003); Eric W. Rothenbuhler and Mihai Coman, *Media Anthropology* (Thousand Oaks, CA: Sage, 2005).

31 Bernard C. Cohen, *The Press and Foreign Policy* (Princeton, NJ: Princeton University Press, 1963): 13.

32 For more on agenda-setting and framing, see David H. Weaver, "Thoughts on agenda setting, framing, and priming," *Journal of Communication* 57 (2007): 142–147. See also, Nikki Usher, Making News at The New York Times. (Ann Arbor:University of Michigan Press, 2014).

33 See also, Sharon Meraz, "Is there an elite hold? Traditional media to social media agenda setting influence in blog networks," *Journal of Computer-mediated Communication* 14 (2009): 682–707; Maxwell McCombs, "A look at agenda-setting: past, present and future," *Journalism Studies*, 6, no. 4 (2005): 543–557; Ari Heinonen gives a good, updated perspective on journalist–user interactions and its effects on newswork in his chapter "The Journalist's Relationship with Users: News Dimensions to Conventional Roles," in *Participatory Journalism: Guarding Open Gates at Online Newspapers* (2011).

34 Susan Jacobson, "Does audience participation on Facebook influence the news agenda? A case study of *The Rachel Maddow Show*," *Journal of Broadcasting & Electronic Media* 57, no. 3 (2013): 338–355.

35 For innovative, digital involvement of the public [sic] see, *The Guardian*'s coverage of the 2011 riots at http://www.theguardian.com/uk/london-riots. In the US, there has also been the creation of the Public Insight Network in which news users can upload answers to journalists' prompts about articles that reporters are working on. For that, see https://www.publicinsightnetwork.org.

36 In other words, what purpose does an "official" news outlet hold if it is sideswiped by YouTube, Twitter, or TMZ?

37 Dan Berkowitz and Robert E. Gutsche Jr., "Drawing lines in the journalistic sand: Jon Stewart, Edward R. Murrow, and memory of news gone by," *Journalism & Mass Communication Quarterly* 89, no. 4 (2012): 643–656; Both Stephen Colbert and Jon Stewart announced the cancellation of their shows in 2014 and 2015, respectively.

38 Bill Carter and Brian Stelter, "In *Daily Show* role on 9/11 bill, echoes of Murrow," *The New York Times*, December 26, 2010.

39 Berkowitz and Gutsche, Jr., "Drawing lines in the journalistic sand," 653.

40 Sarah Stonbely, "The social and intellectual contexts of the US 'newsroom studies,' and the Media Sociology of today," *Journalism Studies* (2013), doi: 10.1080/1461670X.2013.859865.

41 For more, see Martin Conboy, *Journalism Studies: The Basics* (London and New York: Routledge, 2013).

42 Stonbely, 6.

43 To be clear, even in today's expanded and digital era of "Fair and Balanced" news, objectivity remains a dominant normative expectation of "professional" and "good" journalism, as does the debate of whether or not journalism as a field is even a profession since it is not certified or licensed as are others (i.e., accounting and medicine). For more, see Zelizer, *Taking Journalism Seriously*.

44 Stonbely mentions a few such studies: Simon Cottle, "Ethnography and news production: New(s) developments in the field," *Sociology Compass* 1, no. 1 (2007): 1–16; Mark Pedelty, *War Stories* (Oxford: Routledge, 1995); Nikki Usher, "'Marketplace' Public Radio and news routines reconsidered: Between structures and agents," *Journalism* 14, no. 6 (2013): 807–822; David M. Ryfe, "Structure, agency, and change in an American newsroom," *Journalism* 10, no. 5 (2009): 665–683; Sue Robinson, "Convergence crisis: News work and news space in the digitally transformed newsroom," *Journal of Communication* 61 (2011): 1122–1141.

45 Nick Couldry and James Curran, *Contesting Media Power: Alternative Media in a Networked World* (Lanham, MA: Rowman and Littlefield, 2003), 5–6.

46 Ibid., 5.

47 p. 148, emphasis in original.

48 Robert E. Gutsche, Jr., *A Transplanted Chicago: Race, Place and the Press in Iowa City* (Jefferson, NC: McFarland, 2014), 41.

49 For additional reading on "professionalism," see Jesse Owen Hearns-Branaman, "Journalistic professionalism as indirect control and fetishistic disavowal," *Journalism* 15, no. 1 (2014): 21–36; Robert E. Gutsche Jr., "Missing the scoop: Exploring the cultural and sociological influences of news production upon college student journalists," in *Journalism Education, Training and Employment*, edited by Bob Franklin and Donica Mensing (New York and Oxon, UK: Routledge, 2011), 63–77.

50 Warren Breed, "Social control in the newsroom: A functional analysis," *Social Forces* 33 (1955): 326–355; for additional reading on "good journalism," see Homero Gil de Zúñiga and Amber Hinsley, "The press versus the public: What is 'good journalism?,'" *Journalism Studies* 14, no. 6 (2013): 926–942.

51 For review of this and all levels of analysis, see seminal work published in Dan Berkowitz, *Social Meanings of News* (Thousand Oaks, CA: Sage, 1997).

52 For more on examining text and artifacts for cultural meaning, see Terry Eagleton, *Literary Theory: An Introduction* (Minneapolis, MN: University of Minnesota Press, 2008).

53 Berkowitz, *Cultural Meanings of News*, xiii, emphasis in original; See also, Bruno Bettelheim, *The Uses of Enchantment: The Meaning and Importance of Fairy Tales* (New York: Vintage Books, 2010), which provides an interesting historical and literary exploration of how fairy tales construct order; Robert Darnton, "Writing news and telling stories," *Daedalus* 104, no. 2 (1975): 175–194. See also, Mieke Bal, *Narratology* (Toronto, Buffalo, NY and London: University of Toronto Press, 2009). For information on textual analysis as method, see Thomas Lindlof and Bryan Taylor, *Qualitative Research Methods* (Thousand Oaks, CA: Sage, 2010).

54 The third definition, to Berkowitz, however, is "less central" to the arguments and articulations made in that specific volume, "how human interactions carry meanings" in terms of news items and dominant interpretations. For more, see the Introduction of *Cultural Meanings of News*. As background, *Cultural Meanings of News*, is a supplement to Berkowitz's seminal reader, *Social Meanings of News*, published in 1997.

3

Displacement and Punishment: The Press as Place-makers

Chapter Purpose

This chapter implicates the press in constructing and maintaining dominant interpretations of geography that are used to enforce public policies of forced migration and racial segregation. It discusses several instances of localized actions of "news place-making" through the lens of critical race theory and human geography. The chapter deepens articulations of news place-making as a critical component of understanding media control in the United States in terms of building notions of the nation's individual and collective homes as being sites of racial homogeneity through ideologies of White Supremacy.

Guiding Questions

1. How would one identify major characteristics of a "community," in terms of its shared spaces and ideologies? How do members of a community define these characteristics for themselves?
2. What role does the press play in determining the dominant characteristics of a given community?

Key Terms

Banishment: An act that precludes particular social groups from participating in community spaces, social roles, and storytelling

Journalistic Boosterism: Everyday news that promotes mediatized notions of a community's dominant traditions, dominant identities, and potential for future prosperities

News Place-making: The ideological process by which journalists demarcate and characterize geography

White Supremacy: Ideology perpetrated throughout culture that places the needs and interests of white and light-skinned members of society above those of a darker skin

---

HERE IS *NOT* THERE: PLACE IDEOLOGIES IN THE PRESS

On Father's Day, it is customary for US newspapers to carry a profile on "No. 1 Dads" and such—dads who sacrificed, those who have passed, new dads, old dads, soon-to-be dads. On their face, each story appears to be different. They are, in fact, stories about different dads. But, each likely carries the same moral tone—that dads are good, that it is good to be a dad, that it is expected for men to be dads, and for these dads to meet the same level of excellence of influencing their sons and daughters with positive values. So, it was not surprising that the cover of *The Des Moines Register* in Des Moines, Iowa, on June 15, 2014—Father's Day—had a story about a dad (Figure 3.1).

The story begins with a tale of a father's fall from his time as a successful businessman who, when he hit hard times, still worked and sacrificed to keep his family afloat:

> He was a typical 1950s father, his son said. A tall, successful insurance salesman who bought a nice home in Fort Dodge for his wife and two sons, traveled a bit, and honed his golf game.
>
> Then he ran into trouble and lost his insurance. They had to sell the house ....

The father, the story states, aged into a life of poor health that prevented him from working work full-time. Peppering specific details throughout the narrative, the article simultaneously presents a dynamic of "like father like son" in which the son, Gary, himself acknowledged "Nobody's perfect," having, himself, "battled alcohol," having once been convicted of operating a vehicle while intoxicated, and having once lost his driver's license. Both father and son experienced challenge and heartache, the story says, but both men

FIGURE 3.1 The Des Moines Register, *June 15, 2014. Reprinted with permission of* The Des Moines Register, *Copyright 2014.*

were redeemed when the father passed, his true virtues and values revealed, and Gary changing both of their "legacies" while building a sense of national unity. The article reads:

> At the end of that life, at age 82 with cancer, he lived alone in a rental, divorced from Gary's mother. He didn't have much to give by his death in 2008, Gary said, but left "kind of an inheritance"—30 1934 lithographs of the U.S. Constitution that his dad had sold to 184 Iowa schools, libraries and county courthouses.
>
> He left a legacy, too, planting statewide the call to secure liberty for our posterity.[1]

As the story ends, its purpose for building notions of nation and of "Americanization" becomes clear. Writing about the dedication of a copy of the Constitution that was hung in an Iowa courthouse, the newspaper focuses on the next stages of a son trying to see his dad's wishes come true:

> The courthouse was a fitting place to find a purpose after his father's death. It is a place of failings and their corrections. It is a place where no one is perfect.

Motivated by the meanings associated with Father's Day, the story says, the son will carry on his father's quest of planting the hopes and dreams of his father into public places across the state, thereby spreading the most virtuous of all representations of what it takes to live a meaningful life in the United States—and the world. The story concludes:

> The most meaning he (the son) finds in the Constitution's first line—"in order to form a more perfect Union." It isn't happening, maybe can't. But you can try to improve on imperfection.
>
> That's all any son can do with what a father has left him.

The *Register's* Father's Day story holds several normative and cultural meanings in that it is: (1) a heartwarming telling of love between father and son, (2) an affirmation of the power of family ties, (3) a way to reinforce dedication of an individual's purpose to propagate US Exceptionalism from settings within the US Heartland, and (4) a retelling of the nation as being, even in one's most dire of personal situations, the only place in the world where one can find prosperity and freedom at a time of sadness and challenge.

But, on its own, even that story on the cover of the largest paper in a state that launches every presidential election with its political caucuses and that holds to its history of the Americanized work of artist Grant Wood, of *The Field of Dreams*, and of its Protestant Work Ethic, was not enough to validate and legitimize the above paternal/patriotic nature of narratives. What was needed to advance the idealistic notion of fatherhood and of American nationalism on Father's Day in Iowa was a comparison to the dark-side that lives in the same geography as the good. Journalists found that opportunity in hometown stories of urban crime and deviance, subtle hints at the racial influence on societal dilapidation and disarray that threatens dominant US values and traditions.[2]

Also leading the same front page on Father's Day, a story focused on community decline in Des Moines headlined, "Nuisance—160 properties in D.M. deemed nuisances; city pursues $90 million revitalization plan" argued that the city has a major problem that could bring the whole place down: Houses in some neighborhoods have fallen into disrepair, the windows have been boarded, the yards are a mess, and the residents themselves just do not care about the possible implications of their disorder for the larger "community." According to the *Register*:

> … the poor reputation of one deteriorating neighborhood can affect nearby areas, negatively branding an entire portion of the city, said Tom Urban, a former Des Moines mayor who is working on turn around several troubled neighborhoods.
>
> "You do attract groups, gangs for instance, that use those sites as temporary homes," he said. "If crime, which tends to be higher in those neighborhoods, turns out to be of a level that gets reported beyond Des Moines … then we've got a problem."[3]

The paper's explanations for the disorder were also represented in inside pages by thirteen images of small houses titled, "Des Moines worst public nuisance properties" that also carried the locations' addresses, the year the houses were built, the assessed land/building value, and the "assessor's condition rating." The cause of Des Moines' problems, the article explains, were placed within a national epidemic of urban (read, black) decline, in which the city's traditional roots and its future prosperity may fall along the wayside with the rest of the urban cores of the nation's Rust Belt.[4]

The juxtaposition of seemingly counter or unrelated issues and ideas in order to reify dominant ideology is a common trait of news coverage; we need to know what we are "against" to understand what we are "for." In this case, dedication to national pride—even if performed by drunks, the unemployed, and criminals—becomes acceptable if those individuals are white and speak the right rhetoric. The *Register* presented this white, Iowa father as a man who at his core was kind and who may have lived through challenges in life—a divorce, living alone, and bordering on poverty, as the newspaper claimed "[h]e didn't have much to give by his death in 2008"—but who left a legacy of national pride for his troubled-but-recovering son to take on as his own.

And, while such juxtaposition that reifies dominant notions of nation can be achieved by presenting differences between one nation and another, juxtapositions that focus on maintaining a sense of "who we are" locally through the voice of local "authorized knowers" and personalities allow the press to identify what we "are" and what we "are not" within the same space. In turn, the local public can decide, seemingly independent of outside intervention, the necessary means by which to alter local geographies and identities through whatever means necessary to focus attention on our local places as meeting the nation's traditional and acceptable efforts of imperialism and dedication to greatness.

The juxtaposition of rural white lives with urban (again, read black) lives works to reinforce White Supremacy in and through press discourse in which whiteness is the normal and natural, while blackness is the dangerous and deviant. Similar polarizing efforts have been enacted throughout literature, press, and other forms of communication between notions of "the city" and "the country." As Raymond Williams writes, the country has been viewed throughout histories of communication as being feminine, traditional, humble, and wholesome while the city, on the other hand, is engendered with masculine traits of physical strength and danger, with meanings of progress and liberalism, and easily characterized by narratives of vice.[5]

Movements in and out of inner-cities by US blacks even before Reconstruction following the Civil War have presented cities as bastions for racialized deviance and have been practice fields for racialized segregation, economic genocide, authorized murder-by-cops and citizens alike, and the implementation of educational policies that criminalize and oppress dark-skinned students and families. Media, from the press to entertainment and back again, share each other's stories of this deviance. The popular TV show *Law and Order*, for instance, tells stories that are "Ripped from the headlines" in ways that attempt to replicate "reality" of "real-life" crime that has appeared in the press. News media is more than happy to have their stories told and retold, adapted and readapted; after all, everyone wants to be on TV.

The narratives of "the city" maintain commitments of the power elite to strengthen traditional values and stories of home at local levels outside of the urban reach. In recent history, Iowa has become home to an increasing number of inner-city dwellers from across the Midwest, many of whom are black. As of 2014, 3.2 percent of the state's population was black, compared to 1.4 percent in 1980. The percentage of black families in Iowa has increased more than 109 percent between 1980 and 2012. Of today's black population, 55 percent live in four cities, including Des Moines, Davenport, Waterloo, and Cedar Rapids.[6]

This migration has not come without its challenges:

- As of 2012, 12.7 percent of the state's population lived in poverty; within the black population that number was 35.5 percent [7]

- In 2013, the American Civil Liberties Union announced Iowa's blacks were more likely to be arrested for small amounts of pot than white folk by eight times[8]

- Between 2008 and 2012, the number of blacks in the state's Department of Corrections system increased from 15.6 percent to 17.4 percent; the number of whites in the system dropped from 76.6 percent to 74.5 percent [9]

- And, as Iowa Public Television put it in 2008, "If you commit a crime in Iowa, and you're African American, your chance of going to jail is fourteen times greater than if you are Caucasian. That's the worst percentage of racially disproportionate incarceration in any state in the nation ..."[10]

But correlation is very rarely the same as causation. First of all, just because there has been a measured movement of blacks into white Iowa does not mean that blacks are not—and have not been—*from Iowa*. Still, the way the press discuss the state's "changing demographics" is that undesirable black (read, urban) lives are a distraction from indoctrination of traditional Midwest and US values that could not possibly have come from the very same communities that wish undesirables gone. Place-making of the rural/urban dynamic, then, becomes just as much about characterizing the people of those places than about negotiating ideas of those places themselves. Furthermore, by casting local undesirables as "other" from "another place"—or, as Jack Lule calls it "The Other World"—the press and "authorized knowers" hide their hatred for people who really are of their own region and place by replacing them with people from elsewhere.[11]

Efforts made by the community and legitimized in the press, then, maintain a sense of nobility of cleansing a perfect place. In Michelle Alexander's book, *The New Jim Crow: Mass Incarceration in the Age of Colorblindness*, she argues that laws applied more strictly to blacks than to whites—including that blacks are punished for minor infractions at surprisingly higher rates than whites—are means by which to maintain Jim Crow attitudes and processes designed not only to marginalize and segregate our populations, but to increase ideological arguments that cast particular groups as less-than, as deserving of extreme scrutiny, of suspicion.

At the local level, this colorblindness is the veil for racialized hate of fellow citizens. The reason blacks were seen as a last resort to fight in US-led wars, including the Civil War and World War II, was fear among white leaders and citizens that armed blacks might attempt revenge for generations of slavery. Today, the same fear exists, and alarmist non-black attitudes and corresponding social policies ensure subjugation.[12]

My meaning is not to say that subjugation leads to certain complacency, however, but it does stack the deck—a very tall deck—against specific groups, forcing from atop the social structure pressure that other groups do not experience and that is fueled by a neoliberal system of oppression. So, while one group is pushed down, the unrestrained group is not only free to rise but is provided with support to do so. In each case, oppression and support are forces, not outcomes. Consider, for example, that those who have benefited from affirmative action policies within the United States have not been racial and ethnic minorities, but white women—those who have been in the workforce with social status for a far longer (while still unequal) period that has provided them with social and cultural capital to maneuver through bureaucracies and systems to reach their benefits. This consequence of affirmative action policies is not just something that happened—affirmative action policies were designed to maintain difference by veiling them within efforts that were said to do good. In its most brutal—and most accurate—of terms, affirmative action represents the ultimate "mind-fuck."[13]

To propagate confusion-as-reality, news stories like the Father's Day one and its juxtaposed narratives of disorder in the *Register* did not provide any context that might provide any clarity related to social inequalities within the neighborhoods that were described only as being of "nuisance." Specifically missing from the discourse was the degree to which white-based capitalistic approaches to reaching the American Dream—much of which has been written about in recent scholarship but seemingly not read by journalists (see Conclusion for more on journalism education)—is a direct influence on our economic and built environments. Such counter-narratives would likely do little to combat stigma related to some of the nation's homeowners and renters, however, who after two centuries of racist housing policies, land valuation, and lending practices, have contributed to the public denial that we have systematic and culturally embedded problems with affordable and safe housing in today's marketplace.[14]

Instead, by using the characters of father and son from one story as a benchmark for a proper life, the nuisance article used mythical settings of urban areas as a benchmark of what type of life must be avoided. The "nuisance" story mentions, for instance, that "[n]ationwide, cities like Detroit, Atlanta and Chicago have been some of the hardest hit with nuisance and vacant housing." These are three US cities with some of the largest populations of US blacks; they are also cities with some of the darkest histories of racialized oppression in the workforce, of applying methods of racialized capitalism, and of upholding the most troublesome of urban education policies that have, for a century, defunded public schools in the blackest of areas.[15]

Racialized ideographs of "the inner-city" have long appeared in the news as a means of explaining cities as urban jungles, in some cases the undesirable spaces as being characterized as the "other side of town" and cast as places for communities to act out racialized public policies that force the poor out of once undesirable places and to be replaced by desirable residents. Narratives about US cities remain in US media memory, particularly the cities of the 1960s and 1980s, which had grown to serve as geographic crack dens for suburbs and that then turned into places for intrusive policing and economic warfare on black families.[16]

As Jimmie Reeves and Richard Campbell write, TV news coverage of governmental responses to the rise of cocaine and crack cocaine use in US inner cities in the 1970s and 1980s—an effort sanctioned by the CIA to fund military operations throughout South and Latin America—was a form of collaboration between the press and politicians that fostered "journalistic recruitment" in terms of both recruitment *of journalists* to tell racialized and hegemonic narratives of US imperialism and journalists' *recruitment of others* to maintain racist ideologies by supporting press narratives through muted critique and loud contributions of evidence to support journalistic claims of disorder. The authors write that such collaboration:

> ... convert[ed] the war on drugs into a political spectacle that depicted social problems grounded on economic transformations as individual moral or behavioral problems that could be remedied by simply embracing family values, modifying bad habits, policing mean streets, and incarcerating the fiendish "enemies within."[17]

Indeed, US ghettos at the time were not only places for neoliberal money laundering and extortion on the backs of ethnic and racial minorities, but were also scenes of disorder and danger that fed the American desire for gladiatorial entertainment in news coverage of violence and depravity. Today's storytelling that connects local lives *anywhere* to crumbling city cores *somewhere else* relies on the action of dominant ideology—and the ideologies of its "perceived dominant news audience" (see Conclusion)— to provide context, explanations, and "facts" of the imagination—that the problems of Detroit are the problems of Des Moines and the common causes of these problems are the same sets of residents. For example, the *Register* clarified in their tale of urban decline that the concern of city officials, and of some residents, was that the "nuisance" homeowners or renters are not concerned with their property—or the property of others— and therefore purposefully neglect their dwellings. In its supposed diligence, the newspaper attempts a fair and balanced approach by "attempting" to either confirm or deny those claims.

But, one wonders how hard journalists tried to find the voices of those who might live in the dilapidated and even "abandoned" homes before writing them off and turning, again, to desirable citizens to explain their absence in the news—in an almost jarring manner. According to the paper:

> Efforts to reach owners of several of the properties on the nuisance list were unsuccessful. Contact information for the owners either was outdated or could not be found, or telephone calls were not returned.
>
> The unsightly properties upset their neighbors.
>
> Ellen King, who lives across the street from the house on Arlington, said she frequently sees wild animals existing the structure. "I come out here, and I see all these raccoons and possums running around, living in that house," she said. "We really need to get that cleaned up."

Had the journalists found the people who lived there, they just might have found a number of stories of people who either do not own the property or have no legal or financial obligation for maintenance, who likely pay a high rent for the return on their "investment," who live among a range of residents who do and don't care about their properties, or who may say that taking care of a home is too costly and time-consuming. We will not know what these residents would say, and how their comments might confirm or confuse the *Register*'s main thrust of purposeful negligence, because no one asked them.

Whereas in the Father's Day story, the newspaper spent line after line of text explaining away the personal responsibility of one man who drove drunk and of another who could not work full-time and who failed to save his marriage, the reader of the "nuisance" story is left with only one legitimate and authoritative narrative of explanation—and one that is rooted in racialized ideology—as to how and why properties appeared as they did.[18]

Again, my comments are not to be a critique of "good" or "bad" journalism in these cases; rather, I am fascinated by the ideological meanings within the juxtaposition of the Father's Day story and the package on neglect. While both stories may have "just appeared" on the same page of the paper on the same day, the storytelling and meanings embedded in each story independent of each other still hold meanings of their own. In fact, one of the stories addressed here, the failure or decline of the father that led to him having to sell his home and to him wasting away after a divorce was presented as accidental or as an unfortunate influence in his life, while the other story presented the neglect as being representative of individual choice and responsibility. These differences should be enough to raise anyone's eyebrows.

Additionally, we will never "know" what is in someone else's thoughts—in this case, the thoughts of the journalists, photographers, and editors who put these pieces together. We can only go by what people tell us they "think," and we can only surmise as to the potential meanings within a given text, within its language, tone, use of characters, and cultural contexts upon which we base our argument. But, with a foot in historical contexts and in a specific conceptual lens, one can argue as to the potential meanings within media texts, particularly when those texts—and the genre in which the texts appear—maintain a consistent theme of storytelling about people and places.

In the case of these two stories, one sets the standards of what it takes to be a "true American" against which the juxtaposed piece about those who create a "nuisance" is measured. More to the point of this chapter, these stories represent the role of place and geography in news storytelling. Those familiar with the geography of these two stories could most likely recognize the demographics of those living in these place-names—they could recognize that the city where a portion of the Father's Day story took place, Fort Dodge, Iowa, was majority white, as were many of the smaller communities where the US Constitution would be hung. Furthermore, racialized context was embedded in similar, subtle means within the nuisance story.

In that case, journalists provided street names, zip codes, photographs, and quotes from residents and officials to locate the homes in question within a specific geography of Des Moines—a geography that held particular place-meanings built, in large part, upon its density and diversity but still left to the imagination of these places. Properties discussed in the story are located within US Census tracts with large clusters of the city's black and Hispanic/Latino populations that are considered locally as being in and around the city's "ghettoized" area, just north of the city's core. Furthermore, the areas at issue in this article serve as a stark contrast to the white-majority of Iowa and the racial makeup of the *Register*'s news audiences in more affluent and white West Des Moines and neighboring Urbandale.[19]

Throughout this chapter, I build upon my concept of *news place-making*, the ideological process by which journalists demarcate and characterize geography, to identify the power and control in and of geographic characterizations within media that serve to explain social conditions and issues. Most of the chapter continues to discuss racialized place-making in Iowa press to explicate how local news covers neighborhoods and perceived disorder within particular geographies through the lens of *White Supremacy*, an ideology perpetrated throughout culture that places the needs and interests of white and light-skinned members of society above those of darker skin. In the end, the chapter returns to my previous work on place-making in the press and unpacks the depth of news place-making as evidenced by comparisons of press articulations of place in Southeastern neighborhoods of Iowa City, Iowa, and the place-making of residents who live there.

As a result, and when viewed alongside similar ideological practices of the press presented in this project, examinations of press coverage in Iowa City reveal how the press turn to place-making as a means to punish already displaced populations by removing them from the pages of the press and stripping them of the ability to characterize their homes. In sum, I argue that news characterizations of place create stories about a geography or about a specific "community" that intentionally displaces or diminishes undesirable voices from contributing to the dominant media articulations of place. Additionally, I argue that in the process of displacing or diminishing these voices, the press perform an act of punishment for those who are said to operate outside of the "norm" that then contributes to a justification and legitimization for acts of violence against the same populations.

THE POWER OF "OTHERING" IN PRESS CHARACTERIZATIONS OF PLACE AND RACE

"Othering" via US press discourse continues to breed a naturalized difference between "us" and "them" and "here" and "there" that is supported by shared (collective) histories, which drive interpretations of our successes and failures, particularly in terms of rationalizing the conditions—and geographies—in which we live. As George Lipsitz writes, tens of millions of white adults today can "trace the origins of their family wealth" to the Homestead Act of 1862—which like the Federal Housing Act in 1934 and the decades of related redlining and forced black migration—intentionally shaped the very same neighborhoods, schools, places of faith, industries, and political and economic conditions with which we live today.[20]

More important, however, is the degree to which our own experiences with geography and race represent an intersection of public policies designed to oppress through press discourse designed to explain and justify that oppression. In his book *Maps With the News: The Development of American Journalistic Cartography*, for instance, Mark Monmonier writes that location is a central feature of press discourse. Notions of place appear in media descriptions of geography and are reified in news cartography. "News maps," Monmonier writes, "accompany and support words—the written words of the newspaper and news magazine and the spoken words of the television newscast." He adds that these:

> [w]ords structure information linearly, in one dimension, whereas maps structure information graphically, in two dimensions. Readers and viewers seem more at home with words than maps, and journalism uses many more paragraphs than maps to convey its facts and opinions, which are largely nonspatial. But "Where?" is a question of journalistic concern because some news has an important geographic component, most nonlocal news at least has a dateline, and many persons have only a rudimentary knowledge of their own city.'[21]

It is the intersection of the personal experience with dominant communication about geography that drives this project to examine influences of and with mythical explanations of race. Writing about the influences of oppressive policies and development upon personal wayfinding in Britain in the 1990s, for example, David Sibley articulates the role racial characterizations played out in geographic constructions of the mind and of physical space. He writes that:

> the mobility provided by the car, in a city built around the automobile was not supposed to extend to black men who might threaten the white suburbs through their movement, resisting containment where only whites were supposed to drive.[22]

In other words, Sibley argues that a race-space dynamic is central to the creation of modern landscapes of power, and that an investigation of these dynamics reveals racial inequalities inherent in how our geographies are characterized in popular and dominant rhetoric, of which the press are a major contributor.

Lipsitz provides several examples of this racial-spatial dynamic in the US:

- City dwellers (read, urban minorities) lack access to healthy food options. "[I]nner-city poor pay on average 4 percent more for food than suburban dwellers pay," he writes. "In addition, many inner city areas are 'food deserts,' filled with fast-food outlets, convenience markets, and liquor stores but void of stores selling fresh fruit."

- US blacks continue to pay more than whites to borrow money for housing. In North Carolina, one study found that "Black neighborhoods house three times as many payday lenders as white neighborhoods," which tend to charge "an annual rate of as much as 400 to 1,000 percent on money borrowed."

- Whites receive preferential treatment when buying homes. In 2002, "high-income African Americans were three times more likely to be subjected to subprime [home lending] terms than low-income whites."

- US blacks continue to be targets of unfair financial systems that effect the development of residential neighborhoods. In Philadelphia, one study found, two percent of whites "used subprime lenders for home purchases, compared to 20 percent of Blacks." In Chicago, those numbers were 8 percent and 48 percent, respectively.

- Access to health care is stacked against places that have long-been home to racial and ethnic "minorities." In black and Latino spaces of Los Angeles, for instance, "there is one primary care physician for every 12,993 residents, but there is one primary care physician for every 214 residents in the largely white area of Bel Air." Predominantly white, Bethesda, Maryland, "boasts one pediatrician for every 400 children, but the Black neighborhoods in southeast Washington, D.C., have one pediatrician for every 3,700 children."[23]

A vast number of explanations employed by readers, newscasters, pundits, and politicians to understand these social conditions often come from positions of racial superiority veiled by ideologies of whiteness that allow us to ignore the hegemonic functions of society that have become the norm within our culture. In other words, colorblindness has become so normalized that even the most formally educated carry the colorblind belief system as a badge of racial compassion that somehow forgives their own responsibility in constructing inequalities.

An example of how easily colorblind explanations are shared and verified through like-minded rhetoric occurred during one of my own dinners some years ago that might be helpful here in expressing what colorblindness looks and sounds like.[24]

I was at a dinner at Creighton University's School of Law in Omaha, Nebraska, around 2009 with my wife and her friends to celebrate their first year in law school. All of us at the gala—the students, faculty, friends, and family members—appeared to be nonblack, while the majority of those serving us appeared to be black. Admittedly, I was bored, and so I sat back and pondered aloud, ready to watch the spectacle I imagined would follow: "I wonder why all of the law students and faculty members here are white, but all of the people serving us are black." The answers spilled onto the table, each presented with equal conviction:

- "I just don't think African American people want to go to law school"
- "African Americans don't go to college at the same rate as others"
- "There aren't very many African Americans in Nebraska"
- "There aren't many African Americans in Omaha"[25]

My table's explanations were so concrete, so cut and dry, so black and white, that it was clear those around me were having difficulty examining the degree to which we are all indoctrinated into a white system that it becomes next to impossible to even in a friendly way at a dinner table provide an explanation that strikes at the heart of white power. This experience has stayed with me throughout these years as an example of how even the "formally educated" are driven to confusion and distraction in ways that preserve the interests of the power elite.

And, as I discuss later in the book, the education system is geared specifically for this purpose, which has led me to wonder the degree to which journalists—who come into the newsroom with their own backgrounds and indoctrinations, as discussed in Chapter 1—are open and available to alternative ideologies that would be necessary if the mission of the press was to examine complex issues and challenge authority.

In the end, news media are responsible for casting light and shade in stark comparisons that bank upon our incessant need to construct polemics in explaining everyday life and in our interactions with race and place—both social constructions designed to uphold "us/them" dynamics, which center around collaboration with "official sources" and within the authority of business and government. Most troubling, in fact, is when the press celebrate this authority.

Media and place-dividing via boosterism

Journalists have long determined where and how information has been presented to the public, from to which trees info-posters were nailed to where heralders sang information about changing times to where and when police and law were cited as main authorities of explanation of daily events (see Chapter 2). Recent normalization of geotechnologies in media messaging has made these issues of space, place, time, and authority an even more recognizable part of how we interact ideologically and physically with each other:

- We are pushed by tech-driven news and advertisements in terms of determining what is of news interest and what is of economic value based upon where we travel

- We are presented with pathways that are "most convenient" in terms of passing through communities, which sanitize us from experiencing neighborhoods that are just simply "out of the way," and, therefore, marginalized in our own experiences of wayfinding

- And, whether we realize it or not, our business and governmental institutions are bound to regions and place[26]

In turn, because the press function as part of the power elite's physical and ideological mapping of country and culture at both national and local levels, reporters use the structures laid out for them in terms of market economies, urban planning, and local control to privilege particular places and people within those places who subscribe to those dominant meanings. As location becomes even more central to news messaging with the use of tracking and of sensors and of drones that place stories within specific and surveiled geographies, news place-making—and its hegemonic function—will become incorporated as the new status quo (see Conclusion). As I write elsewhere:

As a device, setting provides a familiar terrain through which the reader can see the characters play out the plot. In this case, identifiable physical features of the environment placed in the news story provided legitimacy to the resonance of the news occurring in particular geographies. To local news readers, spaces they can locate on a city map in relationship to their own location and space enhances their physical and psychological connection to the news, where it happens, and the news story's personal meaning.[27]

Indeed, if, as some journalists and scholars suggest, a core purpose of local news is to "build community," the next generation of local news requires an interrogation in terms of what exactly that notion of community is by asking:

- Who is in a community?

- Who defines community?

- Where is the community?

- Who decides these things?

To further help examine the application of media control through news place-making, the concept of *journalistic boosterism*—everyday news that promotes mediatized notions of a community's dominant traditions, dominant identities, and potential for future prosperities—allows us to examine the degree to which place-making in news divides geographies and people. Media hype surrounding the developing Wywood Art District in Miami, Florida, for instance, serves as a good example of how journalistic boosterism indoctrinates the public to dominant ideologies of geography in ways that benefit the power elite.

What was once a light industrial park bordering two largely black neighborhoods of Liberty City and Overtown, the Wynwood Art District has become a mecca for massive public–private events surrounding art, expression, and music. A Miami-area tech hub that is home to "public art," such as the Wynwood Walls, the district represents to many locals a place for progressive and interactive forms of expression.

In 2014, I examined news coverage of Miami's Wynwood, as well as coverage of three other Florida cities that in recent years were, through public and the press discourse, attempting to "boost" particular economically profitable ideas of place while at the same time displacing "undesirable" citizens, such as those experiencing homelessness, low-income and ethnic and racial minorities, to make room for non-black, luxury living. In addition to the Wynwood case, which I explicate below, I was interested in the following places and issues:[28]

- In St. Petersburg, the *Tampa Bay Times* reported on groups of individuals experiencing homelessness in the downtown Williams Park by, in perhaps a drastic move, turning to a local strip club owner—in many communities not the best representative of "welcome" and "legitimate business"—to promote the need to remove homeless and bus routes from the downtown to stop scaring away customers

- The *Sarasota Herald Tribune* in Sarasota—which was titled by the National Coalition for the Homeless as the "meanest city" based upon its public policies related to homelessness—reported that 2012 policies to support the jailing of those experiencing homelessness for charging phones at public electrical outlets in public parks was necessary in order to keep the parks free of "the homeless" and accessible only to local families

- In West Palm Beach, *The Palm Beach Post* reported that a new "luxury" outlet mall would be the best form of development to gentrify nearby neighborhoods and to help restrict the types of people who should shop at the stores and who will live in adjacent "luxury" apartments

My reading of coverage in these cases revealed that journalistic boosterism serves as social *banishment*, acts that preclude particular social groups from participating in community spaces, social roles, and storytelling that is embedded within daily news. In Wynwood, for instance, the press characterized the Art District as having been a geography that brought something to a place of nothing. In fact, one developer is quoted in the newspaper as saying "gentrification is good," with no recognition by reporters that "gentrification" is valued only because of costs deferred to subjugated populations. Indeed, overall *Herald* coverage of Wynwood presented the area as safe until the day a young black man was shot when the paper then referred to Wynwood as a "crime-plagued area."

Additionally, to make the place seem even safer, those who experience homelessness in Wynwood are cast as ancillary characters in news coverage, particularly as those who are being removed to benefit development; one story that explicitly discussed homelessness, in perfect Miami fashion, focused only on the design elements of a new homeless shelter.

To varying degrees within each of these cases that applied boosteristic notions of the community in ways that presented geographies as central to each news audience's sense of identity, I argued in my earlier work, the humanization of these city spaces—where the St. Petersburg park was "troubled," the Wynwood Arts District was "a dying warehouse district" at the "heart of the city" being reborn, and the presentation that troubles within some of these spaces can "bleed" into other parts of the cities—served to make place like people, to build a power structure around these spaces that presented them as having the ability to live and die and able to contribute to a community's life or death.

"Official" and press solutions to "threats" to these spaces, then, became vital for the survival of dominant cultural norms and social traditions of the community. These spaces were, after all, the "lifeblood" of dominant community identities formed by local officials that were left unquestioned by the press, the solutions presented by "authorized knowers" of an expanded journalistic community, including police, business owners, and civic leaders.

In addition to the use of humanization and official sourcing, however, the press applied "legitimate" narratives of impending doom from urban, big cities to mandate public policy changes to oppress racial minorities in ways that would be easily approved by the press.[29]

News about popular places and scary races

In 2015, the city core has once again become attractive, with gentrification occurring both in the inner-city and in rings of cities where expanding economic and racial disparities stretch from the core to the suburbs. Massive development throughout US cities following the 2007–2008 recession created a forced migration of the poor and of the dark-skinned to make room for white investment necessary for a city or a region to become the next popular place. In turn, the press found a need to apply boosterism to make sense of massive neoliberal investments in what once were the ghettos and in what once were outer rings of metro areas in which cities and business had invested for luxury living that, too, have "declined" as opportunities for living and working expanded in the far-off burbs, opening spaces for the "ghetto" to grow.[30]

The press have been caught in a moment of geographic confusion over what is glamorous and what is not, what has contributed to decline and what has not, and who is to blame. In the end, however, the press must protect their own and must show the decline of space as the fault of the minority and the poor, and that any movement of opportunity by the dark and poor to move into white spaces—a sign of the American Dream realized—reveals a threat against dominant white interests. In order to ease the pain of whites who then must live with the "consequences" of black mobility, news coverage must constantly switch what is criminal and what is glamorous in particular geographies, of who is to blame for its decline, and for whom city spaces are designed to benefit the most—or at all. Spaces that were once "bad" become "good" and news coverage must show a constant fight against spatial characterizations that marginalize or confuse the white gaze.[31]

Julian Alfred Pitt-Rivers refers to battles of place-meaning as historic "Us/ Them" constructs that diminish the realities of dominance of one group over another through storytelling in which:

> … always the people of the next-door town who are the cause of the trouble, who come stealing the crops, whose wives are unfaithful, who swear more foully, are more often drunk, more addicted to vice and who do one down in business. In all things they serve as a scapegoat or as a warning.[32]

David Ley describes such divides as "turf-divisions," which appeared between gangs in a 1970s Philadelphia, but where these turf wars occurred in the public light and influenced nearly all parts of life, between all people and places who come to adopt, out of fear, behaviors of particular territories or, at the very least, that treat territories as having natural boundaries. As these fragmented territories become known and authorized in the media, they become stories embedded within publics' "urban memory" and fuel tomorrow's news of cities, transforming, as cities change and capitalism takes its toll, into imaginations of "ruin porn"—the witnessing of decline and destruction that normalizes capitalism's death grip on society through interpretations of beauty and imagination as a way to make us feel better about ourselves through modernity in media, both in its editorial content and advertising (see Chapter 4).[33]

In this process, cities move from being urban jungles to being abandoned places to being spaces to be reclaimed, going from spaces of intentional disinvestment to a reevaluation that benefits from mythical tales of disorder, danger, and of previous efforts of banishment.[34] Boosteristic news coverage applies each of these stages of development, disinvestment, and redevelopment to serve the power elite in several ways, contributing to the following propagandistic outcomes:

- Ideological punishment of the marginalized. News coverage of "disorder" serves as authoritative evidence of the acts of disorder themselves, while the interpretations and explanations of those acts are legitimized through official sources and lay the framework for acceptable ways of dealing with disorder.

- Racialized geographic characterizations. News characterizations of place carry cultural and social influences that shape dominant perceptions of geography and receive further authority when placed within the structure of news storytelling.

- Established interpretations of place and moments of cultural conflict. These meanings of place at the center of news coverage related to social issues influence future meanings of those places and issues in media remembrance.

- The justification of displacing undesirables. Select sources that appear in the news reify dominant ideological explanations for the removal of particular people from particular places.

- The rationalization for increased press surveillance and force. News coverage dependent on racialized ideologies of place and characterizations of perceived disorder provides police and the citizenry with cause for racialized policing tactics.

- Explanation for police violence and military rule. News systems that rely on the above acts and outcomes share authority with police, military, and business communities that provide authoritative meanings for official violence in particular geographies and against particular people.

In the next section, I apply these understandings to implicate the white ideologies inherent in news place-making and to present press characterizations of geography as a key to the indoctrination of nationalistic, US ideologies via everyday media messages in ways that further race and fear and memories vital to the success of media control.

NEWS PLACE-MAKING AS "THE NEW JIM CROW"

In March 2014, the *Chicago Tribune* published a story titled, "Iowa City offers new start to some city dwellers," about the life journey of MeLissia Caston, a black woman and mother who had lived in the South Side of Chicago before moving to Iowa City, Iowa. The story began:

> In Chicago she took no classes, had no job and saw no clear path ahead. And she worried about her children's safety in their violence-plagued South Side neighborhood. She considered the corner store so dangerous that she met their bus from school and walked them home.
>
> Two years ago, she moved to Iowa City looking for a new life. And in this college town ringed by cornfields, she found one.
>
> She is getting A's and B's at nearby Kirkwood Community College, where she is majoring in human services. She works for a youth program at the Neighborhood Centers of Johnson County, a human services agency that helps newcomers settle into Iowa City. Her children are thriving in school and playing sports.
>
> "This is a positive place, a good place," she said.

The story continues by placing Caston in a family-oriented town that offers jobs and a real chance for a better life, where young people are free from gun violence and benefit from plentiful resources and excellent schools. The story quickly moves to discuss some of the ways in which Iowa is not so great for newcomers who carry their Chicago ways:

Some Chicagoans end up in trouble with the law or lose custody of their children to the state's child welfare system.

"Children get taken away a lot," said Sabrena Shields, a social worker at the Neighborhood Centers whose clients are almost all transplants from Chicago.

Especially, she said, from young women who lack parenting role models because their own mothers were on drugs.

"I love my clients, but they are just so lost," she said. "They still want to live that young life, that kind of party life. They come to Iowa City and they have this big-city mentality — but this is not the type of area they should be in."[35]

In this narrative, people from both places—Chicago and Iowa—are cast as representative of single definitions of place in that Chicago equates to "ghetto living" and Iowa to a place of saving grace. The *Tribune* article is not that different from a host of other news pieces that have run over the past thirty years about the haven that is Iowa for people who have been born and raised in the urban jungle.

As I discuss in the conclusion to *A Transplanted Chicago*—and further explicate in this chapter below—the main characters in coverage about particular sections of Iowa to which Chicago natives migrate could be replaced with another section, and they would still read as the same narrative:

[One] *Des Moines Register* article from 2004 details a now-familiar narrative about life in Chicago and quotes Zaida Cruz, a black, unmarried mother who moved "from the trauma of ghetto life" to Iowa about finding food stamps and health insurance for her children that's "covered by a federal program." The story, part of a series on efforts by the state to "lure high-wage, highly educated workers to Iowa" but that attacks "[m]ost newcomers [who] have been like Cruz: poor and looking for opportunities.

Indeed, the *Register's* story continues by presenting Iowa's potential for helping cure residents from the ills of the inner city ghetto:

Were it not for desperation, Zaida Cruz might have stayed indefinitely in the only neighborhood she had known, on Chicago's rough west side. But last year, the former movie-theater worker [*sic*] had no job, no home and no way to protect her family.

With $7 in her pocket and three children under the age of six, Cruz boarded a Greyhound bus bound for Iowa City. The former gang member told herself she would stay long enough to get back on her feet, then head home.

Cruz, who was twenty-four at the time, is quoted as saying, "When you come to Iowa and see all the good things out here, you think of Chicago and you wonder: Man, how did I live like that?"[36]

So, how is it these tales of Chicago, Iowa City, and the people moving between the two places read exactly the same in terms of people leaving desolation in one place and finding solace in the other? Can the stories be that "true," the "realities" that concrete? In response to the *Tribune* article, I wrote a local editorial in which I argued that Brotman had "certainly covered her bases: She told stories of personal struggle, of 'cultural differences,' and of drugs, welfare mothers, jail and program assistance." But, I also pointed out that, like with much coverage of a changing Iowa:

> [t]he stories that weren't told, however, were the ones people never want to read, the ones that keep getting missed — that of indoctrinated whiteness and naturalized racial fear of newcomers, which contributes to an unfriendly and dangerous community for newly arriving blacks.[37]

In that response, I wrote specifically about the story of one person who had shared her story with me that complicates the experiences of some black folk in a white Iowa—Nell, who arrived in Iowa City in 2001, found good work and good schools, but also found that "it was only a matter of time before her kids would stand out in their mostly-white northside school: soon, regular childhood horseplay and fast-talking drew scrutiny. And the situation worsened when one of Nell's three sons, who usually walked his sisters home from school, got suspended." Her story continues:

> After one of the girls got jumped on her walk home, Nell complained to the white principal and was shocked by the response. "Well," the principal told Nell, "if you got off your behind and walked them, then maybe this wouldn't happen."
> Nell lost her composure. The principal called police.
> Nell was banned from the school, charged with "verbal assault" and fined $250. But more than anything that happened from that exchange, Nell said, was that she no longer felt part of the community. That distance grew when people didn't believe her story or chalked it up to whining.

But Nell tells of other, similar stories that have happened since:

- The time when Nell got kicked out of her apartment for making noise, though the next-door white college students partied all of the time and got to stay

- The time a white parent chaperone slapped Nell's kid on a school trip and apologized with a patronizing letter and four coupons for ice cream (not even enough for all of Nell's kids)

- The time when one of Nell's children was told by a white schoolmate, "Ya'll need to get back on a bus and go back to Africa"

By sharing her story with me with the intention of publishing it within the community, Nell said that she wanted others to hear about how Iowa is maybe not the perfect place people think it is. Indeed, Nell was able to interrogate the mythicized Chicago-to-Iowa migration that has moved countless US blacks from larger, metropolitan areas of the Midwest into mainly white and largely, small-town Iowa.

Today, I continue to be fascinated by the role of myth in news place-making, because within stories such as Nell's, there is consistency in the sense that Iowa may provide "good jobs" and "good schools," "safe neighborhoods," and "opportunity," but that within these stories, life is not necessarily "better." In other words, "safe" might mean fewer reported shootings on the street, but does not mean the streets are safezones from other dangers. It is within this framework that I close this chapter by revisiting my initial building of "news place-making" with the intention of (1) examining the interaction of news and geography, particularly in terms of language that is designed to demarcate and characterize place and people and (2) establishing the method of mental mapping that I employed in this initial research to enhance a participatory means that can help us examine the intricacies of communication about geography and interaction with our environments.[38]

CONCLUSION: MEDIA DISPLACEMENT AS PUNISHMENT

Iowa City is placed among cornfields, bordered at the North by Interstate 80 and has long relied on its "Southeast Side" neighborhoods to provide affordable homes and apartments to new arrivals, young families, and the elderly (Figure 3.2). Over the past decade, however, the Southeast Side has become characterized in Iowa press as a black "ghetto," the scene of dilapidation, of policing, of perceived crime, and of racialized news coverage that focuses on the residents' characters as cause for questionable social conditions.

Beginning in the mid-2000s, I began following press discourses of the changing neighborhoods, school classrooms, and public policies related to affordable housing, housing vouchers, and policing in Iowa City, particularly its Southeast Side.

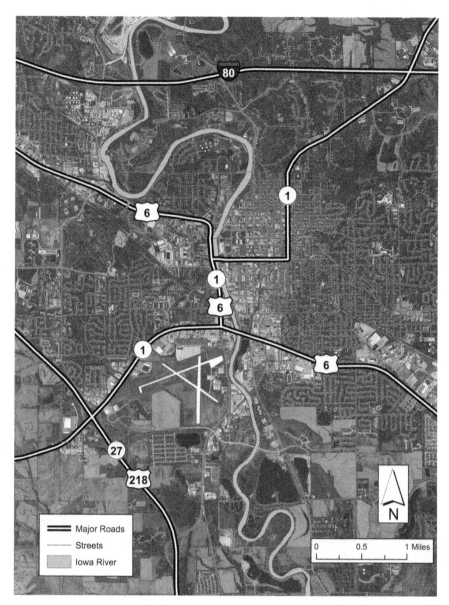

FIGURE 3.2 *Iowa City, Iowa, 2012. Map by Tyler Johnson. Used with permission.*

Imaginations of space: "Southeast Side"
as "Ghetto Scene"

In 2011, I began meeting with Iowa City journalists, public officials who were commonly sourced in news coverage of the Southeast Side, and residents associated with the Southeast Side by either living there or having benefited from resources from that neighborhood's Broadway Street Neighborhood Center. By that time, the press had established the Southeast Side as a home to outrageous crimes, such as loitering, littering, and loud music. The murder of a white landlord by black youths in 2009 continued to hang over the neighborhood's image, though very little crime of that magnitude had occurred there since.

Repeatedly, I was told by residents outside of the Southeast Side that the neighborhood was "the bad side of town." Those not living there told me this with great conviction; residents there, though, said such stigma was not accurate and was merely reflective of white people in the city applying what they "think they know about the ghetto" to a part of Iowa City where black people lived; in fact, the Southeast Side had been regularly referred to in the press as "A No Go Zone" and as "Little Chicago," the first phrase presenting the space as one to avoid at all costs, the second as a reference to the "ghettos" of Chicago.

While I sympathized with residents who wished people did not see their neighborhood as "ghettoized," it seemed little would really change people's perspectives of the neighborhood—at least in the short term—if I merely tried to do research or journalism that attempted to counter dominant narratives. This position was different from my journalistic training, which taught me that I, as a journalist, was someone who could make change by telling the stories of others. But what about the stories of the people themselves, I wondered? Just how would I examine how people experience their environments, and, as I had been hearing over the past few years, how could I explain the hows and whys behind the different stories about the same spaces?

That was the case for my wife, anyway, having grown up in Iowa City, when I asked her to describe the different parts of the city to me in terms of how she came to believe whatever she did about specific neighborhoods—particularly the Southeast Side.

Instead of just telling me what she thought about city spaces, she drew them while at the same time explaining how and why she thought what she thought about specific neighborhoods and who she thought lived there. Especially interesting during this exercise is when she explained that her map—which only included some stops along a route she took from our house to the local law school—encompassed all of her thoughts about Iowa City at that point in her life. I tried to clarify.

"I thought you were going to draw a map of Iowa City," I asked, perplexed, expecting to see a much wider representation of the geography.

"I did," she said. "This *is* my map of Iowa City. It's really all I care about right now."

It struck me that maybe this approach, which I later found had a grounding in what was called "mental mapping," could help residents throughout Iowa City if they were asked to draw what they "cared about" in that the method could help to unveil some deeper meanings about how people in this city came to care for—or at least came to know about—some places and not others. Drawing and explaining people's maps actually became a powerful tool for talking about life in the city in terms of racial hatred, subtle profiling of blacks by whites connected to policing, and inequalities in employment, education, and home ownership. Through the stories of how we interact with our geography, people could express deeper meanings that they may not have been able to articulate otherwise.[39]

Mental mapping in this project, then, provided a wealth of data and stories from which to examine commonalities and differences in spatial interpretation and representation between three sets of people—journalists, official sources, and Southeast Side residents. The maps provided surprising details about how dominant meanings of neighborhoods were created and shared by the press and the local power elite.

Of the eleven journalists who participated in the study, all had regularly covered Iowa City and had reported on issues related to the Southeast Side. One identified as Hispanic, and the rest as white. All six public officials who were frequently sourced in stories related to "the Southeast Side" identified as white, and all sixteen city residents who had either lived or spent much of their time in "the Southeast Side" identified as black.

What came from these maps revealed more about place-making in the news and the construction of racialized discourse in the press than I could have ever imagined: First, journalists and officials held similar interpretations of geographies, particularly in terms of which landmarks were important in contributing to the city's overarching identity; in fact, some maps made by officials and journalists were nearly identical in terms of what and how geographies were presented. Second, Southeast Side residents showed a detailed understanding of the Southeast Side in terms of specific roads, stores, and schools while the remaining parts of the city were less detailed, including spaces in which residents could not draw representations of what was there, because they said that they lacked the ability to be mobile—including through public transportation—and did not know what was in those spaces.

Within the participants' drawings and their explanations of how and why they drew what they drew shed light on the functions of the local journalistic interpretive community and its acts of maintaining dominant, white perspectives of space, place, and its meanings. Below, I present three examples of maps, one from each set of participants that represent the dominant ways those groups explained how they experienced and characterized parts of the city and those who lived there.[40]

Journalistic imaginations of space

Len's map (Figure 3.3) is representative of how journalists blocked-off specific spaces of the city with straight and narrow lines that indicate main streets and identify specific locations as meaningful to the identity of the city which were also considered as being "safe" and "welcoming." These "safe" places included the following: City Hall, which housed the police department and offices for many local officials; schools and the University of Iowa both identified as highly securitized locations where journalists said that

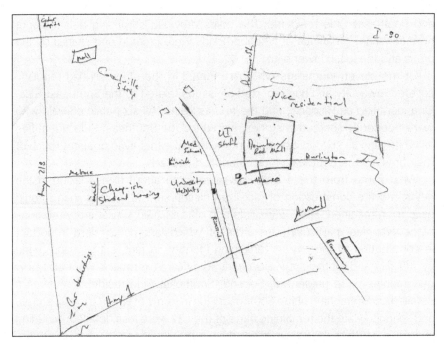

FIGURE 3.3 *A map of Iowa City, Iowa, drawn by Len, a journalist, depicts an orderly city, with specific neighborhoods and streets. Author's image.*

they were welcomed in as guests for sporting events or for feature stories; the downtown business district was a place where families gathered and news emerged; the University of Iowa hospital was a place where public relations professionals indicated to journalists, almost daily, something that would be newsworthy.

Most neighborhoods indicated on journalists' maps also included their own homes and places where their friends and families lived. Other locations included their neighborhood grocery store or place of faith. But specific to "the Southeast Side," this space rarely appeared on their maps. When asked what they thought about this part of the city, journalists said it was seen in the community as largely black and dangerous, evidence of which could be found in city, school, police, and Census data. Ironically, however, local police from 2009 to 2012 largely recorded the downtown—not "the Southeast Side"—as boasting the most violence in the city, the culprits being college students. Indeed, local press reports over the past few years had referred to downtown violence associated with college students as "the exuberance of youth," releasing mainly white college students from responsibility for physical assaults, property damage, and other disorder.

And, such as the journalists explained to me as they drew their maps, racialized narratives of "Chicago" were used to describe where new arrivals to "the Southeast Side" neighborhood came "from" and, in turn, served as evidence of causes for perceived disorder there on "ghetto culture" of its residents.

Official explanations of space

By and large, public officials who had supplied journalists with dominant explanations for perceived disorder and rationales for militarized responses by police in the Southeast Side over the previous few years applied meanings to that space that were very similar to those of journalists. For the most part, these maps—like those of the journalists—revolved around the ways in which officials experienced the city on a daily basis in their professions. For example, a map by Fred, a school official in Iowa City (Figure 3.4), depicts the city based upon the locations of and meanings of schools—the streets included on the map representing major ways across the city from one school to the next.

Other maps, including one by a city housing official, depicts the city in a drawing based on a housing map that was hanging on his wall. In two other maps, these by two police officers made independently of each other, drew the city based upon official police beat maps. In each of these cases, including in the cases of journalists, participants followed "official" and

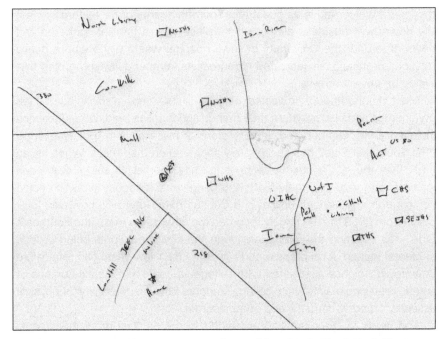

FIGURE 3.4 *A map of Iowa City, Iowa, by a public school official, Fred. The image identifies specific schools that represent corresponding neighborhoods. Author's image.*

"institutionalized' explanations of city spaces and the Southeast Side based upon their professional understandings of how city data and official rhetoric could provide the most relevant and accurate meanings of social conditions in those spaces. For each of these participants, few of their forms of evidence about how and why they came to see the Southeast Side as they did—a rough place to live with black folk from Chicago—were their own personal experiences in those Iowa City neighborhoods.

Additionally, even though officials and journalists were all asked to discuss their experiences with the city not only in terms of their professions, but also in terms of their daily experiences, they relied on their roles as journalists and as officials to explain what these spaces meant. Schools, for instance, according to Fred, were representative of their surrounding neighborhoods with classroom racial, economic, and educational demographics a reflection of students' home-lives and with little explanation of other possible forces that might shape student experiences in school. Maps of city meanings by officials—and of journalists—became even more interesting when compared to the mental maps of Southeast Side residents.

Residents' stories of "home"

Whereas maps by officials and journalists were institutionalized in their explanations and forms of evidence, residents drew maps that focused on their interactions with city environments and with other city residents outside of the Southeast Side as a way to explain their own neighborhoods. A map by Angel, who lived on the Southeast Side (Figure 3.5), for instance, is representative of the types of storytelling by residents that highlighted the people in their lives and the sites, sounds, and feelings they experience throughout the city. By and large, Angel and other residents said that the downtown and university spaces were "unwelcoming" and "unsafe," because the people there were largely white and part of a larger community that did not seem accessible to black residents.

How residents represented streets in Iowa City was also telling: Wide stretches, sometimes with cars drawn on them, showed how much time residents spent crossing major roadways without the safety of bridges or crosswalks. The thin lines that depicted roads, in some other instance,

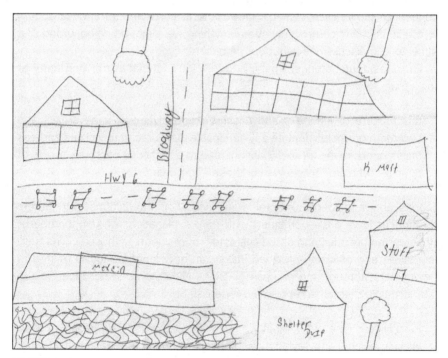

FIGURE 3.5 *A map of Iowa City, Iowa, by Southeast Side resident, Angel, showcases her favorite places and major roadways. The image, she said, represents all of what she knows about the city. Author's image.*

were presented in circles at the center of their maps that residents told me represented bus routes that they relied upon to move throughout the city. Spaces on their maps inside and outside of these circles were often left blank.

Residents told me that these areas inside and outside of their circles were unfamiliar spaces to which they were not able to travel via public transportation. Residents' restricted mobility led to deep storytelling about their everyday lives that also appeared in their maps, such as Angel's, which showed specific details about a particular neighborhood or portion of a neighborhood. In Angel's map, for example, she was able to talk about where her friends and family lived and where she found her favorite store for shopping. She also described the challenges associated with living South of the four-lane Highway 6, which she sometimes had to cross with her children.

Through this experience, residents told me that they were able to present narratives of their neighborhood that were counter to dominant stories about their spaces that they hear or read about in the news. Indeed, by drawing their experiences in the city and with stories about their own lives, perceived behaviors, imagined pasts, and mythical tales of "ghetto ways," residents explained to me what pervades their daily experiences in Iowa City—the concept of "Iowa Nice," what I have come to consider "a rhetorical tool in which conflict and controversy about anything we might be doing wrong that stifles public discussions about our problems."

From residents' stories, I published in a local journal at the University of Iowa that:

> this mixture of kindness and passive aggressiveness, wide smiles and backroom grumbles deplete any actionable discourse to unveil and address racist, oppressive, or hateful actions tied to a particular person—or sets of people—who are "true Iowans," those "from here."[41]

Stories about residents' mental maps and their interactions with others throughout Iowa City—combined with their explanations of neighborhoods, of perceived disorder, and of the characters of residents in those spaces from journalists and officials—provided insight on how longtime locals related to newcomers, through the process of "Iowa Nice," which I described in the journal article mentioned above and republish here:

> Iowa Nice is inherent in what we paste on billboards ("The People of Iowa Welcome You") and saying nice things to your face that don't reflect what we "really think."
>
> Iowa Nice is saying that suspending black youth or sending a disproportionate number of them to special education classes is

pedagogically sound while ignoring conversations about altering teaching style and recruiting (and retaining) diverse teachers.

Iowa Nice is instituting a citywide nightly curfew for the entire city, but then only having enforcing against young blacks while refusing to entertain public discussion about the practice.

Iowa Nice is making black high school students wait hours to get a bus ride home after school—even though "home" is only a couple miles away.

Iowa Nice is believing that these students "enjoy" waiting to get home from the downtown bus terminal while surrounded by police officers with watching eyes and loaded guns.

By taking part in the method of mental mapping, participants were able to examine and explain how communication about built and natural environments, just as much as experiences (or lack of experiences) with geography, largely influence—and are influenced by—imaginations of those places, perceptions of past experiences elsewhere, as well as daily fears, hopes, desires, and needs of daily life that might have otherwise been nuanced, veiled by perceptions what are mere "semantics" and distorted by power in terms of who can set dominant stories of people and place.

Media meanings of mental maps

Mental mapping was also helpful in revealing several characteristics of news place-making in the case of Iowa City's Southeast Side, including:

- The subtlety of place-making in terms of its reliance on everyday experiences

- The stories told about a space throughout a larger geography

- The cultural context of related geographies and the people within them

- The degree to which the myth of "the Southeast Side" and its race narratives were embedded in the place-making approaches of journalists and officials

Southeast Side residents said that they recognized these racialized stories of their neighborhood and used their maps to identify other spaces that were "more dangerous," including the neighboring City of Coralville where residents said police were constantly stopping them for "driving while black" and other "infractions." Most fascinating, however, is the degree to which journalists and officials expressed a need to define city landmarks that represent a single "community" identity.

All of the journalists and officials, for instance, drew the Iowa River on their maps of Iowa City or otherwise indicated in their drawings that the river ran from North to South on the city's West Side and told me that the river was a major physical definer of the city. Among the residents, only one discussed the river or showed it on their maps, many answering my questions about why they might not have included the river at the end of the exercise with questions about where the river was and why it was important. While one may or may not care whether or not the Iowa River appears on a map, it was the inclusion of this feature on maps made by officials and journalists—and not those made by residents—that revealed within the shared interpretive community of journalists and officials an ability to shape dominant narratives related to what the river "is" and what Iowa City "is about." Mental maps of Iowa City also reveal the degree to which these meanings influence the function and process of news place-making that relies on mythical narratives about a place and its people rather than actual "reporting" beyond the involvement of others who have been welcomed into the journalistic interpretive community, such as police and politicians (see Chapter 2).

This finding became especially clear to me through another map I asked officials and journalists to draw, which revealed the role of the press in terms of collaborative place-making among the local power elite. Early on in the project of mental mapping, I needed to identify the area of Iowa City that was considered the "Southeast Side" so that I could to talk with whomever may live there. Iowa City officials do not identify any part of the city by the "Southeast Side" place-name, which truly was a construct of news media through the publication of addresses of police activity there and described via environmental descriptions and photographs that demarcated and characterized the space as desolate and "ghettoized."[42]

During my interviews with journalists and officials, I asked them to identify what they considered the Southeast Side on an image of a Southern region of Iowa City that I had provided (Figure 3.6). To my surprise, each official and journalist described the Southeast Side in the exact same way: There was no one single "Southeast Side," they all told me, but several—each with its own meaning. Drawing lines around the exterior border of the image provided to them, participants identified this first definition of the "Southeast Side" as the "Southeastern portion" of Iowa City where light industrial space met residential, they told me, and where schools and businesses were located.

Participants then drew a second border to identify what they also referred to as the "Southeast Side." This border began with a major highway South of downtown (Highway 6) and stretched to cornfields at the Southern and

The Three 'Southeast Sides'

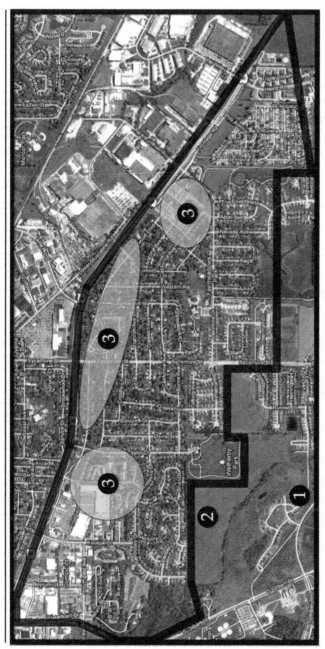

① Borders stretch to city limits and major roadways in all directions; represents ambiguous geography

② Borders follow Hwy. 6 at North, S. Gilbert St. at West, cornfields at South; represents 'Southeast Side'

③ Specific apartments, neighborhood center and road represent people and places of *'what's really meant by* 'Southeast Side'

FIGURE 3.6 *When asked to describe Iowa City, Iowa's Southeast Side, journalists and officials produced the exact three definitions of the geography. Author's image.*

Eastern edges of the city and to a particular street (South Gilbert Street) to the West, which runs parallel to the Iowa River a few blocks further West. This second "Southeast Side," participants explained, was closer to resembling "what people mean when they say the Southeast Side" in that the highway represents a physical and ideological border between a safe and welcoming Iowa City and a portion of the city "known" for its crime and migrant populations.

Yet, it was the third explication of the "Southeast Side" that participants each said "is *really* what people mean when they talk about the Southeast Side." This third definition was associated with three separate locations South of Highway 6, beginning (1) at the East with an apartment complex (the official title of which is the Dolphin Lake Point Enclave), including (2) a stretch of Hollywood Boulevard where the press had heavily covered reported crime and disturbances over the years, and (3) at the Broadway Neighborhood Center further West. These spaces—including the neighborhood center, which provides employment, educational, and daycare services—were said to represent, in the words of one participant, "mostly where black people live."

To me, these maps and conversations correspond with other work from over the past few years that shows the degree to which stories of "here" and "there" influence press coverage and public discourse about mythical inner-cities and corresponding, racialized explanations for perceived disorders in those places. The work presented here on news place-making, I argue, contributes to a lexicon of methodology with which we can examine the degree to which local press influence a community's place-making that is based, in large part, on the interests of the power elite via messages of the press. More specifically, this experience reveals the ways in which journalists and officials work together through shared modes of explanation to create and promote the same stories about social conditions and causes for social disorder that ignore alternative explanations—even if those explanations come from people who live within such conditions and are considered, themselves, to be causes of "disorder." It is important, therefore, to examine the subtle and underlying methods and stories used to introduce and reinforce dominant place ideologies, which is discussed next.

Spaces for news place-makers

One of the subtle—but consistent—landmarks and characteristics of Iowa City used by participants of each set to describe and explain city environments, from journalists to official sources to Southeast Sides residents, included public schools, places that are of constant interest for journalists and that are relatable to most residents who have either attended school themselves or who send their own children there. In turn, journalism about community schools is an effective space for news place-making in which the schools become place-markers that describe and explain a region's cities and neighborhoods in the following ways:

- Since schools tend to be prominently placed within cities and in neighborhoods, in rural settings and in suburbs, they carry cultural and social meanings about our communities, our neighborhood challenges, and our ideological efforts

- Schools provide an identity for the neighborhood or the community and structure the days and experiences of children, families, businesses, and professionals

- For students and their families, schools provide social, civic, and even religious training upon which communities may prosper

- Schools offer opportunities for journalists to make news, partially because public schools in the United States are largely funded by property taxes, making them perfect places to try to address the degree to which news users spend their money through government

- School prep sports and extracurricular activities continue to be areas of immense investment by news outlets—even with massive cuts by many districts to these programs—in part because they draw audiences and advertisers to the media outlets

- Standardized testing of students, an effort supported by state and federal governmental spending and rhetoric, creates moments for quantitative analysis that provides "evidence" related to the value of specific schools and neighborhoods

Rarely, though, do journalists address—or maybe even understand—the complexities of school environments upon which they report. And, if they do, journalists clearly ignore the influences surrounding public education from both sociological and cultural levels. Because schools provide an "everyday" opportunity in the press to indoctrinate audiences to authority in terms of spending and instruction, school news becomes a key tool for media control that becomes just as much about the geography of the schools themselves as the educational bureaucracies or school activities that the press cover.

Understanding school environments

Schools operate within their own social environments; they are their own communities within a demarcated space—sometimes identified with signage, and certainly with more intuitive symbols, such as playgrounds, large buildings, and the presence of children. Indeed, they then become "a school zone." Forced racial desegregation of public schools in the United States—to the degree that schools today are truly integrated—transformed schools into even more of a socializing space that, despite their controlling and dominating nature, enforce cultural interaction and discourse among diverse populations of students from external communities and neighborhoods. Furthermore, schools in the United States tend to be a space over which politics and ideologies of local and national communities are debated, such as in terms of:

- How and what curricula should—or should not—be taught, which contributes to a continued commitment to ban particular books, lesson plans, and pedagogies that challenge the status quo

- How student learning is measured, such as through the controversial No Child Left Behind legislation, the Common Core program, and the increase of privately constructed and privately profitable standardized testing

- The degree to which local control of school boards to make decisions for their schools represents a nationalistic commitment to federalism

- The rhetorical entrance of the role of parents and racialized and elitist notions of "personal responsibility" and the "nuclear family" in terms of influencing policies related to the education of students

Because of the layered ideological meanings of schools, local places of education have reciprocal relationships with their geographic, political structures of governance and civic life in that the school is designed to benefit local social norms, so that, in turn, the local community will provide social and financial support for school activities. Local businesses and community groups (and sometimes national businesses and national community groups) provide funding beyond tax dollars for educational programs through in-kind donations of supplies, faculty and staff, and financial donations. In return, schools train and socialize students to contribute back to the community through work or service.

Furthermore, relationships between neighborhoods and schools also help define what may be considered poor conditions of a school, its students and families, and its corresponding geography. Perceptions related to issues of truancy, violence, poor academic achievement, and social and athletic programming can lead to antagonistic relationships in which schools attempt to limit external forces from within the neighborhoods as to how teachers should educate students. These tensions result in residents and officials blaming schools for failing to provide students with the skills and knowledge to improve communities.[43]

More specifically, however, these ideological connections between schools and geographic space contribute to dominant local characterizations of space. Depending on the degree to which a portion of a student body represents an "urban culture," this can lead to a "ghettoization effect," which consists not just of the real influences of ghettoization upon an individual's psyche, but also the broader effects of characterizing a neighborhood as a ghetto upon the local, regional, and national understandings of place.[44]

School coverage and "the ghettoization effect"

If one were to look at the intersections of school truancy, of the school environment, of neighborhood demographics, and of student home life, the complexities of a student's experience with school is compounded beyond what we read in the press—and, ironically, what we each seem to have forgotten from our own times in school. Research into student academic achievement reveals that neighborhood poverty has a direct impact on a student's school performance, and that crime rates, economic conditions, housing opportunities, and the quality of a neighborhood's social cohesion shape the nature of schools and the experiences of students, teachers, and staff within them.

These ideas have received an abundant amount of coverage in the media, yet without much discussion of the complexities within each category. Lasting demographic changes within many US cities following the destruction of neighborhoods and infrastructure, including schools, from Hurricane Katrina in New Orleans, Louisiana, in 2005, as well as the emptying of the Rust Belt due to large economic changes, have influenced schools systems, particularly in cases of:

- Patterned "white-flight" and middle-class flight from the inner-cities to the suburbs

- The rise of charter schools as a direct competitor to public schools

- The equally outrageous overcommitments of parents and educators to both special education and gifted and talented education as ways to "balance" classroom learning with little critical evaluation of problems associated with teaching to the middle

Public schools across the United States have been influenced by these pressures in several ways, including the depletion of public school funding through the local tax base and through the migration of taxpayers out of city school districts that increase a repopulation of lower-income residents moving in who then have an added burden of funding a defunded school. The student body, then, is of a homogenously dark(er) color than those of highly funded schools—both public and private. The effects of these changes have been massive. In 2010, for example, reports from the US Department of Education and the Metropolitan Nashville Public Schools stated that:

- Black students in that school district were four times more likely to be issued out-of-school suspensions than other student groups in the same schools

- More than half of the black students in nine Nashville middle schools were suspended during the 2007 school year

- Another six elementary schools during the same period suspended *only black students*[45]

Nashville's *Tennessean* had foreshadowed major structural changes when it published a three-part series in 2008 about how middle-class flight from the city schools and neighborhoods to the suburbs and the entrance of charter schools was depleting resources from inner-city classrooms. The blame for potential state takeover of the district was placed on the students themselves. Specifically, the paper stated that "the failure of impoverished high school students to meet math and reading standards" was a "major reason" for the takeover.[46] Relatedly, in Kansas City, Missouri, the Kansas City Public Schools in early 2010 announced that it would close twenty-eight of its sixty-some schools, which attracted national news that focused just as much on local debate about school closures as on changing neighborhoods and demographics of the city and on what was called a "chaotic, almost nonfunctioning" school system administration.[47]

The consistency of language and blame in the press in these cases placed students and their parents as the scapegoats for larger economic and cultural forms of oppression targeted at students of color and their communities. Out of New Orleans in 2010, for example, *Time* magazine reported that changes to the city's schools—including the redevelopment of broken infrastructure, neighborhoods, and leadership—were caused by a natural disaster with little recognition of the role of policymakers and politics involved in decision-making. In fact, local press referred to issues in Kansas City's schools as products of "white flight, forced desegregation, teachers' strikes, revolving-door leadership [of the school system]," a confusing laundry list of human intervention that still skirts issues of a racialized system—or of a racialized press that was covering the system.[48]

In these cases, "the ghettoization effect" contributed, however subtly, to a national narrative in which the schools "cast shade" on their hometowns, and from which the details of the cases have been intentionally forgotten (see Chapter 4), but in which the dominant characterizations of place—and of people—remain.

The violence of protecting place

The power dynamics associated with press coverage of education is quite clear. News coverage of school bureaucracies, public recognition of failing federal standards to equalize education across regional, racial, and socioeconomic lines, today's hyper-militarization of public school hallways, and approaches to discipline and histories of failed efforts—such as school busing policies that were an attempt to diversify student bodies by moving low-income students out of their neighborhoods to "whiter" classrooms—does not lead to an undercutting of the power elite. In fact, as Torin Monahan writes, media are "involved with schools and are thoroughly invested in the images of schools that they project" and that "media thrive on fear and control in schools" through an "oversaturation of rare school shootings [that] attests to the profitability of hyper fear to boost ratings."[49]

To be clear, media operate as they do within the structures and orders of the power elite when covering schools—just as they do when covering our hometowns, public debates about economic development (or redevelopment), and neighborhoods—because schools, like these other places, are treated through media rhetoric not as actual locations with actual people but as imaginaries that can be interpreted, thrust into dominant characterization by the press, and co-opted to serve ideological purposes at particular moments of press coverage.

Place-making in the news that casts schools as representative of neighborhoods, for example, is an effective means by which the power elite can justify using schools as a "school-to-prison pipeline," the process of using professionalized curricula and policing as a form of even the most initial acts of discipline that drives students to negative interactions with educators, police, and employers, greatly increasing their chances of being incarcerated at an early age.

By building dominant perceptions of neighborhoods based upon perceptions of schools reinforces the use of schools to control behavior and language beyond those borders, as well, and to indoctrinate residents from outside those neighborhoods to the desires of the press and policymakers related to appropriate styles of living. And, it is that "desirable living" in those "desirable places" that the power elite and its press are dedicated to protect.

Throughout this chapter, I have attempted to articulate the many ideological arms of press indoctrination based upon the needs of White Supremacy to maintain social authority and cultural legitimacy within the aims of the power elite by focusing on issues of geographic characterization of place, ending with schools. I did so to help identify how media control does not just work in the overt spaces of rhetoric.

The above analyses revealed, among other things, the role of place and punishment in efforts of the press that:

- Indoctrinate audiences to dominant ideologies through the juxtaposition of desirable places and people with the undesirable in ways that audiences can measure, visit, and easily recognize within their own geographies

- Rely on stories of "other places" and "other people" to compare the values, behaviors, and meanings of local norms

- Apply a humanization of geography to boost the economic and ideological value of space in ways that authorize and justify banishment of particular communities

- Displace particular voices from storytelling about specific geographies in ways that empower the local power elite to establish and maintain dominant identities of people and places

The following chapters build upon these efforts and ways of meaning-making to examine how the press, as part of the power elite, use justified violence to protect dominant ideologies of US Exceptionalism and Western (read white) Thought. Whereas the first few chapters of this book have laid a foundation for the conceptual work surrounding issues of the press, power, and place, the remaining pages apply such concepts in ways that highlight the hegemonic functions and approaches of media control by implicating the collaborations between the press and police in ways that support my overarching claim that the press stand within the community of the power elite, alongside the police, and contribute daily to the increased surveillance and investment in weaponry within US society that continues to manifest itself in everyday news.

Discussion Questions

1. What are some other "bad places," maybe even local to the reader, and how have they come to have such a characterization? To what degree does local press coverage shape those dominant characterizations?
2. In what ways may these places be racialized or otherwise characterized as "other," and how might journalists reporting on these places identify such influence on place-meanings?

Notes

1   Mike Kilen, "Son takes on dad's constitutional legacy," *The Des Moines Register*, June 15, 2014.

2   As an aside, Iowa is rarely recognized for its progressive past, which includes being one of the few and first states to have a unionized McDonald's; the Mason City, Iowa, McDonald's joined the United Food and Commercial Workers Union in 1971 and disbanded four years later. For more, see Eric Schlosser, *Fast Food Nation: The Dark Side of the All-American Meal* (New York: Houghton Mifflin, 2012), 64.

3   Grant Rodgers, "Nuisance: D.M. endorses 5-year/$90 million plan to improve blighted properties and spur revitalization," *The Des Moines Register*, June 15, 2014.

4   Daniel J. McGraw, "The complications of our deteriorating inner ring suburbs," *Belt Magazine*, January 5, 2015, http://beltmag.com/complications-deteriorating-inner-ring-suburbs.

5   Raymond Williams, *The Country and the City* (New York: Oxford University Press, 1973).

6   "African-Americans in Iowa: 2014," The State Data Center of Iowa and the Iowa Commission of the Status of African-Americans, http://www.iowadatacenter.org/Publications/aaprofile2014.pdf.

7   Ibid.

8   Kathy A. Bolten, "Blacks in Iowa arrested at rates higher than other races," *The Des Moines Register*, November 19, 2014.

9   Stephen Gruber-Miller and Jermaine Pigee, "Moves in Iowa are aimed at reducing the state's black imprisonment rate," *iowawatch.org*, October 5,

2013, http://iowawatch.org/2013/10/05/moves-in-iowa-aimed-at-reducing-black-imprisonment-rate.

10 "Disproportionate Minorities in Iowa Prisons," *iptv.org*, January 19, 2008, http://www.iptv.org/iowajournal/story.cfm/160/feature.

11 Jack Lule, *Daily News, Eternal Stories: The Mythical Role of Journalism* (New York and London: The Guildford Press, 2001).

12 Michelle Alexander, *The New Jim Crow: Mass Incarceration in the Age of Colorblindness* (New York: The New Press, 2012).

13 For more, see Jennifer L. Hochschild, "Affirmative action as culture war," in *The Cultural Territories of Race: Black and White Boundaries*, edited by Michèle Lamont (Chicago, IL and New York: University of Chicago Press and Russell Sage Foundation, 1999), 343–368. Within these pages, the term white includes those of Anglo descent, though it can be extended in more racially heterogeneous communities based on who is in power to people outside of Anglo groups to people of lighter skin tones.

14 For an overview and application to Iowa, see Robert E. Gutsche, Jr., *A Transplanted Chicago: Race, Place and the Press in Iowa City* (Jefferson, NC: McFarland, 2014).

15 See, John F. McDonald, "What happened to and in Detroit?," *Urban Studies* 51, no. 16 (2014): 3309–3329; David Uberti, "Why the media don't get Detroit—and why it matters," *Columbia Journalism Review* 5 (2015).

16 See also, Lawrence J. Vale, *Purging the Poorest: Public Housing and the Design Politics of Twice-cleared Neighborhoods* (Chicago and London: University of Chicago Press, 2013); Michael Barton, "An exploration of the importance of the strategy used to identify gentrification," *Urban Studies* (2014), doi: 10.1177/0042098014561723; Wesley G. Skogan, *Disorder and Decline* (Berkeley, CA: University of California Press, 1990).

17 Jimmie L. Reeves and Richard Campbell, *Cracked Coverage: Television News, the Anti-Cocaine Crusade, and the Reagan Legacy* (Durham and London: Duke University Press, 1994), 3.

18 Dianne Suzette Harris, *Little White Houses: How the Postwar Home Constructed Race in America* (Minneapolis, MN and London: University of Minnesota Press, 2013).

19 The following chart shows 2010 US Census Tracts; Des Moines data from 2013 estimates; data represent White alone, Black or African American alone, Asian Alone, Hispanic or Latino:

20 George Lipsitz, *The Possessive Investment in Whiteness: How White People Profit from Identity Politics* (Philadelphia, PA: Temple University Press, 2006), 2; Moon-Kie Jung, João H. Costa Vargas, and Eduardo Bonilla-Silva (Eds), *State of White Supremacy: Racism, Governance, and the United States* (Stanford, CA: Stanford University Press, 2011); see also, Laura Pulido, "Geographies of race and ethnicity I: White supremacy vs white privilege in environmental racism research," *Progress in Human Geography* (2015), doi: 10.1177/0042098013478232.

21 Mark Monmonier, *How to Lie with Maps* (Chicago: The University of Chicago Press, 1996), 1; Doreen Massey, *For Space* (London, Thousand Oaks, CA, New Delhi and Singapore: Sage, 2010); Edward W. Soja, *Seeking Spatial Justice* (Minneapolis and London: University of Minnesota Press, 2010).

22 David Sibley, "The racialisation of space in British cities," *Soundings* 10 (1998): 121; for more complete discussion, see David Morley, *Home Territories: Media, Mobility and Identity* (London and New York: Routledge, 2000), Chapters 6 and 7.

23 Lipsitz, see discussion, 28–70; also, Soja refers to such spatial divides as the "socio-spatial dialectic" in *Seeking Spatial Justice*.

	Tract 5	Tract 12	Tract 26	Tract 48	Tract 49	Des Moines
White	26	24	45	39	62	76.4
Black	41	38	29	14	11	10.2
Hispanic	21	22	16	34	16	12
Asian	9	8	3	9	2	4.4

24 Eduardo Bonilla-Silva, *Racism Without Racists: Color-Blind Racism & Racial Inequality in Contemporary America* (Lanham, MA: Rowman and Littlefield, 2010).

25 Around the time of this conversation, the enrollment of US blacks in college was increasing (as a group, however, they still held low retention and graduate rates compared to whites); blacks consisted of 13.7 percent of the Omaha population and 4.5 percent of the state of Nebraska; though black folk were still a "true minority" in the legal field itself. For more, see 2010 US Census data; "Law firm diversity among associates erodes in 2010," National Association for Law Placement, November 4, 2010, http://www. nalp.org/2010lawfirmdiversity.

26 See Eric Gordon and Adriana de Souza e Silva, *Net Locality: Why Location Matters in a Networked World* (Malden, MA, Oxford and West Sussex: Wiley-Blackwell, 2011); Akhteruz Zaman, "Newsroom as battleground: Journalists' description of their workspaces," *Journalism Studies* 14, no. 6 (2013): 819–834; Kristy Hess and Lisa Waller, "Geo-social journalism: Reorienting the study of small commercial newspapers in a digital environment," *Journalism Practice* 8, no. 2 (2013): 121–136; Also, Amy Schmitz Weiss provides a nice synopsis of the spatial influence on journalism in her article, "Place-based knowledge in the twenty-first century: The creation of spatial journalism," *Digital Journalism* 3, no. 1 (2014): 116–131; For more on "communication geography," Paul C. Adams and André Jansson, "Communication geography: A bridge between disciplines," *Communication Theory* 22 (2012): 299–318; Paul C. Adams, *Geographies of Media and Communication* (Malden, MA, Oxford and West Sussex: Wiley-Blackwell, 2009).

27 Robert E. Gutsche, Jr., "There's no place like home: Storytelling of war
       in Afghanistan and street crime 'at home' in the *Omaha World-Herald*,"
       Journalism Practice 8, no. 1 (2014): 68.

28 Robert E. Gutsche, Jr., "Boosterism as banishment: Identifying the power
       function of local, business news and coverage of city spaces," *Journalism
       Studies* (2014), doi: 10.1080/1461670X.2014.924730; John Tomaney, "Region
       and place 2: Belonging," *Progress in Human Geography* 38, no. 1 (2014):
       131–140.

29 For more, see Moses Shumow and Robert E. Gutsche, Jr,
       News, Neoliberalism and Miami's Fragmented Urban Space (Lanham,
       MA: Lexington, forthcoming); Robert E. Gutsche, Jr. and Moses Shumow,
       "'NO OUTLET': A critical visual analysis of neoliberal narratives in
       mediated geographies," *Visual Communication*, forthcoming; Moses
       Shumow and Robert E. Gutsche, Jr., "Urban policy, press & place:
       City-making in Florida's Miami-Dade County," *Journal of Urban Affairs*,
       forthcoming.

30 Alice Skirtz, *Econocide: Elimination of the Urban Poor* (Washington, DC:
       NASW Press, 2012). About how press shape discourse about the value
       of geography, see Moses Shumow and Robert E. Gutsche, Jr., "Urban
       policy, press & place: City-making in Florida's Miami-Dade County," *Journal
       of Urban Affairs*, forthcoming; see also, Kriston Capps, "Minorities and
       the 'slumburbs,'" citylab.com, January 21, 2015, http://www.citylab.com/
       housing/2015/01/minorities-and-the-slumburbs/384680; Alana Semuels,
       "Suburbs and the new American poverty," citylab.com, January 7, 2015,
       http://www.theatlantic.com/business/archive/2015/01/suburbs-and-the-new-
       american-poverty/384259.

31 See Gutsche, Jr., *A Transplanted Chicago*; Tomaney, "Region and place"; Tukufu
       Zuberi and Eduardo Bonilla-Silva (Eds), *White Logic, White Methods: Racism
       and Methodology* (Lanham, MA: Rowman and Littlefield, 2008).

32 Julian Alfred Pitt-Rivers, *The People of the Sierra* (Chicago and London:
       University of Chicago Press, 1971), 30. For related discussions on race
       and space issues, see Scott Rodgers, "The architectures of media power:
       Editing, the newsrooms, and urban public space," *Space and Culture*
       17, no. 1 (2014): 69–84; Peter Parisi, "*The New York Times* looks at one
       block in Harlem: Narratives of race in journalism," *Critical Studies in Mass
       Communication* 15 (1998): 236–254.

33 David Ley, *The Black Inner City as Frontier Outpost* (Washington, DC: The
       Association of American Geographers, 1974); See discussion of "no go zone"
       in Gutsche, Jr., *A Transplanted Chicago*.

34 Nate Millington, "Post-industrial imaginaries: Nature, representation and ruin
       in Detroit, Michigan," *International Journal of Urban and Regional Research*
       37, no. 1 (2013): 279–296; Fred Vultee, "Finding porn in the ruin," *Journal of
       Mass Media Ethics* 28, no. 2 (2013): 142–145; Sandra L. Borden, "Detroit:
       Exploiting images of poverty," *Journal of Mass Media Ethics* 28, no. 2 (2013):
       134–137; Kelley Crowley, "What we do: Detroit in car advertising," *Journal of
       Mass Media Ethics* 28, no. 2 (2013): 145–147.

35 Barbara Brotman, "Iowa City provides fresh start for some urban dwellers," *Chicago Tribune*, March 18, 2014.

36 Gutsche, Jr., *A Transplanted Chicago*, 184–185.

37 Robert E. Gutsche, Jr., "Racism continues to hide in segregated Iowa City," *Iowa City Press-Citizen*, March 21, 2014; see also, Robert E. Gutsche Jr., "'This ain't the ghetto': Diaspora, discourse, and dealing 'Iowa Nice,'" *Poroi* 8, no. 2 (2012):1–4; Robert E. Gutsche, Jr., "News place-making: Applying 'mental mapping' to explore the journalistic interpretive community," *Visual Communication* 13, no. 4 (2014): 487–510.

38 See constructions of related ideographs in Gutsche, Jr., *A Transplanted Chicago*, 184.

39 Methods and background related to this project are outlined in Chapter 5 of Gutsche, Jr., *A Transplanted Chicago*.

40 As discussed in the book, Iowa City has long produced a public transportation system that has very limited weekend service—even entire stretches of hours in which busses do not run—which, as of 2015, had never undergone a comprehensive examination of effectiveness; All mental maps can be found at http://www.robertgutschejr.com/transplantedchicago.

41 Gutsche, Jr., "This ain't the ghetto."

42 Robert E. Gutsche, Jr., "Building boundaries: A case study of the use of news photographs and cultural narratives in the coverage of local crime and in the creation of urban space," *Visual Communication Quarterly* 18 (2011): 140–154.

43 Robert L. Crowson, *School-Community Relations, Under Reform* (Berkeley, CA: McCutchan, 2003); Norman J. Glickman and Corianne P. Scally, "Can community and education organizing improve inner-city schools?," *Journal of Urban Affairs* 30, no. 5 (2008): 557–577.

44 Gutsche, Jr., *A Transplanted Chicago*, 163–164.

45 For review, see Demetria Kalodimos, "9 schools have suspended 50% of black boys," wsmv.com, May 20, 2010, http://www.wsmv.com/story/14795812/9-schools-have-suspended-50-of-black-boys-5-20-2010.

46 Jaime Sarrio, "Saving Nashville schools," *The Tennessean*, May 11, 2008.

47 Susan Saulny, "Board's decision to close 28 Kansas City Schools follows years of inaction," *The New York Times*, March 11, 2010.

48 Karen Ball, "Final bell: Kansas City's effort to save its schools," *Time*, June 14, 2010.

49 Torin Monahan, "The surveillance curriculum: Risk management and social control in the neoliberal school," in *Surveillance and Security: Technological Politics and Power in Everyday Life*, edited by Torin Monahan (New York and London: Routledge, 2006), 119.

4

News as Cultural Distraction: Controversy, Conspiracy, and Collective Forgetting

Chapter Purpose

This chapter focuses on the ideological roles of controversy and "conspiracy" within news during times of cultural trauma to examine how audiences are distracted in ways that allow the power elite to sanitize and whitewash the future while reporting on the present. This chapter examines coverage surrounding the killing of twenty US elementary school students (and six school employees) in 2012 and the murder of a black man in the Midwestern US by a white police officer in 2014 which led to protests about police militarization well into 2015. In both cases, controversy, and claims of conspiracy in news coverage served as a process of "collective forgetting" in which the press operate to indoctrinate today's *and tomorrow's* audiences to dominant explanations of news events and issues.

Guiding Questions

1. What social and/or cultural influences are necessary for an ideology to become considered a conspiracy?
2. What are the purposes for collective remembrance within communities and within the media?

Key Terms

Collective Forgetting: The act by media and public voices that shape dominant interpretations of current-day events and issues in ways that maintain power structures for future remembrance

Conspiracy Theory: A term applied to articulations of power that reveal actions of the power elite and that subjugate alternative explanations through language and rhetoric embedded in policy, dominant ideology, and "common sense"

Cultural Trauma: Challenges associated with the failure of dominant journalistic articulations of values and identities to adequately explain disruptions to mediatized messages and meanings

Neoliberalism: An economic and political ideology that supports increased private investment and operations in public institutions and responsibilities

Normalization: The application of dominant "common sense" principles to incorporate alternative or controversial explanations of social conditions into the mainstream

---

CONTROVERSY OR BUST: MEDIA COMMITMENT TO CRAZY IN NATIONAL CRISES

Adam Lanza had already killed his mother, having shot her four times in the head and leaving the gun he used beside her bed. Later in the morning of December 14, 2012, the twenty-year-old went to Sandy Hook Elementary School, the one he had attended as a child in Newtown, Connecticut. He shot through a glass panel that was part of a locked-door to the school and walked the halls, firing bullets from a gun his mother had helped bring into their household. By the end of the shootings, twenty elementary students would die, as would six school employees.[1]

Days later, the National Rifle Association (NRA) announced it would be presenting a solution to rampant gun violence that had occurred before in schools but never, in recent memory, that had led to such violence in a classroom that was filled with so many young souls. Mainstream media waited during this time period for what NRA officials had only promised would be a "meaningful contribution to help make sure this never happens again." Would this Right-wing constitutionalist organization surprise audiences, media outlets asked, with recommendations to reduce the production and tighten the sale of high-volume clips that can kill a room-full of people with one trigger pull?

Nope. At a December 21 press conference, the NRA's executive vice president, Wayne LaPierre, presented a shocking suggestion for solutions to school violence that was buried within kind rhetoric about the indispensable value of our youth:

As parents we do everything we can to keep our children safe. It's now time for us to assume responsibility for our schools. The only way—the only way to stop a monster from killing our kids is to be personally involved and invested in a plan of absolute protection. The only thing that stops a bad guy with a gun is a good guy with a gun.

LaPierre continued:

Now, the National Rifle Association knows there are millions of qualified and active retired police, active, reserve, and retired military, security professionals, certified firefighters, security professionals, rescue personnel, an extraordinary corps of patriotic, trained, qualified citizens to join with local school officials and police in devising a protection plan for every single school.

We could deploy them to protect our kids now. We can immediately make America's schools safer, relying on the brave men and women in America's police forces. The budgets—and you all know this, everyone in the country knows this—of our local police departments are strained, and the resources are severely limited, but their dedication and courage is second to none. And, they can be deployed right now.[2]

As one might imagine, debate raged in the press about the notion of placing armed civilians as a line of defense of the public, even though this is exactly what the US government endorsed in the mid-2000s when it supported civilians in The Minuteman Project at the Mexican border taking up arms to "protect" the United States from the arrival of illegal immigrants there.[3] In this new proposal, the NRA would seek collaboration with federal and local authorities to arm civilians who would be stationed in each and every school in the country.

On NBC's *Meet the Press* several days later, host David Gregory sat down with LaPierre to discuss the NRA's proposal. Little did some know, however, that Gregory also had plans to, during the interview, violate a local ordinance in the city of Washington, D.C., that bans individuals from possessing high-capacity magazines—or clips—by showing such a clip on-air. Despite having been denied permission to be in possession of such an item by local law enforcement when Gregory and his producers had sought permission, they decided to show the clip on live television anyway. The clip, Gregory said, was similar to what had been used in mass slayings across the United States and that the public should see just what tools are used to create such terror.

With his plan set and the clip hidden under the desk, Gregory pressed LaPierre on the NRA's intentions to reduce school gun violence by putting more guns in schools.[4]

> GREGORY: Because that's your standard is that fewer people should be killed. That's the goal here. And the standard is, if it's possible, your words, if it's possible that lives could be spared, shouldn't we try that? That's your standard, isn't it?
>
> LAPIERRE: I tell you, my standard is this. You can't legislate morality. Legislation works on the sane. Legislation works on the law abiding.
>
> …
>
> There are monsters out there every day, and we need to do something to stop them. And they're not—
>
> GREGORY: If it's possible to reduce the loss of life, you're worth trying it, correct?
>
> LAPIERRE: If it's possible to reduce the loss of life—
>
> GREGORY: That's what you say.
>
> LAPIERRE: Yeah, I want it. That's what I'm proposing.
>
> GREGORY: OK, so let me widen the argument. Let's stipulate that you're right. Let's say armed guards might work. Let's widen the argument out a little bit. [Gregory presents the magazine from under the interview table.] So here is a magazine for ammunition that carries thirty bullets. Now isn't it possible that, if we got rid of these, if we replaced them in said, "Well, you could only have a magazine that carries five bullets or ten bullets," isn't it just possible that we can reduce the carnage in a situation like Newtown?
>
> LAPIERRE: I don't believe that's going to make one difference. There are so many different ways to evade that, even if you had that. You had that for ten years when Dianne Feinstein [a US senator from California] passed that ban in '94. It was on the books. Columbine occurred right in the middle of it. It didn't make any difference. I know everybody—that this town wants to argue about gun control. I don't think it's what will work …

The entire interview, not only the part in which Gregory reveals the magazine, includes an entertaining back and forth between Gregory and LaPierre.[5] Indeed, if we view the Gregory-LaPierre debate as a form of entertainment, the performance easily reads as:

- A journalist outflanking a political hack

- The press contributing information and perspective to public discussion and debate of current issues

- A moment that feeds a public a sense of journalistic watchdoggedness and the role of the press in providing political oversight

- The use of controversy as a main force in the media telling of issues in order to distract audiences from critical analyses of power systems at the moment of public interest in an event or crisis

The exchange is representative of these things, but more than anything it is a moment in which the press presents public policies and private-public collaboration as being rooted in the naturalized notions that the government and its policies and actors, which include suit-wearing reporters, operates within a set of predetermined dictated laws, processes, and language that has been assigned ultimate and virtuous authority. In other words, the Gregory-LaPierre moment of journalistic performance was just that, a moment with which the press, as a tool of and for the government, operated to maintain its authority on monitoring the government but that was designed in such a way that any outcomes related to journalistic examination of public policy and gun laws would only maintain a sense of altruism for the rights of the public good through notions of the Second Amendment and not for the lives of those who are slain each day—including children—by guns.

In fact, two years later—after the deaths of at least four black men (Trayvon Martin [February 2012], Eric Garner [July 2014], Michael Brown [August 2014], Tony Robinson [March 2015]) made national news for being murdered by white police officers, or in Martin's case, a self-described neighborhood watchman—President Barack Obama and local and national officials across the country continued to stand by racialized notions of pure authority of militarized police in the United States (see Chapter 3 for additional victims and Chapter 5 for further discussion.) In March 2015, for instance, following the shootings of two police officers standing guard over protests in Ferguson, Missouri, where Michael Brown was slain, Obama told the US public on the evening talk show *Jimmie Kimmel Live!* that "[w]hoever fired those shots shouldn't detract from the issue" of what was considered by protestors in Ferguson to be a continued attack on black folk by the nation's local police forces. He also said of the suspects:

> They're criminals. They need to be arrested. And then, what we need to do is to make sure that like-minded, good-spirited people on both sides—law enforcement, who have a terrifically tough job, and people who understandably don't want to be stopped and harassed just because of their race—that we're able to work together to try come up with some good answers.[6]

Obama also tweeted from the White House account a simple message to the public: "Violence against police is unacceptable. Our prayers are with the officers in MO. Path to justice is one all of us must travel together." Obama's rhetoric, which resembles calls "for peace" and "for calm" during and after moments of social conflict which is spewed by officials, followed patterns of justification that are made in each moment of such conflict that excuse the violence—or the threats of violence—by police officers in everyday life and especially at times of public protests.

Furthermore, just as the Gregory-LaPierre debate reified dominant constructions of the nation's government and special interests groups as being of concern for the country's children and the safety of all of us but failed to identify the complexities of US gun culture and the media's role in it, Obama's comments were meant to do nothing more than to make a show of the rule of law and to boost the authority of local police.

There also was an attempt in both of these instances to create controversy— or at the very least to recognize public controversy—surrounding the role of guns and militarization in the two news events. The Gregory-LaPierre debate, then, became a moment of focusing on the debate itself, the actions of Gregory, and the rhetoric of LaPierre. In terms of Obama's comments on the shooting of police officers (note, we no longer call them peace officers), the power elite strutted out the Commander in Chief to dictate the rules of "peaceful protesting" and to further confuse the public about a story with uncomfortable and controversial racial elements.

Indeed, by placing Obama, a prominent black figure in US politics and society, as "taking the side" of a police institution—even one that has a history of racialized violence against blacks—audiences were left with a sense that, at the moment, we live in an age of colorblindness. These messages were also meant to create confusion in that if we live within a colorblind society, just exactly what was Ferguson about? Racialized policing? Militarization of local police forces? A bunch of bad (black) apples? It is that controversy that I discuss next as a means to explain how news conflict, when positioned as holding a vast number of perspectives and an emotional tone in the explanations of events protects the power elite from immediate harm.

Using controversy and confusion to cure "cultural trauma"

In the rest of this chapter, I turn to moments of purposeful distraction that is concocted by and with media with the intent to control the interpretations of society in moments of media saturation. I also argue that such journalistic performances are not intended to end with an audience questioning foundational-American-traditionalism and protectionism upon which our laws are formed, but to pretend that any sense of oppression in our society can change if we, the public, will it. The confusion that the US press and public faced following the Newtown mass shooting, like the controversy surrounding claims of racialized police murders and even NSA spying efforts discussed earlier in this book, are examples of how the press create and contribute to controversy in public and press discourse at times of *cultural trauma—* challenges associated with the failure of dominant journalistic articulations of values and identities to adequately explain disruptions to mediatized messages and meanings within the interpretive community.[7]

Moments of cultural trauma, as presented in this project, revolve around challenges to dominant meaning-making of the press during their collaborations with other members of the power elite. In other words, the cultural trauma within the journalistic community that I am discussing is not related to death or destruction of an individual within the community but threats made to the community's dominant explanations that, in the face of opposition, may appear to the public to be as weak as water. The trauma is a jarring of the journalistic community's need to act fast in response to ideological challenges and the difficulty in creating news and cohesive explanations that are consistent throughout the community and, therefore, that match the needs of the power elite. Throughout this chapter, I present several means by which the press institute media control through cultural distraction, including the processes of confusion, controversy, and conspiracy theory.

By presenting news as a product of social confusion, where there are no clear answers to social conditions and crisis (at least, no clear answers the press would be interested in providing that might be counter to the authority of the power elite) the press direct public consciousness away from any avenues that might implicate power structures while working to align the ideologies of the power elite in ways that will pacify audiences. Likewise, controversy as a focus of press coverage delegitimizes any interrogation of the power elite and its role in the very characteristics of the status quo that's contributed to the issues with which the public may be at odds.

The Newtown story, for instance, became about controversy over the NRA's policies—not the publically funded laws that allow for people to own high-volume, military grade weapons or to alter the weapons that they already have in ways that double or triple their ability to spray bullets with a single trigger pull. The endless murder of black men by non-black police or pseudo-police officers became about just how racist the United States is that these deaths occurred but not about the intentionality of dominant culture that applies the fallacy of God-given police authority and autonomy. News discourse about expanded secret mass surveillance and tracking of citizens by both the public and private sectors committed under the premise of protectionism was nothing more than argumentation that naturalized the paternalistic attitudes of US society that leads to justified murder (see Chapter 6).

Conspiracy theory, a term applied to articulations of power that reveal actions of the power elite and that subjugate alternative explanations through language and rhetoric embedded in policy, dominant ideology, and "common sense," becomes another tool for media control when the press wish to avoid real conversations about the public's own responsibility for supporting through elections or through compliance with these laws. The Newtown story, for instance, became a moment for the press to function as distraction and control through conflict, controversy, and "conspiracy theory."[8]

This case is helpful in introducing the third concept, because conspiracy theory was so very well presented in an overt manner during coverage of the shootings as the press worked to realign the power elite's explanations for just how loose gun policies contributed to a rampant culture of gun craziness and gun access. I also begin with a case of news coverage where conspiracy theory is identified overtly in press explanations so that later examinations of conspiracy theory in the press can be extended to include more radical statements of intentional economic and racial oppression and violence that occurs on part of the press and its power elite in more subtle manners.

THE DISTRACTION OF "CONSPIRACY THEORY": NEWS, FEAR, AND THE NEED FOR PROTECTION

On December 24, 2012, a week after Adam Lanza shot and killed his way to the end of his life inside his own elementary school in Newtown, Connecticut, James Tracy, a Communications professor at Florida Atlantic University in Boca Raton, Florida, used his blog "Memory Hole: Reflections on Media and Politics" to post his thoughts about the tragedy. Maybe Newtown, his message suggested, wasn't what it appeared to be. Maybe the Newtown event that was covered in the press, he wrote, didn't really happen at all. He writes:

Inconsistencies and anomalies abound when one turns an analytical eye to news of the Newtown school massacre. The public's general acceptance of the event's validity and faith in its resolution suggest a deepened credulousness borne from a world where almost all news and information is electronically mediated and controlled. The condition is reinforced through the corporate media's unwillingness to push hard questions vis-à-vis Connecticut and federal authorities who together bottlenecked information while invoking prior restraint through threats of prosecutorial action against journalists and the broader citizenry seeking to interpret the event on social media.

It's what Tracy wrote later in the same post that got the most play in the press at the time. The bold text was in his original message:

What can be gleaned from this and similar coverage raises many more questions and glaring inconsistencies than answers. While it sounds like an outrageous claim, **one is left to inquire whether the Sandy Hook shooting ever took place—at least in the way law enforcement authorities and the nation's news media have described**.[9]

On May 11, 2013, Tracy's comments appeared again to attract press attention when he wrote on his blog about The Boston Bombings (see Chapter 1): "Exactly how many people were injured as a result of the April 15 Boston Marathon Bombing (BMB)?" He went on to suggest that his analysis of news and officials reports about the event, its victims, and visuals from that day "do not add up and suggest elements of a manufactured event." Tracy suggested in that post—as he did in posts about the Newtown shootings—that the events of The Boston Bombings were possibly government stunts designed to allow special forces to train for such attacks but also to indoctrinate the US public in believing they are under a constant threat of violence and that US authorities are able to protect them by diminishing individual rights, increasing mass surveillance, and through further militarization of local police forces.[10]

   Later that year, on September 16, following a mass shooting at the Washington Navy Yard in Washington, D.C., in which a man, Aaron Alexis, shot and killed a dozen people and injured at least three others, Tracy's comments on his blog that questioned the validity of evidence presented by government officials and upheld by the press were once again republished and questioned in mainstream news media. One article from the *Broward Palm Beach New Times*, a news outlet local to the geography of Florida Atlantic University, referred to Tracy in the following way:

Publicly funded FAU professor of communications James Tracy is little more than humanoid-shaped automaton programmed to peddle sophistry at times of national mourning and fitted with tousled brown hair.[11]

As of this writing, Tracy continues to operate his blog and has since Sandy Hook made other statements that have been considered by the press to be laughable, if not downright mean. His comments in each of these cases were unwelcome in the press despite a history in which the government and the press have colluded to lie to the US public to harness political, economic, and military support.

As far back as 1898, for instance, US press used the accidental explosion of the USS Maine—which was patrolling at Havana, Cuba, during a time of war between that nation and Spain to protect US interests during the conflict—and to sell papers and to support, to the glee of US government officials, a buildup of the nation's war machine. The phrase "Remember the Maine, to Hell with Spain!" became a common chant for war profiteering at the time. Certainly, media-government collaboration occurred well before the USS Maine, but it is one story of our nation's popular history that is rarely disputed in terms of the media messages that were constructed in ways to benefit (1) the media itself and (2) US warmongering.[12]

Tracy's comments that didn't receive an adequate amount of attention in the press but that did question the role of press-government collaboration in creating dominant meanings for news events included his thought that:

> dramatically shifting factual and circumstantial terrain has escaped serious critique because it is presented through major media's carefully constructed prism of select sound bites alongside a widespread and longstanding cultural impulse to accept the pronouncements of experts, be they bemused physicians, high ranking law enforcement officers, or political leaders demonstrating emotionally-grounded concern.[13]

Instead of highlighting Tracy's long analyses on media coverage in each of these instances in which he unpacked the power dynamics of how news messages see the light of day, Tracy was cast as a "Nutty Professor" in national mainstream press. Coupled with initial media errors made by mainstream press related to the details of Newtown's breaking news, which were identified and criticized by voices on social media, Tracy's controversial comments attacking the power dynamics between news media and other institutions of the power elite were cast as comments rooted in "conspiracy theory."

Dan Berkowitz and Zhengjia Michelle Liu have written that in order for media to maintain the legitimacy and authority of mainstream and legacy press at the time when the institution was being attacked by new media sources and a Communications professor, mainstream journalists protected their boundaries of legitimacy and authority by:

- Questioning Tracy's authority as a Communications professor by representing his questions about media coverage and the indoctrination of the public to unquestioned "official" explanations as not aligning with the standards of a legitimate Communications professor (This act, I argue, is a form of "media shaming," a type of punishment vis-à-vie "media control," which will be discussed in Chapter 5)

- Characterizing Tracy as a Communications professor who operated outside of the most elementary of journalistic communities, thereby maintaining the boundaries of "official" and "professional" journalism in which critiques of official explanations for the crisis would not be made

- Rejecting Tracy's theories "by normalizing his critiques of journalists' errors in initial reporting as 'honest mistakes'" that happen during breaking news events, once again attempting to distance journalists from any lines of questioning that might leak into the journalistic community through Tracy's role as a Communications professor[14]

News coverage of Tracy's questioning of the events of the Newtown shooting—as well as the other events upon which he commented in which he outlined the hegemonic role of the press in validating dominant, governmentally approved "facts" of tragedy based on merit alone—represents how mainstream press takes steps, even in times of breaking news, to maintain acceptable boundaries of what "is" and what "isn't" journalism with the sole purpose of maintaining control over public discourse in ways that reify the position of the press and fellow institutions.[15]

The core of media attacks against Tracy as being a conspiracy theorist were simply because of his critical nature and, quite honestly, his ability to root his critiques within histories of conspiracies between media and governments having been proven to exist—the least of which included the well-documented secrets and media warmongering surrounding the massive US invasions of Iraq and Afghanistan, which were based on lies that the nation of Iraq was harboring weapons of mass destruction related to the 9/11 attacks.

Combined with the power of conspiracy theory to marginalize alternative voices that challenge the status-quo of the press and of the power elite, the power of fear within the public to question what they "believe to be true" about what's covered in the press, of what members of our society's authoritative branches tell us are factual, and the fear that comes with maybe understanding the public policies related to race, hatred, and greed within the borders of our nation, conspiracy theory allows the press and its public to become distracted from asking the tough questions. Below, I further explicate what I mean in this project by "conspiracy theory" before advancing its role in press rhetoric—alongside the processes of confusion, controversy, and collective forgetting—that leads to the justification of press violence and press justification of police and military violence against threats to dominant ideology at local levels of society.

The power of "conspiracy": Protecting ideological investments

In this section, I examine the power of "conspiracy theory" as press employment of fear to argue, as Lance deHaven-Smith does in *Conspiracy Theory in America*, that the notion of conspiracy theory "has become a mechanism of social control, a label with normative implications backed by force," which:

> equates those who voice suspicions of crime in high places with the enemies of reason, civility, and democracy. Those who indulge in speculating about possible political conspiracies are subjected to ridicule, may lost their jobs, and risk being singled out by government agencies for surveillance and restricted mobility.[16]

To a large degree, there is a direct connection between notions of "thought control" and "social control" and of "conspiracy theorems"; yet, my project approaches the idea of "conspiracy theory" as a term that, as deHaven-Smith puts it, "disparages inquiry and questioning that challenge official accounts of troubling political events in which public officials themselves may have had a hand." Throughout this work, I expand upon these words by complicating his notion of "politics" to include not only normative social politics but also larger cultural politics, elements of conspiracy theory work that is frequently diminished, simply because the tales of the conspiracies themselves are so attractive—stories of the Illuminati, of alien cover-ups at Roswell, and that 9/11 was a government operation.[17]

Those are not the conspiracies of which I am interested, however. In fact, I'm really not interested in any one theory over another. Instead, I am interested in the ideological process of assigning a meaning of conspiracy theory. So, while in the discussion that follows I focus on specific cases in which conspiracy theory has been present, it is the role of cultural distraction inherent in the labeling of conspiracy theory that supports, in some cases, the celebratory stories of US heroes and, in most cases, the celebratory stories of US Exceptionalism. That is my interest.

Much of the scholarship related to "conspiracy theory" in the United States focuses on the 1963 assassination of President John F. Kennedy and just who was responsible for his death. Dominant memory that has been cast in the press and in popular media related to his murder include key terms such as "The Grassy Knoll" and the "The Single-Bullet Theory," while images of a Camelot life replaces discourse about his role in the US-led invasions of Cuba and South Vietnam, the implementation of neoliberal, Western views through the establishment of the Peace Corps, and his resistance to civil rights movements in the United States that have been whitewashed by the conspiracy, the controversy, the speculation, and the graphic manner of his death.[18]

Today, national and local press continue to paint a single picture of the man as being a pure American who was lost before his time. Coupled with the voyeuristic image of his skull being blown apart and the intrigue of his relationship with Marilyn Monroe, Kennedy continues to provide an annual moment of nationalistic remembrance; the conspiracy theories behind the murder and the attacks on those who question Kennedy's public policies remind the public to stay within dominant ideological lines. Even Kennedy's smallest connections to local communities throughout the United States serve as a means to localize, and personalize, the story of his dominant legacy and to embed these dominant memories into each of the nation's geographies.

The *Keene Sentinel* in Keene, New Hampshire, for instance, published their own telling of Kennedy's death—and life—in 2013 that, despite the assassination's 50th anniversary, is representative of an annual presentation that's presented each year in local papers across the United States:

> At a small county airport outside Pittsburgh, in fall 1962, Pamela A. Quirinale, her parents and baby brother had the chance to meet President John F. Kennedy.
>
> ...
>
> "I can remember the warmth and sincerity radiating from him. He shook my dad's hand, said hello to us, and then bent over and kissed my new baby brother on the head," Quirinale recalled.
>
> Meeting Kennedy in person reinforced the image of the man she'd seen and idolized on television so many times.[19]

The *Sentinel*'s article goes on to discuss the memories of Kennedy's life and death with several locals who remember November 22, 1963, with sadness related to how the day impacted them, particularly as "Americans." Here, the newspaper again quotes Quirinale:

When (her fourth-grade teacher) told us what had happened, every single student in the class put their heads down on their desks and cried. And then we prayed for him.

Quirinale, like thousands of others that day, said she was shocked that someone would kill America's president, and wanted to know why.

Quirinale's story is just a snapshot of how children throughout the U.S. were feeling that November day. Just like today's youth remember exactly where they were and what they were doing Sept. 11, 2001, so do the children of the 1950s when asked about the day Kennedy was killed.

Even though this story doesn't evaluate the "conspiracy theories" involved in explaining Kennedy's assassination (dozens of hours of cable TV shows and documentaries aired each November do, however), the story's connection between Kennedy's assassination and today's generations who may have experienced the events of 9/11 or the residual effects from that day provides an ideological bridge that deepens the event's meanings to even the youngest citizen. In other words, the grounding of a public in the legends of its history that provide ideological protection against questions and accusations threatening to the ideological peace and calm within which the power elite thrives is vital to maintaining a normalcy against which alternative explanations can be considered threats and, at the very least, abnormal.

In this way, then, "conspiracy theory"—and what Douglas Kellner refers to as "media spectacle"—serves as cultural distraction during which processes of media control reinforce of dominant memory. Social authorities—the "authorized knowers" discussed elsewhere in this book—enter the dealings of the day to shape future interpretations of past and current challenges to dominant ideas, a process discussed later in this chapter as "collective forgetting."[20]

Key to my interpretation of how media characterize alternative explanations in this project through conspiracy theory relies on how deHaven-Smith describes the pejorative connotation of the concept. In his argument, deHaven-Smith writes that *The New York Times* first used the term "conspiracy theory" in 1965 related to the many conflicting "official" reports associated with the potential international plots to kill Kennedy and the role of the Central Intelligence Agency's (CIA) involvement in planting the term in media reports of those who countered the government's explanation that Lee Harvey Oswald had acted alone.

The term "conspiracy theory" itself has since appeared in the *Times* with an immediate growth from barely a mention (under twenty *Times* articles that used the term) in 1965 to spikes throughout the early 1970s, a doubling of the number of articles around 1986 and to between 60 and 120 articles consistently between 1990 and 2011. Through such subtle embeddedness of terms and notions of "conspiracy theory" over the period of time, the power elite are shown to support "hidden associations and implications that reverberate in the national psyche" in terms of stories of national tragedies and in language such as "9/11" that bolster "American" values of virtue told by corporations, politicians, and the press.[21]

When power strikes: Marginalizing control

One of the main purposes of and for cultural distraction, of which conspiracy theory is a process, is to build a dominant narrative with which the press work to create overarching, indoctrinated meanings of the world. These narratives come in handy in even the most subtle moments when the elite's power mechanisms emerge and alternative explanations of the world need to be set aside by members of the power elite. In January 2015, for instance, US press responded in kind to attacks against US virtue during a hearing of the US Senate Armed Forces Committee in which protestors called for the arrest of ninety-one-year-old former Secretary of State Henry Kissinger who had appeared to testify about global security issues. The protestors accused Kissinger of war crimes because of his involvement in US-led violence in Vietnam, Laos, Chile, Indonesia, and Cambodia.

Committee chair and former presidential candidate John McCain denounced the protest in a calm and authoritative manner by saying: "You know, you're going to have to shut up or I'm going to have you arrested." US Capitol Hill police began to escort the protesters out of the room as McCain went on to tell them to "Get out of here, you low-life scum." He also addressed Kissinger by saying: "I've been a member of this committee for many years and I have never seen anything as disgraceful and as outrageous and as despicable as the last demonstration that just took place."

Press coverage of this event focused on the use of McCain's strong language, the scene caused by the protestors, and the role of police in ending the disturbance. Little to no context appeared in terms of the histories that the protesters had referred to. Kissinger's role in such violence was muted. And the power of the government to silence sent a message to the citizens to operate in a particular manner with their concerns and to recognize a naturalized exceptionalism of governing bodies. As *USA Today* wrote: "McCain received applause for his comments and apologized 'profusely' to Kissinger, whom he called 'a man who served his country with the greatest distinction.'"[22]

In effect, McCain's statements—and the press focus on these statements of paternalistic discipline and platitudes—build upon an ideological foundation in this nation that is set on distraction from discourse of controversy and conspiracy based upon the fear that comes from questioning and digging into our collective pasts for complications to the truths that we "know" today. In turn, the punitive and pejorative notions of controversy and "conspiracy theory" persist, resulting in "media control" of status quo messaging. For instance, the easy distancing of the protestors' arguments from "common knowledge" and interpretations of what clearly were war crimes conducted by US military and politicians throughout Southeast Asia—and other places of the world under Kissinger's (and McCain's) rule—come to a head in the following analysis of fear in the foundation of creating the need for distraction during cultural trauma.

Fear as a function of "media control"

Fear as control can best be understood by viewing society as operating amid conflict between the social body and the State—the governed and the governing powers inherent in dominant culture that influence law, authority, communication systems, police, educational structures, and religion. Michel Foucault writes that the "conflictual relationship that exists" within elements of the social body that "shapes the State is in fact one of war, of permanent warfare."[23] And, as I have argued already in this project, journalistic tension with fellow power institutions merely provides a scene of tension that affirms public interpretations that the press operate outside of symbiotic relationships with other institutions, clear of "permanent" and "perpetual" warfare within the social body and the State, and serves to maintain the function of institutions and its "power mechanisms" that provide a tangible process upon which the powerful can rely to distract from the mandates of the elite's wishes. The work and tension and conflict within society to build a civilized community becomes a tension that is the focus of news media, while power elite and press propagate outcomes that, on the surface, appear as having engaged the public.

In this respect, then, the State undergoes constant work to influence its power through economies, war, the maintenance of constant oppression, and the manipulation of alternative meanings through efforts such as controversy and conspiracy theory that drives the behaviors and choices of the citizens. True conflict, which would operate as cultural trauma for the State itself, appears only at moments when public fear is not immediately addressed, though even in those cases the time between the establishment of fear and the State's response serves to bolster the sense of abilities of the State to provide protection. Fear on the part of the State, then, is not that the system will be uprooted and turned against itself; it's about how much profit and authority is lost in the process of maintaining ideological crisis that will have to be rebuilt, often through media intervention.

Indeed, US history is bound in acts of fear that have been enacted through political and media control to marginalize social movements, including, for example, (1) the emergence of unions and worker rights legislation, (2) access to women's reproductive needs, and (3) the continued launching of political-military coups throughout Latin America that hold to veil secrecy and manipulation on the part of governments and corporations within which the true threats to US society are rooted. Yet, our collective "crisis mentality" distracts us from expanding our knowledge of private profits within our war machines of education, technological expansion, and societal repression and blocks us from openly considering the degree to which each of us hold responsibility in societal oppression. Instead, the nation embarks on a united effort to build the economy with which we can maintain a preparedness state for pending doom and in which citizens become mini-propagandists and supporters of whatever paternalistic solution the power structures suggest or implement.

The ideological act of fear that fuels even the most complicated and contested of answers in these cases and in news coverage of most everyday news are the same ideological process of fear that Barry Glassner writes about in his 1999 book *Culture of Fear*. In that work, Glassner presents readers with an innovative reading of the news that suggests "[w]e have so many fears, many of them off-base ... because the media bombard us with sensationalistic stories designed to increase ratings" and, as I will argue, promote "official" explanations and solutions that serve the power elite.[24]

Among Glassner's findings related to fear in news coverage of the 1980s and 1990s is the identification of a consistent narrative of everyday life that appear in the news today—we should fear almost everything. These narratives appeared in several specific notions, Glassner argues, which include that: (1) Everyone is in danger of road rage and that a "disparate new categories of creeps out to get us—home invasion robbers, carjackers, child nabbers, deranged postal workers" who all take to the roads in anger against each of us. Glassner, for example, cites a *20/20* reporter as cautioning audiences about "strangers in their cars, ready to snap, driven to violence by the wrong move" and argues that the press did little to place the frequency or likelihood of such outbursts in context but focused, as *USA Today* did, on road rage as being "a mental disorder";[25] (2) Our coworkers will kill us. Glassner writes that more than 500 news pieces about workplace violence were published in 1994 and 1995 with statistics that included that some 2.2 million people were attacked at work, that murder was the "leading cause of work-related death for women" and "the number-three cause for men." The *Wall Street Journal*, however, reported that only 1 in 457,000 professionals were likely to be killed at work, but that stat doesn't seem sexy enough to stick;[26] (3) Our plane will crash, whatever plane it is. Within two weeks of 110 people dying when a ValuJet plane crashed into the Florida Everglades in 1996 after leaving the Miami International Airport, *USA Today* ran seventy-one articles about the incident. *The New York Times, The Washington Post, Chicago Tribune*, and NBC and CBS nightly news programs ran about fifty pieces each. Glassner argues that plane crash stories are overrepresented in the news and sensationalized, while news about the ability of airline companies *to save lives* rarely appear.[27]

The overarching narrative that the world is full of something to fear and that people like journalists, government officials, police officers, and a united nation are there to save us from each of these instances, reduces the possibility for cultural trauma while maintaining a sense of conflict between what we consider reality in the naturalized power of the power elite and the alternative presentations of reality—the conspiracy theories—that offer nothing but confusion for a public that turns them, once again, to the power elite, which offers all of the answers. In this process—the ideological circle—a news media distract audiences through cultural work of covering news per the demands and interests of the media's own economic and cultural positions and the pressures applied from collaborating and unifying social institutions and actors.

The press have long held a tie to corporate interests that shape the news and keep citizens in constant fear and confusion of social change and US involvement in world and local crises. In turn, efforts like gay rights are seen as an "attack" on the nation's moral compass, the needs for "civil discourse" on college campuses restrict unpopular opinions of its professors who might be "anti-American," and economic potentials of war and police violence are diluted to normative, immediate, and surface meanings of the daily events, thereby assisting the press in avoiding cultural trauma when the press suffer from a lack of adequate, in-the-pocket explanations.[28]

Mark Stein writes that such methods contribute to a type of public hysteria—a "political panic"—that has led to several processes and outcomes, including:

- Public policies and individual actions of ethnic and racial cleansing

- The removal or infringement of human rights for the "benefit" of those surrendering their rights

- Internment and displacement of undesirables

- The instilment of acceptable behaviors upon individuals and communities that maintain the status-quo and demonize noncompliance[29]

In these situations, I argue, hysteria operates in two modes of media control. First, hysteria occurs through the indoctrination of fear among the public by political and media entities that mandate from the citizenry a public action to establish order and protection. Second, political and media entities act in advance of or in response to public cries for protection and order with propagandistic moral tales of paternalism's saving grace and the duty and ability of institutions to protect via specific endeavors, which almost always include physical force.

Directly below, I discuss the first action of media control to answer public hysteria in which the public demands answers and action to establish ideological order and a sense of physical protection. The second type of media control response appears in this chapter's third section, in which I discuss the acts of the power elite to use militarization not only to stave-off public cries for protection but to showcase the elite's ability to reduce future problems through violence.

Initiating ideological order by reducing panic

Two international cases from 2014 operate as examples of how media propaganda and explanations of confusion and of "conspiracy theory" relinquished the United States and its allies from any responsibility for international conflict between Russia and its neighbor, Ukraine. In July 2014, Malaysian Airlines Flight 17, a Boeing 777 carrying more than 280 passengers, crashed in Ukraine during a moment of war between that nation and Russia. All aboard died. The story, as tragic as it might have been, however, presented another opportunity for the international public—and the press—to turn to propagandistic storytelling about who was responsible, building a divide between allies of Russia and allies of Ukraine, and veiling any involvement in that conflict by the United States and other nations.

But to complicate matters, Malaysian Airlines had lost a similar Boeing 777 some 130 days earlier. Malaysian Airlines Flight 370 went missing, possibly somewhere over the Southern Indian Ocean, on March 8, 2014, leading to press coverage of possible explanations for that loss that included the possibility of the flight having been engaged by enemy aircraft, that a technical problem downed the plane, or that a UFO snatched the plane from the sky.

Reasons banking on the public's fascination with "conspiracy" rekindled public fears of airline terrorism and the rise of a global Cold War. Both explanations were prime targets for normative understandings of government propaganda and secrets, which, ironically, served as enough of an explanation for publics—both in the United States and abroad—shown to be in mass panic, crying, hugging, and shaking while waiting to hear what just could have happened over the ocean. Rationalizations for the loss of Flight 370 over the Southern Indian Ocean included the innate dangers of air flight in general and metaphysical possibilities of fiction coming to life: The disappeared was likened in the news to the experiences depicted on the popular TV show, *Lost*, that ran in the United States on ABC from 2004 to 2010, in which an airliner disappeared without a trace and the passengers found themselves in a kind of mystical island purgatory of sorts. Additionally, CNN's Don Lemon—who was included in *Columbia Journalism Review*'s roundup of "worst journalism of 2014"—reported that the crash might have been related to a black hole or something "supernatural:"

> Especially today, on a day when we deal with the supernatural. We go to church, the supernatural power of God ... people are saying to me, why aren't you talking about the possibility — and I'm just putting it out there — that something odd happened to this plane, something beyond our understanding?

Lemon also turned to author and TV personality Brad Meltzer, who writes about "secret societies" and other "conspiracy theories" in US society, who added:

> I'm not one of those believers that aliens came down or anything like that. But you do have to stop and wonder: how does a jet-liner with 200 people on it just disappear?[30]

The crash in Ukraine was different in that the plane hadn't disappeared; it had just disintegrated, spreading debris and bodies across open fields, yet the press covered the event as a political drama that made the story read, with its own conspiracy theories and controversies, as a work resembling that of the late Tom Clancy. An international dispute related to aims of economic and political prosperity embroiled Russia, Ukraine, the United States, and a host of other allies of each "side" of the conflict in speculation about what downed the aircraft. Potential causes, all sides seemed to agree, were closer to the mark than extraterrestrials and were rooted in a contested history of economic and political sanctions by Russia against Ukraine. In turn, this moment of conflict surrounded rhetoric of Ukrainian "independence" from Russia's Cold War hegemony, the rise of Ukrainians wishing for further political and economic distance from Russia, Russian-led forces within Ukraine designed to build disorder and lead to Russian takeover of the nation. The plane crash "just happened," in many of these scenarios.

Still, US media used confusion and controversy about the possible causes of both the conflict and the crash in Ukraine as a propagandistic tactic to marginalize any explanation of possible US and other international intervention into conflict between the two nations in that conflict.[31] At one point, for instance, it seemed US officials suggested "pro-Russian rebels" mistook the plane for a military weapon and shot it down, almost excusing the disaster as simply a mistake and placing the blame on a segment of the Russian military to widened political tensions between the United States and Russia at a time when the United States was attempting to demonize the nation for its commitment to non-US-style democracy.[32]

At the time, Edward Herman—who with Noam Chomsky formulated the Propaganda Model decades earlier (see Chapter 1)—identified the power dynamics embedded within US press coverage within which controversy veiled any evidence of veiled hegemony. His explanation is worth sharing in length:

> ... it is obvious that if there were any evidence demonstrating rebel or Russian guilt in this shoot down, there would have been no delay and obfuscation in publicizing such information. The silence, evasion, delays and agreement to give Kiev a veto power over any findings is telling evidence of Kiev and possibly US responsibility. This conclusion is also compatible with the matter of who benefits from this tragedy. The United States and Kiev have taken advantage of it to vilify the rebels, [Russian President Vladimir] Putin and Russia. Whether the shoot down was deliberate or an error, it has paid off well. The rebels and Russia had no potential benefit from the shoot down, and it has been costly to them. And the power of the Western propaganda system has guaranteed that they would be public relations losers.[33]

In this assessment, US news coverage of the crash represents a moment when debate and confusion obfuscated deeper conversations that could challenge the power elite. Press dedication to its fellow power institutions mandates that "official" statements and explanations as to the cause of the issue at hand are the only ones that may receive adequate and authoritative coverage. As of this writing, debate continued about the cause of both airliner crashes, but what did remain strong in early 2015 was a sense of fear related to the "unknowing" of what happened—and *what might have happened.*

Again, this chapter isn't focused on explaining what *actually happened* in any of the cases discussed throughout it; rather, I am interested in examining the media's obsession with "controversy" and "conspiracy" as a means to shape future memory related to ways that establish a community's collective memory. The process of distraction created by "controversy" and "conspiracy" is designed to increase ideological weaknesses of explanations for events and issues that are counter to press explanations. The press overtly align themselves with their fellow power elite actors in positions of social authority to shape messages for today that will last and influence future thought among news audiences. In so doing, the authoritative voices of government, police and military, and business in the moment of today's event must compete with the alternative explanations, even the "conspiracies" of the day, to show that through the fight, mainstream media can hold to the "truth," which has been indoctrinated.

MILITARIZATION AND MEDIA VIOLENCE: THE VIOLENCE OF MEDIA LANGUAGE

In this section, I discuss what I mean by fear that media control is assigned to counter, which, in its simplest terms surrounds threats to dominant explanations of the world that are rooted in racialized narratives. The fear I am describing, however, is not merely fear of a larger, theoretical nature—it is fear that exists within the dominant ideologies of the power elite that is expressed by the media in ways that present threats to society's dominant ideology as threats to people themselves. In turn, such cases as the police-involved murder in Ferguson, Missouri, which I discuss below, are examples of using violence of media language to approve of and execute threats that we fear.

Paying for fear and protection from it

We may fear the end of a personal or professional relationship that drives us to alter our behavior or to force or influence the behavior of someone else. Maybe this fear provides an opportunity for us to employ our own ideologies to express meanings that reinforce our positions to keep our jobs or to argue for a grade in an academic setting, because we believe these things will better our chances of achieving "The American Dream." But the fear I am speaking of holds at least two levels for individuals and collectives:

- The fear of the State's economic, social, and physical threats that then shape an individual's or a collective's mandates and morals

- The fear that the State uses in its rhetoric to alter behaviors and ideologies so as to avoid direct, overt conflict with the State's power functions

To be clear, by State I mean the apparatus of power and order that is recognized by a collective as its governing body, or, in other words, a portion of and extension of the power elite, and it is from this perspective that I apply Henry Giroux's description of fear-power relations in which I argue for fear to be viewed as a verb, as a power function.

For instance, Giroux writes that fear produces what he calls "totalitarian paranoia," a complex of constant fear of personal and collective demise at the hands of the enemy, "the other"—both the unknown and the known. Planted within a sense of US patriotism that's been guided by generations of historical remembrance and forgetting in which US-led international and domestic violence, manipulation, and colonization has been sanitized to position the nation as naturally just and exceptional, our fear has led to a what Giroux refers to as a "state of perpetual war"—one that includes payments that we make to our authorities for their paternalistic protection.

More specifically, this war operates around acts of securitization such as surveillance, the sousveillance of social networks, the racialized slaughter and incarceration of people of color in the United States, and the neoliberal indoctrination of our education systems that, if unveiled, reveals "a historical conjuncture in which the legacy of totalitarianism is once again reasserting itself in new forms"[34] that are based on the nation's roots of similar acts but which are presented throughout and by the public as traditional and right acts of this nation.[35]

But back to the two types of fear I mentioned above, I do not mean to suggest such forms and acts of fear operate individually. I argue that they work together, the second in collaboration with the first, through which the acts of fear move through a constant transformation of *normalization*, the application of dominant "common sense" principles to incorporate alternative or controversial explanations of social conditions into the mainstream. In other words, whereas, public rhetoric—such as this book—might operate as threats to public/private- or state-issued paternalism and protectionism, the risks associated with this threat is the mass questioning of the validity surrounding notions of "individual rights" that are held under guise of a pre-approved collective good and the indoctrination of paternalism, which often appears in the rhetoric of approved police and security forces, surveillance forces, legal forces, and rationalizations that depict other forms of social life.

This threat, then, is at the core of our rhetorical building blocks to distance US/Western/capitalistic thought from "non-democratic" or "developing" nations. This very system that the power elite wishes to protect, however, has become weakened by increased attacks against society's core ideological positions because of overt normalization of a public/private state, one that is a partnership between public representations of the state—partnerships such as between a local police force or legislative body and the private sector that not only share in the business of police protection through private security forces and military militias also then share in the rhetoric of providing protection through capitalism and White Supremacy.

Private industry continues to provide the citizenry with the protection from everyday threats that are clearly articulated in its advertising and in the naturalization of capitalism as a dominant and "correct" form of commerce. Indeed, corporations tell us that they provide protection against germs with products that "fight bacteria" and "kill 99 percent" of all sorts of things, including weeds, cavities, and influenza. Businesses' cost-saving "sales" "save" the public from no-good capitalists at the neighboring—or the very same—big box store that charges too much for a pair of jeans, jugs of orange juice, or boxes of diapers, "saving us" money while "saving us" from harm of higher prices.

Little do we know, however, just how much we might really be saving without complicated math to determine the reality of price differences (does "buy two get one free" result in real savings?), nor are we aware of the corporation's profit-margins or added costs that are pushed to the consumer and not softened by even the slightest cut to profits. All the while, these promises of protection from the private sector as much as from the public—and almost always the private-public partnerships—is based upon a latent fear of harm, that someone or something is always out to get us and that we, as individuals, must band together with—and pay for—an initiative outside of ourselves for protection, which often involves consumption.[36]

The press function as part of this system, dictating the threats, presenting the likely costs needed to avoid danger, and providing answers for everyday questions and concerns of how we don't "measure-up" within mainstream discourse that's spewed by corporate executives, journalists, government officials, and school teachers. Yet, a national educational system that focuses more on indoctrination of US, local, nationalistic, and consumerist interests, for instance, rather than critical thinking and global perspectives of governance and economic practices, leads to what both the press and politicians have erroneously referred to as apathy or fear of engagement. Voting turnouts, for instance, are assessed in the press with a focus on which age groups participated as a means to determine how well-versed our younger generations are in the affairs of society.

The intellect and sense of community and family values among blacks and racial and ethnic minority groups are measured in the press by their levels of participation in antiquated political efforts that were designed from the outset to be more about governance than citizen participation. And these messages send to the public a call to be concerned that we should participate in "civic" acts, such as voting, or risk being ostracized and categorized as "part of the problem." By no means do elites—nor its press—present the act of not voting as a sign of resistance; the "welfare mother" who doesn't go to the polls is depicted as being too busy or too ignorant to stand in line to vote—sometimes, as evidenced in the 2012 presidential election, for five or six hours—rather than being presented as having the agency to make the choice not to use her time that way. Instead, she may choose to use alternative practices to engage with her community and to avoid voting lines as a political statement related to a corrupt system.

Just as much as casting a vote is a "right," so is the choice not to; indeed, she could very well make the choice to vote, despite the challenge to her schedule and pocketbook, but, like me, opts for other outlets to express herself. Yet within both options—to vote or not to vote—is a form of power in recognizing the fear of marginalization and shame that comes from noncompliance, and only one of the two choices is acknowledged and promoted within the press.[37]

As with press explanations of voting that are meant to pacify through public action, the press provide explanations that marginalize real abilities of the public to create change, which may involve taking-up weapons and rebelling, but that appear in the press as radical and dangerous. Ironically, by pacifying audience through encouragement of public inaction, The Powers That Be are allowed to continue making decisions on our behalf to maintain a norm that feels to us to be so precious and so safe in our daily interactions—often through creating explanations of threats and preventions to those threats that focus on violence. The hegemonic element of this process is in the degree to which news coverage provides opportunities to bark authoritative voices that will, once again, claim the power elite's position of power and to marginalize the alternative voices—at the center of which is the press and its ability to force order.

Slavoj Žižek writes that language operates as a force of control and order. "[L]anguage," he writes, " ... is the first and greatest divider, it is because of our language that we and our neighbors (can) 'live in different worlds' even when we live on the same street." He continues: "What this means is that verbal violence is not a secondary distortion, but the ultimate resort of every specifically human violence."[38] Žižek turns to the word "Jew" to address the power of language and of the assigned ideographs that examine the violence of language that exists within the schema of audiences of speakers and listeners. "What the perpetrators of the pogroms find intolerable and rage-provoking, what they react to," Žižek writes, "is not the immediate reality of Jews, but the image/figure of the 'Jew' which circulates and has been constructed in their tradition." The "catch," he writes, is that individuals, no matter the situation or person, cannot distinguish between a person of faith or the "anti-Semitic image."[39]

As first mentioned in Chapter 3 of this book, images or ideographs—"recognizable, rhetorical symbol(s) of cultural values and ideology"—are embedded by dominant cultural processes so well so that we turn to those within our basket of explanations without even realizing that we do it.[40] Throughout the rest of this chapter, then, I build an argument for understanding the ideological role of "media memory," which relies upon expectations that audiences will turn to the same ideographs to understand and to explain the language and texts of news, as a process of intentional forgetting that serves as a force for control.

To do so, I explicate the function of dominant ideographs and narratives assigned to US urban areas and their residents as a means to justify and normalize the use of physical force, such as what occurred following a police-involved shooting in Ferguson, Missouri, in 2014. My argument is based on a premise that media control operates through "controversy," "confusion," and "conspiracy theory," as I have described them, to initiate and apply violence. More specifically, a main tool for acts of media violence and media legitimization of violence from other sectors of the power elite is related to memory (and forgetting) of geography. Below, I discuss in more detail the degree to which place returns in this book as an ideological device for issuing and maintaining media control, in this case the use of imaginations of the city to create battlefields for the protection of the rest of us.[41]

Warfare of urban memory: Economic genocide and reclaiming "ghetto ways"

Capitalistic destruction of urban environments across the United States—a long-term process that begins at the initial stages of any development—banks on the potential for private profits of capitalism but also reveals its ill effects in manifestations of cultural conflict surrounding labor, greed, education, health, and crime. Yet, in the past decade, these conflicts and resulting physical destruction of urban development has been assigned artistic qualities. As mentioned in the previous chapter, "ruin porn" has led to volumes of photographs and hours of documentaries related to the decline of places such as Detroit, Michigan, the beauty within the destruction of urban housing projects and cores of Chicago, Illinois, and Pittsburgh, Pennsylvania. And while I'm not interested in placing artistic value on the genre of "ruin porn," I am interested in identifying such texts as moments for simulacrum of capitalistic win-lose that has come to dominate so much of the public's understanding of urban "decline" that is then captured for its art.[42]

In fact, I've even written some of this book on tables in a Starbucks that are stamped "RECLAIMED URBAN WOOD," an artistic and "green" trend that has taken the country's hipster nation by storm. *The Michigan Daily*, a student newspaper at the University of Michigan in Ann Arbor, for instance, wrote in a story about a renovated Starbucks there in 2012, that:

> [t]he store received a variety of improvements including new furniture and large chalkboards for community use. The renovation also incorporated a number of environmentally friendly features like tables made from reclaimed urban wood.[43]

In the case of some Starbucks locations, their wood is provided, in part at least, by Black's Farmwood in California and, according to that company's website, much of this reclaimed wood comes from dead or dying trees in urban areas that may also be mixed in with items from not so urban areas—barns being a longtime mainstay of what has been a normal process of building and rebuilding in US rural areas for generations. For me, the ideological process in play here revolves around the term "urban"—one that is often replaced by and used in place of "black."

And while "urban" tends to lack the same distain for black folk as does the term "ghetto," urban manages to move between a sense of coolness (i.e., the Urban Outfitters brand) and danger of "the inner-city" (see Chapter 3). Times when "urban" is an acceptable and "cool" phrase, such as in the case of the tables I have frequented far too much over the past year while writing this project, the receiver of this message is able to walk a line between gritty, hip, and even fresh. More than anything, this investment in the power to take from urbaneness that which we value and leave what we do not, all within the process of creating leisure and entertainment, represents the everydayness of our imaginaries of urban life and the power to subjugate what we imagine is there.

What makes ideographs hegemonic is that they provide the user the ability to ignore alternative, unpopular, or uncomfortable explanations for the same term. Users of "reclaimed urban wood," for instance, are expected to gain a sense of self-worth, to feel as though they have somehow contributed to the reclamation of the wood by contributing to customer demand for "green alternatives" in the marketplace. Additionally, though, the user is presented with the duality of this ideograph in which "urban" represents the grittiness and hipness of recycling and "renewal," not just from destruction and waste but also from an acknowledged, dangerous, and dark urban environment. Such a duality is clear in the demand of consumers for the remnants of disassembled urban cores, of which Detroit has become the most popular archetype.

Since around 2010, the City of Detroit has razed abandoned homes and other buildings—sometimes as many as 1,000 houses per month—in a city thats population has dropped from a peak of 1.8 million in the 1950s to around 700,000 in 2013. The massive demolition project—and preceding economic genocide—has left entire neighborhoods empty and has encouraged continued processes of racialized defunding of public services. In 2014, the city announced it would sell "valuable building materials—floors, fixtures and moldings" from buildings—including homes—that have been abandoned so that the items could be "reclaimed" and placed again on the market.[44]

The *Detroit Free Press* reported in December 2014 that Reclaim Detroit, a nonprofit, "is gaining national attention as a leader in the burgeoning deconstruction movement, where trained workers remove valuable material in homes set for demolition, and then resell it, creating jobs and sparing landfills millions of tons of debris." According to the *Free Press*, the group is attempting to gain from 80,000-some abandoned homes products that can be sold and remade into building supplies, tables, and even "one-of-a-kind guitars," the paper writes, quoting one man who used wood "from a home on Carpenter Street in Hamtramck"—a city outside of Detroit—as saying: "To throw material like this away, it's almost like a crime against culture. People love that there is a story behind this wood."[45]

But what exactly are the stories behind these items, this art, this altered urban landscape? If left to the press, the stories of abandonment will be of people who have chosen to leave, thereby "abandoning" their homes and neighborhoods. What is left to be "reclaimed" is removed from any sense of previous ownership that has been devalued, reappropriated, and commoditized. Given the historic racial makeup of these urban areas and the racialized process of a forced migration through gentrification and the violence of language related to capitalistic explanations for "redevelopment," narratives that run counter to those of the power elite and that will be ignored and "forgotten" by the press is of a long-standing process of reappropriation of black history and culture for white profit.

Such appropriation of black culture has revealed itself, most recently, in silly "flash mob" renditions of the Harlem Shake in the early 2010s—an Ethiopian style of dance that was Americanized by black dancers in Harlem in the 1980s and which appeared in black hip-hop music for two decades before wealthy and light-skinned college students, public officials, school teachers, and social mediates took control of the dance in an online flurry with no overt recognition of its African and black backgrounds that have been shaped by dominant memories of African tribes, urban ghettos, and a future that could only be tarnished by releasing the beasts.

A similar cooption of black culture for white profit, which also fueled an online and media hysteria in the last decade includes the releasing of white twerking, a dance move that had long lived in black hip-hop music but was reduced to a mainstream, white artifact by white pop star Miley Cyrus in 2013. Both of these instances received as much straight-laced coverage from news outlets at national and local levels in the United States as they received from entertainment press; the dances were presented in mainstream media as "cultural phenomena" but only of the day's dominant white culture.[46] Before these cultural texts were mainstreamed to white audiences, if they appeared to white audiences, they were considered representative of "ghetto blackness" in which the quick movements of the dance represented a savageness of US blacks and their African roots.

Once "civilized" by technophiles (in the case of the Harlem Shake) and white pop music fans with disposable incomes who were looking for their own personal sense of "edginess," these movements and this music, at appropriate times and in appropriate places, became acceptable—even desirable. In the process, any "blackness" inherent in these dance moves was diminished to a novelty, the profits of which were directed not to the people and places who created the artifacts but to the white producers who had successfully sterilized any dominant connections to black culture. In the case of other forms of reclamation, such as profiteering in an "abandoned" Detroit, the value of homes and buildings that once housed local businesses, public services, playgrounds, and hospitals, was stripped from the people who lived there long ago in a time-intensive process of reevaluation that benefits the marketplace outside of Detroit.

Indeed, one can only wonder about the strangeness of eating on a door that was from an empty house in Detroit, sitting on furniture that once was a roof or the walls of a house from which black folk have been expelled, observing with awe ransacked and burnt public school classrooms where black education was purposefully dismantled by white capitalism. In mainstream media, these artifacts appear in glowing stories about art exhibitions and renovated suburban coffee shops when in another reality, we have taking boards from a slave ship and made them into a building's exposed rafters.

At the core of the dominant press are explanations for this process of destruction/revitalization that veils not only the positive attributes of our cities, their neighborhoods, and the wealth of intellectual innovation, and love that took hold in neighborhoods and emerged to benefit larger society. So, too, are stories of intentional violence by governments and police at the core of press tellings that oppress and segregate and that become hidden and "forgotten" in current—and future—tellings of changing landscapes. Violence of language and physical manifestations of force—or in threats of force—continue to dominate popular notions of urban landscapes within news audiences. Jacquelin Burgess, writing from the UK, argues that the ideograph of "The Inner City" paints urban environments as "alien place(s), separate and isolated, located outside the white, middle-class values and environments," as was committed by British press in coverage of riots there in the 1980s.[47]

As I have elsewhere examined, such a notion of "The Inner City" in press coverage of locations throughout the United States, has become even clearer to me as a dominant means of explaining urban environments. In Miami, where I live now, for instance, I am much more likely to see news coverage of police activity busting crack dealers in the black neighborhood of Overtown than of drug-busts in the wealthy high-rises (and light-skinned neighborhoods) near the ocean on Collins Avenue. It is not just that the police patrol one place more than another—which is not unique to the cities' policing culture—but that the press present news of the everyday, including crime news, in particular ways based on geography. Building upon work on "The Inner City" by Burgess, I argue that the press cover these urban imaginaries in three ways:

- By describing the environments in which the violence occurs as morally rotten, as humanized spaces of intentional waste, absent of influence from outside its geographic borders

- By describing people in these spaces based on race and class positions, as the opposite in lifestyle and human desire from the financially wealthy outside of its geographic borders, and as the best representation of the lowest of human qualities

- By applying language that characterizes the geography's dominant cultures as being those rooted in violence and with little regard to "civilized" living

As I write in *A Transplanted Chicago*, where I examine press language related to urban environments in more detail, I recognize how notions of "The Inner City" cast undesirable, city spaces as being "rough, poor, crime-invested area(s)" that suffer from neighborhood "pathologies" based on constructs of "black culture." Furthermore, I argue that these "labels of racialized hatred [that] were placed on those from the 'inner city' from the outside—private business, governmental policies, and public disgust for city life" represent the intricacies and connections of and between the power elite and the press.[48]

It is here where I wish to indicate that these ideological processes of cooption based on mythical representations of place (and people) throughout media function to veil "black culture" and history as a white product that can safely be sold and appropriated without the stigma and potential dangers of "blackness." Our capitalistic system is able to separate what it seems most valuable from these neighborhoods—the culture to be coopted—from traits that may also hold value to larger society and to those who have lived in and have experiences with wide ranges of social support systems, relationships, art that, if identified for their value, would alter the ownership of the culture being commoditized. Instead, stories of urban violence and of negative value in these geographies and of the related artifacts maintain their monetary value in that they can be incorporated into products and ideologies of vice and sin and into the militarized protectionism of private-public police industries, though such value is further mired in a rhetoric of mythical normalization in terms of what's long been deemed especially dangerous in society.

From both of these cooptions of "ghetto blackness," media is able to shape a collective "urban memory" of fear that may operate amid cultural distractions of controversy related to issues of urban education, employment, crime, and policing. Furthermore, because these fears associated with dominant urban memories are so rooted in US society and in common perceptions of urban life, those who present counter-narratives such as appear in this chapter may, among the public, be aligned with the "deranged and pernicious" conspiracy theorists but quickly escape interrogation, because the facts of the inner city are so greatly established throughout our nation's history of remembering— and forgetting—that maintains stories of its exceptionalism. In fact, the traits of US Exceptionalism—of peace-keeping and democratization—appear at the core of our society's commitment to the financial solvency of "global market" demands upon which our nation's military, technological, and strategic communication efforts are based. We use the fear of the local "other" as we would if these "others" were in geographically distant parts of the world and from the respective news audiences within which we participate.[49]

Operating a "virtuous war": Killing black kids

Efforts employed by the power elite internal to the United States—as well as externally—to maintain the polemics associated with "appropriate" and "approved" violence and "disorder" operate through media control in ways that solidify a grasp on perceived disorder that would ultimately damage US hegemony. Often, this includes moments of physical violence against undesirable people and communities that would not be publically acceptable if issued against dominant cultural and social groups. James der Derian describes such violence as a "virtuous war" at the center of which "is the technical capability and ethical imperative to threaten and, if necessary, actualize violence from a distance—*with no or minimal casualties.*" More specifically, der Derian is writing about acts of approved violence abroad, over long distances, and that is veiled in coded language about the "war's" purpose of protection against a demonized "other." I adopt his definition here with the understanding that the distance still exists, both physically and ideologically, between news audiences and those whom suffer the violence of language and physical force—even within the same geographic region.[50]

I adopt der Derian's expansions on his definition of "virtuous war" in that it relies upon "networked information and virtual technologies to bring 'there' here in near-real time and with near-verisimilitude" in ways that exercise "a comparative as well as strategic advantage for the digitally advantaged." Casualties in this case are those within our society—even within our own local communities—who have been identified as undesirables, frequently those who (1) are experiencing homelessness, (2) are racial, ethnic, religious, and economic minorities, (3) speak or act against dominant social actors and ideologies. I make the connection to the local level because the notions of a "virtuous war" should not be limited in perspective only to actions abroad.

The literal "hands-off" approach to warfare *within the United States* through the empowerment of technologies within police forces and within media processes and practices (i.e., the use of drones) will never surpass the benefit of approaches where the powerful keep their hands clean while others do the work for them. Put another way, as a child I watched "there" become "here" through some sort of imaginary that recorded for me the physical and psychological connection of war and US imperialism and violence as video recorded bombs striking the Middle East that were played—and replayed—over the nightly news for decades (see Introduction). And ever since, I've watched—and in some cases helped report—connections between one domestic US landscape to another, a common approach to news place-making that appears to help make the news culturally salient to the widest audience.

Domestically, the virtuous war operates amid local crime, local attacks against the same sense of nation and against local ideology and interests of the power elite, of which the press are set to be propagandistic and violent in protecting through dominant community identities and meanings. Put simply, press reporting on urban environments through "urban memory" as I have identified it, allows news audiences to "enter" warzones of the urban landscape from their living rooms or mobile phones, far away from the direct "dangers" and with the security of social capital with which they sense protection from any urban uprising that may leak into their own spaces. To explicate my meanings, I apply such an approach to the analysis below related to press coverage of 2014 violence in Ferguson, Missouri, from which I argue for a radicalization of "collective memory" by recognizing the ideological and violent actions inherent in media remembrance, which identifies memory itself as an act of violence.[51]

"Ferguson": A briefing

The US public saw media control's violent abilities throughout much of 2014 following the August 9 murder of Michael Brown, an eighteen-year-old black man, by a white police officer in Ferguson, Missouri—a St. Louis suburb. Autopsy reports indicate that Brown had been shot six times, the fatal shot being to his head. Some in Ferguson—many black—questioned the degree to which the shooting was justified, as witness reports contradicted official reports of aggressive behavior on Brown's part that, as the officer said, led to him fearing for his life. Even members of the grand jury that would on November 24, 2014 decide not to indict the police officer for the shooting, it would later be revealed, questioned the degree to which the shooting was "good."[52]

Those who countered official reports that Brown threatened the officer argue that the patterns of bullet holes on Brown's arms indicate he had raised them up in a sign of submission, leading to the mantra "Hands up, don't shoot" used by protestors across the country. St. Louis Post-Dispatch coverage following the shooting and then again after the grand jury's decision built upon "urban memory," providing moments for the media to construct narratives of massive protests against police militarization and brutality in Ferguson in ways that benefited a violent collective forgetting of alternatives explanations for the shooting. Even national coverage in these moments propagated perceptions of race and racial tension in ways that cast black men as hyper-aggressive and dangerous and the protests of racialized policing practices as disobedience.

(De)Valuing black lives

Following initial reports of the August 9 shooting, local press highlighted how the effects of the shooting and controversy surrounding the shooting might influence the local economy. Black lives were assigned an economic value with which audiences were able to measure against power elite responses to threats to local ideologies related to curbing public discontent. One August 11 business story in the *Post-Dispatch*, for instance, highlighted how the region surrounding Ferguson had recently experienced an "economic hope" that was now in danger of complete destruction, given the negative attention by national press provided by the Brown shooting and racialized discourse associated with it.

Ferguson itself was described in the story as "a picture of pleasant suburbia, with trees lining streets in front of tract houses built during the 1950s and 1960s" but that had suffered recent threats associated with a diversifying population; North County, where Ferguson is located, the *Post-Dispatch* reported, had undergone "a racial transition, from 52 percent black in 2000 to 66 percent in 2012."[53]

Yet, articles like this one that pinpointed the newspaper's concern over potential economic impacts represents the degree to which the press has been incorporated with the power elite and serves a propagandistic function, in this case by focusing on the degree to which property values and the potential for investment would be negatively impacted by "TV images of buildings burning could have a psychological impact, damaging business and the housing market in Ferguson and surrounding towns." Even though the press required a single explanation for the police shooting and its possible threats to the power elite, even more so the press needed time to provide possible characterizations related to upset black folk in Ferguson and a militarized police response which resulted in the launch of some 150 police officers in riot gear shooting rubber bullets and manhandling protestors by August 11, riling crowds. At its core, the first characterizations of the disorder (by police and the public) were directly connected to the possible effects of "looting" and "vandalism" of a dozen businesses and property damage upon the power and persistence of capitalism.[54]

Confusing the problem

By August 14—after five days of what the *Post-Dispatch* referred to as "rioting," including hundreds of people carrying signs surrounded by some seventy police officers in SWAT gear—the press portrayed police officials as being hopeful that the contested information about what led to the shooting—

Brown's alleged behavior. However, by this point, normalized racial tensions in and around Ferguson that had led, to some degree, to corresponding concerns that police had been acting with hyper-aggression, approaching and stopping, arresting and battering, black protestors as though these residents were undeserving of determining appropriate social norms in their own community.

The Post-Dispatch helped solidify the authority and virtue of local police by marginalizing black residents' complaints of institutionalized racism, leading to profiling, militarization, and brutality. Quoting the Ferguson police chief, who is white, the newspaper reported that "mending the strained relationship between his department and the African-American community is imperative for the city and region to move ahead." He continued:

> We have always had real good relations with all of the neighborhoods associations. Apparently, there's been this undertow that now has bubbled to the surface, and it's our first priority to address it, to fix what's wrong.[55]

By presenting the concerns of protesters as operating outside of the realizations and interpretations of police officials and, assumedly, other public officials who could have informed the police chief about *just what was wrong* in Ferguson, the press painted a picture of altruistic public officials open to understanding citizens' complaints. Confusion then became part of the distraction created by the press. To do so, journalists needed to place blame—not for the police violence against Brown or for the police violence against protestors—but of the "disorder" of US citizens rising up against the power system.

Hiding blame by rationalizing eradication

A day later (August 15), the *Post-Dispatch* posted on its cover statements from officials, including President Barack Obama, who stated that there is "no excuse for police to use excessive force against peaceful protests," along with other "official" criticisms of militarization and alleged suppression of free speech, including that of journalists (Figure 4.1). The rhetoric was nonsense, though, and served only as a moment to validate that the police were operating outside of the norms, when they really weren't: They were following orders not only of their superiors but of the public-at-large, a public in the United States that demands the suppression of black culture, the oppression of black freedoms, and brutality against people of color.

Motivated by memories of the urban environment, which dictates that black outrage occurs only in the grit and vile of the city, not in the safety and

FIGURE 4.1 The St. Louis Post Dispatch, *August 18, 2014. Courtesy of* The St. Louis Post Dispatch *and newseum.org. Used with permission.*

niceness of the suburbs, one story in that day's paper, for instance, hinted at an escalation of violence against police forces and traditional "American culture" in that the reporter wrote that while US residents have seen protests and police retaliation before, they have never seen such violence "on wide open suburban streets. After all, this is Ferguson, pop. 21,135." The reporter continues by stating that:

> (t)he images are striking, and all the more frightening, because of the backdrop. Ground zero for the chaos is a torched QuikTrip, a convenience store built on the edge of the four-lane road across from a carwash.[56]

The story also quotes one city council member as saying: "In the other riots, you think of the high-rise public housing and the city backdrop, but this has a different feel because you are not dealing with a major city." Media violence through language soon appeared in press storytelling and performed two ideological functions that supported a narrative of a police/citizen and approved behavior/deviance dynamic that would be told for a period of two or three months in Ferguson coverage—and that had been told over the course of generations in press coverage of urban spaces and police action.

First, journalists' words from the example above, such as "frightening," "riots," and "high-rise public housing," tapped into a single definition of urban spaces, including that those who live in public housing do so because of a sense of desired poverty. In fact, the police—who were not presented in the press as a group, or as residents of these neighborhoods in which the violence took place—were not cast as causing fright or riots (Is it even possible for police to riot?) despite their acts of violence to someone else's person and property. Nor was their public involvement in the violence ever presented as being acts of public servants or in any other ways that would reveal a public-involvement or endorsement of their violence. In turn, the police were shown to be fighting the "other" *in someone else's home* and to be doing so not to save the homes of their own community but to keep at bay those who might leak out into the spaces *of other peoples' homes.* The violence associated with this marked the enemy at the time and the hero and justified the needs of and for physical violence.

Second, press language served a violent purpose by connecting the day's battles in the burbs on the part of the protestors with immense violence and remembrance associated with, among other previous elements of domestic and international terrorism, terms such as "Ground zero" that reflects an environment of force and violence associated with murder of US innocents. The term, frequently used as a proper noun in relationship to the World Trade Center during and after the 9/11 attacks, also has a history in discourse related to effects of nuclear war in that what occurs at Ground Zero during a nuclear blast dilutes the focus of the event from the act of the blast itself to that which transforms a place being of things to being of nothingness. "Ground zero," writes Peter Schwenger, "is itself a somewhat oxymoronic term." He continues:

> Ground melts away at the point of an explosion, and the figurative ground of our conceptual systems disappears as well, swallowed by the yawning zero. It is that zero which, more than anything else, serves as a sign for what is, or is not, at the blast's center.

The "the shape of this symbol is significant, for it is, of course, a circle around emptiness," which if such meaning is applied to its use in case of Ferguson disorder, casts the space as absent of humanity and, therefore, ripe for further eradication.[57]

Echoing a media chamber

Following another night of protests, national media attention created a national concern about the militarized force of local police officials. By August 17, Missouri's governor had placed local policing in Ferguson under the control of the Missouri State Highway Patrol, and protestors on that day faced tactical units and the continuance of a nightly curfew. At this point, news coverage focused on the images of the police, the return to some calm based on the forced curfew, and public/political debates about the degree to which the police, both before the shooting and then in the times of protest following the shooting, were sound and justified. Media echoes related to concerns locally—and now nationally—about the degree to which local police forces were able to curb black crime and threats from black communities across the nation and fueled national discourse about brewing hostilities in black spaces.

   This echo prevented the press from hearing and/or articulating the voices of protestors that presented a counter-narrative. One *Post-Dispatch* story from August 17, for instance, headlined "I have never seen anything like this before" coopted the words of a Ferguson protestor to tap into the echo chamber in which the quote was more easily read as referring to never having seen street violence, the riots, and in the experiences of one resident quoted in the piece who reported seeing "'things' hitting the ground around her and then exploding, before releasing the gas."

   Yet, the words that appeared in the headline came from yet another source—one who was commenting on the solidarity of Ferguson folk as part of a group of demonstrators, "the Brown justice chasers," who had come from Nashville, Tennessee, to join the fight. Her full comments appeared in the story's last sentence, a mile away from the headline: "I have never seen anything like this before, a whole neighborhood coming together today." Had the woman's commentary about a neighborhood "coming together" to protest unequal treatment by brutal police forces appeared, the reader would be left to wonder just what "the story" was and whose story should be believed.[58]

Readers were up against a strong presentation of authority in the explanations for those days of violence in which the press benefited from the authority of the sites and sounds of policing that reinforced press discourse about what groups were violent and what groups were protecting the public. The August 19 *Post-Dispatch* cover (Figure 4.2), for example, is representative of the aggressive nature of policing during these days of unrest that provides a visual of force—and of the news coverage of force both locally and nationally—that created an echo chamber of politicians, police, and the press who shared in storytelling of virtuous acts of violent policing as a means by which to create calm. In other words, the show of police force was also a show of press force. In fact, the August 19 front page headline "**STREETS FLARE UP**" and its subheads told a consistent story that placed protestors against their own community:[59]

- "TEAR GAS FLIES, PASTORS LOCK ARMS TO BREAK UP CROWDS"

- "NIXON LIFTS CURFEW IN FERGUSON, CALLS IN NATIONAL GUARD"

- "PRIVATE AUTOPSY FINDS 6 SHOTS"

The design of that issue's front page also contributed to the authority of press commentary. By placing the newspaper's flag above the massive bold text that showed the streets swamped in flames and related subheadlines that included names as sources and quantifiable evidence of disorder, the newspaper was placing itself as an "authorized knower" of sorts—so much so that to make the design work, the newspaper removed its tagline: "THE NO. 1 ST. LOUIS WEBSITE AND NEWSPAPER" (see Figure 4.1), to distance any association with capitalism and media systems that then reified the social and cultural legitimacy—and objectivity—of the press. Power associated with the page one image of a police officer firing gas into the street protests, fire raging from the barrel, bookended the text that came above it in ways that the press shared in the physical force of fellow power institutions. In summary, the cover served the press narrative of legitimizing police brutality against black folk by showing the degree of force that was "necessary" to

FIGURE 4.2 The St. Louis Post-Dispatch, *August 19, 2014. Courtesy of* The St. Louis Post Dispatch *and newseum.org. Used with permission.*

subdue alternative explanations and acts of protectionism of a community *against* the power elite.

At least one other police shooting in and near the St. Louis area around this time contributed to more tension between protesters and police, placing the press in a position to extend their common explanations that diminished those of angry citizens with the calm and collected excuses from officials. On August 19, 2014—right in the middle of protests related to the Brown killing—another black man in his twenties was shot and killed by a police officer, this time after the man allegedly stole energy drinks from a gas station and, carrying a knife, came within three or four feet of officers. In the end, however, this echo chamber of voices calling for calm via police action ignores a history of police abuse in this nation, of racial profiling, of the use of excessive force, and of unequal treatment of citizens by the press in favor of protecting the power elite's militant arms.[60]

Endorsing angry media violence

The act of using the press to provide calm despite acts of the same police forces that instigating violence *in order to* incite even more violence reveals an ideological connection between police and the press that supports a dedication to entertaining the public and to providing protection-promising of paternalism by public officials. Fast forward three months to when the press began waiting for the grand jury's decision about whether to indict the police officer involved in the Brown shooting. Roughly two weeks before the jury's announcement was expected, on November 11 Missouri's governor released the National Guard onto Ferguson streets in preparation for—and expectation of—street violence. The press spent these two weeks not only speculating about the grand jury's potential decision but also stoking fires with their "media waiting" (see Chapter 5), all in order to present a narrative not surprising to anyone when the jury did announce their decision not to indict: The citizen-led violence was "much worse" than in the past and even worse than expected, even though street protests lasted but a few days.[61]

On November 26, for instance, two days after the grand jury announcement, cable news and local press continued to show only tight shots of the violence, removing the depth of context of scenes throughout the city, in which acts of violence were sparce, to show limited views of specific instances of violence. Focusing only on one or two moments of violence—for instance, by showing one car fire with a tight shot of the flames and ignoring that it was the only one within a radius of five blocks—justified the unjustifiable use of smoke bombs, tear gas, rubber bullets, and a militarized presence of police in SWAT gear.[62]

In turn, members of the public and journalists took to criticizing any press coverage that touched too close to home in terms of how its rhetoric identified a hegemonic system that could be implicated for its part in creating situations such as Ferguson. CNN's Don Lemon—who was briefly mentioned at the top of this chapter for being among the worst journalists in 2014—was taken to task by fellow journalists for reporting about Ferguson violence following the grand jury decision in ways that reified urban memories of the past when the police went up against black communities, justified by "niggerized" behavior of drug use, anger, and threats to communities outside of the ghetto. The *New York Daily* News, for instance, covered Lemon's journalism this way:

> As Ferguson erupted into anger, bullets and flames Monday night, Lemon ham-handedly drew tear gas into his own gas mask, whined for water and a device to contact his producers, and then made a culturally insensitive comment about protesters smoking pot.
>
> Tuesday Lemon was further blasted by critics online for imitating the "St. Louis accent" and for retreating to a "safe room" while other CNN reporters stayed out on the scene.
>
> But it was his useless observation that he smelled drugs in the air that polarized critics.
>
> "Maybe a minute, two minutes ago we heard a gunshot and watched people scattering," Lemon said. "And we're watching people on the roofs of cars, on the tops of cars and, er, ... Obviously there's a smell of marijuana here as well."[63]

I watched Lemon that night, his comment on the "safe room" reminding me of when US Vice President Dick Cheney was rushed away to "an undisclosed location" on 9/11, and while I, too, was surprised by his style of reporting that night, he seemed to be reporting exactly what the US public already thought was happening inside US city cores—not only in Ferguson at the time. It was a bit surprising, then, when Lemon was called-out for his rhetoric since it really was representative of dominant societal imaginations of "blackness."

Deadspin's Greg Howard helped fill in this gap in our self-reflection following the Ferguson shooting in August that became more meaningful as Ferguson coverage played out in the second half of 2014. "The United States of America is not for black people," Howard wrote. "We know this, and then we put it out of our minds, and then something happens to remind us." Within days of Brown's murder, Howard noted, "... what's happening in Ferguson is about so many second-order issues—systematic racism, the militarization of police work, and how citizens can redress grievances, among other things."[64]

Such a focus on Lemon's reporting, however, not only served to distance journalists from what they considered "poor journalism" that may upset some in US society who have social capital to question the system but to extend public controversy and confusion to hide the deeper issues of US racism—particularly in the press. Local press in the United States benefited from this paradigm repair to forget their own acts of journalism that might be considered "bad" or "poor" but which was equally as compelling and "true" as what Lemon produced.

Reinforcing virtuous acts of press protectionism

The "virtuous war" in Ferguson relied on visuals of journalists working alongside police in the streets, capturing the stories, humanizing the destruction—not of police but of protesters—and suffering the consequences of "rioters'" actions by breathing in and coughing out air fouled by police smoke bombs. And even though the police and the press were on-scene for these acts of governmental violence against fellow citizens, the very media system that transmitted the visuals maintained a connection between audience and journalists as domestic war correspondents. Combined, national and local press rhetoric related to Ferguson and the presentation of racialized violence at the local level as an indication of how militarization contributed to the construction of a fair and just "virtuous war" in which the power elite followed the rules of engagement with the public through:

- Quantifiable evidence of protestors and the number of police officers watching the protests

- "Transparent" presentations of information that was presented by journalists who were on-the-scene, eyewitnesses to the disorder

- Entertaining and visually stimulating "shock and awe" showings of force in ways that also justified the use of force against citizens

Certainly, moments of "virtuous warfare" in the streets of the United States have appeared before in modern history, specifically through the power elite's act of using the press to bring into living rooms of the 1960s blacks who were increasingly being raped of power through efforts surrounding passive resistance, and who were often depicted as victims of police actions at the end of fire hoses and barking dogs through which blacks were presented as able to be controlled and therefore, perhaps, worthy of additional consideration of their grievances. Virtuous wars of the past benefited societies' versions of the power elite via military acts against places far away, which were presented and explained in news reports of attacks against savages in need of being tamed by civilization.

The home-front's imaginaries, then, were fed imperialistic rage against the savage that deepened the need for physical power to conquer and murder. Each citizen of the warring party was cast as a soldier in battle, or at the very least, potential casualties that demanded action by the power elite (for more, see the book's Conclusion). What's especially virtuous about our domestic wars today, as the Ferguson case exemplifies, is that they are, as discussed above, perpetual and show themselves only in brief moments of battle. The normalization of the war, then, becomes the basis for its manifestations, a reminder to the audience and to the public that the wars have never ended, particularly wars with "urban" populations (i.e., black folk)—even non-black folk who don't live in urban areas.[65]

CONCLUSION: COLLECTIVE FORGETTING AND MEDIA CONTROL

Examinations of cases discussed in this chapter have been built around notions of journalistic confusion, controversy, and applications of "conspiracy theory." I have also relied on notions of "urban memory" as a way to explain how— and why—the press present narratives of explanations, particularly of urban environments, as they do to contribute to the justification and legitimization of violence against the citizenry. Therefore, I close this chapter with a discussion about the role of memory in media control. Instead of viewing issues of "urban memory," for instance, as being of "collective memory," the process of constructing a collective's shared interpretations of history, urban memory has come to include the phenomena of media memory—"the systematic exploration of collective pasts that are narrated by the media, through the use of media, and about the media."[66]

I consider the process of memory as a power mechanism. This process, which I call *collective forgetting*—an act by media and public voices that shape dominant interpretations of current-day events and issues in ways that maintain power structures for future remembrance—is interested in the ways of developing explanations for today's events that erase alterative explanations so that they are no longer on the books when today's moment or event is remembered.

Those who study collective memory do so by examining memory *as an outcome* in ways that examine how members of the press remember the past. In this way, the media events are presented as operating within a timeline of events that are connected and can explain today based through power explanations of past events. There is no doubt that memory work in Journalism Studies reveals issues of power, in part by implicating media memory as holding an agenda-setting function, but dominant approaches on outcomes of memory within the news field, such as the degree to which memory fulfills the setting of an agenda, largely ignore the ideological functions of journalism in the ways that force us to forget moments of the past—or in other words, that make us remember in particular ways.[67]

As this chapter has presented, processes of controversy and conspiracy theory within press explanations distracts the audience—in the moment—from the intentionality of press presentations that benefit the power elite. Additionally, however, and as the notion of "urban memory" shaped press discourses related to violence (by both protesters and by the police) in Ferguson, the news of these many moments in 2014 also constructed popular and "official" histories for future audiences. In that case, the police may have been called into question related to their practices of violence, but their purposes of providing "protection for the public" were never challenged. Still, protesters were challenged for both their actions and their intentions, continuing a press commitment to "police myth" of virtuous "officers of the law" (see Chapter 5) and an engaged citizenry as rabble-rousers.

A similar ideological function of forgetting in the case of the Newtown shooting also constructed a simple, consistent memory for future press application. It is easier to remember the "Nutty Professor" and the distain to which the public and the press addressed alleged "conspiracy theory" than to discuss, in any meaningful way, a culture of gun violence. In turn, the shooting will go down as the act of a deranged man, similar to the dominant explanation of the Kennedy assassination, without any cultural context of that moment in time. Memory—like so many other concepts discussed in these pages—is an ideological act, a hegemonic process of indoctrination that relies as much on forgetting as on remembering and should be considered, as I have argued, as "collective forgetting" to complicate the very notion of memory in journalism and to identify its elements of force.

Whereas collective memory approaches power dynamics in terms of who and what is "remembered" as a way to interpret contemporary times, "collective forgetting" speaks more directly to how the press shape and maintain dominant interpretations of everyday life and events in ideologically conservative interpretations of news *at the moment* of the event or issue that might be remembered in the future.

More importantly, I argue, this "forgetting" is intentional, not just a process that occurs over time as in ways we may "forget" someone's birthday, the dates of the US Civil War, or our many passwords to our online bank accounts.

In this way, media remember by forgetting (which can include processes of marginalization or the exclusion of information) alternative explanations but even explanations that, at the time of an event, are not alternative but may not be in full support of the power elite—such as the use of drones to spy (and kill) US citizens at home and abroad, NSA surveillance of anyone and everyone, and collaboration between private industry and public life to influence social control policies. Collective forgetting is an effort to align collective identity and cultural continuance based around approved ideas and voices of yesterday and today *and tomorrow*.[68]

Henry Giroux makes similar articulations of how society forgets by turning to David Price's concept of "organized forgetting," a social process in which:

> ... anti-public intellectuals are part of a disimagination machine that solidifies the power of the rich and the structures of the military-industrial-surveillance-academic complex by presenting the ideologies, institutions and relations of the powerful as commonsense.[69]

In other words, and as with Price, Giroux suggests that forgetting is embedded throughout society in shared and collaborative ways, using institutions and social processes to create explanations for issues and events that will be used tomorrow. He writes elsewhere, for instance, that '[a]s historical memory is erased, critical thought is crushed by a sterile instrumental rationality under the guise of mass information and a data storm" and continues to state that:

> It is only a rebirth of historical memory that will enable the merging of dangerous thinking, critical knowledge and subversive action into a movement capable of reviving the dream of a future in which the practice of radical democratization prevails.[70]

This process of "organized forgetting," Giroux writes, is rooted in violence and is in and of itself a violent act. Though Giroux applies this articulation to processes of the State, I argue here (and in the following pages) that as a member of the power elite, in which the State is a mechanism of power maintenance and delivery, so, too, do the press function with similar aims of forgetting. From Giroux:

> State violence cannot be defined simply as a political issue but also as a pedagogical issue that wages violence against the minds, desires, bodies and identities of young people as part of the reconfiguration of the social state into the punishment state. At the heart of this transformation is the emergence of a new form of corporate sovereignty, a more intense form

of state violence, a ruthless survival-of-the-fittest ethic used to legitimate the concentrated power of the rich, and a concerted effort to punish young people who are out of step with neoliberal ideology, values and modes of governance.[71]

And, just as media can "remember" and "forget," for the benefit of the power elite, collective forgetting's function within acts of "media memory," of maintaining a constant paradigm of "good journalism" and approved journalistic practices, should not be limited to understanding journalistic ideological forms and functions outside of the journalistic interpretive community (see Chapter 2). This forgetting operates as a form of paradigm repair, as well.

For example, Dan Rather—the famed anchor for CBS News—left the network in 2006 after forty-four years (twenty-four of them as anchor) over debate about potential connections to the power elite that had helped President George W. Bush dodge serving in Vietnam. The evidence upon which CBS based their claims about Bush's military record was suspect, however, and later found to be doctored and supplied to CBS through a source who was no friend of Bush.

Not only did Rather find himself placed outside of the "journalistic community"—even though for most of his career he was a curmudgeon and sometimes abrasive to colleagues and sources, which hadn't led to his dismissal from the professional sphere—but he was being erased from the network's remembrance of its historical coverage when CBS prepared to air a program related to the fiftieth anniversary of the Kennedy Assassination. Even though CBS aired Rather's footage from that event, they did not invite him to reflect on air about the coverage and his role in it. "They are trying to airbrush me out of their history, like the Kremlin," Rather said at the time. "What's next—I'm airbrushed out of Watergate coverage? Vietnam? Tiananmen Square? 9/11? Where does this lead?"[72]

The ability—and ideological need—of collectively forgetting on behalf of the press protects the many sectors of the power elite in moments of initial rhetoric and explanation for the world and reinforces the homage that "News is the first rough draft of history."[73] More importantly, the concepts discussed in this chapter that function within the act of forgetting are most effective when the costs to the power elite are the highest, particularly when the potential to threaten the power elite is most potent in that threats may fragment communities of the elite or may divide the public's dominant sense of support for the elite's explanations and social institutions. Indeed, "forgetting" about portions of the past—and of the present—as I have discussed, serves as a process of "media control" that shapes the news as entertainment and as ideological indoctrination, harkening on collective memories of past uprisings and wars against the powerful (and the related social and cultural norms).

In the end, the process of "collective forgetting" reifies the positions of the power elite and serves to justify the actions of its many sectors, including the press, to maintain the status-quo, as the press will always find a way to position itself and its power colleagues as the victors. In the next chapter, I present three other processes of media control that not only shape the understandings of today's audiences similar to the processes discussed here but that directly contribute to public punishment via the press.

Discussion Questions

1. What methods do media and other social institutions perform to normalize dominant explanations of the past that influence discussions of modern times?
2. What other forms of "media control" occur in moments of journalistic cultural trauma?

Notes

1   Louise Boyle, "Adam Lanza hated his mother he shot dead because he thought 'she loved the students at Sandy Hook more than him,'" *Daily Mail*, December 28, 2013, http://www.dailymail.co.uk/news/article-2530371/Adam-Lanza-shot-dead-teacher-volunteer-mother-thought-loved-students-Sandy-Hook-him.html.

2   See transcript at http://www.washingtonpost.com/politics/remarks-from-the-nra-press-conference-on-sandy-hook-school-shooting-delivered-on-dec-21-2012-transcript/2012/12/21/bd1841fe-4b88-11e2-a6a6-aabac85e8036_story.html.

3   For review of Minuteman Project, see https://en.wikipedia.org/wiki/Minuteman_Project.

4   Though NBC producers had sought—and were denied—permission to have and show the magazine, neither producers nor Gregory were charged by local authorities. For more, see Peter Hermann, "Police: NBC asked to use high-capacity magazine," *The Washington Post*, December 26, 2012, http://www.washingtonpost.com/local/crime/police-nbc-asked-for-high-capacity-clip/2012/12/26/4c8f77da-4f76-11e2-8b49-64675006147f_story.html; J.K. Trotter, "David Gregory won't be going to jail over his NRA interview after all," thewire.com, January 11, 2013, http://www.thewire.com/politics/2013/01/david-gregory-wont-be-going-jail-over-his-nra-interview-after-all/60917/.

5 Read the full transcript here, http://www.nbcnews.com/id/50283245/ns/
meet_the_press-transcripts/t/december-wayne-lapierre-chuck-schumer-
lindsey-graham-jason-chaffetz-harold-ford-jr-andrea-mitchell-chuck-todd/#.
VK_mt4rF_1s.

6 Soraya Nadia McDonald, "Here's how President Obama responded to the
shooting of two Ferguson police officers on "Jimmy Kimmel Live!," *The
Washington Post*, March 13, 2015, http://www.washingtonpost.com/news/
morning-mix/wp/2015/03/13/heres-how-president-obama-responded-to-the-
shooting-of-two-ferguson-police-officers-on-jimmy-kimmel-live.

7 Jeffrey C. Alexander, "Toward a theory of cultural trauma," in *Cultural
Trauma and Collective Identity*, edited by Jeffrey C. Alexander, Ron Eyerman,
Bernard Giesen, et al. (Berkeley, CA: University of California Press, 2004),
1–30; Robert E. Gutsche, Jr. and Erica Salkin, "Who lost what? An analysis
of myth, loss, and proximity in news coverage of the Steubenville rape,"
Journalism (2015), doi: 10.1177/1464884914566195.

8 See, Lance deHaven-Smith, *Conspiracy Theory in America* (Austin, TX:
University of Texas Press, 2013).

9 James Tracy, "The Sandy Hook Massacre: Unanswered questions and
missing information," December 24, 2012, http://memoryholeblog.
com/2012/12/24/the-sandy-hook-massacre-unanswered-questions-and-
missing-information, emphasis in original.

10 James Tracy, "The Boston Marathon Bombing's inflated injury tallies," May
11, 2013, http://memoryholeblog.com/2013/05/11/the-boston-marathon-
bombings-inflated-injury-tallies/.

11 Terrance McCoy, "FAU professor James Tracy implies Navy Yard
shooting was faked," October 4, 2013, http://blogs.browardpalmbeach.
com/pulp/2013/10/james_tracy_navy_yard_shooting.php; James Tracy,
"Artifacts from the DC Navy Yard Shooting," September 18, 2013, http://
memoryholeblog.com/2013/09/18/artifacts-from-the-dc-navy-yard-shooting.

12 For more example of "alternative" histories of the United States that identify
issues of power, see Oliver Stone and Peter Kuznick, *The Untold Story of the
United States* (New York: Gallery Books, 2012).

13 Tracy, "The Sandy Hook Massacre."

14 Dan Berkowitz and Zhengjia Michelle Liu, "Media errors and the 'nutty
professor': Riding the journalistic boundaries of the Sandy Hook shootings,"
Journalism (2014), doi: 10.1177/1464884914552266: 10.

15 Matt Carlson and Seth C. Lewis, *Boundaries of Journalism: Professionalism,
Practices and Participation* (London and New York: Routledge, 2015).

16 deHaven-Smith, 36–37.

17 Ibid., 41.

18 Frank Rich, "Who was JFK?," *The New York Review of Books*, February 20,
2014.

19 Alyssa Dandrea, "Area residents recall the day of JFK assassination," *Keene
Sentinel*, November 22, 2013, http://www.sentinelsource.com/news/local/

area-residents-recall-the-day-of-jfk-assassination/article_efbd0020-63c1-57e4-
b7d8-6c1950ba8763.html; For another example of local glamorized coverage
of The JFK assassination, see Cathy Horyn, "Jackie Kennedy's pink suit,
preserved in memory of violent day, is kept out of view," *Idaho Statesman*,
November 15, 2013. Horyn's name appeared above a *New York Times News
Service* byline.

20 For more, see Douglas Kellner, *Media Spectacle and Insurrection, 2011:
From the Arab Uprisings to Occupy Everywhere* (New York and London:
Bloomsbury, 2012); Barbie Zelizer, *Covering the Body* (Chicago and London:
University of Chicago Press, 1992), 3.

21 deHaven-Smith, 125; 155.

22 Catalina Camia, "McCain to Kissinger protesters: 'Get out of here,
you low-life scum,'" onpolitics.usatoday.com, January 29, 2015, http://
onpolitics.usatoday.com/2015/01/29/john-mccain-henry-kissinger-
protesters; Eric Bradner, "McCain boots 'low-life scum' from hearing,"
cnn.com, January 29, 2015, http://www.cnn.com/2015/01/29/politics/
mccain-boots-low-life-scum-from-hearing; Peter Cooney, "John McCain
calls protesters 'scum,' tells them to 'shut up,'" reuters.com, January 29,
2015, http://www.reuters.com/article/2015/01/29/us-usa-mccain-protesters-
idUSKBN0L22V520150129.

23 Michel Foucault, *Society Must Be Defended* (New York: Picador, 1997), 88.

24 Barry Glassner, *The Culture of Fear: Why Americans are Afraid of the Wrong
Things* (New York: Perseus, 1999), xx. Glassner reissued this book a couple
of years later to include issues related to 9/11, but I prefer the first edition.

25 Ibid., 6.

26 Ibid., 27.

27 Ibid., 191–196.

28 Henry A. Giroux, "Totalitarian paranoia in the post-Orwellian surveillance
state," *Cultural Studies* 29, no. 2 (2015): 108–140.

29 Mark Stein, *American Panic: A History of Who Scares Us and Why* (New
York: Palgrave MacMillan, 2014); For more, see Jay Feldman, *Manufacturing
Hysteria: A History of Scapegoating, Surveillance, and Secrecy in Modern
America* (New York: Pantheon, 2011).

30 Evan McMurry, "CNN's Don Lemon wonders whether something
'supernatural' happened to the Malaysian plane," mediate.com, March 17,
2014, http://www.mediaite.com/tv/don-lemon-cnn-guest-wonder-whether-
something-supernatural-happened-to-malaysian-plane; Josh Feldman,
"CNN's Don Lemon: 'Is it preposterous' to think that a black whole caused
Flight 370 to go missing?," mediate.com, March 19, 2014, http://www.
mediaite.com/tv/cnns-don-lemon-is-it-preposterous-to-think-a-black-hole-
caused-flight-370-to-go-missing; David Uberti, "The worst journalism of
2014," *Columbia Journalism Review*, December 22, 2014, http://www.cjr.org/
darts_and_laurels/the_worst_journalism_of_2014.php?page=all.

31 For more, see Dan Falcone, "Mainstream news coverage of Ukraine,
Malaysia Airlines Flight 17 shows Western propaganda machine at work,"

truthout.org, October 10, 2014, website; Also, Fred Kaplan, at slate.com, writes about his coverage of the US-downed Iran Air Flight 655 in 1988 that killed 299; he claims the US government attempted to cover up the event and argues that the media and government officials, alike, have "forgotten" it ever happened. Read at http://www.slate.com/articles/news_and_politics/war_stories/2014/07/the_vincennes_downing_of_iran_air_flight_655_the_united_states_tried_to.html.

32 Catherine E. Shoichet, Josh Levs, and Kyung Lah, "MH17 crash: Did Russia pull the trigger? Ukraine says yes," cnn.com, July 23, 2014, http://www.cnn.com/2014/07/22/world/europe/ukraine-malaysia-airlines-crash.

33 Falcone.

34 Giroux, "Totalitarian paranoia in the post-Orwellian surveillance state," 131.

35 For more, see Anthony DiMaggio, *When Media Goes to War: Hegemonic Discourses, Public Opinion and the Limits of Dissent* (New York: Monthly Review Press, 2009); For more on the use of language in creating a state of "perpetual war," and a critique of Noam Chomsky's approach to such via "cosmopolitanism," see Bruce Robbins, *Perpetual War: Cosmopolitanism from the Viewpoint of Violence* (Durham and London: Duke University Press, 2012).

36 For more, see Feldman, *Manufacturing Hysteria*.

37 While I acknowledge that voter turn-out can also represent the function of marginalization through the forced removal or intentional barriers constructed to restrict people from participating in their governance, I have spent this time to provide yet another interpretation of voting and the interaction of power and agency to operate against the status-quo.

38 Slavoj Žižek, *Violence* (New York: Picador, 2008), 66.

39 Ibid., 66–67.

40 Robert E. Gutsche, Jr., *A Transplanted Chicago: Race, Place and the Press in Iowa City* (Jefferson, NC: McFarland, 2014), 102.

41 Motti Neiger, Oren Meyers and Eyal Zandberg, *On Media Memory: Collective Memory in a New Media Age* (Hampshire and New York: Palgrave MacMillan), 1.

42 See also, Michael Darroch, "Border scenes," *Cultural Studies*, 29, no. 3 (2015): 298–325; For examples of "ruin porn," see Chuck Beard and Linda Benedict-Jones, *Abandoned Pittsburgh* 3 (2014); Andrew Moore, *Detroit Disassembled* (2010); See also "ruin porn" of rural areas in Christopher Payne, *Asylum: Inside the Closed World of State Mental Hospitals* (Cambridge, MA: MIT Press, 2009).

43 Liana Rosenbloom, "Starbucks Coffee on South University reopens following renovations," *The Michigan Daily*, January 10, 2012.

44 Paul Beshouri, "Detroit to begin salvaging materials from abandoned buildings," detroit.curbed.com, May 16, 2014, http://detroit.curbed.com/archives/2014/05/detroit-to-begin-salvaging-materials-from-abandoned-buildings.php.

45 L.L. Brasier, "Reclaim Detroit finds city's treasures in abandoned homes," *Detroit Free Press*, December 26, 2014.

46 For the Harlem Shake, see Emily Dugan, "A brief history of the Harlem Shake," *The Independent*, March 2, 2013, http://www.independent.co.uk/ arts-entertainment/theatre-dance/news/a-brief-history-of-the-harlem- shake-8518071.html; On twerking, see Mark Graham, "A complete history of twerking (1993–2013)," vh1.com, August 7, 2013, http://www.vh1.com/music/ tuner/2013-08-07/twerking-complete-history/2.

47 Jacquelin Burgess and John R. Gold, "News from Nowhere: The Press, the Riots and the Myth of the Inner City," in *Geography, the Media and Popular Culture,* edited by A. J. Burgess and J. R. Gold (London and Sydney: Croom Helm, 1985), 193.

48 Gutsche, Jr., *A Transplanted Chicago*, 53.

49 Mark Crinson, *Urban Memory: History and Amnesia in the Modern City* (London and New York: Routledge, 2005); deHaven-Smith, 36; For more on fear, see Jesse Walker, *The United States of Paranoia: A Conspiracy Theory* (New York: HarperCollins, 2013).

50 James Der Derian, *Virtuous War: Mapping the Military-Industrial Media- Entertainment Network* (New York and London: Routledge, 2009, xxvii, xxxi, emphasis in original).

51 Monica Davey, Jon Eligon, and Alan Blinder, "National Guard troops fail to quell unrest in Ferguson," *The New York Times*, August 19, 2014; For a timeline of events, see Emily Brown, "Timeline: Michael Brown shooting in Ferguson, Mo.," *USA Today*, December 2, 2014, http://www.usatoday. com/story/news/nation/2014/08/14/michael-brown-ferguson-missouri- timeline/14051827.

52 Jonathan Capehart, "Why 'hands up, don't shoot' struck a chord," *The Washington Post*, December 2, 2014, http://www.washingtonpost.com/ blogs/post-partisan/wp/2014/12/02/why-hands-up-dont-shoot-struck-a-chord.

53 Jim Gallagher, "In Ferguson, optimism about the city's revival turns to worry," *St. Louis Post-Dispatch*, August 11, 2014, http://www.stltoday. com/business/local/in-ferguson-optimism-about-the-city-s-revival-turns-to/ article_3729e091-4a27-5ffe-b905-345f1c596bc4.html.

54 Jeremy Kohler, "St. Louis police chief says he does not support militarized tactics in Ferguson," *St. Louis Post-Dispatch*, August 14, 2014, http:// www.stltoday.com/news/local/crime-and-courts/st-louis-police-chief- says-he-does-not-support-militarized/article_b401feba-b49e-5b79-8926- 19481191726f.html.

55 Kim Bell, "McCulloh blasts Nixon for replacing St. Louis County Police control," *St. Louis Post-Dispatch*, August 14, 2014, http://www.stltoday.com/ news/local/crime-and-courts/day-five-wrapup-mcculloch-blasts-nixon-for- replacing-st-louis/article_0806541b-ed48-5d06-9267-323531ad6cf1.html.

56 Nicholas J.C. Pistor, "Suburban backdrop creates shocking images of Ferguson unrest," *St. Louis Post-Dispatch*, August 15, 2014, http:// www.stltoday.com/news/local/metro/suburban-backdrop-creates-shocking-images-of-ferguson-unrest/article_f5bb06cd-2bfe-5763-bc71-3fee226042cf.html.

57 Peter Schwenger, "Circling ground zero," *PMLA* 106, no. 2 (1991): 251–252.

58 Ken Leiser, "Police, protesters clash again Sunday night," *St. Louis Post-Dispatch*, August 17, 2014, http://www.stltoday.com/news/local/metro/police-protesters-clash-again-sunday-night/article_16467491-df06-5cf4-a156-f2dd328ef97b.html. [Previous version of the headline was as indicated in the related book text.]

59 See also, *Post-Dispatch*, "Some flare ups, tear gas flies after gun shots," *St. Louis Post-Dispatch*, August 19, 2014, http://www.stltoday.com/news/local/metro/some-flare-ups-tear-gas-flies-after-gun-shots/article_f794b446-1ee7-56f1-b4f5-03c5663b596f.html?utm_medium=twitter&utm_source=twitterfeed; for example, see *Post-Dispatch*, "Outburst interrupts night of peace," *St. Louis Post-Dispatch*, August 20, 2014, http://www.stltoday.com/news/local/metro/outburst-interrupts-night-of-peace-in-ferguson/article_375eff87-6a6b-534b-abcc-a8664e7d3ba2.html. This coverage and the photo of the police officer with fire erupting from the barrel received a Pulitzer Prize in 2015.

60 Amanda Holpuch, "St. Louis police fatally shoot 'erratic' man with knife near Ferguson," *The Guardian*, August 19, 2014; On December 23, 2014, a white police officer in Berkeley, Missouri, shot and killed an eighteen-year-old black man who was carrying a gun after he left a disturbance at another gas station, about five miles Northwest of Ferguson, see Kevin S. Held, "Videos released of officer-involved shooting," ksdk.com, December 24, 2014, http://www.ksdk.com/story/news/local/2014/12/24/police-shoot-kill-armed-teenager-in-berkeley/20849209; Jane Onyanga-Omara, "Videos show officer shooting armed teen near Ferguson," *USA Today*, December 24, 2014, http://www.usatoday.com/story/news/nation/2014/12/24/man-shot-killed-berkeley/20849045.

61 *Post-Dispatch*, "Businesses burn, police cars torched as violence 'much worse' than August," November 25, 2014, St. Louis Post-Dispatch http://www.stltoday.com/news/local/crime-and-courts/in-ferguson-businesses-burn-police-cars-torched-as-violence-much/article_47fc89b3-b0d2-5c41-a1fa-f4636673aac0.html.

62 Tim O'Neil, "Tear gas deployed after protesters burn police car, break windows at Ferguson city hall," *St. Louis Post-Dispatch*, November 26, 2014, http://www.stltoday.com/news/local/crime-and-courts/tear-gas-used-after-protesters-burn-police-car-break-windows/article_4e930309-b1b5-581d-85ed-04cd0a8f7921.html.

63 Don Kaplan, "CNN's Don Lemon, reporting from Ferguson, is under fire for poor journalism, skills and alleged bias," *New York Daily News*, November 25, 2014, http://www.nydailynews.com/entertainment/tv/cnn-don-lemon-disgrace-article-1.2023460.

64 Greg Howard, "America is not for black people," deadspin.com, August 12, 2014, http://theconcourse.deadspin.com/america-is-not-for-black-people-1620169913; see also, Tamara K. Nopper and Mariame Kaba, "Itemizing atrocity," truthout.org, August 17, 2014, http://www.truth-out.

org/opinion/item/25612-itemizing-atrocity; Sarah Goodyear, "The Fergusons we already forgot," citylab.com, August 15, 2014, http://www.citylab.com/crime/2014/08/the-fergusons-we-already-forgot/376129.

65 For more, see Nicole Maurantonio, "Remembering Rodney King: Myth, racial reconciliation, and civil rights history," *Journalism & Mass Communication Quarterly* (2014), doi: 10.1177/1077699014550094; See also, Mohan Dutta, Susan Brockus, and Laura Vercler, "Television coverage of Operation Iraqi Freedom," *The Journal of International Communication* 18, no. 2 (2012): 155–173; Benjamin Ginsberg, *The Value of Violence* (Amherst, NY: Prometheus Books, 2013).

66 Neiger, Meyers and Zandberg, 1.

67 See Neta Kligler-Vilenchik, Yariv Tsfati, and Oren Meyers, "Setting the collective memory agenda: Examining mainstream media influence on individuals' perceptions of the past," *Memory Studies* 7, no. 4: 484–499; Sue Robinson, Sandra Knisely, and Mitchael L. Schwartz, "A news negotiation of a state's 'history': Collective memory of the 2011 Wisconsin protests," *Journalism Studies* 15, no.4 (2014): 431–448; Jill A. Edy, *Troubled Pasts: News and the Collective Memory of Social Unrest* (Philadelphia, PA: Temple University Press, 2006); Rachel Somerstein, "Newspapers commemorate 11 September: A cross-cultural investigation," *Journalism* (2014), doi: 10.1177/1464884913519033; Carolyn Kitch, *Pages from the Past: History & Memory in American Magazines* (Chapel Hill, NC: The University of North Carolina Press, 2005).

68 Charles B. Stone and William Hirst, "(Induced) forgetting to form a collective memory," *Memory Studies* 7, no. 3 (2014): 314–327; Elizabeth J. Marsh and Barbara Tversky, "Spinning the stories of our lives," *Applied Cognitive Psychology* 18 (2004): 491–503; Nicole M. Dudukovic, Elizabeth J. Marsh, and Barbara Tversky, "Telling a story or telling it straight: The effects of entertaining versus accurate retellings on memory," *Applied Cognitive Psychology* 18 (2004): 125–143.

69 Henry A. Giroux, "The violence of organized forgetting," truthout.org, July 22, 2013, http://www.truth-out.org/opinion/item/17647-the-violence-of-organized-forgetting; David Price, "Memory's half-life: A social history of wiretaps," *counterpunch* 20, no. 6 (2013): 14.

70 Henry A. Giroux, "Data storms and the tyranny of manufactured forgetting," truthout.org, June 14, 2014, http://www.truth-out.org/news/item/24550-data-storms-and-the-tyranny-of-manufactured-forgetting.

71 Giroux, "The violence of organized forgetting."

72 Melissa Clyne, "Dan Rather: CBS 'airbrushed' me from history, 'like Kremlin,'" newsmax.com, November 14, 2013, http://www.newsmax.com/US/rather-cbs-jfk-assassination/2013/11/14/id/536692.

73 There is some debate about who coined this phrase. For more, see Jack Shafer, "Who said it first?," slate.com, August 30, 2010, http://www.slate.com/articles/news_and_politics/press_box/2010/08/who_said_it_first.html.

5

Normalizing Media Surveillance: Media Waiting, Watching, and Shaming

Chapter Purpose

This chapter examines overt collaborations between the press and other power structures by discussing how news contributes to a surveillance and control state operated by the power elite. Analyses in this chapter identify three main processes of media control—waiting, watching, and shaming—that function in and as a surveillance institution. Cases analyzed include press coverage of value-laden "waiting" and "watching" surrounding a black street festival, Urban Beach Week, in Miami Beach, Florida, and "shaming" that occurred in media telling of testimony given in the 2013 murder trial of a young black man in Sanford, Florida, by a white Hispanic neighborhood watchman.

Guiding Questions

1. How might the press contribute to social surveillance that benefits the policing of behaviors and ideologies by police and private enterprise?
2. How is it possible for media to "shame" members of the public? What would such shaming look like, and what would its purpose be?

Key Terms

Control: The process by which individuals and collectives are forced to conform to the demands and expectations of the powerful through psychological, ideological, and physical means of violence

Media Shaming: The act of informally punishing through public displays of disapproval, including humiliation and immense unexpected exposure by the press

Media Waiting: The process of fear-construction related to what "might happen" in a pending news event

Media Watching: The process by which the press "watch" in a traditional sense of surveilling with the intention of employing moral overtones to what is otherwise "objective coverage"

MEDIA WAITING: FEARING SOUTH BEACH'S URBAN BEACH WEEK

Each Memorial Day weekend, Miami's South Beach becomes inundated with hip-hop music and scantly clad dancers—it is Miami Beach's Urban Beach Week, which began in 2001 as an iteration of historic Freaknik, a street party that began as a form of Spring Break for Atlanta's black college students that quickly turned into melees, attracting participants from far and wide. Historically, press coverage of Freaknik focused on violence and policing, particularly in the 1990s, that highlighted disorder surrounding racialized characterizations of black male savagery, in part because of reports of black women being frequently accosted, groped, and assaulted.

Instead of focusing on these instances as being moments of sexual assault and harassment during the event, though, local TV reporters cast the women who were assaulted as "jezebels," hyper-sexed savage women who wanted and deserved sexual violence. Because these archetypes tapped into dominant narratives of the "savage black," writes Marian Meyers, assaults against black women by black men were presented in the press "within a racialized context that blamed locals rather than students for any acts of violence and initially failed to recognize sexual harassment as an issue."[1]

And it is that narrative of devious blackness that continues to be applied to participants of Miami Beach's Urban Beach Week, which each spring launches an exodus of the neighborhoods' residents and business owners as some 300,000 partiers—most of them black—make festive noise. Furthermore, since 2011 when local police shot and killed an unarmed, black driver that they said tried to run over officers—spraying more than 100 bullets through the streets; sixteen hit the twenty-two-year-old male victim—Urban Beach Week becomes a place of sick pleasure of the press and police, armed with their cameras and guns, waiting for violence to break out and the chance to punish perceptions of blackness with media and police violence.[2] Tones of hypersexuality, of "gangsta style," and of "ghettoization" by local journalists in 2012 and 2013, for instance, influenced non-black owned businesses on South Beach to announce that they would close en masse because of the perceived, potential problems that might arise.

Despite the fact that major violence—and murder—*that had occurred* during the festivities in 2011 was conducted by the police, it was the violence of that year that contributed to increased surveillance of the festival by police and press in the years to come, with reporters promoting the new policing technologies, military vehicles, and shows of force applied as a means not to diminish public fear about South Beach's black crowds but to ignite it.[3]

In effect, immense reporting on local law enforcement's preparation for the event constituted a legitimate, "virtuous war"—one that is presented as righteous, clean, and distant from the war-makers—against attendees (see Chapter 4). And, the virtuous war got great PR from local news outlets. Miami's local CBS station, for example, presented an "Exclusive look at Urban Beach Week security measures" in 2013 with a tone that characterized police as heroes preparing for an assault on the local community. According to that report:

> Cameras, both mobile and stationary, have been installed throughout the city. Ready to be deployed throughout the city of Miami Beach are a total of 62 light towers, twelve [sic] visual messaging boards and three watch towers.
>
> Roughly 400 officers per shift from multiple agencies will pack the streets of Miami Beach.
>
> In addition to extra bikes and ATVs, the Police Department has a new vehicle on loan referred to as an LTV.
>
> CBS 4 News had the exclusive first look at this 140-thousand dollar light tactical all-terrain vehicle, similar to the ones used in the military.
>
> "This is the only one of its kind," an officer explained to CBS 4's Lauren Pastrana. "There's no other vehicle like this on the market at this time."[4]

Furthermore, Urban Beach Week in 2013 was presented as being as dangerous as an "inner-city" that was in need of police protection. The CBS report above, for instance, justified the fear audiences already had about what could happen during the Memorial Day event by quoting one local police officer as saying that during "[a] dark beach at night, I would compare it to a dark alley in a big city," and that, in the reporter's words, a new camera that the police department would employ will keep a constant eye on nearly every single partier that street lights might miss. The camera, the reporter states, with assistance from the police officer:

> … uses infrared technology to detect heat signatures on the beach, so even in the dead of night, officers can see people on a small screen mounted inside the vehicle.
> "We could easily pick up a heat signature on this camera close to 3/4 of a mile away," the officer explained.

As I will argue throughout this chapter, local news coverage of preparations for Urban Beach Week, even as late as 2014, as well as coverage of other local events and issues across the country in recent years, reveal media control's involvement in an increased police and surveillance state by conducting *media surveillance*—social monitoring with the intention of controlling the behaviors, activities, and ideologies of individuals and collectives. More specially, I examine how media surveillance serves White Supremacy by dictating dominant rhetoric of violence against blackness and perceived disorder related to black folks while at the same time rewarding people and places of non-blackness that are valued for their cosmopolitanism and capitalistic potential. In fact, Miami's Urban Beach Week coverage, when compared to press discourse of Miami as a "global city" and as a place of "luxury," maintains mediatized segregation based on race, class, uneven public and private investments in geography and infrastructure, and sweeping gentrification.

In 2014, media surveillance of another large, public party—the annual international Art Basel event on Miami Beach—also controlled public behaviors and dominant identities of Miami but did so by rewarding crowds who were about to descend throughout the Miami area; news coverage even highlighted businesses that "rush(ed)" to open. As one story states, the 75,000 people who come annually to Art Basel—a majority of which are non-black—"hint at the spending power" associated with the crowds and the desirability of the event itself. While Urban Beach Week, with its black crowds and their disposable income and quadruple the numbers, was presented as something to avoid, Art Basel on Miami Beach and in Miami's Wynwood Art District and other "hip" and "urban" landscapes was referred to in the press as "an essential business tool for developers and businesses in South Florida" and an event for which 1,800 journalists were credentialed to tell stories about "the world's largest art gathering."[5]

Lastly, that media coverage didn't connect previous and current police activity and public violence to Art Basel was a clear act to maintain a sense of normal innocence of those who attended—and patrolled—those streets. In fact, when the *Miami Herald* did cover the police murder of a young, male graffiti artist in Wynwood in December 2014, the newspaper provided a clear discussion about the death and what it meant to the Art Basel event and the hipster Wynwood neighborhood. Journalists wrote that Delbert Rodriguez Gutierrez, twenty-one:

> was spotted by police gang unit members as he was "tagging" a privately owned building near Northwest Fifth Avenue and 24th Street about 2 a.m., police said. When officers began chasing him, Rodriguez fled.
>
> He turned a street corner, then ducked between two cars to try to get rid of his spray paint can, police said. As Miami police Detective Michael Cadavid turned the corner, police said, Rodriguez jumped out from between the cars and was struck by the detective's vehicle.
>
> . . .
>
> The timing and the location of the incident could not come at a more sensitive time for Miami police: Rodriguez was struck at the height of Art Basel week, as thousands of visitors descend on Miami Beach and Miami for one of the biggest art fairs in the world. Wynwood, which has gained international renown in large part because of its street art, has become central to the festival.[6]

Rodriguez, the story says, was in fact the second "tagger" to be killed by police in the Miami area in as many years. Eighteen-year-old Israel Hernandez-Llach was killed in 2013 when he was tased by a police officer in Miami Beach after he ran from police who allege he was spray painting the side of an abandoned McDonald's. But these deaths, at the hands of an aggressive police force, didn't change any of the press narratives related to these two events: Art Basel didn't hold a hint of danger; Urban Beach Week was a public event with potential for violence.

In this chapter, I continue with an analysis of Urban Beach Week coverage to explicate the police function of media control by identifying three processes of its actions in terms of surveillance, which include:

- *Media waiting*, the process of fear-construction related to what "might happen" in a pending news event that then provides the press with an ability to set the dominant scene for future coverage and influence public discourse and action based upon interests of the power elite at the time of the event and as the event unfolds

- *Media watching*, the process by which the press "watch" in a traditional sense of surveilling with the intention of employing moral overtones to what is otherwise "objective coverage"

- *Media shaming*, the act of informally punishing through public displays
  of disapproval, including humiliation and immense unexpected
  exposure by the press

Collectively, these processes of media control help us in this chapter
to radicalize the notion of social surveillance by the media and to identify
characteristics of journalistic reporting and storytelling as an active searching
for moments of social conflict with which to pass moral judgment on behalf
of the power elite and to inflict punishment upon those who act outside of
the norms. Each section of this chapter expands upon a specific process of
media surveillance, beginning with "media waiting" and concluding with
an explication of media control as a machine of violence and violence-as-
entertainment in which press share in the duties and benefits of police. In
this way, I argue that by sharing in the social and cultural policing function
of the power elite that surrounds hype related to fear and solutions that
include force, the press operate as members of society's police forces that
fight our fears.

Waiting for the inevitable violence

Miami Herald coverage leading up to Urban Beach Week as early as 2010
explained local debate about the event's purpose and virtue as revolving
around South Beach residents' "outrage by the annual spectacle of crowded
streets, never-ending parties and piles of trash." Other local residents, the
paper writes, "maintained [that] the neighborhood concerns were based in
part on race and that police had been overzealous" in their policing, a haunting
foreshadowing of the next year's shooting involving twelve police officers
who fired 115 bullets at an unarmed black driver of a car near the festivities
on Collins Avenue.[7] A bystander who video recorded the shooting unleashed
it on the internet. The video included police approaching the citizen who was
videotaping the situation, telling him to stop recording, and then arresting
him. Autopsy reports released two years later—and a few weeks before the
2013 event—showed the driver's blood-alcohol level to be .14 percent, almost
twice the legal limit.

Police had also announced that they had allegedly found a handgun
wrapped in a blanket inside the dead man's car. Little to no evidence,
however, suggested that the driver had attempted to—or succeeded in—
shooting or driving at police with intent to harm, and the police chief at
the time told reporters that finding the gun in the car was "good news"

in that it helped to clear his officers of any wrongdoing. The newspaper stated, in related coverage, that in light of this news, police in 2013 "will be ready to deal with anything" in terms of the expected crowds but provided little detail as to just what the police intended to do to holster their weapons.[8]

Coverage about the pending party in 2013 began with a rumble of cautions to citizens by police and businesses, which were said to be "bracing" for the Memorial Day event. One *Herald* article claimed that "Miami Beach is holding its collective breath through Monday, hoping to dodge the human stampedes, tear gas and deadly police shootings that have marred recent Memorial Day weekends." That same story focused on the businesses that have closed—or have "been forced to close" in the past—because of the large crowds. Amid this coverage, overt mentions of race—that this party was a black party—appeared in photographs of previous events, in which dark-skinned revelers were shown in massive crowds or in individual poses featuring women's "booties" in short shorts.[9]

Journalistic nods to perceived notions of "blackness" also appeared loud and clear in the use of "hip-hop" as a classification of the music that's played at the party; the very word "Urban" in the event's title of "Urban Beach Week" referencing to geographies associated with black folk and, therefore, "black culture," dominant perceptions of which include elements of pathological disorder (see Chapter 4). Therefore, journalists couldn't outright ignore the racial elements of the party and local concerns related to fears of potential violence. In their process of "waiting," the press did however, include references by local civic leaders who spoke out about police profiling and harassment of black visitors, though these concerns were not presented with a level of legitimacy equal to "official" reports of police preparedness. Rather, discourse about racism in the behavior and ideologies of local police officials—and some South Beach residents and business owners—from the perspective of civic leaders interested in racial equality appeared only in relationship to the institutions' ideologies about structural racism.

Rhetoric that focuses only on "structural" or "institutional" types of racism—in which racial inequality is suggested to have been normalized within patterns of social behavior, rules, and law—releases individuals, such as politicians, business leaders, journalists, and average citizens from a responsibility to consider and address prevailing ideologies of whiteness by presenting the racialized rhetoric and social conditions as a natural element of life. There is no room in descriptions of "structural" or "institutional" racism for racialized hate, something that in those manners of explaining racism allow for measurement of quantifiable evidence.

However, the *Miami Herald*, in an effort to provide "balanced" coverage on the point of racial inequalities related to structural elements of how local officials approached Urban Beach Week, quoted a leader of the local chapter of the American Civil Liberties Union who said that Miami Beach officials should work to be more inviting to Urban Beach Week tourists "who happen to be black, the same way it welcomes visitors to every other big event, like Art Basel or the boat show." Rather, the leader said, "city leaders have been working hard to suppress this one group."[10] Still, the source's position is buried in a story that focuses on efforts of the police to protect the citizenry from the pending onslaught of Urban Beach Week so as to provide "journalistic evidence" that reporters provided "both sides" to the story. In fact, journalists were always quick in their narratives to diminish comments that were critical of local officials and police by heralding the efforts of local law enforcement. In the same story, for example, the newspaper listed the efforts of force or threats of force to maintain order during the Memorial Day event:

> Police will deploy a plan first rolled out last year that includes license-plate readers and DUI checkpoints on causeways, driving and parking restrictions south of 23rd Street, increased patrols, zero-tolerance enforcement of drug and trespassing laws, and more lighting along dark stretches of beach.[11]

As another example of burying racialized themes of conflict related to Urban Beach Week within *Herald* storytelling, the newspaper turned to local residents to humanize and to strengthen the position of the local power elite that (1) the public should be afraid and (2) that such fear isn't rooted in racism, but in a normal and natural interpretation of the event's history. One resident, Alexander Gomez, told the paper:

> I mean, if you're visiting from out of town, it's got to be great, no? It's just too packed with people. No matter what race or color, it's just too crazy and swamped with revelers for my taste.[12]

The above examples represent coverage of Urban Beach Week between 2012 and 2014 in which any slight reference to issues of race in terms of police activity before and during the event was presented as something distant from individual action, thoughts, choices, and application through policy and policing. When racism is present—such as in the "colorblind" statements of Gomez, which dismiss race as being an element of social and cultural identification—news reports pass over the mention as though critical challenges to the ideographs of Miami, Miami Beach, and its residents (a place home to historically marginalized communities) are outside of acceptable definitions of that place.

The massive police presence that was proposed and implemented over the years in preparation for black crowds, particularly in 2013, was legitimatized in the press as an effective means by which to address perceived disorder related to loud music, public drinking, specific attire, and the gathering of dark-skinned people. But the military style execution of force, which included high-tech surveillance systems and cameras, weaponized beach patrol units and watchtowers, was only acceptable because of the crowds the force was being used against and the mediatized fears associated with them during stages of "media waiting" before the event.

Violence against "the other"

By 2014, media waiting leading up to Urban Beach Week was much more subtle in terms of explanations of hyper-vigilant police and their hopes to curb "black culture." For that year's event, a ramped-up police presence had already been justified and normalized in 2013 news coverage that presented the police presence as something that was natural and just part of the event's environment. I first noticed this change in coverage related to police activity when I saw on the homepage of the *Miami Herald* on May 19 in an image that characterized Urban Beach Week—and it's "urban" meanings—as a form of "tourism." To me, the prominence all but ignored the presence of a police surveillance watchtower in that photo (see Figure. 5.1) that represented the voyeuristic appeal of the event in terms of the entertainment value of waiting surrounding potential violence and disorder.

I was so struck by the normalized presentation of such surveillance that I asked *Herald* editors for permission to run a screen shot of the homepage for this book project. At first, I was denied. Instead, I was allowed to republish a section of the paper's website, which shows a different version of the same image that appeared earlier in the day on the homepage and the subject of a screen shot I had shared with editors. The original image from the *Herald*'s homepage carried the headline similar to the one in the image that I was allowed to republish—"Miami Beach preps for holiday weekend crowd."

But the image that I wanted appeared under a tagline of "TOURISM," and, the image itself was cropped just to the right of the police watchtower that appears in Figure 5.1, which highlighted the presence of that tower while also painting it as a normal feature of Miami Beach. The caption of the first image was different too: "Miami Beach is once again bracing for massive crowds

FIGURE 5.1 Miami Herald, *May 19, 2014. Used with permission.*

this Memorial Day weekend as up to a quarter-million revelers are expected to flock to the Beach for hip-hop performances."

In negotiations with the editors, they mandated that I use another screen shot—the one that does appear in this book—because, they said, it shows "context" related to the image. At first, I thought I would not be able to represent my meanings associated with the context that I had seen in the original image—that black people (tourists?) were, in the words of the caption, "flocking" in "massive" crowds to the degree that local residents needed to "brace" themselves, and that, in turn, demanded police surveillance.[13]

But the interaction with editors over which image to use in and of itself holds its own interesting meanings related to the role and purpose of media watching that when placed within the larger context of how the *Herald* has covered preparations for Urban Beach Week. By focusing on militarization and economy, not on the hip-hop artists and attendees who might attend for the music, violence was bound in and by racism but was denied within propagandistic rhetoric of the local power elite.

Take, for instance, these headlines from 2013 that showcase a clear discourse about the "virtuous war" on Miami Beach but that in the stories themselves—which I summarize—remove any challenge as to the rationales for war:

- "Holiday weekend crowds way down from boom in Miami Beach."
  In this story, DJs and hotel managers discuss the profits and the
  crowd levels related to increased "new security measures including
  highway checkpoints, roadblocks and surveillance cameras" that the
  newspaper states have appeared to "work" in the past.[14]

- "Heavy police presence tames Urban Beach Weekend festivities." A
  photo cutline indicates that "[a]gainst a background of hyper police
  [sic] preparedness, the crowds on and around Ocean Drive were light
  and mellow .... " (Figure 5.1).[15]

- "Crowds, arrests down at Memorial Day Weekend in Miami Beach." In
  this story, "revelers" are characterized as "sedate," though one young
  man tells the reporter, "To be honest there are a lot of beautiful young
  ladies here"; and, the reporter notes, "(the interview was cut short
  when five women walked by wearing short shorts and bikini tops)."
  The event, the story notes, has largely been attracting "throngs of
  mostly young, black men and women" since it began in 2001.[16]

- "Urban Beach Week comes to an end—very quietly." Enter a sigh
  of relief, because in this piece, police sources highlight the success
  of their efforts to "provide a safe and secure destination," while one
  tourist was quoted as saying, "I understand why they (the police) are
  here, but it makes us feel like Miami is scarier than it is."[17]

In effect, 2013 coverage of Urban Beach Week operated within the three
ideological processes of media control via media surveillance mentioned
above that then paved the way for news presentations a year later that didn't
require further explication. First, that the crowds were "tame(d)" by police
as though the visitors were animals and savages, as they were presented in
coverage of Atlanta's Freaknik and in a long history of racialized rhetoric about
US "black culture." This use of news myth is indicative of media waiting in
that news articles consistently contained a vigilant recording of police arrests,
levels of authorized physical social surveillance, and an on-the-ground "eye-
witnessing" and "watchdogging" of police and revelers through narratives of
disorder—including that restaurants suffered from tables left empty as regular
and desirable patrons avoided South Beach.

That process of storytelling represents a second process of media
surveillance through media watching, which occurred after the press
determined the tone and facts of the story and the dominant explanations for
Urban Beach Week. With the stage set, the press functioned to present moral
overtones to the story's settings and characters, where men and women

were presented as hypersexualized savages that at any moment could break through barriers of control and harm the larger citizenry.

Through fear appeals, the press was able to enact the third process of media surveillance—media shaming—through two means. First, the press shamed those who would attend Urban Beach Week, casting all of the revelers as trouble-makers and dismissing any potential interests or experiences of enjoying the art of music during the event. Indeed, the few moments of enjoyment that appeared in the coverage was embedded with an overarching narrative of disorder. Second, the press positioned the police within a questionable degree of adequacy. Media remembrance of 2011 police violence during Urban Beach Week served as "flak" to distance media from any potential shaming they may have been required to cast on police in order to maintain the paradigm of a "virtuous war."

Below, I continue my dissection of media surveillance by examining the process of media watching before moving into an analysis of how these processes help to reveal the violence inherent within press discourse.

MEDIA WATCHING: THE FUNCTIONS OF MEDIA SURVEILLANCE

Press salutations of police militarization and übersurveillance of "potential threats" in the case of waiting for Urban Beach Week appeared in ways that assumed news audiences would adequately interpret news characterizations of police "protectionism" as being related to the potential threat of urban blackness. In turn, the press act of waiting served to apply the "ghettoization effect" that corralled audiences into a state of belonging surrounding the role of media surveillance, one that was rooted in racialized paranoia. In this section, I examine what is meant by surveillance and begin explicating the role of media in what is an established industry of the power elite that's designed to justify even the most egregious of militant acts against the citizenry.

Understanding surveillance

William Staples identifies two types of surveillance that are helpful for this project. First, soft surveillance includes "seemingly benign and relatively inconspicuous forms of monitoring and assessment," such as the use of video cameras in coffee shop that are tucked into the ceiling, systems that record ISP addresses when accessing databases, or software that tracks our purchases online and suggests other items we may want to buy. These soft forms, Staples writes, operate "behind the scenes." Second, hard surveillance is more overt and is "often designed to uncover the truth about someone's behavior, to test an individual's character, and, more generally, to make them consciously aware that they are indeed being watched and monitored." This definition of surveillance is usually the most-recognized, because of its physical manifestations, such as in direct questioning by members of authority and the use of magnetic and electronic scanners by the Transportation Security Administration (TSA) workers at airports. In between these two types of surveillance, Staples writes, is a spectrum of forms that move back and forth in terms of their meanings, where on one end information may be provided voluntarily, for instance, and on the other, taken by force.[18]

And it is within the "liquidity" of today's surveillance state—the embeddedness of surveillance tactics into daily experiences that makes it more difficult to identify specific surveillance acts or tools—where media control's processes of surveillance operate and where we should focus our concern in this project. Indeed, as Zygmunt Bauman and David Lyons write about "liquid surveillance":

> Surveillance is a growing feature of daily news, reflecting its rapid rise to prominence in many life spheres. But in fact surveillance has been expanding quietly for many decades and is a basic feature of the modern world. As that world has transformed itself through successive generations, so surveillance takes on an ever changing character. Today, modern societies seem so fluid that it makes sense to think of them being in a "liquid" phase. Always on the move, but often lacking certainty and lasting bonds, today's citizens, workers, consumers and travellers also find that their movements are monitored, tracked and traced. Surveillance slips into a liquid state.[19]

Members of such a surveiled society are left bemused, confused, or absent in the process of being watched and—as this chapter will further develop—of being punished by the very same media said to be offering entertainment and protection. Within these media acts, meanings of surveillance become reappropriated or, at the very least, are provided a singular meaning in press discourse and explanations that veil the interests of media itself to control audiences.[20] Media surveillance is not new, however. As a means of addressing the development of modern surveillance within the communication field, Josh Lauer presents the ways in which forms of "new media" have occurred in historic interpretations of what we may consider today to be "old media," such as the phonograph, the telephone, and the portable camera. In each of these cases, Lauer suggests, public anxiety about the interjection of new technologies into daily life led to an interaction between moral panic and a desire to experience the promises of innovation.

Furthermore, he notes that these technologies gained attraction among the elite and celebrities in ways that extended their uses within society. Beta users tested the technology and the marketplace and set the standard for the use and practices associated with the technology. They also influenced the distribution, economic costs, and class/racial/geographic divides that emerged from unequal degrees to which the technology was infused into portions of society. Early users help form dominant ways of using technology and validate the initial, dominant meanings associated with the technology and its uses so as to create a public anxiety surrounding overt signs of a potentially rising protected and privileged class.

As these users, via communication, express the wide usability of technology within appropriate means and for approved purposes, the public is presented with a calming message to overcome any initial concerns. Over the course of time, for instance, the photograph of one's self, of a family, of a landscape, of a public gathering, and of breaking news events, became normalized and accepted—even desired—as a means of remembering, of creating evidence, and of presenting norms of society to the masses.

Still, the early days of the photograph must have been somewhat frightening (not to mention threatening to particular cultural and religious positions) in terms of the uncertainty related to:

- The technical operation of related devices
- Who has the knowledge, financial ability, and power to take photographs
- Who controls the release and use of captured images
- When individuals within the "masses" would be able to participate as users

Media turned to these fears of technology within previous generations—as it does today—as a means of "waiting" on the development of elite definitions and applications of such technologies in order to coopt early notions of the technologies' ability to be used by an individual or collective for social change outside of social norms.

Debate since the mid-2010s about the private—and journalistic—uses of drones, for instance, has been stalled by intervention of "official" government agencies and decisions as to who can fly a drone, where, for how long, how high, and for what purpose. The process of determining the federal laws related to using drones—in which the press has been most regulated—has allowed the worlds of officialdom and businessdom to collaborate on ways in which drones can be used, first and foremost, for military/police surveillance and physical force. Only when business has laid its claim to the dominant uses of drones for commerce will the regulations at the federal level relax enough so that other members of society can experience any personal value of the technology.[21]

Lauer conceptualizes media history of surveillance tools in such a way that casts early forms of surveillance—and the power and social costs inherent within it—as being "something more than the history of rationalization and control." Rather, he argues that:

> [t]ensions between the liberating and oppressive uses of new media— the dream of perfect communication versus the horror of continuous inquisition—is directly related to the indeterminacy of media as tools for producing evidence. It is not the proliferation of new surveillance technologies per se that threatens privacy or creates power asymmetries, but the proliferation of *mediated evidence* that institutions and individuals produce, preserve, and scrutinize.[22]

"Mediated evidence," which Lauer defines as "texts, images, sounds, data by which individuals might be identified, their motives and thoughts inferred, and future behavior predicted" is volunteered by media users as much as it is captured by the technology itself and is used as a way to define the meanings associated with technology and its surveillance mechanisms. He writes:

> A media-saturated society is evidence rich. We give and give off more evidence about ourselves than perhaps at any previous time. Though much of this evidence is institutional and compulsory—we must leave transactional clues as a *condition* of communication when using the internet or mobile phones, for example—we also use new media as a source of self-expression and pleasure in constructing identities, histories, and webs of affiliation.[23]

In return for this evidence, audiences participate in an environment of control and surveillance that becomes naturalized and within ways which individuals still feel as though they have the ability to identify and articulate the degrees to which they may—or may not—operate with a controlled and surveiled state. Such *control*, then, which has been and will continue to be a dominant definition throughout this project, is seen as a process by which individuals and collectives are forced to conform to the demands and expectations of the powerful through psychological, ideological, and physical means of violence. But just how do the press control as they surveil?

Enacting control through media watching

As a constant act of transformation, the "waiting" that press conduct becomes "watching" in moments when "media memory"—and "collective forgetting"—cast potential doom as an inevitable social condition that the press has waited to cover. In other words, the press is always prepared for "breaking news" of disaster and controversy and willingly join forces with their governments and police forces to fight whatever challenges faces their initial interpretations of the event as the event unfolds for control. For example, in terms of the second Gulf War, marked by the US-led invasion of Iraq in 2003—which occurred a year after the US invasion of Afghanistan as retaliation for the 9/11 attack—US press turned to metaphor in their stage of waiting as a means by which to present war as "inevitable."

Jack Lule argues, for instance, that TV news media in the early 2000s presented governmental actions surrounding growing tensions as a "timetable for war," while other news channels reported from "war rooms" of their own as the "clock" was "ticking" on war as the only solution to tension between the nations' governments. As the war unfolded and the decision to invade was challenged by enough of the public that maintained a sense of social capital (i.e., the exposé by Richard Clarke about what the US government knew about the potential for an event like 9/11), the press transformed from "waiting" to "watching"—a switch that allowed journalists to maintain their arguments for war within an admitted fallibility that was rooted in seeking justice.[24]

The transition from waiting to watching is not only a process of a national press and is not limited only to international events. Without a doubt, US society has become so reliant on violent methods of press rhetoric that following debate about the militarization of the nation's local police forces, such as what occurred throughout 2014 and into 2015 (see Chapter 4), has cast violence as such a common experience within US society that languages of violence, control, and surveillance have become not only norms of a just society but so, too, are the related acts. Two examples: (1) images of war are brought home to our location to support notions of protectionism from a common enemy, and the authority of that use binds us together in ways that support increased scrutiny over our daily lives and authorized violence "at home"; and, (2) surveillance tapes of store robberies and police mugshots are incessantly republished and replayed in local news coverage of disorder—and perceived disorder—with little information about what we are actually seeing, what happened before, during, and after the footage, or what appears outside of the frame, both in terms of vantage point and time (see discussion, below).[25]

Harold Lasswell writes that media systems have long held a tradition of enacting a "communication process in society" that performs three media control functions within surveillance. These functions operate to further embed into our daily lives a naturalized and shared purpose of surveillance, and they are:

- Conducting surveillance of societal environments that identify threats to a local community and the values of said community that may be challenged

- Providing correlations within society that are used to inform a response to the environment and challenges to the environment

- Transmitting "social inheritance" to future generations in terms of articulating and applying acceptable ideologies through mass media, literature, and culture[26]

In the 1960s, Charles Wright borrowed from Lasswell's articulations of how press surveil the social environment and added another function—to entertain—through which:

...the collection and distribution of information concerning events in the environment, both outside and within any particular society, this corresponding approximately to what is popularly conceived as the handling of news.

Additionally, Wright states, this approach to media surveillance identifies how the press:

- Transmit both information and interpretations of information as a means to prescribe "conduct in reaction" to events of the day

- Provide "warning and instrumental functions" in that news functions as a tool for helping inform audiences about ways to protect themselves from potential dangers, and simultaneously, to present the press as a key tool for the security and prosperity of society

- Assign "prestige" to those who inform themselves through mainstream press by casting them as well-informed, civically engaged, and of greater value to the masses[27]

Embedding the news with ethical and moral meanings that would be acceptable to this "well-informed" class is a crucial component of media messaging. Media "ethicizing" of a social condition or issue is an act of moral application by the press to reify social control over populations by applying moral codes in what and how the news is covered. In turn, social and cultural maintenance of news narratives that are familiar to dominant news audiences further aligns audience interaction with news text to reinforce the process of indoctrination to the power elite's ideological strengths and weaknesses. As a result, media surveillance—as it has been discussed here—serves as a function of human survival. Indeed, news-as-surveillance, writes Pamela Shoemaker, operates as such because of the public's: (1) "desire to receive and transmit information about the environment [that] is both biologically and culturally derived" and (2) because "biology and culture have [operated within society in ways that they have] had a profound impact on the form that news content has taken."[28]

Shoemaker continues by saying that because "[f]ear and anger," for instance, "could have interacted with early humans to stimulate the surveillance mechanism," biological reasons for communication focus on maintaining a safe environment and have transformed over time to serve as cultural functions of control. In that respect, the press perform surveillance on behalf of audiences, but the media surveillance that is being discussed in this chapter, while it might present the actions as being on behalf of the public, is in fact surveillance of the public *on behalf of* the power elite. In turn, news media have become a surveillance and control business, one that benefits from social and economic outcomes around which it revolves its very purposes of accessing information and its ability to create and distribute information and its interpretations to the public. Without access to gain, craft, and distribute information, as discussed in Chapter 1, news would not be able to partner with fellow power elite institutions with which to surveil. More specifically, without these partnerships, the press would be unable to perform its power functions in terms of applying violence as a means to control, which I further examine below.

Violence of media watching

Debate about uses, purposes, and the definitions of surveillance has become even more polemic and contentious in recent years as the global economy continues to demand investment and production of weapons for watching and for violence. In one sense, as mentioned above, surveillance can be seen as a means by which to protect from harm to individual lives, property, and collective ideologies, whereas others argue that surveillance is a threat to some of the very same things. The complexities of debating surveillance, in its normative sense, emerge when one asks: "Who is watching whom, and for what purpose?"[29]

Common interpretations of how we view one another in terms of access by which to understand and express power through surveillance is based on initial understandings of the "panopticon"—an architectural style of early prisons that maintained order through gazes of power and space. This approach ultimately contributed to Michel Foucault's articulation of power and surveillance in his work, such as in *Discipline and Punish* (see also Chapter 1).

Inside the panoptic prison, prisoners were placed within its spaces in ways that forced them to:

- Conduct self-discipline as a modern form of societal regulation of ideologies and behaviors

- "Supplant" forms of physical discipline by members of authority with self-discipline of coercion and brutality

- Emphasize classification of disorder and the disorderly through which power structures apply specific forms of punishment and meanings for specific categories of behavior[30]

In recent decades, the function and perspective of panopticism has been altered as scholars examine new processes and products of control and surveillance related to technological advancement and corresponding complications of how societies institute power, control, and punishment. Still, the most basic of Foucault's assumptions about the panoptic approach hold heavy weight, particularly in terms of how he describes processes of surveillance and, as Chapter 6 discusses, of sousveillance. Thomas Mathiesen describes the panopticon at these early stages, by writing that:

> [t]he life of the young prisoners is regulated by rules down to the most minute details, from the first drum roll in the morning, making the prisoners rise and dress in silence, through prayer, working hours, meals, education, rest, the washing of hands, the inspection of clothes, and finally order, silence and sleep ... [31]

Instead of identifying specific physical outcomes of punishment, this approach to discipline identifies social—and cultural—elements that have created a means by which people are expected to punish themselves through self-discipline (including repression) and punishments of which they place upon each other that extend beyond acts of formal, institutional control. Mathiesen, for instance, helps to identify the human element of self-punishment and citizen-on-citizen control by describing Foucault's explanation of panopticism as a process that leads to the "tortur(ing) of the body to the transformation of the soul."[32]

Therefore, I argue that media function to create a panoptic environment in which the public enjoys and participates in ideological acts of "waiting" and "watching," both of which hold the intent and issue the outcome of violence to support the positions and possibilities of the power elite. Media operate through a lens of watching that is rooted in a militarized presentation of news, entertainment, and cultural storytelling that provides a foundation of normalized violence with which journalists provide cultural explanations of the everyday. John Huxford writes that news visuals represent a "war of images" that empower news images to fulfill social functions of surveillance, of witnessing, and of spectatorship. Photojournalism presents a "truth" related to stories of the day that connect the viewer to the "decisive moment" of the photographer and places the viewer within that moment so that what's captured and shared with the public forms a bond of "watching" between the audience and the artifact. As Huxford writes:

[i]n surveillance, the content concentrates on information pertaining to the health and welfare, directly or indirectly, of the self, while the validity of the communication process rests on the observer adopting a position of trust or belief to the source.[33]

Meanings of news images rely on a sense of shared fear within the audience and the degree to which the images provide information of either security or danger. Even in images of social and civic participation such as voting in an election, of children playing in a park, of police giving teddy bears to children, there is a sense of pending doom that revolves around the scene, of *what could happen* if too much of the citizenry didn't vote, if our economy and environments were not maintained for the children to play in blissful ignorance, and if police were not deeply invested in our understandings of life. The image, then, and its related watching and witnessing is for those who are not able to be at a scene—bridging geographic divides and spaces of time in which the news media are awarded authority of meanings.

Verisimilitude engages the viewer as an eyewitness, herself, that leads her to feel as though she is seeing the event for herself. As a result, the viewer carries a sense of participating in history-in-the-making and contributes to the "seeing" of the event that will be paved for future generations (see Chapter 4). The live nature of the news image and message maintains that the witness/viewer/pseudo-eyewitness captures a moment in real-time and, in some cases, provides images in real-time designed to "(invite) the eyes of the voyeur, the curious gaze, or the fixed stare." Especially problematic, however, is that news audiences are—and have been since the beginning of information—bombarded with images of war and violence that blur the difference between visual representations and social explanations that appear in the news and those that are projected onto the movie screen.[34]

Media watching, which in the main is about providing explanation of an event or issue, functions as a form of entertainment that demands a confusion between content deemed news and content deemed, in its normative sense, entertainment media of popular culture. Producers of both media types depend on a similar application of simulacra that provide meaning to the images and explanations in ways that are then humanized and applied to the individual observer. Popular films such as *The Matrix* (1999) and *Minority Report* (2002), for example, explained to early digital technology users the means by which such technology can be employed as a form of social networking, economy, entertainment, and of individual compliance with its authority as a means to foreshadow what would be decades of technological innovation and incorporation. Indeed, these films focused on the potential (and real) "negative" effects of technology but in a way to maintain a sense of individual agency within the moral panic of a high-tech world, the meanings of which infringed on senses of "personal privacy" and added confusion with the possibilities for added individual security.[35]

In effect, these "popular" media artifacts and the processes of production surrounding them occur within a "watching" media, one that has waited for an event to unfold and maintains watch over potential threats to dominant explanations that have been outlined by the power elite. For example, dystopian films such as *Atlas Shrugged* (2011), *Total Recall* (2012), *The Hunger Games* (2012), *Dredd* (2012), *Elysium* (2013), *Ender's Game* (2013), *The Purge* (2013), *RoboCop* (2014), and *The Divergent Series: Insurgent* (2015) benefited at the box office because of the "reality" of the threats to modernity by effects of climate change, the failing economic model of capitalism, and the rise of authoritarianism in even the most "democratic" of nations that appear in daily presentations of news and personal experience.

A most striking example of the "realness" of popular culture media that functions to explain social conditions in a more "official" form of communication is the news related to the 2012 release of *Red Dawn*—a remake of a 1984 film of the same name in which Soviets parachuted into the Western United States as part of a major takeover. The 2012 version, however, told a story of a modern-day invasion of the United States by North Korea, which spoke specifically to growing tensions between the two nations since the early 2000s. As it turned out, however, the production—even more than the product—spoke to larger social and cultural tensions between the United States and other nations, particularly China.

Originally, the more recent *Red Dawn* producers intended to cast the Chinese military as the invading army but early on replaced them with North Korean armed forces so as not to threaten the political-economic ties between the United States and China and to further demonize a nation that US officials and businesses had attempted to ostracize from the world community because of its own form of "democratic" governance. Ironically, the news media followed a similar path of appeasing those with an interest in economic alignment with Chinese businesses when, in 2013, editors at Bloomberg News reportedly ordered their reporters who cover China "to tread carefully" or risk having editors "spik(e) stories deemed too sensitive out of fear that Beijing will make it impossible for [Bloomberg] to continue operating in the world's second-largest economy."[36]

Effects of military-industrial-media-entertainment complex

Entertainment associated with military violence and media coverage of such violence operates within a "military-industrial-media-entertainment complex," a system in which "made-for-TV wars and Hollywood war movies blur, military war games and computer video games blend, mock disasters and real accidents collide, producing on screen a new configuration of virtual power."[37]

Normalized media surveillance allows for news and entertainment media to "watch" and comment on itself through film and performance as a means to defuse any accusations of connections between on-screen representations of conflict and—in the case of *The Interview*, US-sanctioned assassination of another head of state, as discussed in Chapter 1—and news representations of a US-led overthrow of governments across the world.

The confusion that emanates from attempting to understand the correlations between entertainment and "real life" does no more than to reify a sense of "reality" in the messages and meanings that the two arenas present. In other words, both what is presented as news and what is presented as entertainment (though, as I have argued, they can be and are one and the same) carry the same meanings of American Exceptionalism, of capitalism as a God-delivered solution to all crises, and of violence as, when authorized by acceptable official means, a natural, acceptable, and rational response to conflict. These meanings are further reinforced in the normalization of "media violence" that appears in a sexual voyeurism within news media and are sold to the public in entertainment media as "blockbuster hits."

Here, too, we see film as indoctrination that requires financial investment on part of the viewer who once has entered into the imaginary world of the film's construction is able to safely and with distance of mixed realities, space, time, and physical freedom, experience visions of war that present a hero and a villain. These messages, the viewer will find, are rooted in hegemonic symbols of nationalism that are retold on the nightly newscast and in news rhetoric such as that which is built upon military explanations of violence similar to what appeared in the naming of "shock and awe" as the United States first entered Iraq with "calculated" devastation in 2003.

The press operate upon their presentations of history and their stories of today in ways that reflect this "military-industrial-media-entertainment complex" as a chosen ideology that shapes the way media watch events unfold—both at home and abroad. Through constant moral telling of events, presented to audiences by a watchful press, fellow institutions of the power elite take cues in how to properly respond to any challenges to dominant explanations of institutional action that might arise. And it is within this response to challenges that media move into a third process of media surveillance, that of "media shaming," which employs a disciplinary function of "media control."

MEDIA SHAMING: NORMALIZING "CORRECTION"-AS-CONTROL

If the power elite's media can appropriately identify the enemy to dominant ideology and instances in which the enemy acts against the power state— which I have argued is the purpose of both media watching and waiting— operations of discipline for the purposes of control can be initiated and, perhaps, these operations will hold an additional effect of "correcting" future misbehavior within the citizenry. Wishes for social correction and control today and *for tomorrow* is the primary function of media; indeed, the function of the news product is to align society to single interpretations of "naturalized" events, social action, and ideas through media-enforced punishment.

The media "walk of shame"

The history and purpose of the "perp walk"—when police escort a suspected or convicted "perpetrator" of crime past lines of press and public for mass viewing—has since its conception been a public form of punishment, and one that has constituted the attention of the press. Whereas a public court trial or a public hanging applies punishment at the hands of a clear authority, the perp walk, while planned and announced in advance, places the subject of the walk in a controlled space, often constrained in shackles and surrounded by authority. But the punishment isn't issued by the interaction with the space, restraints, or armed escorts; the punishment is in the "being watched" and the subsequent judgment of the public—and of the press. The punishment is in the "shaming" of the act. The *New York Post*—ironically, because like most mainstream press, participates in the perp walk—reported on the history of the "perp walk" while it also covered a string of high profile perp walks in 2011 in a piece titled "Innocent until perp walked":

> Though the origin is unclear, the perp walk is a descendant of other shame-inducing American spectacles such as the stockade and the scarlet "A"s adulterers were forced to wear — the difference, of course, being that the latter two were punishments visited upon the tried-and-convicted.[38]

Scholarship on public discipline indicates that the "perp walk" serves as punishment that relies upon at least three conditions—each of which helpful to identifying the act of "media shaming," which is discussed in this section, as punishment. In order for the walk to be effective public discipline, it must:

- Include harsh treatment in which physical force or depriving one of access to liberties is executed in *view of the public*

- Be in response to a *specific wrongdoing* of which the punishment is expressed as a consequence

- Be performed by "*appropriate*" authorities[39]

Especially concerning about this media "walk of shame"[40]—and its very core of effectiveness—is the degree to which the walk applies a sense of guilt upon the suspect who is walked. Since these events are announced ahead of time in communication between members of the court and of the police and of the press, the "perp walk" is an embedded, normal part of a court/police/press ritual so much so that journalists are not only aware of its pending occurrence but build their own routines around the event.

In effect, the "perp walk" serves as a means to appease the press—and the public—while also works to maintain the authority and legitimacy of the court system. The walk reminds the "public" that they, too, are involved in the capturing and scrutinizing of their fellow citizens and are brought into these acts through the processes of media waiting and watching so as to provide a shared sense of power in determining and applying punishment.

Media surveillance as shaming

At the root of media surveillance, watching is transformed into *media shaming*, the act of informally punishing through public displays of disapproval, including humiliation and immense unexpected exposure by the press. Without a larger societal structure and corresponding cultural norms that, together, justify public shaming—and shaming particularly by media, as journalists present themselves as acting outside of the authority of "official" acts of policing and punishment—public critique of citizens by reporters would be viewed as distasteful by news audiences. From this vantage point, the press—in collusion with other social and cultural authorities—cast meaning on the news event, reporting from the scene and republishing images and other forms of "journalistic evidence" of the event throughout future coverage.

And, just as the "perp walk" is presented by and through avenues of authority and normalcy, the press use the moment—and other moments of "watching"—to enact their own justice through rhetoric. While claiming "free speech" and "the public's right to know" about criminals—and alleged criminals—the press maintain such institutional rites as a form of social control and a maintenance of the power structure for market value, feeding a public and a media sphere dedicated to violence and public humiliation. As Jim Ruiz and D.F. Treadwell write:

> ... the news and entertainment media have fostered a conception of the police as rugged crusaders whose job is glamorous, tough, and often fraught with danger. With the perpetrator's (or "perp's") apprehension, the "crime-fighter" demonstrates his or her effectiveness and worth.[41]

Frequently enough, Ruiz and Treadwell note, the damage to one's reputation, safety, and future prosperity if convicted in the public's eye through events such as the "perp walk" and related discourse facilitated by the press (see coverage of The Boston Bombings suspects in Chapter 2) can manipulate the "justice" associated with the public's expectations for protection. Indeed, even if acquitted, or if the charges against the suspect are dropped or reduced, which occurs in many cases, the press rarely are able—or interested—in publishing the development. And, if they did, the level and length of discourse surrounding it would be threatening to the institutions who had indicted the suspect's guilt in the first place. Put simply, the institutions would, for one reason or another, appear to have had their power overturned and their judgments and actions brought into question.

But it is not enough to view "media shaming" as an unfortunate outcome of societal and institutional actions. Media shaming should be viewed for its intentions—to punish those who operated outside of the norm and to "correct" any future actions by individuals or collectives in society who *might act out*. Several acts of "disciplinary power" work to normalize the functions of social control through moments of media "naming and shaming." They are:

- Naming individuals who are to be shamed

- Announcing the act and the punishment to audiences in order to spread awareness of the issue and people to be shamed

- Applying language and narratives to individuals or collectives to be shamed that will create a public interest in extending shame[42]

In these acts, the press rely on fellow institutions within the "criminal justice system" to solidify easy access and interpolations of images and news about alleged delinquents, crimes, and related unapproved behaviors. Indeed, because the press has been an active institution in creating laws and regulations within the criminal justice system—such as helping form laws in some states that create legal standards for removing press cameras from courtrooms—the news media is an active participant in a prison industry that shapes "evidenced deviance."

The press, then, take these forms of evidence from their collaborations with the police and military to repurpose from just news to messages of social control. Law enforcement officials in Phoenix, Arizona, for instance, release video captured by jail cell cameras that are then broadcast over the internet as a means to publically shame inmates and to maintain behavior throughout society. Images of what it's like in jail, officials say, threaten potential troublemakers by showing the results of lawlessness. Through the release of these images—and accompanying press reporting about them—the consequences of unapproved acts are presented out of context, without any recognition of the social conditions or situations that led to any potential infractions. The power of these images lives within the public imaginaries of the crime *that could have been committed*.

The imagination, then, provides the commentary that demands viewers recognize the supreme authority of "the system" and that harnesses their desires to act otherwise, no matter the social circumstances of their experiences and the veracity of their (alleged) acts being "just." Furthermore, imaginations of the "reality" associated with this virtual shaming and punishment treat *all crimes* as equal and present the consequences of *all crimes* as potentially leading to incarceration.[43]

An even more popular form of media shaming that relies on police/press collaboration is the republishing of jail booking photographs—otherwise known as mug shots—on news websites, sometimes with captions that include the individual's name and initial charge. This free content—again provided under legal and rhetorical demands by the press for "the public's right to know"— appears in photo galleries where people can click to gaze upon the spectacle of violence and punishment and to allow their own imaginations to examine the potential events that led a person to have their image placed among detained deviants—sometimes with watermarks of the law enforcement agency that released the image stamped on their faces.

Whereas mug shots and basic information about local police calls and activity once sat in police blotter or logs that were reprinted, verbatim, in local news spreads, online galleries provide news audiences with an opportunity to employ a voyeuristic gaze. As of early 2015, for instance, the *Chicago Tribune* ran its galleries under the title, "Mugs in the news." The images that appear are associated with news stories that had been run about alleged crimes and police activity; a hyperlink connects the user to news articles about what the paper labels "Defendant," their "charge" listed. Faces correspond with charges of murder to the "unlawful delivery of cannabis" and appear under a disclaimer at the top of the webpage that hedges acknowledgment of the newspaper's responsibility in assigning meaning to the images and allegations against the subjects:

> Arrest and booking photos are provided by law enforcement officials. Arrest does not imply guilt, and criminal charges are merely accusations. A defendant is presumed innocent unless proven guilty and convicted.[44]

The *Tribune* is not alone in its use of mug shot shaming; it is actually a feature on news websites across the United States:

- The *Sun Herald*, which covers Biloxi and Gulfport, Mississippi, for instance, presents these photographs each week
- The *Eugene Daily News* in Eugene, Oregon, publishes them each day

- *The Post-Standard* out of Syracuse, New York, even provides a searchable database for citizens to find arrests[45]

And it is not just news media that capitalize on "public access" to mugshots. Placing them online is becoming big business, with non-news websites popping up across the country—and websites, even print formats, are now popular venues for user-produced artifacts of voyeurism and capitalism; in many cases, people whose mugs appear online must pay a fee to these private companies if they wish the images be removed from the sites.[46] Still, the normalization of these images throughout media—both in terms of news and of entertainment—provides validation that these images represent successful tactics of control and, when used in the press, present journalists as partners in crime-fighting in that they are posting their "catches" for a public spectacle of shaming.

Media shaming of "the ordinary"

"Media shaming" does not only apply to suspects of crime, nor does media shaming appear only in such overt connections to specific legal language and criminal proceedings. More often than not, the everyday shaming in which this project is interested appears in everyday news, in which the meanings related to the specific act deserving of punishment are embedded in banality. A reposted blog article published on Fort Lauderdale, Florida's, *Sun Sentinel* website, for instance—"Report: Teen wearing only bra and panties busted for DUI" (the headline states a video is included)—reveals not only the influence of the police state in providing content for the press (the video was recorded by a police officer's dash cam), but represents the desire to shame those which the public views, as in this case, as merely an opportunity to apply its hegemonic masculinity upon the female gender.

In this case, the suspect is not shamed for an alleged unlawful act of "driving under the influence," but for "being hot" and "stupid." In fact, this story was published with a tagline of "FloriDUH: WEIRD, WACKY, STRANGE, [sic] NEWS FROM THE SUNSHINE STATE," that also included a mugshot of the apparently white, eighteen-year-old woman who stated that she was merely returning home from work in Fort Pierce, Florida—more than hundred miles North of Fort Lauderdale—when she was pulled over.[47]

The 2013 video shows the light-haired teen in a long Shaquille O'Neal jersey, participating in a field sobriety test. Her jersey appears to barely reach below her behind, making it appear as though she is neither wearing shorts, nor—according to the discourse on multiple news websites (and even a few porn sites)—panties. As a result, the dashcam video, the woman's name, and commentary about her level of "hotness" appeared on local news websites across the United States, garnered attention from websites such as The Huffington Post, and was plastered on sites across the pond in the United Kingdom. It is a wonder that if designed neither to shame nor to provide a kind of soft porn for audiences why this video was of interest to so many news sites. It is a sexual pleasure of employing power of the gaze that alters the video and its meanings into multiple interpretations, all of which, however, revolve around the scantily clad young woman and her sex.

Another shaming news article, which gained national and international media attention in 2014, focused on the arrest of a man who couldn't fit into a police car after having been arrested for an alleged domestic disturbance. In this story, published by The Daytona Beach (FL) News-Journal and titled, "Deputies: Man arrested was too large for patrol car," the "6-foot-tall, 500-pound" man in Deltona, Florida, was said to have:

> ... resisted being handcuffed, then refused to walk out of the house using his weight against the deputies and falling to the floor.
>
> Deputies dragged Hendrix to the patrol car only to find out he was "too large to put in a patrol vehicle," they (the police officers) wrote in their reports.[48]

The story concludes with what charges were to be filed against the man; yet, despite the allegations that he had assaulted a woman earlier that night, the details of which were collected and distributed through the police report, there is little to wonder the degree to which the man would have made the paper—along with his jail mugshot—had he not been fat. This example reveals how the power elite and respective ideologies benefit from access to this free and authoritative news having been supplied by law enforcement officials to the degree that it ignored "domestic violence" as an acceptably common occurrence—so much so that the story wasn't about violence, but rather was about obesity. Indeed, the degree to which this story not only sets the standards for appropriate weight, it also shames others who may not fit such standards, beginning with the subject of the story.

The above examples represent the types of stories journalists are trained to capture, those supplied by the police or found in a courthouse that are focused on moments of gossip and innuendo that blocks the public from examining deeper the elements of social and cultural conflict inside daily news, which might reveal the acts of the power elite. In fact, I remember being trained at a newspaper in Wisconsin to stop by the police department each shift and sift through all of the printed arrest reports. We did so, of course, because such information is "public" and because the police were "required" by open-records laws to provide these reports. But we really did it to find arrests of local celebrities, popular names, or wacky stories.

This was "free news," after all, with little need to do our own reporting; we certainly did not seek to confirm information in these reports with the subjects of the arrest report (even though their contact information was most always listed). These pieces of news don't require obvious signs of journalistic verification to hold a sense of social authority. In addition to providing attribution to police records, these news briefs rely on the headline for immediate authority, applying symbols such as "Police:," "Report:," "Officials:," "Cops:," "Deputies:," "Police Chief:," "Officer:" to validate the report itself, to veil the journalists' interest in and ability to "make the news," and to be recognized as being aligned with legal and police forces that justified press punishment via shaming.

Kristy Hess and Lisa Waller examine the role of media shaming of "ordinary people" and argue that while there has been a long history of shaming public officials and celebrities in Western press systems, today's websites—including YouTube and LiveLeak—aggregate videos from across the world to showcase behaviors, events, and personalities that are deemed to occur outside of the ordinary, leaving a "lasting mark of shame." And while media shaming is not always associated with formal policing, I argue, institutions of the power elite, including the press, operate in unison at times of shaming to:

- Release similar messages of what is to be shamed
- Verify the legitimacy of the shaming process itself
- Authorize and expand shaming through society related to gender, race, and "undesirable" behavior
- Identify approved targets of shaming[49]

In return for these actions—particularly once specific targets for shaming are identified within media—journalists, police, and authorized punishers receive public permission to seek discipline through shame, which, as a further result, creates a public call and validation for violence against targets that move beyond punishments of shame to physical assault and murder (see Chapter 6). In this chapter's final section, I examine the role of media surveillance as punishment, particularly through shaming.

CONCLUSION: MEDIA SURVEILLANCE AS PUNISHMENT

Media surveillance, through the act of "media shaming," was applied as punishment in clear form during the 2013 court trial of neighborhood watchman George Zimmerman. Zimmerman was prosecuted for the murder of Trayvon Martin in Sanford, Florida, the previous year—the details of which attracted public and press attention across the nation as discourse about "racism" emerged in a moment of cultural distraction from the processes through which racism is formed, maintained, and distributed. News coverage focused on shaming blacks for stigma associated with "ghetto culture" and press involvement and physical presence cast the story within explanations of "urban memory" (see Chapter 4) that was intended, I argue, to shame entire communities of black folk in the United States through the intense shaming of one particular black woman—the last person to have spoken with Martin before he died and who found herself on trial for her "devious blackness."

Shaming "black culture"

Press "watching" of the trial—as was the case with "media waiting" up to the trial—focused on the alleged actions of Zimmerman, a white Hispanic who was charged with shooting and killing Martin, a black seventeen-year-old, at an apartment complex near Orlando, Florida. Zimmerman, a pseudo-police officer (he was a self-described local "neighborhood watchman") thought Martin was going to harm him and, he said, shot out of fear for his life. News that Zimmerman might not think favorably toward US blacks and questions related to the degree to which Martin was considering or was even capable of killing Zimmerman, contributed to protests across the United States to bring attention to the value of black lives.

In fact, the Martin case reappeared in national and local media in 2014 during coverage and protests surrounding the death of Michael Brown, mentioned earlier in this book, and the police-involved death of another black man, forty-three-year-old Eric Garner in Staten Island, New York, in July 2014. Even more protests occurred in 2015 related to other murders of black men by police.[50] In Garner's case, two white, local police officers approached him for allegedly illegally selling cigarettes. When Garner became vocal about what he claimed was harassment, a police officer placed Garner in a "chokehold" or "headlock" (debate about which "hold it was" continues), and Garner went limp; he died later at a hospital. A grand jury failed to indict the officer who many claimed had applied undue force. To complicate matters, the events that had led to Garner's death were recorded by a nearby citizen, the video was widely shared via mainstream press and influenced the popular hashtag #ICantBreathe, which was used in protests about police violence throughout 2014 and 2015. Garner can be heard on the recording telling officers, "I can't breathe," as he was pressed into the sidewalk.

Racialized shaming of Trayvon Martin had appeared throughout much coverage leading to the trial, with journalists discussing his possible "gangsta ways" and his record of bad behavior. But the most effective way to shame an entire group of people is to find a scapegoat, to take on the stereotype of disorder not through a direct attack against a dead man but against someone who can be cast as being too stupid to defend herself in the harsh limelight of public ridicule. Certainly, characterizations that clouded rosy pictures of Martin as a harmless young man appeared in local and national media throughout the United States, but only contributed to a more direct moment of media shaming involving Rachel Jeantel, a nineteen-year-old Miami woman of Haitian and Dominican descent who was reportedly the last person Martin spoke with, besides Zimmerman, before his death. Jeantel had been on the phone with Martin when he was attacked and was to be an early and important witness for the prosecution to recall what she heard in relationship to the incident between Zimmerman and Martin in which, Jeantel would testify, Zimmerman continued to pursue Martin in the dark of the night, even though Zimmerman said he was afraid that Martin could hurt him.

Jeantel became something more than a witness to anything related to the Martin murder when defense attorney Don West, on cross-examination, questioned her about what she heard Martin say about Zimmerman during their interaction that night. On one day of testifying, the press focused on Jeantel's physical presence and her mannerisms, her life experience and her language, based, in large part, on the fact that she was of a darkskin color, spoke in broken Standard American English, and had been friends with a young black man, Martin, who had been cast in the press as deviant and from a "ghettoized" background.

Indeed, from the beginning of the trial (and the weeks leading up to it as the media "waited"), press coverage of Zimmerman's actions that night and in his role as a neighborhood watchman—including multiple phone calls he had made and that were played in the courtroom in which he is heard asking "for police to come to his subdivision and check on suspicious strangers, often black"—was diminished in relationship to discussions of Martin's "black culture."[51]

During her testimony, Jeantel became the subject of racialized tension between her and West, particularly in the moment when the two were discussing Martin's interaction with Zimmerman:

WEST: At that point, he [Martin] decided to approach this man [Zimmerman] and say, "Why are you following me?"

JEANTEL: Yes, sir.

WEST: And he [Martin] could have just run home if he wasn't there.

JEANTEL: He was already by his house, he told me.

WEST: Of course, you don't know if he was telling you the truth or not.

JEANTEL: Why he need to lie about that, sir?

WEST: Maybe if he decided to assault George Zimmerman, he didn't want you to know about it.

JEANTEL: That's real retarded, sir.

UNIDENTIFIED VOICE: I'm sorry?

JEANTEL: That's real retarded to do that, sir. When you don't know the person, why a person—Trayvon did not know him.

WEST: OK.[52]

In such transactions, Jeantel became a benefit to Zimmerman's case, in part, because of confusion between her and West in terms of their language, positions of power, and intentions for her testimony. Immediately, the media story of the day was that the witness called to testify in the Martin murder trial was illiterate, black, overweight, and deviant—elements of "niggerized ghettoness."

Of particular interest to West—and to the press—was that on the phone with Jeantel, Martin had reportedly called Zimmerman "a creepy-ass cracker" who had been following him through the apartment complex. Jeantel testified that Zimmerman approached Martin and engaged in violence. The testimony did not go as the prosecution might have expected (though there is some credence to the idea that the prosecution designed a case that was meant to fail) when press coverage of Jeantel became about shaming her via the presentation of white righteousness that was upset because of Jeantel's degree of "blackness."

Watching white hostility

On the third day of testimony (June 27), press reports smacked of missing context related to the interactions between West and Jeantel that positioned him as a hostile white man and her as an "Angry Black Woman" and a dullard, a project of "the ghetto." At issue between the two was a letter that Jeantel said she had written to Martin's mother in which Jeantel described the last phone call she had had with the young man. But it was also a letter that Jeantel said she couldn't read, because it was written in cursive. As it turned out, Jeantel admitted that she hadn't written the letter herself but had dictated for someone else to write. As one TV station reported, Jeantel had "admitted to lying about being in the hospital during Martin's funeral and lying about her age to try to avoid telling her story to Martin's family and the public."

Furthermore, the headline to one online article characterized the interactions as such: "Witness gets combative with defense attorneys in Zimmerman trial;" a television station out of Louisville, Kentucky, published a story from ABC News titled, "George Zimmerman witness can't read letter she 'wrote' about shooting" in which Jeantel was shamed for expressing her struggles with reading as the defense attorney attempted to paint Jeantel as a liar and an unreliable witness. The TV station reported the story this way:

> A teenage friend of Trayvon Martin was forced to admit today in the George Zimmerman murder trial that she did not write a letter that was sent to Martin's mother describing what she allegedly heard on a phone call with Martin moments before he was shot.
>
> In a painfully embarrassing moment, Rachel Jeantel was asked to read the letter out loud in court.
>
> "Are you able to read that at all?" defense attorney Don West asked.
>
> Jeantel, head bowed, eyes averted whispered into the court microphone, "Some but not all. I don't read cursive."
>
> It sent a hush through the packed courtroom.
>
> Jeantel, 19, was unable to read any of the letter save for her name.
>
> Jeantel was subdued on the stand today, in contrast to her openly hostile demeanor towards Zimmerman's lawyers on Wednesday. Her behavior was so different that defense lawyer Don West asked Jeantel, "You seem so different from yesterday. I'm just checking, did someone talk to last night about your demeanor in court?"
>
> Jeantel replied that she had gotten some sleep.[53]

Who crafted the letter was less the story, though, than the way West—and the press—"ghettoized" Jeantel through hostility that presented her response to disrespect and arrogance as that of the "Black Bitch" archetype. As John Rickford writes on the blog "Language Log":

> On talk shows and social media sites, people castigated her "slurred speech," bad grammar and Ebonics usage, or complained that, "Nobody can understand what she's saying."
>
> ...
>
> But a lot more involved grotesquely racist, misogynistic and dehumanizing attacks on this young woman, devoid of any sensitivity to

the fact that she was testifying about the murder of a friend she had known since elementary school, and that she was racked by guilt that she'd been been talking to him by cell phone moments before he died but couldn't prevent his murder.

Another, eager to demonstrate that ignorance and viciousness were equal opportunity traits, fumed that: "She has to be the most, ignorant, ghetto, uneducated, lazy, fat, gross, arrogant, stupid, confrontation Black bitch I've ever seen in my fucking life. Yes, I said it ... and I'm Black."

Not everyone was this negative, fortunately. In TV appearances and in a commentary on Times.com [sic], linguist John McWhorter explained that Jeantel's "Black English ... has rules as complex as the mainstream English of William F. Buckley." I tried to do the same in a short segment on the National Public Radio program, Here and Now. But you'll notice from the comments on these sites that we both attracted critics and detractors.[54]

Yet another archetype constructed around Jeantel was that of "Stupid Black Kid" that made Jeantel out to be a caricature representative of public sentiments related to the failings of "urban areas" to produce desirable citizens, particularly in terms of developing "proper" language. As Hal Boedeker, a media critic for the *Orlando Sentinel* in Florida (located about 30 miles from Sanford) wrote on June 27 in his story, titled "Strangest show in TV":

The 19-year-old was talking to friend Trayvon Martin shortly before he was fatally shot by Zimmerman in Sanford. On the witness stand Wednesday, Jeantel gave conflicting answers, acknowledged lies and acted combative with defense attorney Don West.

She supplied bizarre, original drama to the high-profile trial. In years of watching legal dramas, have you seen anything quite like Jeantel's testimony? Jeantel ensured that this trial will be studied for decades to come.

Boedeker also wrote that on CNN's Anderson Cooper's evening show how commentator Sunny Hostin—who "described Jeantel as 'a credible witness' who was raw and uncoached"'—was countered by commentator Jeffrey Toobin who said Jeantel was "'compelling, even if you couldn't understand half of what she said.'" The *Sentinel's* article ended by stating that the trial could be "memorable TV. Wednesday afternoon certainly was .... You will want to save the tape."[55]

Local and national press alike attacked Jeantel with a consistent reference to race relations in the United States; yet, the press response was not such just because West was white and aggressive (some would temper this by saying he was merely assertive, as any lawyer would be on cross-examination). The press responded as they did because of the power with which Jeantel resisted white power and white arrogance. When West questioned Jeantel's ability to understand English, for instance, she said that she often did not understand what West was trying to ask—a moment in which Jeantel revealed her ability to know when she was being coopted and railroaded, her words and stories being complicated in order to confuse her.

West went on the attack:

> WEST: Are you claiming in any way that you don't understand English?
> JEANTEL: I don't understand you, I do understand English.
> WEST: When someone speaks to you in English, do you believe you have any difficulty understanding it because it wasn't your first language?
> JEANTEL: I understand English really well.[56]

Unable to adequately explain this and similar exchanges between the two in ways that did not reveal the order of White Supremacy over the criminal justice system, the press struck back against Jeantel's resistance to white power and white arrogance with "shame" associated, in the view of the press, with being black. White arrogance also made itself apparent during the trial when West took some flack after his daughter posted a selfie of her, her sister, and him eating vanilla ice cream cones from a local restaurant drivethru with the statement, "We beat stupidity celebration cones #zimmerman #defense #dadkilledit." The post included emoticons of a party horn with confetti, a vanilla ice cream cone, and a smiley face, though the West family contended that the image was not related to the father's grilling of Jeantel.[57]

Insight related to the exchange between West and Jeantel that mainstream (white) press couldn't—or opted not to—provide, BET prepared a clear assessment of the complications in ways that should have schooled mainstream media. Some major statements included:

- ... (Jeantel's) time on the stand was so protracted because defense attorney Don West constantly asked her to repeat herself, to talk slowly, as if he were seeking to understand the language of an alien from another planet.

- The daughter of Haitian and Dominican immigrants, Jeantel's first language was Creole. She later picked up English and has clearly become conversant in the language of urban Miami. But West continued to speak to her as if she were some outlandish extraterrestrial rather than a teenager.

- (West) asked her about the expressions used in "your culture," as though teenagers of all races don't have their own linguistic idiosyncrasies.

- Jeantel is a teenager who has been thrust into an extraordinary situation. She is a star witness in one of the most highly watched trials in modern times, testifying about a phone call with a friend who was killed shortly after their telephone conversation.

- (Jeantel) never hid who she was or how she felt. Clearly she was reluctant and displeased about being there.[58]

In the end, the press performed its punishment duties through shaming people for their perceived "blackness" as a means by which to identify undesirable citizens and behaviors and to reify the authority and purpose of police, legal justifications of examination and punishment, and the role of the press in "covering" events and providing meanings. Having drawn a landscape for understanding the role and function of media surveillance, the next chapter argues for a sense of media sousveillance—the watching of society by societal members of the power elite to issue moments of power, control, and violence—that aligns the press with the institutional aims and actions of the police.

Discussion Questions

1. What press acts might *not* be considered surveillance, and how might *these acts* operate outside of the lens of surveillance, as defined in this chapter?
2. To what degree does "media shaming" function as discipline, and how can one measure the impact of such punishment?

Notes

1   Marian Meyers, "African American women and violence: Gender, race, and class in the news," *Critical Studies in Media Communication* 21, no. 2 (2004): 102; For more recent coverage of Freaknik, see Nedra Rhone, "300,000 hit streets, but cops keep activities under control," *The Atlanta Journal-Constitution*, April 19, 2010; Megan Matteucci, "Freaknik throng hardly parties," *The Atlanta Journal-Constitution*, April 18, 2010; Nedra Rhone, "Freaknik: A new day or blast from the past?," *The Atlanta Journal-Constitution*, April 17, 2010.

2   Robert E. Gutsche, Jr. and Moses Shumow, "NO OUTLET: A critical visual analysis of neoliberal narratives in mediated geographies," *Visual Communication* forthcoming; Moses Shumow and Robert E. Gutsche, Jr., *News, Neoliberalism and Miami's Fragmented Urban Space* (Lanham, MA: Lexington, forthcoming); Moses Shumow and Robert E. Gutsche, Jr., "Urban policy, press & place: City-making in Florida's Miami-Dade County," *Journal of Urban Affairs* forthcoming; See discussion of hip-hop and rap music genres in Chapter 4 of Robert E. Gutsche, Jr., *A Transplanted Chicago: Race Place and the Press in Iowa City* (Jefferson, NC: McFarland, 2014).

3   A shooting in 2007 on South Beach around the time of Urban Beach Week, which included the rapper Fat Joe, also gained media attention and contributed to local memory about violence and the event.

4   Lauren Pastrana, "Exclusive look at Urban Beach Week security measures," miami.cbslocal.com, May 21, 2013, http://miami.cbslocal.com/2013/05/21/ exclusive-look-at-urban-beach-week-security-measures.

5   Hannah Sampson and Evan S. Benn, "With Art Basel crowds about to descend, Miami businesses rush to open," *Miami Herald*, November 30, 2014.

6   Charles Rabin, "Grafitti 'tagger' dies after being hit by Miami police car," *Miami Herald*, December 5, 2014, http://www.miamiherald.com/news/local/ crime/article4296547.html.

7   Audra D.S. Burch, "Urban Beach Week brings revelry, revives dialogue," *Miami Herald*, May 29, 2010; See also, David Smiley, "Urban Beach Week's hard-partying crowds have Miami Beach police on alert," *Miami Herald*, May 29, 2010.

8   David Ovalle, "Most records in Miami Beach Urban Beach Week police shooting to remain secret," *Miami Herald*, April 3, 2013; David Ovalle and Evan S. Benn, "Autopsy: Man killed by Miami Beach police on Memorial Day 2011 shot 16 times," *Miami Herald*, May 8, 2013; see also, Evan S. Benn, "Miami Beach police to business owners: We are ready for Urban Beach Week," *Miami Herald*, May 8, 2013.

9   Christina Vega and Evan S. Benn, "Miami Beach residents, businesses, police brace for Memorial Day crush," *Miami Herald*, May 22, 2013.

10 Ibid.

11 Ibid.

12 Ibid.

13 Personal correspondence, May 22, 2014. My agreement to republish the image restricts me from sharing even the original image online. I am amicable to sharing the screenshot via email, upon request.

14 Hannah Sampson and Chabeli Herrera, *Miami Herald*, May 24, 2013.

15 Marc Caputo, Dorothy Atkins, and Christina Vega, *Miami Herald*, May 25, 2013.

16 Evan S. Benn, Chabeli Herrera, and Michael Vasquez, *Miami Herald*, May 26, 2013.

17 Chabeli Herrera, Evan Benn, and Glenn Garvin, *Miami Herald*, May 27, 2013.

18 William G. Staples, *Everyday Surveillance: Vigilance and Visibility in Postmodern Life* (Lanham, MA and Plymouth, UK: Rowman & Littlefield, 2014),2.

19 Zygmunt Bauman and David Lyon, *Liquid Surveillance* (Cambridge, UK and Malden, MA: Polity Press, 2013), vi.

20 Charles R. Wright, "Functional analysis and Mass Communication," *The Public Opinion Quarterly* 24, no. 2 (1960): 614–615.

21 Daniel Byman, "Why drones work," *Foreign Affairs* (July/August 2013): 32–43; See also, Medea Benjamin, *Drone Warfare: Killing by Remote Control* (London and New York: Verso, 2013).

22 Josh Lauer, "Surveillance history and the history of new media: An evidential paradigm," *New Media & Society* 14, no. 4 (2011): 579, emphasis added.

23 Ibid., 579.

24 Jack Lule, "War and its metaphors: News language and the prelude to war in Iraq, 2003," *Journalism Studies* 5, no. 2 (2004): 179–190; See also, Alfred McCoy, "Surveillance and scandal: Time-tested weapons for US global power," truth-out.org, January 20, 2014, http://www.truth-out.org/news/item/21332-surveillance-and-scandal-time-tested-weapons-for-us-global-power; Richard A. Clarke, *Against All Enemies: Inside America's War on Terror* (New York: Free Press, 2004).

25 Lily Hay Newman, "LAPD body cams will automatically start recording when police use Tasers," slate.com, January 8, 2015, http://www.slate.com/blogs/future_tense/2015/01/08/the_lapd_is_ordering_more_than_3_000_smart_tasers_that_will_activate_body.html; Marie Gillespie, "Security, media and multicultural citizenship: A collaborative ethnography," *European Journal of Cultural Studies* 10, no. 3 (2007): 275–295; Karen Qureshi, "Shifting proximities: News and 'belonging-security,'" *European Journal of Cultural Studies* 10, no. 3 (2007): 294–310.

26 Harold Lasswell, "Structure and function of communication in society," in *The Communication of Ideas*, edited by L. Bryson (New York: Institute for Religious and Social Studies, 1948), 37–51.

27 Wright.

28 Pamela J. Shoemaker, "Hardwired for news: Using biological and cultural evolution to explain the surveillance function," *Journal of Communication* 46, no. 3 (1996): 33, 36.

29 Gordon Fletcher, Marie Griffiths, and Maria Kutar, "A day in the digital life: A preliminary sousveillance study," SSRN, http://papers.ssrn.com/sol3/papers.cfm?abstractid=1923629; For more, see http://www.whoiswatchingwho.com.

30 David Lyon, "The search for surveillance theories," in *Theorizing Surveillance: The Panopticon and Beyond*, edited by David Lyon (Devon, UK and Portland, OR: Willan, 2006), 3.

31 Thomas Mathiesen, "The viewer society: Michel Foucault's 'panopticon' revisited," *Theoretical Criminology* 1, no. 2 (1997): 216.

32 Ibid., 216.

33 John Huxford, "Surveillance, witnessing and spectatorship: The news and the 'war of images,'" *Proceedings of the Media Ecology Association* 5 (2004): 5.

34 Ibid., 5–7; see also, Jan Mieszkowski, *Watching War* (Stanford, CA: Stanford University Press, 2012).

35 For an analysis of blockbuster hits *Selma, Citizenfour and American Sniper*, see Henry A. Giroux, "Hollywood heroism in the age of empire," truth-out.org, February 18, 2015, http://www.truth-out.org/news/item/29175-hollywood-heroism-in-the-age-of-empire-from-citizenfour-and-selma-to-american-sniper.

36 Russ Fischer, "More MGM Fallout: Red Dawn Delayed, Perhaps Indefinitely?," June 10, 2010, http://www.slashfilm.com/more-mgm-fallout-red-dawn-delayed-perhaps-indefinitely; Daniel Politi, "Report: Bloomberg News spikes stories that could anger China," slate.com, November 9, 2013, http://www.slate.com/blogs/the_slatest/2013/11/09/bloomberg_news_reportedly_spikes_china_stories.html.

37 James Der Derian, *Virtuous War: Mapping the Military-Industrial Media-Entertainment Network* (New York and London: Westview Press, 2009), xxvii.

38 Maureen Callahan, "Innocent until perp walked," *New York Post*, May 22, 2011.

39 Bill Wringe, "Perp walks as punishment," *Ethic Theory Moral Pract* (2014), doi: 10.1007/s10677-014-9545-5, emphasis mine.

40 The double entendre that "walk of shame" is often used to describe a gendered (often female) walk "home" after "spending the night" elsewhere is not lost on me. And while I wish to use the term as I do in this project, I do not mean to add credence to the dominant definition as a derogatory word related to women—or men. See, http://en.wikipedia.org/wiki/Walk_of_shame.

41 Jim Ruiz and D.F. Treadwell, "The perp walk: Due process v. freedom of the press," *Criminal Justice Ethics* (Summer/Fall 2002): 45.

42 Jacob Rowbottom, "To punish, inform, and criticise: The goals of naming and shaming," in *Media and Public Shaming: Drawing the Boundaries of Disclosure*, edited by Julian Petley (London and New York: I.B. Tauris, 2013), 1.

43 Mona Lynch, "Punishing images: Jail Cam and the changing penal enterprise," *Punishment & Society* 6, no. 3 (2004): 255–270.

44 "Mugs in the news," *Chicago Tribune*, January 12, 2015, http://galleries.apps.chicagotribune.com/chi-mugs-in-the-news.

45 See, http://www.syracuse.com/crime/police-blotter; http://eugenedailynews.com/c/news/news-mugshots; http://www.sunherald.com/2015/01/11/6011927/south-mississippi-mugshots-for.html.

46 David Kravets, "Mug-shot industry will dig up your past, charge you to bury it again," wired.com, August 2, 2011, http://www.wired.com/2011/08/

mugshots; Thom Goolsby and Tim Moffitt, "Under scrutiny, mug shot publishing industry evolves," wral.com, June 24, 2014, http://www.wral.com/under-scrutiny-online-mugshot-industry-evolves/13756083.

47 "Kristen Forester, wearing only bra and panties, busted for DUI: Police (VIDEO)," The Huffington Post, November 8, 2013, http://www.huffingtonpost.com/2013/11/08/kristen-forester-bra-and-panties-dui-video_n_4240127.html; Barbara Hijek, "Report: Teen wearing only bra and panties busted for DUI | Video," sun-sentinel.com, November 8, 2013, http://articles.sun-sentinel.com/2013-11-08/news/sfl-flduh-bra-and-panties-dui-20131107_1_bra-undies-teen; "Kristen Forester arrested for DUI wearing ONLY panties and bra," georgianewsday.com, November 11, 2013, http://www.georgianewsday.com/news/regional/186533-kristen-forester-arrested-for-dui-wearing-only-panties-and-bra.html; "Florida teenager, 18, arrested for drunk driving wearing ONLY her panties and bra," *Daily Mail*, November 11, 2013, http://www.dailymail.co.uk/news/article-2501172/Kristen-Forester-arrested-DUI-wearing-ONLY-panties-bra.html.

48 Patricio G. Balona, "Deputies: Man arrested was too large for patrol car," *The Daytona Beach News-Journal*, October 20, 2014.

49 Kristy Hess and Lisa Waller, "The digital pillory: Media shaming of 'ordinary' people for minor crimes," *Continuum: Journal of Media & Cultural Studies* 28, no. 1 (2014): 101–111; Rachel Cooke, "So you've been publically shamed and is shame necessary?" *The Guardian*, March 15, 2015; Kelly McBride, "Journalism and public shaming: some guidelines," poynter.org, March 11, 2015, http://www.poynter.org/news/mediawire/326097/journalism-and-public-shaming-some-guidelines. For more on the disciplinary function of the news in relationship to institutions and journalistic practice, see Teun A. van Dijk, *News as Discourse* (New York and London: Routledge, 2009), specifically Chapter 1; and discussion of the "lexical style of news" in Chapter 2.

50 See the video here: http://www.theguardian.com/us-news/video/2014/dec/04/i-cant-breathe-eric-garner-chokehold-death-video.

51 That he was wearing a "hoodie" sweatshirt, for instance, became a symbol of his "urban" deviance.

52 "Trayvon Martin described 'creepy-ass cracker' in final moments," wtxl.com, June 26, 2013, http://www.wtxl.com/news/florida_news/trayvon-martin-described-creepy-ass-cracker-in-final-moments/article_1cb153aa-dea8-11e2-b5d5-0019bb30f31a.html; see transcript and discussion at http://www.democracynow.org/2013/6/28/at_zimmerman_murder_trial_defense_tries.

53 "George Zimmerman witness can't read letter she 'wrote' about shooting," whas11.com, June 27, 2013, http://www.whas11.com/story/news/local/2014/10/14/15782678; WFTV, "Witness gets combative with defense attorneys in Zimmerman trial," wftv.com, June 26, 2013, http://www.wftv.com/news/news/local/judge-may-rule-calls-first-eyewitness-testifies-zi/nYWXq.

54 John Rickford, "Rachel Jeantel's language in the Zimmerman trial," Language Log, July 10, 2013, http://languagelog.ldc.upenn.edu/nll/?p=5161. Cites from within the selected text: http://hereandnow.wbur.org/2013/06/28/n-word-language and http://ideas.time.com/2013/06/28/rachel-jeantel-explained-linguistically. For more on the "Black Bitch," see Meyers, "African American women and violence."

55 Hal Boedeker, "George Zimmerman trial: Strangest show in TV," *Orlando Sentinel*, June 27, 2013.

56 See John McWhorter, "Rachel Jeantel explained, linguistically," ideas.time.com, June 28, 2013, http://ideas.time.com/2013/06/28/rachel-jeantel-explained-linguistically.

57 Lisa Lucas and Corky Siemaszko, "Trayvon Martin trial: Daughter of defense lawyer posts odd Instagram after another day of gripping testimony," *New York Daily News*, June 29, 2013, http://www.nydailynews.com/news/national/trayvon-martin-straddling-george-zimmerman-confrontation-neighbor-article-1.1385077.

58 Jonathan P. Hicks, "Commentary: A witness for Trayvon who stands her ground," bet.com, June 27, 2013, http://www.bet.com/news/national/2013/06/27/commentary-a-witness-for-trayvon-who-stands-her-ground.html.

6

The Violence of Media Sousveillance: Identifying the Press as Police

Chapter Purpose

This chapter implicates the press as being a member of a larger social and cultural police force. Identifying relationships between police and the press contributes to the book's overarching purpose of challenging the traditionally reductive notion of the journalistic community as being a collective with distinct, if even fluid at times, boundaries that exclude direct influences on the news from the outside. To begin, my analysis of news coverage of press and public calls for an increased police presence in Miami Gardens, Florida, during a time of increased "black-on-black" violence—even when the police were secretly recorded snooping through a private business and harassing its patrons—explicates the ideological function of "police myth" that maintains police (and its partner, the press) have natural authority to institute and maintain order.

Guiding Questions

1. How is it possible that the press, in its capacity as a "watchdog" of social institutions, could share the same interpretive community as the institutions it is said to monitor?
2. In what ways do popular media and scholarship describe institutional relationships between the press and police?

Key Terms

Inverse Surveillance: The observation of behavior and ideologies of self and of and within a collective

Media Sousveillance: A form of inverse surveillance enacted by media upon themselves and partners within the power elite, performed to identify ideological disjuncture and to perform paradigm maintenance

Police Myth: An ideology that police are awarded as a natural right to "serve" the public through methods deemed effective and necessary

Virtuous War: The technical capability and ethical imperative to threaten and, if necessary, actualize violence from a distance—with no or minimal casualties

---

POLICE MYTH: MEDIA ADOPTION OF POLICE POWER

Residents and city officials in Miami Gardens, Florida, spent much of the summer and fall of 2013 attempting to understand and to address gun violence that had claimed some twenty-five lives in 2012 and another twenty-three in 2013—ten of which occurred within eleven days in October of that year. The shootings—which took the life of a twelve-year-old girl in late 2013 who was inside her grandmother's house while getting her hair done for school when bullets flew into the home, hitting her in the head—was cast in public and press discourses as "black-on-black" violence that was out of control and representative of the city's urban "blackness." News coverage of the violence in a city that was at the time 76 percent black was associated with racialized images of black families mourning their losses, black protestors rallying against crime, and connections with conversation about gangs.

News coverage did not involve black folk simply because of their numbers in the city; local journalism used the opportunity to paint Miami Gardens not as a black city but as a ghettoized one, ripe with disorder, gangs, innocence lost, and undesirables. Even in news coverage of the young girl's death, her mother identified her daughter as an innocent who needed to be presented as being separate from the dominant characterizations being made about the city and its people. "I want to clear the air on this issue," she told a local TV station.[1] "My daughter tequila [sic] was not a gang member. She was an innocent bystander." But something needed to be done, no matter the causes for disorder, residents and officials agreed, and with the violent language of the press that reified the authority and virtue of local police as being central to the solution.

One *Miami Herald* article from July 27, 2013, for instance, about the "teary, spiritually rousing funeral service" of a seventy-year-old minister and her twenty-year-old grandson who had been killed earlier in the month at their home failed to serve the purpose set forth by its headline—"With tears, community mourns for murdered minister, grandson"—by turning to a tale of police authority in solving local crime. The article stated that during the eulogy, the presiding pastor told the audience that "they caught the person" who was thought to have committed the murders but then, minutes later, clarified that he was mistaken. "They didn't apprehend them yet," the minister said, "but they know who they are." For the rest of the story, the newspaper focused on the efforts of the police, turning away from the lives that were being remembered at the funeral to celebrating the power of the police. Said Miami Gardens Police Detective Michael Wright: "What we're doing is monitoring this case very closely."[2]

By the end of 2013, even journalists were calling for increased policing throughout Miami Gardens, the idea being that more cops with more guns would reduce "gang activity" and any related vigilante behavior in one of Miami-Dade County's "ghettos." Police efforts were presented as the perfect solution—only if residents would comply with their efforts to gain law and order. Wrote one *Miami Herald* columnist in October:

> Miami Gardens police have stepped up efforts, but despite the rallies and tough talk, they still don't get enough meaningful community support. Not one person, for example, from the dozens of people at Bunche Park, where a child was one of four people shot in 2011, has been willing to come forward.
>
> The lack of involvement is so prevalent that the city installed Shot Spotter technology to alert them when gunshots are fired, partly because residents won't call police when they hear gunshots. And, insiders tell me, even residents active in Crime Watch who should know better remain silent until violence and death personally affect them.[3]

The media was also assigned—by those within its own ranks—a role to play in creating a safer city by adopting an active role of investigating crime, in one instance by examining the effectiveness of officials and police at keeping guns out of Miami-Dade schools, including those in Miami Gardens. In September 2013, for instance, the *Herald* interviewed their own reporter, David Smiley, about a report he had filed on the issue. Wrote one *Herald* reporter about the other:

> As the summer began, *Miami Herald* education writer David Smiley set out on a fact-finding mission. "Most of the time you don't hear if a gun is found in a school," he said. "We wanted to know 'What are local schools really dealing with?'"

Smiley requested all police reports from 2009 to 2012 involving gun-related incidents at all public schools in Miami-Dade and Broward, the fourth and sixth-largest school districts in the country, respectively. It took months to gather the information, then sift through the 200 cases to hone in on the incidents that involved guns inside schools or on school property.

It was a painstaking endeavor, a first-time effort to get a full picture of the problem locally.

. . .

Smiley's reporting found that 75 percent of the schools in Miami-Dade did not have a single gun-related incident during the last four years, a lower rate than some smaller Florida school districts. However, of the six schools that had five or more cases, all are clustered in Miami and Miami Gardens.

"Generally they are doing a good job of keeping guns out of school," he said. "And when they do find their way into schools, they have a good safety net of student and parent tipsters and aware teachers and police."[4]

And though the story went on to discuss that guns are found in schools— turning to an example from *a full three years prior* when a student in a Northwest Miami-Dade County school was found to have a .22 caliber gun and a hundred-some bullets that the student said he meant to sell in schools—the newspaper quoted *Herald* reporter Smiley once again to boost the efforts of police in keeping places safe, in this case, by saying that the police are "trying to do everything they can to keep guns out of school without turning schools into a vault."

Amid calls for increased policing in and throughout Miami Gardens in 2013 the people of Miami Gardens would receive a shock that November when local police officers were found to be some of the very same troublemakers in the city that the public wished to stop. A local convenience store owner released to the *Miami Herald* press surveillance videos that had been recorded for over the course of more than a year depicting Miami Gardens police officers harassing black patrons and snooping, without authorization, throughout the convenience store owner's office and his personal belongings. The news story emerged as the store owner prepared a legal case against the police department and as several residents emerged to discuss with the press their specific experiences with police harassment and racial profiling—not just at the convenience store but across the city.

As debate unfolded about the degree to which police were part of the city's disorder, both the press and police attempted to explain just how the same institution that had been endorsed as providing protection to the community could also be guilty of misdeeds. Throughout the discussion, press presentations of police explanations and their overarching role in the community held to mythical characterizations of the police as being just, vigilant, and innocent heroes. In other words, even as the *Miami Herald* released images from the store owner's surveillance cameras that showed police officers breaking their code to protect and to serve, local journalism pitted unacceptable forms of black/gang/urban crime and violence in Miami Gardens against acceptable violence and disorder of the police.

While some stories provided "flak" in the local media's propagandistic presentation of police misconduct, the overarching narrative that police—as an institution—could never do wrong formed a single story and explanation for what the police contribute to the community and how, in cooperation with the press, protect the community by maintaining watch over public and private efforts to stop "unacceptable" violence.

Therefore, whereas Chapter 5 examined how the press perform media surveillance—social monitoring with the intention of controlling behaviors, activities, and ideologies of individuals and collectives—here I wish to present media control's monitoring functions as a means by which to identify two specific elements of these cases examined in this chapter: (1) that the press function as police in maintaining forms of social surveillance of citizens and (2) that forms of media surveillance contribute to a validation of physical force—or threats of physical force—against citizens. At the core of these arguments is that even in times of "watchdogging," the press merely enact "flak" that presents ideological separation (or disjuncture) between the press and police without which would reveal their shared space within the power elite and support narratives of a virtuous police and press.

And, as I argued below, discourse surrounding disorder in Miami Gardens reveals a moment in which the myth of police exceptionalism was threatened, creating cultural trauma within not only the police community but within the press community in terms of the local power elite's ability to band together to protect the validity and legitimacy of the police and of the press. Here, then, I discuss the elements of press coverage of the Miami Gardens case to reveal the process of maintaining mythical representations of the police and—in turn—of the press within journalism that, when applied to other cases of cultural trauma, build an ideological and power connection between the press and police that cannot be broken.

Collaborating to create explanation

From early on in public calls for added protection throughout Miami Gardens, the press and police collaborated to provide authoritative explanations that additional police forces would curb crime and that this solution was not only in the public interest but would be supported—and even enacted—by the public itself. On August 1, the *Miami Gardens News* applied a singular, supportive tone for a 7–0 vote by the City Council to "adopt a No Tolerance Pledge for the City and residents," which was, in the words of the paper, "aimed at further reducing violence, illegal activities and promoting increased involvement in community programs."[5]

Assigning a sense of legitimacy to the local resolution, the paper used the full title of "No Tolerance Pledge" in its description of the act that had to do with "adopting"—not "applying"—a mandate that as presented in the press was to "promote peace and non-violence" with little mention of the corresponding police activity that would emerge as a means to "keep the peace."

The July 26 vote for the pledge, which was part of a "For the Children Sake Campaign," came along with a pledge that the Council voted to encourage homeowners to sign, a portion of which reads:

I am answering the call! I am taking a stand for a better Miami Gardens. I agree that we have lost too many of our children and family, to gun violence. I agree that too many of our children are at risk of dropping out of school, getting pregnant, or using drugs. I agree that too many of Miami Gardens residents are not activity involved in making our community better. I am joining the efforts to help save lives and transform our community. We all deserve a safe and peaceful place to live. We will work together to make our neighborhoods and community better. I will no longer tolerate these challenges in my community. I will do my part! I will take a stand For the Children Sake.

Among corresponding bullet points on the pledge for residents to sign is that they agree to non-violence solutions to local crime and to complying with an armed police force. By signing, residents stated that they would:

- Make a family commitment to non-violence and not be involved in illegal activities

- Make a commitment to solve issues in a non-violent way and get connected with groups and organizations that are providing positive alternatives and opportunities

- Speak Up and Step forward [sic] with information and make the commitment to work with the Miami Gardens Police Department to prevent and solve violent crimes

Problematic, however, was that while news articles stated that the city and its residents would now work "more closely with the Miami Gardens

Police Department to prevent and solve violent crimes" little in the press described just what that working relationship would entail. In fact, in August, the *Miami Gardens News*—a public-private partnership to present community news from the city government—made a similar report about the petition and the city's dedication to non-violent tactics to gain peace, stating that "City of Miami Gardens leaders and police have a stern message for bad guys: illegal activity, firearms and illicit drugs will not be tolerated in the City ...."[6]

As "proof" of the officials' ability to reinstate order (or at least order under the rule of police) after months of shootings, the story highlighted the work of Operation Smoking Gun III, what the publication called a "law-enforcement crack down" that included city police, the State Attorney's Office, the US Attorney's Office, and other federal and state agencies that had made sixteen arrests and issued federal charges against twenty-two people involved in drug and other crime ventures. Another eighty people were arrested for alleged drug and weapon violations. The data related to police power continued with a dramatic list of what the police collected from "bad guys":

> Police removed from the streets 248 firearms, including a sawed off shotgun, 342 grams of crack cocaine, and a host of powerful prescription drugs, more than 15-thousand grams of marijuana and five bullet proof vests.

Such quantitative data served as evidence of police power and complemented press language and press interpretation of crime and crime-solving that expressed to audiences what it takes to enforce order.

Details about the city's new "peace-keeping" initiative appeared in the *Herald* on August 2 and adopted language and explanations for the initiative that were consistent with local government officials; in fact, further coverage in the newspaper focused on proposals by city officials to increase taxes in an effort to "*help fund* the addition of 10 officers to the city's police force."[7] Coverage focused on police responses and intervention in violent crime throughout Miami Gardens over the next few months maintained a commitment to "acceptable" police violence and an increased police presence, with very little other coverage providing alternative efforts that would be as successful at curbing crime.

One October 12, 2013 article titled: "A city, a family fight to end cycle of violence" didn't read as a story about a family's efforts to end violence much at all, for example, but focused instead on (1) what the police were doing to "stop crime," (2) what residents "say" they are afraid of in their neighborhoods— "gang violence," mostly—as a means to create a single enemy, and (3) efforts by some in the city to host walks to promote non-violence but that, in the end, are cast as being unorganized, trivial, and ineffective. More than anything, instead of diving into the causes of the violence, the efforts and organizational practices of local residents to take action against violence, understanding the degree to which gangs may operate in the city beyond quantitative evidence from police agencies, and even talking with residents to address their assumed fears and proposed solutions, the *Herald* spoke broadly in terms of the "sense of fear and violence."[8]

Furthermore, in an effort to humanize the story that rationalizes journalists' ignoring of a story with deeper meanings, they turned to the family of the young girl, mentioned earlier in this chapter, to provide authority to the newspaper's interpretation and articulation of just who were "authorized knowers" of local values, culture, and meanings of what it takes to stop the violence and what types of organization (read organized police action) will save the city. The article reads:

> The presence of these gangs comes as no surprise to the mostly working class residents of Miami-Dade's third-largest city, where the rat-a-tat-tat of gunfire is known to shatter placid evenings.
>
> Cristal Forshee, 10, Tequila's younger sister, can matter-of-factly recite the names of the gangs in her Miami Gardens neighborhood. She knows which gang wears red bandannas, which one wears black bandannas. "I found out from people at school," said the fifth grader.
>
> Even as Miami Gardens police step up their efforts to tame the growing gang activity, city residents say these loosely organized groups—at least 14 known gangs of mostly preteen and teenage kids—are terrorizing the community.
>
> "We are seeing a rise in the kids getting started in this earlier and that's troubling," said Miami Gardens Deputy Police Chief Paul Miller, who declined to disclose the names of the gangs.
>
> The story does, finally, turn to talk to the Tequila and Cristal's father—whose first name isn't mentioned—"is speaking out." The story continues:
>
> At anti-violence walks, prayer rallies and town hall meetings, Forshee recounts his bitter loss and urges residents not to follow in his example. Pay attention, he implores.
>
> "If we don't look, we're going to pay," he said at a recent town hall forum. "I paid. I didn't look. It took me losing my child to look and I grew up here in Miami Gardens for 33 years."

At this point, the news article begins to read not as a story about a community "taking back their streets" but as a police battlefield where only cops know how to create a peaceful community:

Miami Gardens police acknowledges [sic] it will take a community partnership to stamp out the five or six gangs they say are the most active of the known gangs operating in the city. Most of the gang-related incidents and shootings are clustered in the Carol City and Norland neighborhoods.

Indeed, the article focuses on unsourced, general statements about what residents there think and feel about violence in their city:

Though not as organized as better known gangs, said Rawlins, gangs in Miami Gardens are violent and can grow powerful within communities if left unchecked.

"We see that there are some Miami Gardens residents who are very, very afraid when we knock on the doors where the shootings take place," he said. "There was one woman who was just afraid to step out of her door. You do see residents where this has impacted their way of life."

And while elected officials regularly tout the city's overall reduced crime rate in recent years, it all seems overshadowed when tragedies—like the slaying of 12-year-old Tequila—strike the community.

The above statements make the story read as though the newspaper and its reporters have their ears to the ground, their hands on the heart of the matters, and the ultimate authority to speak on behalf of "the community" without the need for specific evidence to support their claims. Police sources appear because they are part of the press team—the power elite—but citizens of the city are presented as though they are almost a community separate from the press/police in that the reporter must be sent out to the bush to gather information and return it to civilized society, generalizing as she must, and confirming her own claims with sources of a civilized organization.

Yet another article at the end of October continued similar rhetoric about residents with no verification of the assumptions that only local gangs are what make citizens fearful and that police have been authorized by those same citizens as a shared source of saving:

Residents blame much of the violence on local gangs, noting that at least 14 known gangs of mostly preteen and teenage kids are terrorizing the community.

In recent months, Miami Gardens has hosted anti-gang walks, town hall meetings and peace rallies in response to the violence.

Miami Gardens police will hire 10 more officers to allow for more of a focus on violent crime, and the department has also put technology in neighborhoods to alert police when shots are fired.[9]

The story ends with a call to connect citizens with the police and financial incentive to participate in stopping crime.

Anyone with information about Saturday night's shooting in Miami Gardens can remain anonymous in contacting Miami-Dade County Crimestoppers [sic] at 305–471 (8477) or 1 (866) 471–8477. If the tip leads to arrests, the tipster may be eligible for a reward. You can also leave an anonymous tip at the Miami Gardens Police Department website: http://www. miamigardenspolice.org/contact.php.

It is interesting that the press often close their stories about crime with information on how the public can contact police or police-authorized sources such as Crime Stoppers but in stories that talk about local activists who are organizing efforts to curb crime ways for the public to make direct contact to help in those ways are left finding their own contact information. It is this type of obvious participation of outsiders in the mission of the press that reveals how journalists align themselves with police interpretations of law and order—even when that interpretation might be questionable.

Paradigm problems abound

On November 21, the *Miami Herald* reported a story that challenged police exceptionalism and threw the police and the press into a moment of cultural trauma. Since June 2012, the paper reported, Miami Gardens convenience store owner Alex Saleh had used fifteen surveillance cameras to capture police harassment of patrons inside and outside of his store. In fact, Saleh told the newspaper, his business had never been robbed; he had installed the cameras in order to "protect him and his customers from police." Since they were installed, the newspaper stated, the cameras had collected more than twenty-four videos—some of which *Herald* reporters had viewed—that showed Miami Gardens police officers:[10]

- "[S]topping citizens, questioning them, aggressively searching them and arresting them for trespassing ... "

- "[C]onducting searches of Saleh's business without search warrants or permission"

- Using "what appeared to be excessive force on subjects who are clearly not resisting arrest"

- "[F]iling inaccurate police reports in connection with the arrests"

Beginning with its initial report, the *Herald* needed to explain how Miami Gardens' saviors, if they could fall from grace, could save others from danger and disorder that the press and public had demanded for months. In a first round of defense when police officials refused to comment about accusations against members of the force, reporters allowed officials to maintain their legitimacy as protective (and protected) authorities of a vital and virtuous institution by naturalizing the fact that officials do not need to be held accountable by the press and, instead, can have their sentiments published by issuing a press statement. The *Herald* wrote that:

> Repeated phone messages and emails to Miami Gardens Police Chief Matthew Boyd and City Manager Cameron Benson asking for comment on this story were not returned.
> Boyd did release a statement, saying that the department is committed to serving and protecting the citizens and businesses in the city.

At this point, not only did the press and the police need to address major questions in order to repair a paradigm of protectionism in terms of police authority, including, "How could the police explain their role as protectors of the public while also, at the same time, being part of the problem?" But the media needed to address another question related to their own paradigm: "How could the press, which had largely supported the increased policing as a solution to crime and misdeeds in Miami Garden, maintain legitimacy after revelations that even the police cannot maintain order of their own?"

For the next several weeks, the *Herald* presented police actions that had been caught on camera as maybe not quite justified but still characterized *the institution of the police* as proper, genuine, and necessary. For instance, one November 22 article in the *Herald* headlined "Miami Gardens defends cops accused of harassing, rousting store's clientele" focused on police reports related to initial investigations into misconduct that "did not provide sufficient evidence" for the department's internal affairs unit to pursue a full investigation.[11] Furthermore, the newspaper stated that even a day after the *Herald* released the surveillance story, the Miami Gardens city manager had "not yet become familiar" with the case, and while news columnists at the

Herald, including Fred Grimm, questioned the actions of police officers in the surveillance case, they largely ignored or marginalized voices of local residents that might justify further investigation into police misconduct. Instead, these journalists blamed citizens of Miami Gardens for their own problems that somehow explained why the city deserved and needed "vigorous policing." As Grimm wrote:

> Over an 11-day stretch beginning in late October, 10 people were gunned down in the city, including an 11-year-old girl. Last year, Miami Gardens, a working-class town of modest homes and a population of about 110,000, suffered 25 homicides and 369 robberies.[12]

Attempting to strike a balance—even in opinion journalism—between "watchdogging" local police and "shaming" residents of Miami Gardens was indicative of an attempt to align public paradigms of police and press rites and responsibilities to protect dominant ideologies with maintaining a sense of "objective" journalism so as not to encourage a revolt based on press rhetoric by the citizenry or to erode the public's understanding of dominant ideological functions of the power elite. Even when in December 2013, the Miami Gardens police chief announced he would retire—as one local television news station put it, "amid officer harassment allegations"—the story heralded him as being "the city's first and only police chief" and clarified that he had "originally planned to retire in January (2014)." The change in his plans, journalists said, was related to an announcement by the National Association for the Advancement of Colored People (NAACP) that the organization was going to seek an investigation into police misconduct by the US Department of Justice.[13]

Press meanings of "police myth"

These moments when the press needed to align public paradigms of police authority with press legitimacy, relied, at its foundation, on the power of myth. Throughout this chapter—and further solidified in the Conclusion—I approach police and journalistic practices and ideologies as those of a single journalistic interpretive community that build upon each other's social and cultural legitimacy and authority through *police myth*, an ideology that police are awarded as a natural right to "serve" the public through methods deemed effective and necessary. This mythical characterization provides a framework for examining the close connections between police and press—a connection that scholars might have identified in the past—but which continually fails to articulate dominant explanations of press-police power in the field of Journalism Studies.

Just as the press operate among several levels of understanding, from the individual level of "journalistic self" to news as a social institution and as a cultural pressure, examinations of media and police through myth allows us to move beyond the social levels of journalistic inquiry into the cultural realm of explaining the world, specifically the ways we identify the cultural meanings of news in assigning authority to those who protect and save us—the press and the police. As Teun van Dijk writes:

> Stories about problems, conflicts, or disasters also require happy ends. That is, in the simulation of possible problems, we also need models of problem solving, and the reestablishment of the goals, norms, and values shared in the group or culture. Hence, the special attention in crime news for the role of the police. And in disaster stories, we expect prominent attention to rescue operations and to heroes that solve the problem ...[14]

Peter Manning writes that police myth becomes a force for maintaining legitimacy and authority of police explanations of their own institution and of issues of the day because police mythology is built upon foundations of six major suppositions.[15]

First, Manning writes, police myth operates amid a correlation of "themes that are in reality unacceptable or bipolar into integrated or holistic units." By this, Manning identifies the rhetorical function of taking information that would be counter to our expectations (such as police officers, themselves, operating outside of the law) or rationalizations that, on their face, hold little validity (that even though police are breaking the law, for instance, they are the sole ones to enforce laws against others) and maintaining a sense of legitimate meaning that diminishes confusion about who is in charge—and why.

Second, the power of police myth allows for those communicating police power to remove the issues at hand "from everyday discourse" and to place them "in the realm of the nebulous and mystical, that which stands to serve *all* in a removed and fair, almost dispassionate, fashion." In the case of Miami Gardens police misconduct, for instance, newspaper columnists, police officials, and local leaders presented dispassionate and quantifiable explanations related to a need for increased policing that would benefit the larger public. Placing the meaning of daily life and police activity in the hands of myth via the press without, as individuals, becoming involved in our communities, in policymaking, and in challenging mainstream media in meaningful ways allows for the power elite to shape both the efforts of the press and the police through a lens of unquestioned altruism.

Third, police myth provides an opportunity for alleviating "societal crisis by providing a verbal explanation for causes, meanings, and consequences of events that might otherwise be considered inexplicable." In the case at hand, Miami Gardens city and police officials operated in unison by withholding judgment about *specific* alleged police misconduct while speaking out against the larger concept of misconduct by police as though such acts would—or could—never happen.

As a fourth mode of police myth, related storytelling identifies "the actors in the drama of crime, gives them faces and names, and makes them subject to predictable scenarios with beginnings, middles, and ends." Journalists and Miami Gardens officials spent much time in the storytelling of the convenience store owner and the criminal pasts—or alleged pasts—of many patrons who had claimed harassment by police while veiling the identities and stories of the police officers involved, thereby maintaining an aura of authority by enveloping them within the collective identity of police.

The idea of "concentrat(ing) public attention upon (police) force and conserving potential even in times of rapid change" operates as a fifth process of police myth. In coverage of public meetings and forums about police conduct during which Miami Gardens residents were presented as unorganized (or "packed" into meeting rooms), unlawful and hyperbolic (or "rowdy"), and loud and unruly (or "vocal") while city and police officials were cast as calm (officials "co-hosted" the meeting), quiet (the police chief "did not comment directly" about recent misconduct), powerful (having "eliminated gangs" throughout the Miami area), and rational through diction (one official stated that it is necessary to have "a prevention component" to solving crime).

Lastly, police myth relies on the ability of freezing "the organization in time and space, giving it a reified authority over the thing it opposes, and establishing in timeless dynamic a Manichaean *pas de deux* between the two poles of social life." Such an element of "police myth" appeared in coverage of seeking a tax increase before the surveillance story emerged and that was carried into coverage following the story with headlines such as "Miami Gardens defends cops accused of harassing, rousting store's clientele" in which the city's mayor pits the store owner against a police department, which has—in the mayor's words—"reached out" to investigate the incidents but who also states that the owner "hasn't been cooperative."[16]

Joseph Gusfield, in his edited volume of works by Kenneth Burke, writes that "police myth" represents Burke's approach to myth itself in terms of explicating an organization's symbolism of recognizability and power that is rooted in language, "evidence," and argument. Gusfield writes that "[t]he use of crime rates, the frequent depiction of the police as crime fighters, the emphasis on the gun—all present a performance in which police are the direct enemies of crime."[17] And so, too, do the press carry a dedication to such evidence and use of language, in which local television journalists frequently present themselves in news segments fighting for the rights of individuals against "white collar crimes" and in which consumers are pitted against local small businesses, landlords, a host of usually unimportant businesses, and even the occasional low-level politician. But, the press adoption of police myth requires a development of audience desire for press and police control.

Aligning the police and the press

Police myth becomes an easy process for the press to adopt in terms of (1) supporting police authority through the mythical explanations and (2) aligning themselves with their own sense of police authority. Indeed, both press and police institutions perform remarkably similar physical representations of their social roles that put members of both individual units within close quarters of socialization. It is again at the cultural level of understanding where connections between the press and police are most aligned, particularly in terms of the support and violence used by both groups to protect dominant ideologies in everyday situations and during cultural trauma.

Most interesting to this project, then, is the similar means by which the institutions of press and police apply myth and narrative in ways that protect the power elite and that are applied in such tandem that the ideological relationship between the two groups has become normalized among audiences. For example, the economic function of news has been established as both a natural expectation of what journalism looks like, as what it does, and as an indicator of its success. Police and the press are tied together with the same bonds of interpretation and protectionism through the cultural and financial commodification and sales of "police myth" that pays in terms of social and financial capital. TV news segments titled something similar to "On Your Side" are used to "police" local issues of consumer fraud, though these are rarely the segments used by journalists to tackle Big Business, governmental collusion to cheat citizens, or the role of business in expanding private surveillance of public spaces that contribute to private-public policing that becomes normal and natural for society. And it is this collaboration that should be of most concern for readers.

JOURNALISTIC INFORMATION AND (QUESTIONED) COLLABORATION

As I have argued throughout this project, there is no divide between "the power elite" and "the press"; rather, information is created, captured, and disseminated all within the shared ideological community of the press and police and identified based upon their shared practices.[18] These practices are summarized here and examined throughout the remainder of this chapter:

- Adapting to being watched. News is a culture in which journalists are seen as local or national celebrities and entertainers and who are otherwise recognized by officials and citizens as "authorities" that work so very much in a public light that the press capture and reuse for future remembering.

- Militarizing the press. These are efforts through which the press cooperate in official militarization by (1) learning and sharing the technical details of weaponry with the public as a means to familiarize the public with tools of violence and (2) presenting the weapons as tools "of violence" "for peace" by showcasing them in the hands of authorities before and during times of official use.

- Justifying virtuous violence against domestic citizens in ways that support police and press presentations of their own authority to determine for these same citizens the appropriate actions to provide safety for the greater masses.

Each of these have been well established throughout this project, but it is a fourth practice that demands special attention in aligning the efforts, interests, and communities of press and police—that of playing what Manning refers to as "informational games" by which the press and the police search for information on events, issues, and individuals that form a coherent and authoritative narrative in support of dominant ideological positions in presentations of the information to the public.

Police and press authority is ultimately reified in ways the institutions "find"—and create—information about society at both levels of the collective and of the individual that is applied through communication. In terms of both the press and the police, information that is gathered is frequently volunteered by citizens to police and to the press, which then is coopted and turned into "evidence" for the purposes of ideological discourse.

Such information collected in even the most basic contact with the police (think of a simple traffic stop or contact on the street) and the press (consider how journalists observe crowds at events, conduct interviews, examine documents) includes one's names, ages, addresses, and other demographics. But with the press—and maybe inadvertently, depending on the situation with police—people share political positions, career, and financial information, history of social activism, and social networks, and relationships. In these ways, the "informational game" functions with the assumption that the information-seeker has to work at getting what she wants; therefore, processes by which journalists and police go about gaining information are presented as acts of public service. Put another way, in terms of the press, journalists provide enough "positive news" where people are shown divulging their demographics, ideas, and associations in ways where citizens are revealed to hold a wealth of valuable personal information that can be shared with the public through the media, recorded as part of a collective's "history" and commoditized by news outlets to meet corporate aims that argue that sharing such information is a rite or ritual awarded to worthy individuals.

In addition to publishing such information within the context of a particular story, journalists save this data in electronic formats—also known as archives, an advanced version of media outlets' spaces of keepsaking once called "the morgue" or the "clip file"—that can be solicited and read by consumers, subpoenaed by prosecutors (the success of which varies), and owned via copyright by media companies upon which future profits may be based. For example:

- A comment from a witness to an event is owned as "journalistic evidence" that such an event occurred, the information from which is first shaped to maintain dominant ideological explanations of the event that journalists can return to in the future to serve the maintenance of that interpretation

- A photograph or video of a group or individual is published, copywritten, and repurposed for profits that remain with the media institution; such images are especially profitable if they are part of a large or popular event (read 9/11) or are nominated for and win a Pulitzer

- Police blotter and reports republished in the news, basic quotes of a person's perspective on a social issue or causes told to a reporter, and private information that is captured through police and legal means and released to the public through media are also used to monitor people and to create public images of individual citizens or communities

Most problematic in the act of "informational games" is its ability to help the press track individuals and collectives, particularly of those who operate outside of the status quo, and that serve the power elite with readily available information on the citizenry. As I wrote in *A Transplanted Chicago*, for instance, it is not unusual for public officials and police to turn to the news to find potential troublemakers, such as those who have been arrested, charged with a crime, suspected of misbehavior, or shamed for some reason and to use that information as their own justification for further punishment. This has certainly become the case in terms of how social media is used by employers—and even of private citizens—to track and to punish.

Additionally, as Raymond Boyle writes, police forces and their public relations arms have been influencing the media by providing journalists access to police scenes and to data and supplying verification that information is "newsworthy," "factual," or "of interest" to the public. In fact, a common task at news outlets is to make "cop calls," for instance, where reporters dial through a list of police agencies to ask whether there is "any news," an extension of the days when reporters would be assigned to specific police houses to await anything that might happen there.[19] In this and other ways, then, I argue that the police and the press are socialized to work with each other with particular aims in mind in order to identify and articulate for the power elite threats to its institutions.

These aims are reached by:

- Finding information that is of interest to the power elite in terms of maintaining the elite's positions of authority, legitimacy, and control

- Sharing information among fellow institutions for validation, shared authority, and further distribution of meanings that fuel ideological and physical acts of violence

- Distributing information in ways that, for the most part, reflects one's ideological positions of the "facts" related to the actions of police and press

- Protecting the structures and ideologies of power elite systems through "flak," if necessary, to present the appearance of ideological differences between institutions

- Punishing and disciplining individuals and collectives in order to correct current and future social actions and to present a common narrative for future remembering

- Validating the use of physical force, or the threat of physical force, within the violence of language and the affirmation of official acts of local police and military to support power elite efforts to maintain power and control

Within this collaborative "informational game" that the press and police play, institutions mandate individuals operate amid an "approach-avoidance scenario," in which members of both institutions—but of the shared collective, as I argue in the book's Conclusion—balance the needs and expectations of their own organizations in terms of the gathering, interpretation, and sharing of information. Such efforts are to reduce the amount of energy spent on shared paradigm maintenance surrounding the ideological practice of "flak" to insist they maintain a divide between their interests and efforts and to reduce any overt and lasting evidence of any relationships between institutions of the power elite that will allow for harmful remembrance.

Functioning within collaborative forgetting

Just as claims against the press as being controlled within their shared community of the power elite are attacked through a lens of "conspiracy theory," attacks against a "press-as-police" argument face similar rhetoric from the public and from the very same institutions that are under scrutiny. Claims against the approach include arguments that a lack of policing would lead to "anarchy" and that police are a necessary and virtuous connection to a "peaceful" and "free" life. Additional arguments that policing is merely "the price we pay for our freedoms" and that police officers and journalists hold agency to act otherwise if and when their units become "corrupt" operates from a virtuous position rooted in propagandistic media, political, and military histories that diminish histories of the poor, the minority, the "other," and the true rebel.

There is a reason, of course, why our nation does not cherish the rabblerousing of Thomas Paine but celebrates the conservative efforts of other "Founding Fathers" in our collective memories, particularly those approved memories of our nation that cannot be shown to endorse radical political positions. In turn, public rhetoric marginalizes people who—even centuries ago—were viewed as founding a New World.

Each of the above criticisms of critiques of press-police collaboration operate in a social and cultural context that means to (1) distract the public from alternative explanations for social conditions and to (2) help the public "forget" alternative explanations that occur each day. Indeed, because alternative explanations occur multiple times a day, every day, either in our own minds, in conversations with friends and enemies, and in the thankless voices of the subaltern, media marginalization of such ideas and voices makes it possible for us to collectively forget counter-narratives rather than to address the complexities in our shared histories that reveal collaborative violence between press and police.

In some ways, forgetting merely means leaving behind some of the details of counter-histories to make the most effective narratives of "journalistic evidence" part of the nation's consciousness (see discussion on incorporation in Conclusion). Public and press mistrust of US corporations during the days of muckraking journalism—to the degree that such a movement holds to our nostalgia of it today—is presented in popular histories that suggest those journalists solved financial inequalities in society. In turn, journalists and the public have been released from a critical reading of modern-day unfair land grabs by corporations, racist forms of consumer and business credit backed by the US government, racialized housing policies adopted by local communities, the establishment of predatory payday loan stores as an industry of its own, and public-private ventures and hyper-professionalization of education.[20]

Additionally, specific historical moments in US politics in which officials and police physically stop and abuse protesters operating within the freedoms of the nation's "democracy," such as during the 1968 Democratic National Convention in Chicago in which the police attacked journalists, is set aside as isolated incidents, just as will public action in Ferguson, Missouri, and in other US cities in recent years. These more recent events will be forgotten in terms of the organizational tact and bravery of protestors and the brutality of the police and will merely join a long list of the public whining for "equality."[21]

Other moments of history are also forgotten in ways that diminish the power collaborations of media and police. Press partnership with US drug officials and local law enforcement to hype concerns related to drug culture in the 1980s in ways that veiled increased and intentional disinvestment and brutality of blacks in US cities is almost never spoken of today and is easily written off as liberal propaganda and "conspiracy theory."[22] And when moments of today's racialized acts of the police and press emerge, institutions of the power elite present these stories as though they are especially rare and have never happened before. Little is remembered in public rhetoric, however, that these events happen all of the time, including a very public spotlight on the role of police officers in the deaths of three men in the 1990s in New York who died while in custody.

At the time, debate raged about the degree to which the officers were responsible for these three cases—the NYPD was, as a result of investigations into the deaths, found to be home to a massive drug and corruption ring—but which was also treated by the press at the time as a struggle to maintain police authority.[23] More recent efforts of police-press collaborations that have already been "forgotten" through marginalization and press distraction includes the lies made by US officials associated with the development and holding of weapons of mass destruction in Iraq that led to war in the mid-2000s and the blatant use of nationalistic applications of weaponry and the drama of CIA spying in media entertainment that indoctrinates the public to the hype and patriotism of such efforts.[24]

Even with a long list of historic and current deeds that reveal the collaborative nature of the press and police, the public opts to either ignore or to explain away potential and real power and purposes of our authorities when revealed. In early 2015, for instance, the North Miami Beach Police Department was found to have been using mugshots of local black men as targets for police sharpshooter training. A group of local Florida Army National Guard soldiers reported to the press that during a visit to an area shooting range that had just been used by North Miami Beach officers, they found targets such as what appears in Figure 6.1 "riddled with bullets."[25] One of the faces was the brother of one of the soldiers who saw these targets and reported them to the press.

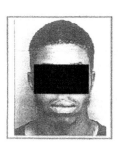  

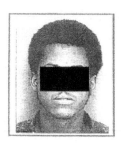 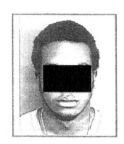 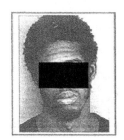

FIGURE 6.1. *The North Miami Beach Police Department in January 2015 was found to have used this image of actual residents who had been photographed by police as targets for sniper practice. This doctored version of the original target, released by police officials, included black squares to conceal the men's eyes.*[26]

As a way to sanitize the evidence for future remembrance, at least from an official source, the police department released a version of the target with portions of the men's faces blacked out, though the images published in the press showed the full faces with bullet holes in the skulls of each image, holes square in the forehead of the image in top right and blowing away an eye of the man in the bottom right corner.[27] Even though the police department and the city's mayor refused to acknowledge any connection to racialized profiling or hatred, the city stopped using these targets once the images hit international media.

So if these "big moments" come before our eyes so easily and so frequently, why don't we choose to apply critical lenses and connect these instances together? One rationale is that because the press has incorporated these events into normal practice of society the very overt presentation of such acts hide the violent purposes and nature of the power elite. And, as I explicate in the book's final chapter, myth related to the police—and the press— operates as an act, not as an outcome of categorization or characterization but *as a process of rhetoric* to distract audiences (sometimes by apologizing, sometimes through rationalization) from attacking power systems directly. In the next section, I apply the act of journalism and its mythical processes of violence to further explicate the police acts of the news.

CONTROLLED MONITORING AS MEDIATED PRACTICE

In the cases mentioned throughout this chapter, media surveillance functions as a way to watch and assign meaning to the actions of the power elite in moments of acknowledged misconduct within the elite community. Instead of "punishing" the police for recorded misconduct or "shaming" them, the act of media punishment was replaced with justification of their acts. This difference in how the press conduct surveillance as an act of media control indicates that the third stage of "media surveillance" discussed in Chapter 5, in which morals and values noted through "media watching" are applied in an outcome of punishment, can also result in outcomes of ideological maintenance. In terms of the Miami Gardens case, "shaming" occurred in a mild form only, with few explanations of police activity and authority operating within a realm of press legitimacy to shape dominant interpretations of how police—and the public—should deal with perceived public disorder that don't include additional police.

It is surrounding this approach to local power systems that I wish to expand upon the notion of media sousveillance as contributing to the force of "media control." I do so for two reasons: (1) to identify the inverse approaches and purposes of maintaining the internal stability and external validity of the power elite and (2) to discuss the connections between the press and the police as sharing an interpretive community of power-makers directed by the power elite. In the end, the following pages attempt to place the press as a member of the power elite's police force in ways that challenge articulations that have appeared in both normative, professional, and scholarly rhetoric about press/police relationships, particularly in terms of these communities as being distinct and separate.

To continue this conversation, however, it is helpful to see the term "policing" (and its relative terms, such as "law enforcement") as verbs—just as many terms in this book, including "media," are presented as ideological acts with specific power functions. This clarification allows for us to examine the acts and aims of both the press and the police to enact media control—ideologically and physically—through a mediatized practice of monitoring. Through active watching and collaboration with fellow sectors of the power elite the press reify ideologies that rationalize, legitimize, and economize acts of surveillance and related hyper-vigilantism of public-private armed forces at our very doorsteps.

The press then also share in the benefits of White Supremacy with other power elite institutions that emerge out of our nation's dominant paternalistic positions of "protecting" ourselves from the "other" and from the "subordinate" through law, regulation, social restriction, and the promotion of desired behaviors of consumption that appears in media. The press benefit by publishing consistent ideological meanings of media and press purposes, which argue that:

- Some members of the press and police may operate outside of the communities' norms without reflecting upon other members of the community

- Press and police institutions, at their roots, are designed to provide a public good

- Maintenance associated with repairing public perceptions of institutions during moments of cultural trauma dictates a return to traditional and believable narratives of protectionism

- The traditional and believable narratives assume that a return to normalcy is in the best interest of the public and that the norms of policing and of journalism function as acts of peace

Daily press and police operations operate through a form of *inverse surveillance*, the observation of behavior and ideologies of self and of and within a collective, that allows the press to act as though they operate outside of the spheres of control shared by fellow institutions of the power elite but that, in fact, serve to maintain the elite's shared ideologies of order. At the center of this form of surveillance, the press assist police in the urbanization/ghettoization and demonization of cities by covering crime as a natural occurrence. In non-city spaces, such as the suburbs and rural areas, journalists present neighborhoods and dominant communities of these geographies as a kind of "The Heartland," home to the forming of a region is and nation's moral fiber that, like houses of faith, influence ideological positions that contribute to policies of control via force.[28] Press constructions of the "ghetto," even if hours and miles away from press coverage of a particular event outside of a city, is used as a baseline against which to maintain local dominant norms in order to avoid the immoral, violent, and racialized elements of the urban United States.

Before expanding upon media sousveillance, which appears in the last section of this chapter, I wish to discuss how the press become socialized not only to watch but *to be watched*.

Socialized to be watched: The normalization of media sousveillance

The ultimate goal of the police and the press collaboration, as this chapter explicates, is to police the possible threats that comes from communication in which the press become part of the story and are increasingly shown as celebrities. The interaction between public watching of journalists and of journalists of each other forms a business model of news that is no longer a covert cause for coverage but becomes a central focus of a normalized scenario where the press, in many ways, are public (and police) figures.[29]

In 2015, for instance, NBC's Brian Williams faced public scrutiny, despite his popularity as a regular feature in the network's sitcoms and programs such as *Saturday Night Live*, for questions related to his coverage of involvement in covering war in the Middle East. His suspension from the news desk created a storm of discourse throughout the press and entertainment news sites, as well as on social media, where people treated his decline not as a strike against journalism but as a hit against a popular entertainer.[30]

In more serious events, such as the Ferguson, Missouri, protests in 2014, media training website Poynter.com covered how the media covered itself through videos, tweets, and photographs of reporters to show "who's in town" to report on the events. One tweet that the website republished showed three reporters smiling in a parking lot with the message: "My view from the MSNBC shoot just now. Pity this crew freezing on an empty lot in #Ferguson. Not glamorous."[31] But what effect might there be in journalists being in the spotlight? Just as Chapter 1 discussed, the "journalistic self" is a constantly changing identity that is morphed by experiences journalists have throughout their professional and personal lives. These experiences, which can be examined through processes of socialization, but should also be examined through the ideological process of indoctrination, influences how journalists not only see themselves in the world but how they can explain the experiences of others as citizens describe similar interactions with their environments and fellow citizens.

The effect of a hypersecuritized world on the ability of the press, as a group of individuals, to recognize the increasingly intrusive nature of technology on social monitoring emerged for me during a January 2014 visit with a colleague to the *Sun Sentinel* newsroom in Fort Lauderdale, Florida. Having worked in media most of my life, I am used to locked doors that one must pass to enter a newsroom, the need for a visitor's pass to have a source or guest welcomed into the space, and the initial measures an employee may need to go through to gain clearance—depending on the location, the decade, and the corporate ownership—to gain access to one's very own work station.

Yet, I was shocked by the difficulty for members of the citizenry to access members of the press at the *Sun Sentinel*, which I must admit is similar to other newsrooms in metropolitan areas. If memory of that visit serves, which I think it does, not only did two locked glass doors stand between us and the newsroom but a security guard sat behind a command station in the lobby and asked for our names and with whom we had an appointment. All of that seemed legit and within expectations, but before our host was beckoned to welcome us, we were required to give the guard our driver's licenses, which he scanned into a database.

We were then asked to position ourselves in front of a webcam that took photos of our faces that were then placed into the same database that now held our addresses, our license numbers, dates of birth, heights and weights, and whether or not we would donate our organs. It would not be beyond reason to wonder whether the scanning system could also record any data stored within bar codes on the license. That such technology was instituted by their employers normalizes for members of the press themselves a system through which they can recognize the "normality" and even the "common sense" of such "security." The concern, then, is the degree to which our own normalization to these technologies influences our abilities to think and act critically elsewhere, particularly when similar efforts "for security" are reported in some communities as related to violence.

Consider, for instance, the replaying of the Rodney King video—the images of police repeatedly striking King with batons and kicking him—or the US missiles from the First Gulf War pounding into enemy lands, or the blasts pushing from the World Trade Center on 9/11. At what point does the showing of the violence within media serve as violence itself in a way similar to the productions that media outlets constructed and published related to lynching in the United States South that not only captured a moment of punishment but that also provided entertainment to the audiences who wanted to be captured, smiling, in photographs, and sent a message of punishment to stop potential wrongdoing in the future?

In the same way, then, to what degree does the personal experience of the journalist with securitization, particularly in the newsroom, normalize the lies of the technology's ability to provide protection? Indeed, that it is so damn hard just to get to a reporter or an editor—if you have recently tried email, Twitter, or phone, you will know that is no easier than getting past a locked door—what does this distance in the interest of "security" say about the notion of today's public sphere or the role of the press in serving the public?[32]

The media themselves operate within an increased, normalized industry of surveillance that makes moments when we are required—or require others— to participate in similar moments of social monitoring as the cost of doing business. Complexities of the surveillance system that is applied to media as a function of its control requires an added level of complication to include the participatory nature of journalism. In this way, the press become a militarized force of "media control" that can be expressed as *media sousveillance*, a form of inverse surveillance enacted by media upon themselves and partners within the power elite and that is performed to identify ideological disjuncture and to perform paradigm maintenance.[33]

Elizabeth Bradshaw's work, which examines these complexities, is vital for making this transition from media surveillance to media sousveillance. In her work, Bradshaw encourages an analysis of the intersection between:

- Foucault's application of surveillance beyond the panoptic from the prison to the institution of the everyday in which the "few" watch the "many"

- Mark Andrejevic's notion of "lateral surveillance," in which ordinary people watch each other

- Thomas Mathiesen's idea of "synopticism," in which the "many" watch the "few" and which may lead to a "transparent society"[34]

The notion of sousveillance as "inverse panopticon" or as "inverse surveillance" is the process of one monitoring another within a social sphere; it is often associated with wearable viewing and recording devices that monitor the public as an act of counter-surveillance, a means by which to question the authority of those who surveil and to surveil the surveilers. Steve Mann, Jason Nolan, and Barry Wellman write that acts of sousveillance are "a type of critical reflectionism which challenges bureaucratic structures by mirroring their practices back at them." Additionally, they state that:

> [r]eflectionism becomes sousveillance when it is applied to individuals using tools to observe the organizational observer. Sousveillance focuses on enhancing the ability of people to access and collect data about their surveillance and to neutralize surveillance.[35]

Sousveillance has taken many new meanings in relationship to media. Paul Reilly writes that the increased participatory nature of journalism, which has increased the use of citizen-constructed media into the mainstream press, has altered the surveillance function of the news by introducing the citizen as one who is able to watch, constantly, and to comment on the "news" while also making the news, which either supplements mainstream messaging or replaces it by subverting power.[36] Conversations about surveillance and sousveillance in the first decades of the twenty-first century revolve around privacy and the risks involved in creating moral panic or hysteria related to further implementation of new technologies in daily life. For instance, Simon Cole and Henry Pontell write that the media influence public fears related to technology in ways that attack personal concerns on financial and physical health and safety:

> Media accounts typically begin with a sample horror story in which a person becomes aware of having been victimized, cancels his or her credit cards, and then experiences the now-familiar Kafkasque dilemma of trying to restore his or her financial identity ... Experts comment on the seemingly helplessness of consumers, financial institutions, and governments to stem the rising tide of identity theft ... They bemoan the lack of security regarding personal information in society, and blame is apportioned, usually to credit card companies and other businesses and government entities that collect and hold such data.[37]

Yet while news coverage banks on the imaginary power of technology as oppression and as a threat to individualism, the press confuse audiences by also legitimizing a hyper-surveilled world, one built around watching and waiting for the news or the danger to happen, and waiting and watching for the moment in which society can impose its dominant ideologies and solutions for acts of unpopular disorder. The protectionism of the status quo—and the values and rites within the status quo—are cast as the always-hero with the ability and expectation of instituting order through technology. Indeed, media function within what scholars refer to as the "surveillance assemblage," which Vian Bakir clearly articulates as being "loosely linked systems" that are:

> ... emergent, unstable and operates across state institutions and others that have nothing (directly) to do with the state, such as supermarket and credit card transactions. In the assemblage, rather than individuals passing through spaces of panoptic enclosure, surveillance works by computers tracking persons, abstracting bodies from places and splitting them into data flows to be reassembled as virtual data-doubles.[38]

As the definitions of media become more complicated surrounding the role of user-created content—including comments made on news stories that are posted online, tweets and Instagram posts that provide records of our movements and thoughts, "eye-witness" reports of news events, such as in the case of The Boston Bombings, and the blurring of these messages between the private and the public, those of which we may be aware and those which we may not—the movement from media surveillance to media sousveillance functions to identify as the "sousveillant assemblage," which "compris[es] the surveillant assemblage, but data-fattened by the proliferation of web-based participatory media and personal sousveillance that we willingly provide online."[39]

Below, I examine the violence associated with the participatory nature of media sousveillance that blends and blurs what information is gathered by officials of the power elite and what is given to them.

CONCLUSION: THE VIRTUOUS VIOLENCE OF MEDIA SOUSVEILLANCE

Press operations that constitute actions of police agents appeared in news coverage of the Occupy Movement in the United States, which began on September 17, 2011, in New York City when thousands of people gathered to "occupy" physical spaces of economic oppression driven by capitalism's demand not just to profit but to gain as much profit as possible—despite the costs to humans. Over the next few years, Occupy morphed into tent cities in locations across the country, and rhetoric involving protestors associating themselves with each other as being among "the 99 percent," which represents the idea that the majority of the wealth in the United States is maintained by 1 percent of the population. The protests provided local press outlets and police departments around the country to conduct violence against the "democratic process" that had been seen during the World Trade Organization protests in Seattle in 1999 and the 2004 protests in Miami during the meeting of the Free Trade Area of the Americas. During Occupy, tens of thousands of protestors clashed with police, with nearly 8,000 as of this writing having been arrested, some after feeling the fists of police power.[40]

As in each of the protests mentioned above, from Seattle to Miami, press coverage cast protestors of Occupy as terroristic threats to the average American that should either be put down by police or marginalized as a threat only in terms of creating a generation of hippy (and hipster) citizens who will dismantle efforts for "an American Dream," even if to the detriment of their own success. Despite the symbolism instituted by police for the benefit of silencing possible protests in the future, and despite the real, physical brutality felt by scores of those arrested or merely assaulted by police during the several years of pop-up protests, the movement forced the press to at least acknowledge public challenges to the system in light of financial recession in the mid-2000s that led to massive home foreclosures and layoffs.[41]

It was also understood by the press and much of the public, however, that no one was going to take out the business class—especially from among the ranks of young hoodlums that formed Occupy who were positioned ideologically by the press as being counter to order and in need of heavy policing and press monitoring. Indeed, as John Whitehead writes, the public

> is now on a fast track to raising up an Orwellian generation—one populated by compliant citizens accustomed to living in a police state and who march in lockstep to the dictates of the government.

He continues that new generations are being introduced in ways that justify these generalizations in order to slow any future forms of dissent. Whitehead writes that:

> with every school police raid and overzealous punishment that is carried out in the name of school safety, the lesson being imparted is that Americans—especially young people—have no rights at all against the state or the police.[42]

Seeing sousveillance as traditional social control

Today's police-press state is reliant on emerging media technologies and communication lines but which at their core represent methods of monitoring that these units of the power elite have always used to coopt and to produce surveillance through stealth and oppressive securitization. Building upon Foucault's "three great variables" of institutional order— "territory, speed, and communication"—Joshua Reeves and Jeremy Packer note that media, which they define as not just the press but as "all technologies used for the collection, storage, and processing of data," provides police with tools for information-gathering and for the extension of police surveillance of the public through collaboration via lines of communication to and with the public.[43]

The use of media—from "Wanted" posters in post offices to online galleries of local mugshots on news outlet websites (see Chapter 3)—has always functioned to spread the appearance and existence of police authority while shaming and protecting members of the public. Media efforts have included the use of high-tech and protruding surveillance cameras, flashy police cars, prime-time police dramas, shiny badges, and prominent placement of police news in the press.

Today, however, media help gather information, institute order, and oppress through the constant need for one-upmanship of and by police forces following the terrorist attacks of 9/11 that have sent the press into PR overtime reporting on the best and brightest new police tools and toys: By 2012, the US Department of Homeland Security had awarded some $34 billion in grants to communities as small as Fon du Lac, Wisconsin, and Fargo, North Dakota, and awarded millions of dollars to single locations, including more than $4 million that went to Johnson, Rhode Island, from the Pentagon in 2010 and 2011. Increases in local SWAT team numbers are also alarming: roughly 30,000 of US towns with populations between 25,000 and 50,000 held SWAT teams in 1995. That number grew to 45,000 by 2001 and grew again to between 50,000 and 60,000 by 2005.[44]

The rise of affordable, unmanned drones for non-military use has, in recent years, also led to their use by local police forces—a use that local news sources love to promote. In 2011, for instance, the *Houston Chronicle* wrote that the Montgomery County Sheriff's Office planned to use an unmanned drone with a seemingly unclear purpose:

> Unlike UVA used by the military, which are used chiefly to gain intelligence, the ShadowHawk will give deputies a "bird's eye view" of crime scenes,

search-and-rescue missions and large-scale emergencies, Chief Deputy Randy McDaniel said.

Later in the story, the chief deputy said in response to concerns about possible government spying, "We have better things to do, and spying is not our role."[45]

But even in 2011, the US drone wars had formed a measurable impact on the world: former President George W. Bush had approved a reported fifty drone strikes in his time, whereas by mid-2013, President Barack Obama had signed-off on an estimated 400, with results including the deaths of some 3,000 "terrorists" throughout the Mideast and—in 2011 alone—900 noncombatants, 200 of which were children. And, even if the Chronicle's article suggests that local police will use their new toys to observe the public only in times of crisis, if history is any indication, the police will use their new tools to conduct surveillance in specific urban neighborhoods and of specific, dark-skinned publics, not in the back yards of suburban neighborhoods to see what deviance occurs there.[46]

Technological advancements in sousveillance and surveillance by the media turn local news outlets into "agents of social control" through a "system-maintenance" role that conduct traditional policing behaviors.[47] By watching each other and the rest of us, reporting on the actions of fellow media outlets and units of the power elite, as well as average citizens, the press conduct private policing that benefit from an "open" public process of discipline. In fact, write Richard Ericson, Patricia Baranek, and Janet Chan, the courts of the "criminal justice system," of "due process," and of civil law "allow journalists to meet their claim that they are standing in on behalf of the public to see that governmental processes are just and that government officials are accountable." And because, only on few occasions do members of the public crowd courtrooms for these processes, "[t]he 'public' aspects of court hearings is defaulted to journalists, and their selection of what cases and what details the public should know."[48]

Ericson, Baranek and Chan also write that the media's "policing knowledge" influences selections of what the press cover in terms of monitoring physical manifestations of public disorder and of embedded traditional values—such as the now defunct "Family section" of newspapers—that are integrated into daily news stories of today. Media policing of "institutional site(s)" such as "the family" in such instances operate amid:

good-news items underpinning the consensual values the family is supposed to embody [that] are blended with good advertising items underpinning the consuming wants the family is supposed to emulate.[49]

The introduction to news media of private footage and information, including the journalistic use of surveillance videos in the news (see Chapter 5), then, come to operate amid a trio of what Astrid Gynnild writes are three functions, each of which I argue reveal the press as companions of the surveillance state led by police and the power elite. The three functions are:

- Crowdsourcing that allows private citizens to contribute videos via the media to help "solve crime" and to set social and cultural expectations for others within a collective

- Use of published surveillance video—and other private evidence—that influences the operations of the legal system and potential outcomes of the legal system, including expanding the power of the authority to the press and public

- Publication of private moments of disorder in the news that presents a "preventative warning"[50]

Through these processes, several outcomes emerge:

- Members of the press become participants themselves as consumers of media

- Members of media use items from the public to humanize the news and connect the press as an institution and cultural force with the viewer/reader/user

- The viewer/reader/user experiences the items supplied by their peers through the press and, therefore, adopts the meanings of the items as though they were their own

- The watching of the press—and of press participation—means to help maintain social order and social standards

Through these processes and outcomes, the viewer/reader/user and producer/advertiser/source become members of the public that is charged with contributing support to a social system in which violence becomes a rationalized function of survival. This process is similar to what William Staples refers to as "power seeing," which operates within a mechanism of force and threats of force that can be issued for compliance.[51] Therefore, issues of surveillance in these conversations of journalism should not be viewed only through the lens of a single operator or oppressor or of a group of people sitting around a table, watching every move and predetermining outcomes of social actions. While such an operation may exist in some cases, as Kevin Haggerty and Richard Ericson make clear, "the power of surveillance derives from the ability of institutional actors to integrate, combine, and coordinate various systems and components."[52] It is in the Conclusion, then, when these signs of integration and coordination are put to rest in an analysis of the journalistic training and educational systems, as an analysis of the means by which journalists and police are combined within a single interpretive community.

Discussion Questions

1. In what ways do the forms of press surveillance effect our everyday lives? What are some examples, and how do they reveal the interests of the power elite?
2. What challenges to the argument that the press operate as police exist, and what evidence is provided to support these challenges?

Notes

1   Maggie Newland, "Girl killed when shots fired into Miami Gardens home," miami.cbslocal.com, August 15, 2013, http://miami.cbslocal.com/2013/08/15/girl-killed-when-shots-fired-into-miami-gardens-home; see also, 2012 data available at http://www.fdle.state.fl.us/Content/getdoc/a7980a71-a59a-49d9-a33d-719ad9a4abd7/CoMuOff2012annual.aspx; 2013 data: http://www.fdle.state.fl.us/Content/getdoc/2c79e16b-8846-4383-be92-c7c16e227813/CoMuOff2013annual.aspx.

2   Katia Savchuk, "With tears, community mourns for murdered minister, grandson," *Miami Herald*, July 27, 2013.

3   Fabiola Santiago, "In Miami Gardens, a start in breaking culture of silence," *Miami Herald*, October 24, 2013.

4   Aminda Marqués Gonzalez, "*Herald* reporter tracks weapons in public schools," *Miami Herald*, September 22, 2013.

5   "City Council votes No Tolerance Pledge," *Miami Gardens News*, August 1, 2013; "For the Children Sake Campaign," miamigardens-fl.gov, June 12, 2013, http://www.miamigardens-fl.gov/pdf/community/children-sake-campaign.pdf.

6   Julia Yarbough, "Not in our city: Miami Gardens Police partner with federal agencies to tackle gun violence," *Miami Gardens News*, August 1, 2013.

7   Nadege Green, "Tax rate likely to increase for Miami Gardens residents," *Miami Herald*, August 2, 2013, emphasis mine.

8   Nadege Green, "A city, a family fight to end cycle of violence," *Miami Herald*, October 12, 2013.

9   *Miami Herald*, "Miami Gardens shooting leaves four hospitalized," *Miami Herald*, October 27, 2013.

10 Julie K. Brown, "In Miami Gardens, store video catches cops in the act," *Miami Herald*, November 21, 2013.

11 Lance Dixon and Julie Brown, "Miami Gardens defends cops accused of harassing, rousting store's clientele," *Miami Herald*, November 22, 2013.

12 Fred Grimm, "Miami Gardens police make much ado about nothing in arrests," *Miami Herald*, November 24, 2013.

13 Janine Stanwood and Ben Candea, "Miami Gardens Police Chief Matthew Boyd retired amid officer harassment allegations," local10.com, December 12, 2013, http://www.local10.com/news/miami-gardens-police-chief-matthew-boyd-retires/23435220; To be clear, the city was incorporated and its police department formed in the early 2000s, making this chief the first for the city.

14 Teun A. van Dijk, *News as Discourse* (New York & London: Routledge, 2009), 123–124.

15 Peter K. Manning, *Police Work: The Social Organization of Policing* (Prospect Heights, IL: Waveland Press, 1997), 324–326.

16 Lance Dixon and Julie Brown, "Miami Gardens defends cops accused of harassing, rousting store's clientele," *Miami Herald*, November 22, 2013; Lance Dixon, "Miami Gardens residents vent over police problems," *Miami Herald*, January 7, 2014.

17 Joseph R. Gusfield, *Kenneth Burke: On Symbols and Society* (London & Chicago: University of Chicago Press, 1989), 20.

18 See discussion of mugshots later in this Chapter.

19 Raymond Boyle, "Spotlight Strathclyde: Police and media strategies," *Corporate Communications: An International Journal* 4, no. 2 (1999): 93–97; Robert Chrismas, "An arranged marriage: Police-media conflict & collaboration," *Canadian Graduate Journal of Sociology and Criminology* 1, no. 1 (2012): 43–55; Louise Cooke and Paul Sturges, "Police and media relations in an era of freedom of information," *Policing & Society*, 19, no. 4 (2009): 406–424; Edson C. Tandoc, Jr., "Breaking news or breaking the newspaper?: Print journalists, online journalists and their medium-based loyalties," *Tandoc* 11, no. 1 (2014): 172–191; Luis A. Fernandez, *Policing Dissent: Social Control and the Anti-Globalization Movement* (Piscataway, NJ: Rutgers University Press, 2008).

20 Manning Marable, *How Capitalism Underdeveloped Black America* (Cambridge, MA: South End Press, 2000).

21 Jill A. Edy, *Troubled Pasts: News and the Collective Memory of Social Unrest* (Philadelphia: Temple University Press, 2006).

22 Jimmie L. Reeves and Richard Campbell, *Cracked Coverage: Television News, the Anti-cocaine Crusade, and the Reagan Legacy* (Durham, NC & London: Duke University Press, 1994).

23 Regina G. Lawrence, *The Politics of Force: Media and the Construction of Brutality* (Berkeley, Los Angeles & London: University of California Press, 2000), 112–138.

24 Robert M. Entman, *Scandal and Silence: Media Responses to Presidential Misconduct* (Cambridge & Malden, MA: Polity, 2012); Oliver Boyd-Barrett, David Herrera, and Jim Baumann, "Hollywood, the CIA and the 'war on terror,'" in *Media & Terrorism: Global Perspectives*, edited by Des Freedman and Dayna Kishan Thussu (London, Thousand Oaks, CA, New Delhi & Singapore: Sage), 116–133.

25 McNelly Torres and William Shepard, "Family outraged after North Miami Beach Police use mug shots as shooting targets," nbcmiami.com, January 17, 2014, http://www.nbcmiami.com/news/local/Family-Outraged-After-North-Miami-Beach-Police-Use-Criminal-Photos-as-Shooting-Targets-288739131.html.

26 The North Miami Beach Police Department released this image along with several other examples of targets used by police departments on January 16, 2015 at this link: http://www.citynmb.com/index.asp?Type=B_BASIC&SEC=%7B7CF2B20B-DDBA-4F51-A939-0BF8CA815F84%7D&DE=%7B654946AA-EBE9-413B-A3D4-55C0D782D599%7D.

27 Torres and Shepard, "Family outraged after North Miami Beach Police use mug shots as shooting targets."

28 Katherine Fry, *Constructing the Heartland: Television News and Natural Disaster* (Creskill, NJ: Hampton Press, 2003).

29 Stuart Hall, Chas Critcher, Tony Jefferson, John Clarke, and Brian Roberts, *Policing the Crisis: Mugging, the State and Law & Order* (London: Macmillan, 1978); Robert Reiner, *Law and Order: An Honest Citizen's Guide to Crime and Control* (Cambridge, UK & Malden, MA: Polity, 2007), 15; Lee Humphreys, "Who's watching whom?: A study of interactive technology and surveillance," *Journal of Communication* 61 (2011): 575–595.

30 To see Brian Williams as celebrity, Robbie Vourhaus, "Brian Williams—the last celebrity news anchor," The Huffington Post, February 12, 2015, http://www.huffingtonpost.com/robbie-vorhaus/brian-williams-the-last-c_b_6663212.html.

31 Kristen Hare, "As the media waits in Ferguson, it begins covering itself," poynter.org, November 21, 2014, http://www.poynter.org/news/mediawire/282987/as-the-media-waits-in-ferguson-it-begins-covering-itself.

32 Stephen Graham and David Wood, "Digitizing surveillance: Categorization, space, inequality," *Critical Social Policy Ltd* 23, no. 2 (2003): 227–248; Astrid Gynnild, "Surveillance videos and visual transparency in journalism," *Journalism Studies* 15, no. 4 (2014): 449–463; Similar arguments can be made of popular social media tools, such as Facebook and Twitter, as being forms of surveillance that includes that which conducts "social sorting." For more, see Daniel Trotter, *Social Media as Surveillance: Rethinking Visibility in a Converged World* (Surrey, UK & Burlington, VT: Ashgate, 2012).

33 Kevin D. Haggerty and Richard V. Ericson, *The New Politics of Surveillance and Visibility* (Toronto, Buffalo & London: University of Toronto Press, 2006).

34 Elizabeth A. Bradshaw, "This is what a police state looks like: Sousveillance, direct action and the anti-corporate globalization movement," *Critical Criminology* 21 (2013): 447–461; Thomas Mathiesen, "The viewer society: Michel Foucault's 'panopticon' revisited," *Theoretical Criminology* 1, no. 2 (1997): 215–234; Mek Andrejevic, *iSpy: Surveillance and Power in the Interactive Era* (Lawrence: University Press of Kansas, 2007); David Brin, *The Transparent Society: Will Technology Force Us to Choose Between Privacy and Freedom?* (Reading, MA: Perseus Books, 1998); For more, see Zygmunt Bauman and David Lyon, *Liquid Surveillance* (Cambridge & Malden, MA: Polity, 2013).

35 Steve Mann, Jason Nolan, and Barry Wellman, "Sousveillance: Inventing and using wearable computing devices for data collection in surveillance environments," *Surveillance & Society* 1, no. 3 (2003): 33; Vian Bakir, *Sousveillance, Media and Strategic Political Communication: Iraq, USA, UK.* (New York & London: Continuum, 2010).

36 Paul Reilly, "Every little helps? YouTube, sousveillance and the 'anti-Tesco' riot in Stokes Croft," *New Media & Society* 17, no. 5 (2015): 755–771.; Geert Lovink, *Dark Fiber: Tracking Critical Internet Culture* (Cambridge, MA: MIT, 2002); See also, Robert E. Gutsche, Jr., Charnele Michel, Juliet Pinto, and Susan Jacobson, "Participatory (and problematic?) newswork: An examination of teen involvement in creating local, mainstream science news," in-progress.

37 Simon A. Cole and Henry N. Pontell, "'Don't be low hanging fruit': Identity theft as moral panic," in *Surveillance and Security: Technological Politics and Power in Everyday Life*, edited by Torin Monahan (Oxon, UK & New York: Routledge, 2006), 126.

38 Bakir, 19.

39 Ibid., 165.

40 See http://occupyarrests.moonfruit.com; Noam Chomsky, *Occupied Media* (Brooklyn, NY: Zuccotti Park Press, 2012); Mark Bray, *Translating Anarchy: The Anarchism of Occupy Wall Street* (Winchester, UK & Washington: Zero Books, 2013); Matthew Morgan, "The containment of Occupy: Militarized police forces and social control in America," *Global Discourse* 4, no. 2–3 (2014): 267–284.

41 Joel Penney and Caroline Dadas, "(Re)Tweeting in the service of protest: Digital composition and circulation in the Occupy Wall Street Movement," *New Media & Society* 16, no. 1 (2014): 74–90; Sarah Jaffe, "Post-Occupied," truthout.org, May 19, 2014, http://truth-out.org/news/item/23756-post-occupied.

42 John W. Whitehead, "The police state mindset in our public schools," truthout.org, August 13, 2013, http://truth-out.org/opinion/item/18147-the-police-state-mindset-in-our-public-schools.

43 Joshua Reeves and Jeremy Packer, "Police media: The governance of territory, speed, and communication," *Communication and Critical/Cultural Studies* 10, no. 4 (2013): 359–384; Michel Foucault, "Space, knowledge,

Power," in *The Foucault Reader*, edited by Paul Rabinow (New York: Pantheon, 1984), 244.

44 Radley Balko, *Rise of the Warrior Cop: The Militarization of America's Police Forces* (New York: Public Affairs, 2013), 254; 308.

45 Nicklaus Lovelady, "Sheriff's office adds to law enforcement arsenal," *Houston Chronicle*, November 7, 2011.

46 Even as far back to the late 90s, scholars have identified "driving while black" as a consistent show of racialized force by police against blacks. Of course, "driving" and any other verb while black goes back much further than that, but renewed interest in policing and race relations in the 1990s revealed blacks in some regions were twice as likely to receive a driving-related ticket from police than non-blacks. David Harris, writing in 1999, argues that US legal systems—including previous decisions made by the US Supreme Court—or decisions to not hear specific cases, a decision in and of itself—blankets the police from legal accusations of racial profiling in these moments. Instead, police are "free to use blackness as a surrogate indicator or proxy for criminal propensity"; Daniel Byman, "Why drones work," *Foreign Affairs*, July/August (2013): 32–43; see also, Medea Benjamin, *Drone Warfare: Killing by Remote Control* (London & New York: Verso, 2013).

47 Gray Cavender, "Media and crime policy: A reconsideration of David Garland's *The Culture of Control*," *Punishment & Society* 6, no. 3 (2004): 335–348; Michael McKee, "Are we depending too much on the military's media management?," truthout.org, November 8, 2013, http://www.truth-out. org/opinion/item/19722-are-we-depending-too-much-on-the-militarys-media-management; See also, Nick Turse, "America's black-ops blackout: Unraveling the secrets of the military's secret military," truthout.org, January 7, 2014, http://truth-out.org/news/item/21085-americas-black-ops-blackout-unraveling-the-secrets-of-the-militarys-secret-military; Francis Dalisay and Masahiro Yamamoto, "Local newspaper coverage and endorsement of a U.S. military buildup in the Pacific," *International Journal of Communication* 6 (2012): 2780–2800; Robert E. Gutsche, Jr., "There's no place like home: Storytelling of war in Afghanistan and street crime 'at home' in the *Omaha World-Herald*," *Journalism Practice* 8, no. 1 (2014): 65–79.

48 Richard V. Ericson, Patricia M. Baranek, and Janet B. L. Chan, *Negotiating Control: A Study of News Sources* (Toronto, Buffalo & London: University of Toronto Press, 1989), 260.

49 Ibid., 263.

50 Astrid Gynnild, "Surveillance videos and visual transparency in journalism," *Journalism Studies* 15, no. 4 (2014): 449–463.

51 William G. Staples, *Everyday Surveillance: Vigilance and Visibility in Postmodern Life* (Lanham, MA: Rowman & Littlefield, 2014).

52 Kevin D. Haggerty and Richard V. Ericson, *The New Politics of Surveillance and Visibility* (Toronto, Buffalo & London: University of Toronto Press, 2006), 4.

Conclusion

The Myth of Being "Post-Media" & Why Americans Will Always be Media Illiterate

Chapter Purpose

In this conclusion, major arguments and outcomes from this project are summarized and, in the discussions that follow, the reader is challenged to revisit the aims of indoctrination within structures of formal education systems in ways that examine the degrees to which media producers—and users—are influenced to interact and interpret the news. Additionally, this chapter examines the failures of past media literacy efforts in the United States and the mythical expectations of today's journalism training within higher education to argue that movements to educate the citizenry about media production, use, and power has been diminished and undermined by a growing anti-intellectualism both in and outside of institutions of higher learning.

Guiding Questions

1. What are the main purposes and aims inherent in the construct of formal education, and what groups or individuals benefit from this education, and how?
2. In what ways may formal education that occurs outside that of specific journalism training influence the socialization of journalists?

Key Terms

Digital Distraction: Normative rhetoric that "digital media" technologies and ideologies hold inherent power to evoke social change while ignoring issues of control, power, and subjugation inherent in the very rhetoric of technological development

Incorporation: The process of adopting alternative, subordinate ideologies into dominant ideology as a means of pacification and normalization.

Press Pacification: Acts of indoctrination and socialization to normative ideologies that are pressed upon or that occur within the journalistic interpretive community that result in diminished antagonism between the press and fellow power institutions

---

MEDIA CONTROL: AN ASSESSMENT & REMINDER

The intent of this book has been to radicalize specific arguments about ideological forms and functions of today's news through the lens of "media control." When I began this project, US media was loaded with discussions about surveillance and secret secrets about us held by the government and corporations (see Introduction). By the time I have come to write this chapter, such discussions have become muted, replaced by a string of stories about the murder of black men by white police officers in cities across the country. No doubt, by the time these pages make it to press and into the readers' hands, narratives of local militarization of police forces and discourse about "race relations" in the United States will have become incorporated into another theme or trend.

But it is the discursive pattern of the news—and of public discourse—to incorporate threats into dominant ideology, as this book has discussed, that will still be of my central concern. The cases discussed throughout these chapters are important, if for no other reason than for the meanings associated with them are real to someone, because they involved a person or group of people, because they signified moments of individual and collective agency, and because they implicated the power elite through its arms of the press and police as being institutions and agents of force. However, the arguments made here are not stuck to the respective cases in this book. In other words, the cultural work that the press perform can be identified among a set of news events and issues and can involve entirely different casts of characters and sources and environments.

These final pages move away from specific cases of news events and analyses of press processes to provide a discussion about the ideological challenges facing today's journalists and media users that, if acknowledged and acted against, might alter the look and feel of news in ways that could benefit more people outside of the power elite. I caution that this discussion does not provide a "solution" to any normative assessments of "bad journalism." Neither does this conclusion suppose that public recognition or action related to the issues addressed here will take journalism closer to the idealistic realm of its purpose and practice. As I have discussed throughout the book, journalism is a cultural construct. We are living, though, in an ideal realm of what journalism "is" or what it "should be," but while journalism operates with pressures that can be identified, measured, and altered, we should realize that the journalism we have today—and that we have had—is the best it is going to get if we continue to look at journalism within its own strict boundaries of hyper-professionalization and collaboration with capitalism.

In large part, I am speaking mainly right now about mainstream news media; however, alternatives to the mainstream should not be given a pass, either, but that analysis—which I discuss in brief terms in this conclusion—is for another day and another project. Indeed, that discussion, too, with its reliance on alternative financial arrangements and a widely expressed and celebratory relationship with digital "innovation," falls short of moving far beyond the elite charges of what media "is for" and who it benefits.

First, however, this conclusion is focused on examining reasons for why those concerned with media education, media literacy, and creating journalism "as it should be" have largely failed in recent decades within the US educational and telecommunications structures to meet their aims of creating a mass of critical media users who, as Art Silverblatt, the editor of *The Praeger Handbook of Media Literacy*—one of a host of books by similar names and with similar efforts to trace media literacy efforts and extend their idealistic notions to the next generation of media consumers—writes are the major principles of public media education.[1] The principles are to:

- Create critical thinking skills that allow users to independently select and interpret media messaging

- Understand how media is produced and functions, its intended audiences, and its social purposes

- Articulate the potential influence of media messaging on individuals and collectives

- Prepare ways of analyzing media messages that will lead to critical conversations about media and social issues

- Interpret media as cultural "texts" that embed meanings of today's world into messages

- Increase enjoyment and appreciation of media products

- Help media producers to create more effective and responsible content

As I will state later, however, these efforts—which are generally accepted by media literacy educators and scholars as being core to the aims of media education in the United States—are coopted by media educators themselves to meet the needs of corporate interests; to benefit the individual educator or scholar herself; and to maintain a status quo in terms of the influence of journalism as a cultural function. Indeed, this conclusion isn't to cast "positive" or "negative" value upon media; rather, it is to extend the critical analyses of media control to some of its social sources of influence, many which are daily contributors to how media is created and expressed and its meanings applied.

At the core of this discussion is the ability of interpretations through the lens of "media control" to attack a rampant anti-intellectualism within higher education in the United States. In the end, it is the denial of deeper thought, the rejection of complication, and the distain toward processes of learning that maintain oppressive systems of learning and communication. As discussed below, just as the media, we experience today through the demands of traditional functions—to "democratize" through oppression and subjugation—via institutions of education, including higher learning, which are designed to maintain order of the masses.

But it is with frustration and perhaps ire that I attempt to buck the system of which I am part as a means to irritate the status quo and present arguments against which those who wish to maintain the norms of journalism education must then confront.

To begin, I provide a brief overview of the elements that build to notions of "media control" as I view it. I then examine these elements in terms of the educational and anti-intellectual environments of newsrooms and journalism curricula within which professional journalists may be trained. While I recognize that in the US journalists need not be formally educated—the processes of socialization and training discussed in Chapter 2 are rooted in a history of "professionalization" in journalism that has been influenced, in large part, by formal educational institutions and journalism programs. Here, I present six statements that summarize the conceptual points examined throughout *Media Control*:

- Media are not observers looking in on a system of the power elite. The press operate within that system and conduct forms of surveillance and violence in ways that balance the needs and expectations of their own organizations—such as in terms of gathering, interpretation, and sharing information—with creating messages that reduce the amount of energy spent by the power elite on countering threats to dominant ideology. (see Chapters 5 and 6)

- Media serve to subjugate individuals and collectives by applying dominant ideologies in press rhetoric and through the functions of news myth. News myth and narratives of explanation are ideological acts of, not outcomes of, journalistic storytelling and function by veiling the moral meanings and threats of force and control—or rationalizations of force and control—against the public within recognizable and authoritative tales. Processes involved in this effort include those of "media surveillance" and "media sousveillance." (see Chapter 4 and 6)

- Edward Herman and Noam Chomsky's Propaganda Model is critical for examining today's news media. However, to be effective, the contested approach needs to be expanded to understand how ideological acts of news operate at a local level. Such local efforts include the hegemonic "positive" process of "journalistic boosterism" and in geographic characterizations of "news place-making," both of which appear in everyday news and news about life in the everyday. (see Chapters 1 and 3)

- Journalism is a bullhorn for White Supremacy. Operating within a culture that is dedicated to the interests, experiences, and efforts of "non-black" citizens and collectives, the press function to present the news in ways that make meaning through a lens of whiteness. In order to maintain a sense of order surrounding whiteness and the status quo, the press engage in shaming and forms of the virtuous war against the "other." (see Chapters 4 and 5)

- Fifth, journalism intentionally provides a lack of context in the news to make room for immense consumerism, anti-intellectualism, and popular explanations for social events and conditions that are rooted in capitalistic and "Americanized" ideologies. (see Chapter 2 and Conclusion)

- Sixth, the interests of the power elite are placed at the forefront of media explanations, a process veiled by news of controversy, confusion, and conspiracy theory that still meet the needs of explanation for the "perceived dominant news audience," which is defined below. (see Chapter 4 and Conclusion)

In the section below, I argue for understanding the degree to which US media users will never meet the standards of media literacy in the ways that educators have intended—certainly not as long as these same educators continue to operate with the premise that we live in a "post-media" society.

THE DEATH OF MEDIA LITERACY: THE FORCE OF DIGITAL DISTRACTIONS & CORPORATIZATION

The digital news age has not moved us forward. Media is not more inclusive, more open, more transparent, and more engaged—at least not in the ways that are useful to creating social change. That is a hard pill to swallow, for some, and one that is countered with notions of the "Arab Spring" (see Chapter 4), the role of user-influence on media content (see Chapter 6), and the moments when the press critique fellow institutions of the power elite (see Chapter 5).

Our mediatized nation still lives in times of immense—and growing—divides in terms of digital access. Media continue to benefit those with "smart phones" and seems to be shocked when others have, for whatever reason, antiquated "dumb" ones. Efforts at creating media in which the messages and production values are shared with the citizenry, where the media must relinquish dedications to branding, to "standards," to notions of proper language and presentation have not come to pass. And, with mediaites' heads in the clouds about the "promise" of the digital age and the fact that we might just have reached some of those promises, the ability of outsiders to enter into the journalistic community, to have their voices heard without marginalization, becomes a darker possibility.[2]

Just as we tell ourselves we live in a post-race society (see Chapter 3), we want to tell ourselves that we are "post-media," where media has become so integrated into our lives and into the lives of "digital natives" that we somehow believe human cognition has been able to advance within the period of decades the same degree to which it would take us to develop in a millennia. Early and consistent introduction to digital technologies creates new habits and processes that can be adopted and that, with repeated use, can become a learned behavior. But the user is still stuck in a cognitive dilemma, where the ability to use the brain is adaptable to new stimuli, and yet the invisible influences of culture that are embedded in this media and in these media experiences are left to wane and be ignored, to become adopted as virtuous or advanced, and the harms and hurts—or more to the point, the potential to identify these harms and hurts—are cast aside.

In terms of our media lives, we live in what Ronald Wright calls a "progress trap," which simply put, is the loss of the individual or collective at the moment of recognizing "progress" to critically evaluate future scenarios of one's investment in that moment. In other words, the trap is when this lack of critical thinking and problem-solving—with the moment of progress enamoring the individual or collective—fails to examine prior moments of society before progress was recognized beyond nostalgic memories and casts for the future a dedication to maintaining the joy of the moment, despite the potential costs. For example, Wright uses the advancement and adulation of weaponry from the Stone Age through current times as a movement away from alternative means of survival and conflict resolution to nuclear proliferation, as the advancement of the weapons itself is viewed as the progress that should continue as a means for enabling future resolutions in times of conflict.[3]

In terms of media, the progress trap exists within even the most critical analyses of media power today (see Chapter 2) in which scholars and educators say that they operate within a system and with an interest that uses technological advancement for the betterment of society. This betterment surrounds the solution that media must become further integrated into our daily behaviors, into our explorations and examinations of daily issues and environments, and into how we gain and build "relationships" and "social networks." Media, then, become our life, our message. We become media.

What is lost in this movement of and to progress within a "post-media" society is the ability to see beyond ourselves and beyond each other. Our media selves carry culture, the oppression of our days today and of before, the places where we have been or are or will be, the ideologies of our behaviors and our choices. This is an isolated, insular world, one that is focused on the media of the self and that rejects that which does not become a dominant focus of that self. Alternative explanations are cast out, away from our media self; identities become polemic and fragmented, validated but also cursory; and the media selves of others to which our self is not attracted are oppressed through "biological explanations" of race, class, gender, sex, geography, and difference.

Our media self is about today and how much more mediatized the self can be tomorrow with little understanding of the past and its circle of history and the potential and certainty of oppression—and repression—during times of technological advancement. As I stated earlier in this project, mine is not a cry of "moral panic" or "hysteria," as is often interpreted by dominant media selves in this post-media world, nor are these the claims of the pejorative luddite—if only to save myself from being categorized in some strategic means of dismissiveness. It is with years of experience in a changing (yes, if you must, "advancing") media world as individuals, consumers, and creators that even the past decade of movements to post-media have been ignored, incorporated into dominant ideology, or accepted—not blindly but with intentionality on part of the media user and producer to further develop the media self and, in the process, to provide further avenues for control of those not associated with that self.

What is lacking is a commitment by journalists, journalism educators, and scholars of Journalism Studies to understand the dimensions of the rhetoric of being "post-media." In the United States, this phase of life for my generation and the next has been to focus on the "positive" outcomes of social media and the use of technology with little background or preparation in critical and cultural histories and media interpretations that circle through and back through again the times in which we live: economic genocide of racialized communities abound; women continue to earn less in the workplace, suffer sexual abuse, repression, and judgment at staggering and personal levels.

This book has been packed with experiences and statistics, evidence of all kinds, that reveal the hegemonic approach to interpreting life through media messaging, much of which has been set within efforts for building national and capitalistic hegemony, yet these concerns are cast aside in the "post-media" world as being things that just cannot be solved—even if through advanced, technological media intervention—and the personal agency of the individual has become so downtrodden (though with little acknowledgment of the medias' role in such an effort) that one cannot approach issues beyond one's self alone and even with the assistance of the media that we worship.

These messages of what is possible and what is not are formed with intentionality in mind—intentionality that is focused not on helping one find the agency within herself but to marginalize that agency and, ironically, kill a sense of individualism upon which the United States is built to become part of a "greater good" but a "greater good" of individuals who have been trained to trust in the tech gods and the greater media selves of others, who also have been stripped of a sense of agency, to make change. This sense of unity, in the United States anyway, is centered around what my friend Stephen Heidt refers to as the "democracy promotion industry," a notion referred to by out-going President George W. Bush who had recognized the "growth" of US "democracy" as one that is and should be spread around the globe.[4]

This industry—of which the US government, its media, and its citizens are the workers—applies within explanations of world distress and disorder metaphor and literary, devices similar to those discussed in this project (see Chapter 1), to indoctrinate audiences to an "American way of life." In particular, rhetoric initiated by US presidents over recent decades has instituted what Heidt calls "light/dark" metaphors within common discourse about US value-laden involvement both at "home" and "abroad" in which "America is a beacon, appearing most often when the presidents need to justify, authorize, or generate support for foreign assistance and democracy promotion." Other metaphors include those related to "waves" on the "sea" in which the movement of US-led democracy can cascade across the world in times of trouble to help societies rise-up.

Presidents have even used metaphors of disease to counter threats to US ideologies and actions around the globe, which function to:

> orient American conceptions of international danger and, in the context of democracy promotion, suggests that inoculating America from the disease of disorder is best accomplished via the extension of democracy.[5]

The influence of dominant political rhetoric and the media self is not slight. The efforts of the power elite to indoctrinate the local level, as discussed, reveals a continued commitment through media to connect the individual's alignment of the mediatized self to dominant ideology. As Herbert Gans writes, as recently as 2014, news media "report on government and politics with top-down reports of what public officials and others in the political elite (and more recently, also some of the economic elite) have done and said in the pursuit of their duties."[6] For example, election coverage, Gans writes, is a mainstay of unhelpful news coverage. Elections are an increasingly popular venue for news media to show themselves off to the world, to gain recognition within the power elite, and for showcasing their ability to harness technology: in 2008, for instance, CNN debuted its "election night 'hologram,'" which projected the images of correspondents and entertainers onto the digital set that made them appear three-dimensional (on-set, though, the people appeared only on a monitor.) Still, as CNN reported about itself:

> It was an election night like none other, in every sense of the phrase. In addition to the obvious—the selection of the nation's first black president— Tuesday night's coverage on CNN showcased groundbreaking technology.[7]

The rise of satire journalism over the past two decades in US and global media and the understanding of entertainment not just of the comedy but of the violence, the conflict, the controversy, and the distraction that is news itself has provided some respite for the "progress trap" in terms of questioning how media is produced, for whom, and by whom. Yet, what is covered in satire journalism are stories still revolving around the mainstream that may attack notions of power within social and cultural institutions— including the press, itself—but that fail to provide conceptual and acceptable forms of shared knowledge to counter dominant ideologies. The alternative journalism of satire journalism has become mainstreamed in its continued call for "effective" journalism but journalism that does not operate outside of a capitalistic form and is focused in its major discourse as presenting interpretations of the narrow articulations of social issues and events that appear in mainstream media.[8]

The very social and cultural structures of journalism—not merely the corporate influences upon the news—protect journalists from critical examination related to coverage of society and public policy that could create political participation or, God forbid, rebellion and revolution to overthrow the very structures that were designed through rebellion and revolution. "Although media critics tend to blame the shortcomings of mass news media coverage of politics and the economy on journalists and their employers," Gans writes, "the major causes of these shortcomings are built into the structure of America's politics." He continues to write that:

> [a]s long as the members of the news audience have such infrequent political duties and also learn little from political news that is personally relevant, they will have little incentive to pay attention to political and related news.[9]

Still, Gans is assuming that the political stage, as it stands now and as it has stood since the beginning of US Exceptionalism, is open and malleable for real public participation. It is not and has never been. For those who have made changes, or who have wished to make changes, the degree of angry fighting and battling against the systems in place that are designed to placate the public and to normalize the authority and forceful oppression against those who wish to challenge institutions costs dearly. The costs are so much so that the selfishness that appears in the media self in this post-media world relies not on the promise of the technology to overcome adversity for the greater good but on the potential protection of selfishness as a shield against harm.

The normative rhetoric that digital media technologies and ideologies hold inherent power to evoke social change, while ignoring issues of control, power, and subjugation functions as an act of *digital distraction* that moves audiences away from critical thought. Therefore, it is the shield of the media self in a digital age that halts efforts to alter media in meaningful ways and that, instead, produces the status quo of a veiled system of media control as being in and of itself a representation of slight progress. In other words, that media control does not show itself in terms of overt forms of physical death and destruction—at least without significant evaluation and uncomfortable inquiry—serves to harness any overt ill aims of media and its operators from being seen as diminishing individual autonomy from the system.

The anti-intellectualism of journalism education

At the center of the challenges I have presented is a growing sense of anti-intellectualism within halls of higher education and related efforts designed to embark on any meaningful efforts at civic education. Kathleen Hall Jamieson, for instance, notes that civic education faces challenges based on debate about the ideological values that can—and maybe should—be engrained in such efforts.[10] Ideologies related to engagement that could include the overturning of oppressive systems and the organizational strategies of social change are threats directly to the power and purposes of universities themselves to maintain the status quo of power elite dominance. In turn, then, civic and media education operate as extensions of the power elite to train the public to expect—and, perhaps, to demand—an idealistic but oppressive form of democracy and an "objective" press to "watch" over it.

Furthermore, collaborations between the corporatization of higher education and of journalism training focus on professionalization and skills-training coupled with diminishing public investment in the arts, humanities, and public governance that limits scholarly explorations of media power and control in ways that allow only for the identifying of tangible functions and outcomes of repressive communication while obfuscating embedded elements of power. Especially troubling is the corporate funding of efforts that are focused on "innovation" and technology, social media, and "engagement" efforts rooted in creating sustainable economic models to fund media that are veiled by avenues for public participation in creating media.[11]

Media literacy efforts over the past half century have attempted to address the influence of capitalism on media production and civic engagement, but each has had a limited effect in creating anything more than a normalized, conservative approach to media production and use:

- Pre-1960: Early efforts by popular figures such as of Marshall McLuhan and John Culkin contributed to public-private initiatives that resulted in a shared interest among educators to create media literacy curricula, though many of the efforts from this time period were difficult to fully establish given the socially conservative political environment of the times

- 1960s: Experiments related to teaching critical media use and interpretation included the creation of the first elementary school TV studio, the *Media Now* curriculum established by educators in Iowa, and corporate funding of media production efforts by organizations such as the Ford Foundation

- 1970s: Programs and curricula, including those produced by church groups such as *Television Awareness Training*, provided new challenges through the creation of value-laden curricula about how to address media and some of its content

- 1980s: Initiatives outside of the US, including UNSECO's "Grunwald Document," launched international efforts for media literacy and applied pressure to educators in North America, particularly in the US, to create a set of basic principles of media education that would guide future media literacy efforts

- 1990s: The National Council of Teachers of English recommended educational approaches for media literacy programs, and other organizations, such as the Aspen Institute and Harvard University, held public symposia on media education and shared outcomes with media educators

- 2000s: An attempt to enhance what had been fairly scattered and unsuccessful efforts to publicize and institutionalize media literacy principles, countless reports, conversations, and publications, emerged from the newly-formed Alliance for a Media Literate America and the US Department of Education[12]

Despite these efforts, acts by branches of the US government that have been repulsively restrictive in terms of civic use and fair access to media of all types—such as the increasingly massive deregulation of telecommunication industries and oppressive educational policies built upon No Child Left Behind—effective media literacy programs throughout the United States are battlegrounds for political and corporate distraction. Instead of discussing critical and cultural theory related to media production and use, which undoubtedly leads to challenges to dominant ideologies of religion, identity, and nationalism, efforts to educate the public about the media have instead come to celebrate the lies of social media and the digital self. In turn, these efforts provide cover for the power elite to maintain activities that restrict public access to media, including the internet.

Robert McChesney, in his 2014 book, *Blowing the Roof off the Twenty-First Century: Media, Politics, and the Struggle for Post-Capitalist*

Democracy, writes that four major efforts in recent years related to media literacy in the United States have limited educational opportunities to general discussions of:

- Government regulation of media
- The role of independent media in society
- Media education and critique of journalistic training
- Abilities and actions of the individual media producer to challenge the mainstream[13]

Yet these areas—and how they are addressed—are steeped in a confused and debated history of the role of the press in US democracy; therefore, resulting in understandings of media systems that emerge as being agreeable to the masses—and to the power elite—that focus on sociological explanations of media, particularly in terms of political economy in a digital age. Little of this descriptive information and understanding, though, is effective to counter a power system without conceptual articulations that can be used to challenge the ideological forces in play.[14]

Today, writes Paul Mihailidis in *Mediated Communities: Civic Voices, Empowerment and Media Literacy in the Digital Era*, media literacy:

is about making sense of a messy, complex, and fast-paced media word. It is about critical analysis of content, of course, but increasingly about navigating peer-to-peer spaces at the point where news and entertainment, the personal and public, meet.[15]

Indeed, not much has changed in how media educators look at media literacy. Instead of tackling the real issues of subjugation, gender inequality, murder-by-police, racialized ideologies that are perpetuated through media messaging, and the effects of our obsession with media selves, media literacy is still focused on "critique, analysis, and evaluation" of the same old processes of opening shared media spaces without acknowledging that the these "shared spaces" operate within a closed system.[16] And even though the book in which Mihailidis' words appear—a project edited by a dear friend of mine, Moses Shumow—provides international perspectives on media literacy approaches, the larger messages inherent in each of the cases and pedagogies presented rely on an idealistic and unclear interpretation of democracy—that, through education, one can become an active participant and a critical member of society.

To drive home that point, Shumow relies on John Dewey's words in *Democracy and Education* that democracy "is more than a form of government; it is primarily a mode of associated living, of conjoined communicated experience"—a perspective Dewey bases, but does not acknowledge, on a world wrapped in White Supremacy. Shumow— like many social mediates bent on definitions of democracy rooted in deterministic notions of a digital democratic—also turns to the mainstay Jürgen Habermas and his often under- or misinterpreted "public sphere" to reveal, in Shumow's words, that:

> [t]he rapid and widespread adoption of digital communication around the globe has led to the revelation of injustices long suspected but previously hidden; deeply entrenched and endemic corruption has been brought to light; decades of authoritarian roadblocks have been removed nearly overnight; and a newfound power of mass protest has been embraced as people take to the streets, spurred to action through understanding and the discovery of a common cause with fellow citizens.[17]

I am not blind to the potential for such idealism; indeed, I hold to the promise of my own idealistic wishes. Nor do I reject the individual moments when social media or digital technologies have appeared in the public light. However, as *Media Control* has argued, the press manipulate the meanings of these moments and the role of media early on in their processes of development. Serendipitously, the same media that reports favorably in terms of social media and technological advancement for the good of the masses, particularly when the press use such technology, operates within a media system that assisted in taking the internet, supposedly designed to be de-centralized, and centralizing it around interests and access of corporations, militaries, the massively wealthy, and members of the public with social capital enough to navigate its potential but who have just enough capital that we become blinded by our own selves to apply the potential power of our agency via technology to service others.

If we were to assume for a moment that as with other aspects of governance, public policy, and communication structures that the messages and meanings of news media are crucial to the selection and implementation of society's programs, policies, and other initiatives within our changing classrooms and cities and that news coverage has the potential to shape public opinion and involvement in how people and communities can operate within forms of social and governmental structures, then understanding that news coverage and how it may relate to larger issues of funding and public support is worthy of consideration through the lens of media literacy—maybe even one that does hold idealistic and celebratory constructs of the digital age.

But these outrageous outcomes cannot be accomplished through today's media literacy efforts, nor can these things be fully accomplished in much of today's journalism curricula where partnerships with corporations and with histories, lessons, and ethics statements focus on maintaining distance from "the people" and a hegemonic financial equation. In fact, Robert Kubey writes that efforts at media literacy in the United States face an "inoculationist-protectionist aim"[18] that focuses on maintaining a paternalistic and elitist explanation of the role of media in society that, as I mentioned above, naturalizes a system in which the public need not participate in order to be "protected." And, as McChesney writes, public policies are developed and described between politicians and their corporate partners behind closed doors just as much as in "open" forums of city council meetings and live sessions of Congress.[19]

Indeed, McChesney states that outcomes of our privatized public society results in:

- The absence of the public from boardrooms and back-door meetings of our corporations and governments—even though the decisions made by both private and public sectors have a direct impact on our lives

- Language of laws and policies that are convoluted and contradictory as a method of involving only a select few of society—the formally educated—who then charge the masses insurmountable and damaging costs to translate

- Processes of law-making that are expensive and time-consuming and that make it impossible for the average citizen who is riled in consumer and educational debt and in the desire to achieve "The American Dream" from participating fully in such processes

- Dissent that may emerge from members of the public that is marked as domestic terrorism at the extreme and as public disorder at the most latent; both interpretations, however, that lead to public punishment and acts of or threats of violence and discipline

Most troubling is the degree to which these naturalized practices appear in the press through public discipline and rhetoric that "our system" is better than any alternative (see Chapter 2). Indoctrination of journalists to follow blatant nationalism requires an authoritative method of socialization, which is discussed next.

MEDIA SOCIALIZATION AND PRESS PACIFICATION THROUGH JOURNALISM EDUCATION

In early 2015, the Knight Foundation—a champion of journalism education and, ironically, one of its biggest detractors and an enemy of intellectualism within journalism programs—released *Above & Beyond: Looking at the Future of Journalism Education*, a manifesto that aggregated previous research on journalism education, industry trends, and commentary from some of today's most industry-friendly journalism schools in the United States. Like dozens of reports that have come before it, the report dismissed pedagogical and curricular concerns and focused on the economic function of journalism programs to benefit a media system that has always—and continues to be— profitable, despite the thousands of layoffs in print newsrooms over the past five years, mergers that have reduced the amount of original content being produced in the field to keep profits as high as possible, and the injection of fear tactics in discourse with journalism faculties, students, and professionals that media may not be dying but that without massive changes it might.[20]

The report also tapped into cultural challenges within many journalism units at universities across the country—and the globe—to strengthen the narrative that the corporate structure of higher education is all that can protect journalism. Only hyper-professionalization and a dismissal of intellectual content and content providers within college programs, the report argued, can save journalism programs from themselves. Borrowing from a 2013 Poynter Institute study on journalism education, the 2015 Knight document highlighted "a troubling divide between academic and professionals over the value and quality of a journalism degree" that helped to explain why "enrollments in journalism programs *seem* [my emphasis] to be stagnating or on the decline." Enter the quantitative data (verbatim below, but with my own emphasis):

- Ninety-six percent of journalism educators believe a journalism degree is very important to extremely important when it comes to *understanding the value of journalism*. Only 57 percent of media professionals agreed.

- More than 80 percent of educators but only 25 percent of media professionals say a journalism degree is extremely important when it comes to *learning newsgathering* skills.

- Thirty-nine percent of educators say journalism education *keeps up with industry changes a little or not at all*. Editors and staffers are even harsher, with 48 percent saying J-schools are not keeping up with changes in the field.

- Thinking back to the last person their organization hired, only 26 percent of media professionals say the person had "*most*" *or* "*all*" *of the skills necessary to be successful.*

Not surprisingly, then, the report contributes to an echo chamber of anti-intellectual and corporate reports that it references and links to that focus on using university classrooms—many of them public classrooms, paid for with public monies—to supplement the costs of training media professionals for corporate profits. Rarely, however, do these profits make their way back to universities in meaningful ways. When they do, they often come in awards to particular programs through a vetting process that matches the popularity contests of middle and high school. Faculty and staff members at universities across the nation spend vital amount of time and energy applying for these funds—sometimes hundreds of applications arrive at donor's feet for small amounts of monies. Even $100,000 is chump change for media organizations, and with the many restrictions placed on funds and the bureaucracies of university's even this amount does not cover nearly as much as one might think, particularly when technology is at the core of many of our programs and efforts.

Corporate profits also do not make their way directly to our students in reasonable and dignified salaries that cover the debt or costs they might have spent on internships and related costs associated with providing cheap—and more frequently, free—labor. Entry level—and even advanced—positions within the media industry do little to cover the amount of debt students have taken out and the vast amounts of money that taxpayers, faculty members, or endowments at private universities have invested into training the student (now the new employee). Indeed, the Knight report, which I analyze below in terms of how it represents the larger—and ignored—problems of journalism education, is presented as fulfilling a needed role in understanding the potential and promise of journalism to contribute to a healthy "democracy" through capitalism (which, in fact, is one of the core problems).

What was missing—which is seemingly always missing in reports such as this—was any recognition of the cultural monopolization the media hold on today's social issues and the needs of journalism education and training to recognize the complexities of media ecosystems through the adaptability and acknowledgment of social and cultural theory. Throughout this section, I treat the Knight report from 2015 and another report—*Searchlights & Sunglasses: Field Notes From the Digital Age of Journalism* by Knight Foundation senior advisor to the president Eric Newton and published in 2013[21]—as representative of the corporate and anti-intellectual rhetoric that's been spewed for decades and that is presented as being in the best interests of journalism education, journalism schools, and the public good.

Searchlights & Sunglasses seems to be an extension of a list of "radical" ideas for reform within higher education that Newton published in 2012 but expanded within an interactive, multimedia experience on the web, and so it is with these three documents—one from Poynter and two from Knight—that I conduct the following analysis of how the corporate model of journalism education represents the process of *press pacification*, acts of indoctrination and socialization to normative ideologies that are pressed upon or that occur within the journalistic interpretive community that result in diminished antagonism between the press and fellow power institutions.

In turn, this process of pacification baulks at the basic tenets of even the mildest of progressive aims that are (and should be) at the root of higher learning and that reject traditional ideals of disruption upon which US journalism is said to be built. Below, I present four major problems of current discourse related to journalism education, the last one being all-encompassing in terms of the major recommendations being made to create journalism classrooms of the future.

Problem 1: "The teaching hospital"

From somewhere around the mid-to late-2000s, loud voices within journalism education called for journalism schools to follow a "teaching hospital model" in which students operate as community reporters and content creators, not merely as students. In this dynamic, according to Newton's *Sunglasses* report:

> students, professors and professionals work together under one digital roof to inform and engage a community. They experiment with new tools and techniques, informed by research and studied by scholars, in a living laboratory.

The "teaching hospital model"—which seems to be built on the idea of teaching hospitals where medical students work alongside licensed doctors and professionals as they learn their trade—adopts the idea that teaching hospitals are not just places to train future doctors but that as the students learn and work, they provide an important—and more affordable—service to the community.[22] The ironic part of this movement is that journalism programs have been working this way since Day 1. Journalism is a trade that is practiced, to which one is socialized (see Chapter 2). The idea that journalism programs focus only on stuff inside books with no focus on "practice" is misguided.

But the principles of the "teaching hospital model" have been misguided, as well. As both the 2013 and 2015 reports indicate, journalism education has become an industry of its own, following the neoliberal movements of learning across fields, and one that must shed its intellectual components to increase the profitability of its practice. To satisfy these voices within journalism education, journalism programs should come to look at themselves as mini-corporations led not by "thinkers" but by "doers." Though the 2015 Knight report does not explicitly call for the removal or reduction of tenured faculty members to be replaced by professionals in the classroom, the documents do highlight views of "innovators" across the field that suggest "[s]low turnover among longstanding, tenured faculty can make it more difficult to bring fresh perspectives, innovation and currency into higher education in general," which the report then "confirms" with arguments that the journalism programs and efforts within journalism programs that don't make the grade are on the backs of the same faculty members that should be kicked to the curb.

The target of this approach, of course, is the misunderstood and undervalued function of tenure. While I do not wish to extend the lengthy conversation of tenure and its pros and cons to these pages—thereby providing credence to an attack on a process and function of building university structure that does, in fact, lead to innovation in practice as much as in thought—I also do not mean to argue that the field and profession of education is in a good spot. Indeed, people have taken the institution of higher education to task in effective and critical ways, such as Michèle Lamont did in her 2009 *How Professors Think: Inside the Curious World of Academic Judgment*.[23] I will, however, say that despite the debates about tenure—ones I was happy to embark upon as a reporter and college student without understanding the vital role of the process—tenure and the role of the tenured professor contributes more to society, to communities, to students, and to the university than just to their home departments and areas of specialization.

Faculty spend most of their time on committees working within university structures, fighting—almost as my father did in his bureaucratic world of work (see Introduction)—for advancements in process, for fairness in policies and curricula, and in maintaining a hold on financial management of our institutions. By and large, faculty care about student development; how students live and experience the world; the structure of building comprehensive learning environments across the institution; saving the Humanities and Social Sciences from neoliberal attacks; finding ways in tight budgets "to do more with less;" fixing problems; putting out fires; and building intellectual thought.

At least all of those things are what I like to think we do, and I worry why many people think otherwise: maybe it is because professors and teachers in general are not good at explaining our jobs; maybe some of us are assholes that turn off too many in the public with our conceptualizations and arguments; maybe we are just too damn busy doing our jobs that fighting public perception is not at the top of our list when maybe it should be. Still, seeing reports like those that come from leading voices such as the Knight Foundation—because they are also leading funders—that acknowledge problems of divides between practice and theory but that also clearly present their own single interests concerns some of us who wish to see a deeper dedication in our classrooms to examine and critique today's power structures. Only passing mentions of thinking in reports that are designed to drive the thought of faculty and administrators—if those faculty and administrators want to receive monies from these foundations—is troubling.

Denying the depth of the learning process, the application of pedagogy, the creation of means by which students can identify their agency, and the dedication to aims beyond those of profits for the already profitable is particularly important to someone like me who dropped out of college when my birth mom died and went full-time into a newsroom. Leaving school—and trying to get back in—provided me an opportunity to learn the most I ever could about life, about who I was (and am) as a person; about the role of education not only in finding money to pay rent but to find meaning in life; and about the purpose of love and learning when I fought—with the support of so many people—to get back into the classroom.

Not all of my students, thank God, are like I was—focused only on the profession. Many of my students are hungry for critical and cultural examinations of the world—and of their work—and push through the uncomfortable moments of the learning process to see how journalism fits into their lives and into the meanings they wish to make for themselves and for others. We need students (and professionals) like that, and we sure as hell need more from the loud voices in the field of journalism education—and in the field of education, generally—that place value on the lived experience. The people our students are "practicing on" in the "teaching hospital" need faculty, funders, and journalists who care about their lived experiences, too.

Before continuing, I should note that I have not escaped the benefits of the same types of funding that I am critical of in this chapter. In 2014 and 2015, I was part of a team of faculty members at my university that received a grant from the Online News Association in order to "crack the curriculum" in ways that would challenge the ways in which journalism is taught through technology and community engagement. This $35,000—funded by several organizations, including the John S. and James L. Knight Foundation, the Robert R. McCormick Foundation, the Excellence and Ethics in Journalism Foundation, the Democracy Fund, and the Rita Allen Foundation—led to the creation of a web project, eyesontherise.org, which examined the effects of sea level rise in South Florida through journalism and scholarship.

Over the course of an academic year, we worked with students and community partners to produce journalism about the environmental impacts of rising seas in South Florida that are infiltrating pockets of fresh water with salt, eroding the region's infrastructure, and flooding neighborhoods with waters full of toxins and pollutants. Efforts paid for by the grant gave my school and students a national spotlight—including time on NBC's TODAY—and allowed us to build upon work already being done in my department and at my university to discuss changing environments of South Florida.

When we started the project, I thought the experience was going to be about journalism education—pushing the boundaries of what we could do as a field. But that really was not the case. While other awardees who also received that round of funding provided opportunities for their students to engage with issues in their communities—including applying pressure on public officials to maintain clean and safe housing for the underserved, to manage public funds in a transparent manner, and to clean the environment—discussions among the funders and fellow university teams rarely focused on pedagogical and educational changes that could emerge from journalism "innovation."

My team was fortunate enough to merge our college courses with those at a magnet STEM (Science, Technology, Engineering, and Math) high school located on our university campus to push our curricula and learning outcomes. The collaboration led to much success: students from the high school taught college journalism students about the science involved in understanding sea level rise; college students took to mentoring the high schoolers and teaching them effective means of communicating complex environmental stories.

But the students—and the faculty members—involved in this project got lessons and experiences of another type, as well, as we became mired in a political battle with local officials, businesses (and even fellow professors outside of our unit) who wanted to collaborate with us but who also wanted to control the conversation about rising seas in ways that protected local tax bases. Even the most conservative estimates on sea level rise put places like Miami-Dade County underwater by 2100. While our project began with concerns about how we might address the controversial and politically volatile debate about what causes sea level rise (i.e., climate change), we soon learned that no one in South Florida gives a damn anymore about any controversy surrounding climate change—let alone sea level rise.

What we found to be off-the-table for open discussion among local professional media, politicians, and economic tycoons, however, was the potential economic effect of a changing environment on the ability of developers to take whatever profits they can from local residents who are moving en masse to new high rises built on sinking land. The controversy surrounding our efforts increased following a thoughtful piece about the political infighting surrounding sea level rise in South Florida that appeared in *The Washington Post*.[24]

As Joby Warrick wrote from Miami Beach in October 2014:

At least twice in a normal year, the Biscayne Bay rises to swamp the streets of this fashionable resort town in an event known as the "king tide." Water spills over seawalls and gurgles up through storm drains in what scientists say is a preview of life in Florida in a warming climate.

But this is an election year, when even nature becomes a foil for competing political narratives. When a highly anticipated king tide hit the Florida coast last week, state and local officials surged into action to ensure that any flooding was kept out of sight.

Crews went to work at daybreak Thursday to fire up brand-new pumps installed to prevent seawater from inundating expensive bayfront real estate. By late morning, the TV reporters who arrived in wading boots to film flooded streets instead saw only puddles. By Oct. 10, when the state's two gubernatorial candidates met for a televised debate, the streets were completely dry, and the Republican incumbent was able to deflect a question about the impact of climate change on the state.

"We put $350 million into flood mitigation," Gov. Rick Scott told viewers of the debate with Democratic rival Charlie Crist.

The scramble to limit the damage from rising waters—practically and symbolically—illustrates the challenges and pitfalls faced by politicians this year in dealing with the divisive issue of climate change. Particularly in hard-hit coastal states such as Florida, where rising sea levels are now an inalterable fact, the effects are becoming harder to ignore or suppress, though officials regularly still try.

In early 2015, it was revealed that Florida's governor had banned the use of the term "climate change" from appearing in any official state communication.[25]

For a "teaching hospital" to work, there needs to be a commitment from universities and donors as, in our case, to navigate the political and possible legal matters associated with students practicing journalism. This is especially true in such a strong anti-intellectual and anti-university climate.[26] Indeed, our coverage and involvement in issues of sea level rise in South Florida led to the disinvestment of a previously negotiated partnership and funds in the tens of thousands of dollars between our faculty and one of the city's most at risk for massive sea rise problems. Most shocking, however, was the polite but telling pushback we got from one of the donors to our very own grant in which one of the project managers emailed, saying that our once-a-week (at most) tweets about our project, "since they mention sea level rise," is "sort of confusing to our audience given we don't focus on the issue directly .... you probably don't need to mention our support for the project quite as frequently."

Embedded in this message and in our subsequent phone call, was that the tweeting was not the issue; rather, it was the political (and possible financial) implications to his own organization, because we were implicating them in helping fund efforts that challenge the motives and efforts of developers and politicians building on the hopes that the seas don't rise. In the end, the grant provided an opportunity for our students to affect social change through communication and involvement, but it also shed light on the inner-workings of how these grants function—that, coupled with the rhetoric of many of the funders themselves, these opportunities are not about challenging or changing the status quo but socializing students to maintain it.

Problem 2: "Innovation"

"Innovation" has become a key word in journalism education, as schools attempt to create a Googlish culture that provides students with the ability to create their own platforms, technologies, and techniques for journalistic reporting and storytelling. In calling for such a cultural shift within these units of universities, Knight's 2015 *Above & Beyond* report didn't disappoint:

> Journalism schools have for decades structured curricula around the core journalistic values of truth, commitment to the public good, editorial independence, watchdogging the powerful, effective storytelling, and objectivity and balance. Schools hired faculty with the appropriate expertise to teach both content and skills courses grounded in these core values, and that expertise, once established, enjoyed long staying power.
>
> Today, currency—the capacity to identify and master emerging market trends and media technologies and to integrate them quickly into journalistic work—is as critical to credible journalism education as command of Associated Press style and the inverted pyramid used to be.

I love innovation, and I strive to extend that passion to my students, and, honestly, many of my students are innovative even without me. But journalism students—by and large—might not consider themselves to be creative. To guide innovation, one must be empowered to make their own choices, to fail, to recreate, and to have time and distance to think, let alone have the financial and physical spaces and resources to do so. What universities really want—and the only reason journalism schools are on board with "innovation" without the necessary training, pedagogy, affective support and resources— is the potential in innovation to provide patents and products that can be sold to the marketplace.

My broad statements are not meant to ignore the wonderful work that many of my colleagues do, but the innovation of those who have the most influence on students and on the field, on our communities and on our future, are of those who are focusing their innovation efforts on understanding the process of innovation just as much as working to an end product. It is in the process of learning, of thinking, of doing, that the potential of and for innovation thrives. And that potential includes the potential—and the certainty—for failure. Indeed, the *Above & Beyond* report challenges university faculty to provide more opportunities for innovation, but in its apparently acceptable narrow view of "credible journalism education" as being one that is constructed around the "command of Associated Press style and the inverted pyramid," faculty members and the work of the university is reduced to practices of rote memorization.

There are dozens of coherent facts I can remember from journalism school, and I am thankful for the educators and other students who provided my training in the field. But what I took with me more than anything else from the University of Wisconsin was its focus on the "Wisconsin Idea"—that the role of the university system is to reach beyond its borders, beyond its surrounding communities, and beyond the state line. What we did in those classrooms, the conversations and debates, papers and presentations, fit within an environment that placed ourselves in a larger society.

Somehow—perhaps because many of the professors and staff members and students I knew took the Wisconsin Idea to heart by supporting a system and network of state universities and colleges, its extension offices, and the schools' direct influence on respective communities—these ideas made their way into how I view the role and function of messaging. More than anything, though, the Wisconsin Idea influenced us to explore social problems and potential solutions, often at the cost of power structures. Not surprisingly, then, did the state's governor, Scott Walker, in 2015 attempt to remove the Wisconsin Idea from state legislation and language, a move that when it became public, he claimed was a clerical error.[27]

The reports and rhetoric that come from voices attempting to direct journalism education as an industry include a blending of fear tactics (programs that do not innovate will be disbanded and defunded) and emotional support. According to *Searchlights & Sunglasses*, for example: "You can create both new uses of software and new software itself. Anyone can create the future of news and information. Anyone includes us." This rhetoric is helpful in making faculty feel like *something they might do* would be appreciated. But armchair leadership ignores the processes and potentials of things like the Wisconsin Idea and other ideological influences designed to create vision and direction toward a better society.

Faculty members are then left to figure out how to balance the desires of universities that are already focused on a customer service model of coddling and placating to (some) students and launching degree programs and courses only if they are "self-sustaining" and fit into "market rate" equations. Students have been trained from early classroom experiences of standardized testing, of hyper-authority, militarization, and fear that by the time they reach our journalism classrooms they have employed their savvy to have completed most—if not all—of their general academic coursework and have their sights set on full-time employment. In addition to the part-time (and too-often full-time) work that many of our students must have in order to afford college, the intellectual and pedagogical purposes of the classroom become second- or third-level interests and aims. Overworked faculty, then, follow suit and the classroom becomes a mirror of the dysfunctional and schizophrenic industry that touts traditional values of "serving the public" but institutes paywalls for people to access content said to be vital for creating a "public sphere."

These barriers become financial barriers that require subscriptions that, even for journalism professors, place the cost of news too far out of reach for consumers. (I estimate that for me to access all of the news I need online through subscriptions would cost me roughly $1,900 a year.) As long as media companies are so profitable *and* claim to provide resources for the public that are supplemented by the public through tax incentives, mailing rate reductions, education for training employees, and socio-cultural initiatives discussed throughout this book that provide wonderful public relations through news for the power elite, I will hope for access to a "free" media.

Using the industry as a benchmark for media production and social investment, students and faculty become confused about the degree to which journalism is critical in covering low-income or marginalized populations who cannot afford to purchase and participate in media. But it is not just economic deficiencies that remove journalists-as-executives from the larger public. As I discussed in Chapter 6, journalists are intentional—and innovative—in creating distance between "us" and "them."

One of my favorite experiments with my journalism students to prove this point is to give them a short time period, roughly thirty seconds, to find the names and contact information, including phone numbers, for reporters and editors on a local newspaper website. I then give students the same amount of time to find information on how to subscribe and to advertise with the newspaper. Time almost always elapses before students can find the details for a reporter or editor, but they find advertising and subscription information almost immediately. News outlets do not want to hear from "citizens," this tells us, only from "customers." How is that message reflected in journalism classrooms, curricula, and training?

Apparently, the authors of decades of reports similar to *Above & Beyond* and *Searchlights & Sunglasses* have subscribed to a similar approach—one that will only bring journalism programs in-line with the rest of the university. Writes Henry Giroux:

> What is new about the current threat to higher education and the humanities in particular is the increasing pace of corporatization and militarization of the university, the squelching of academic freedom, the rise of an ever increasing contingent of part-time faculty and the view that students are basically consumers and faculty providers of a salable commodity such as a credential or a set of workplace skills.[28]

The thing that drew me to journalism and to journalism school, in the first place, and what keeps me in the field, is the degree to which—in principle—the role of journalism is to create disturbances in power structures. Even now, when that idealistic function is in question, even in my own mind, I am troubled that the field I have loved and hated most of my life has been suckered into a neoliberal mode of anti-intellectualism that is so blatant and so hateful. Given the nature of my own field as I have explored it in this project, however, maybe this ideological position is right where journalism and journalism education belongs.

Problem 3: "Collaboration"

Above & Beyond and *Searchlights & Sunglasses* approach the economic implications of innovation—including high-priced technology and salaries to steal professionals away from the private sector—by arguing for "collaboration" with other university's and established media enterprises. *Above & Beyond*, for example, quotes professionals and professors from across the country who speak in code about collaboration as a way to add economic value to the added reach of content through collaboration with media outlets. According to one interviewee quoted in the *Above & Beyond* report:

> Culturally, I think journalism schools have to think about collaboration and partnership as a huge value; the concept of exclusivity no longer exists.
>
> If you really want to leverage your work for impact and reach, especially in an investigative nonprofit space, it's all about distribution, traditional and nontraditional unique storytelling, and creating a culture where impact is thought about and valued.

I have also been associated with efforts in media collaboration, and I am not opposed to the learning—and possible public benefit—that can come from partnerships. In 2009, I helped launch the Wisconsin Center for Investigative Journalism at the University of Wisconsin and that same year co-founded The Iowa Center for Public Affairs Journalism at the University of Iowa. These online, non-profit media centers were designed to seek funding from private donors and organizations to produce journalism that can be shared and republished throughout the media ecosystem at no cost to other outlets. They are an admirable effort and represent perhaps some of the best initiatives of the modern day to counter a capitalistic system of media control.

That said, the embeddedness of media-for-profit still influences the ideological and economic values that drive news production, making these non-profits, in many way, not so different from our for-profit cousins. As I wrote with a colleague in 2012 about our early experiences in non-profit news:

> Contrary to any implication of financial freedom and independence in the emergence of nonprofit regional news outlets in the U.S., journalists have no sanctuary from market-driven pressures.
>
> Even among nonprofits, financial considerations play a significant role in news coverage. While nonprofits may operate independently from shareholders, corporate forces and advertisers, they face pressures created by the constant need to attract donations.
>
> The reality that news workers must maintain long-term financial stability splits the journalists' focus between news, networking, and self-promotion. This weakened "wall" between editorial and business in the nonprofit newsroom contributes to what may be an even larger issue—its potential influence on journalism.
>
> We've found through our experience that such a focus on funding can create money-conscious, self-censoring reporters and editors who may subtly shape content to best fit a donor's mission. Self-censorship, which chills the journalistic mission, runs counter to the missions of many nonprofit initiatives, particularly those in which we've been involved.
>
> More concerning, however, has been the lack of open conversation among nonprofit news workers and media scholars about the potential problems involved with this form of journalism. Only with further investigations into the nature of nonprofit news work can we reveal the challenges—and possible conflicts—to better the work of journalists.[29]

At their core, collaborations that place faculty members and working professionals in the same space of news production with professional and student reporters are spaces in which students are allowed to apply what they have learned, fail, and recover through challenge and support. Absent of any pedagogical influence, however, educators are experts only in their fields and are released from being required to have equal knowledge of cognitive and affective processes. In turn, faculty members—and students—become employees of and for a media industry without reaping the financial and social profits and providing a public good, as journalism is said to do.[30]

Problem 4: "Knowledge"

Above & Beyond argues that solutions for saving journalism education from a dark future "(rest) not in the retraining of every legacy journalism faculty member, but in the creation of new ways to deliver expertise to our classrooms." Additionally, the report states, programs should focus on creating "a startup, digital-first program with all new systems, structures and operating assumptions, designed to ensure that all faculty, in every classroom, are teaching what they know." Setting aside the financial implications of such efforts and the lack of unrestricted funds coming from media companies to *all* of the country's journalism programs—not just the most popular ones— arguments for training and retraining faculty members to produce a skills-focused education sounds promising and would be welcome, I am sure, by many of us who teach both skills and theory courses.

The concern here is that knowledge that faculty members *already have* in terms of their research, journalism, creative work, community involvement, and individual values and perspectives is secondary in a "retraining." In fact, only one of the recommendations for journalism programs in *Above & Beyond* recognizes what faculty already bring to the table in that programs should "[l]everage the disciplinary expertise of the full-time faculty while creating new delivery structures for skills-based learning." Other than that one conciliatory nod to intellect, two other recommendations for journalism programs suggest that they should (1) "[e]stablish a digital-first academic startup, the educational equivalent of the ProPublicas, FiveThirtyEights and Vox Medias of the news-and-information marketplace" and (2) "[c]reate a mission-specific accreditation process for programs that define as their core mission the preparation of twenty-first-century journalists."

In the section below, I explicate the ideological and social problems that emerge from journalism's—and journalism education's—isolated and corporatized model, which include:

- Funding mechanisms for training the needs of the industry from which profits are rarely returned to the classroom in meaningful forms of investment

- Media purposes and approaches grounded in Western, hegemonic processes of professionalization and anti-intellectualism

- The targeting of power at popular and technologically savvy forms of journalism and training

- Co-opting the sense of agency within one's self through digital distraction that perpetuates racist presentations of the world in daily coverage

CONCLUSION: COMPLICATING MEDIA CONTROL'S COLLECTIVE IDENTITY

In this final section, I take the time to address the deep connections made throughout this project between journalism and race as a means to also address the above concerns about journalism education by turning to the role of education and socialization of journalists and the indoctrination of the news worker to the racist ideologies of US society and dominant culture. Through the process of formal education, from the first moment in a classroom at the youngest age, we are introduced to authoritative means of understanding the world and the imperialistic function of US explanations that present positions of the United States and of US citizens as being exceptional and virtuous. In fact, the journalism classrooms where I teach (Figure C.1) are decorated with the remembrance of the expected nationalistic commitment that those within the room should be aware.

The lessons and discussions therein are cast in a nationalistic light, the questioning of US tendencies to violently invade "lesser-than" nations and justify such action through rhetoric of expanding democracy watched by the flying flag of oppression and repression. We are always reminded "where we are" and "who we are" and, as journalists and educators, we must face the options of questioning all that we know to be true about where we are and who we are, despite the consequences of speaking against what we are expected to praise and revere.

US ideology is rooted in racism, and the degree to which the classroom is a space to challenge the status quo without the reprisal of the classroom environment itself and the dominance of hegemonic structures of education and nationalism that appear within it, is vital for effecting change or attempting to operate outside power structures, where possible, through journalism and journalism education. In his ethnographic study of newsrooms, for instance, Don Heider discusses the intentionality of white coverage of black issues, of the indoctrination of journalists that may have occurred outside the realm

FIGURE C.1 *The flag of the United States protrudes into nearly every classroom in which the author has taught at Florida International University—a sign of US dedication to itself. Photographs by Alicia Sandino. Used with permission.*

of journalism training and education but that was reified by the journalistic system itself.

Heider presents the story of one news editor in Albuquerque, New Mexico, as an example. The editor told Heider that he denied racial bias appears in the reporting done by journalists at the newspaper, turning to the police scanner and information from officials and authoritative institutions, such as police, as being free of racial meaning. Heider writes that the editor considered "his police scanner [to be] color blind" and "that all crimes were reported by the police dispatcher without mention of race-ethnicity" and in ways that did not spark racialized rhetoric within the news. But as Heider argues, "to make this assertion one would have to know whether the police presence is the same in all areas of a city, if all groups within that city report crime at the same rates, and to what crimes police themselves decide to pay close attention."[31]

In other words, the lived experience of the reporter and her interpretations of the world, of her neighborhood, of other people's neighborhoods, and of the legitimacy and virtue of police—in this case, anyway—influences what she does with the information that she gains from outside herself. Sonya Alemán, an assistant professor of Communication and Ethnic studies at the University of Utah, writes that because these experiences and interpretations of what I call the "journalistic self" (see Chapter 2) are rooted in dominant ideologies of White Supremacy from outside of the classroom, formal education should be a place where these ideas are assessed and challenged. But they are not, she writes, in that:

> current journalism pedagogy may be understood as perpetuating whiteness and promulgating a worldview that excludes the perspective of racially disenfranchised communities—even when students of color are enrolled in the classroom.[32]

Alemán bases her findings on some twenty-five hours of observation over a dozen class periods of introductory and intermediate news writing courses to examine how issues of race, privilege, and social context emerge in students' discussion of news values and journalistic decision-making. Additionally, her critical analysis of a popular journalism textbook, *Reporting for the Media* and of a chapter from *Working with Words: A Handbook for Media Writers and Editors*, which both reflect the types of writing and approaches taught in introductory journalistic writing courses, revealed an educational environment that benefits the experiences of whiteness that are presented as normal and expected against which perceived difference is measured.

These measurements of "what's normal" and of "what's different," particularly in terms of race, become compounded outside of the classroom where there is little structure and organization available to guide critical discussion and analysis of gut reactions and journalistic explanations based on individual and personal interpretation. That self-examination of self-decision-making is rooted in an ideology of oppression and is maintained by structures of indoctrination and socialization that is media control. Journalists are trained to turn to "authorities" on matters of society and culture, the very same who, too, have been indoctrinated to the system and to systematic and measured explanations that benefit the power elite.

In effect, then, the efforts to maintain a normative sense of journalistic "objectivity" is an ideological method of maintaining bias toward power systems and control by and of those systems. And because journalists hold credible those who reinforce their own meanings and interpretations of what is in the news, they share not only in the understandings themselves but within the communities of those understandings.

Despite the efforts of journalists and scholars who wish not to see journalists sharing in the interpretive communities of other social and cultural institutions—or more likely to avoid having journalists share their own community with other social and cultural institutions—journalists are viewed as functioning separately as interpretive communities of their own making, with boundaries and borders that are maintained to keep them separate from non-journalists and any other unapproved influences that could challenge the preeminent meanings of journalism. Matt Carlson, in the introductory chapter to the edited volume *Boundaries of Journalism*, explains that journalistic boundary work is not to reduce "boundary struggles to a cabal of conniving, power-hungry plotters," which would "be to shortchange the range of motives among players and stakeholders."[33] Indeed, that might sound too much like a conspiratory construction close to that of the power elite.

And while in that same volume David Domingo and Florence Le Cam argue that journalism scholarship should examine the "diversity of actors playing a role in news narratives ... regardless of their position inside or outside journalism as a profession"[34] as a way to complicate the notion of journalistic boundaries that, though possibly malleable given the moment in time and the rationale to be fluid, such approaches to the journalistic interpretive community focus on the social production of news related to the journalist-source relationship and forms of professionalization of the field to discuss how news may be "co-constructed."

Defined by Dan Berkowitz and James TerKeurst as "a geographic community's culture and power structure" that "shape(s) both decision-making processes and news coverage" about a community's central identities and decisions that need to be made,[35] there remains great potential which has not yet been reached within Journalism Studies to highlight the elements of power and the direction and intentions of those power flows to argue that the journalistic interpretive community does not send power outside of itself but maintains the flows of power within its borders, which include institutions that have largely been viewed as operating within their own units of ideological interpretation.

Examining the "mediated social capital" of small-town newspapers in Australia and the United Kingdom, for example, Kristy Hess argues that several ideological processes operate to connect the power flows of the press and fellow power institutions in ways that, I argue, reveal intentionality of journalism as an institution to capitalize on the methods and means of a shared ideological community of which the press, business, military/police, nation-builders, and educators coalesce. These processes are:

- Bonding—the creation of the press to build connectedness and community through news explanations of values and geographic characterizations that make audiences appear to be one unit

- Bridging—the function of the press to broker relationships and commitments between the people and communities during times of crisis and celebration

- Linking—the act of news explanations that "link" local audience to the issues, concerns, and solutions of the elite[36]

Borrowing from Pierre Bourdieu, the "mediated social capital" of the press, Hess argues, holds the role of negotiating conflict between one side of an issue and argument and the other (or, more to the tone of this project, one explanation over another). In this process, the press becomes what Georg Simmel refers to as *tertius gaudens*—"the 'third' who benefits" from mediatized (and mediatizing) debate by operating as "a broker [that] can spontaneously seize opportunity by controlling information relating to the conflict between two others." Indeed, the press benefit from this accumulated social capital not by solving conflict, but by expanding it.[37]

It is within this press operation of mediatizing conflict and benefiting from the navigation of debate and then catapulting themselves at the climax to the winning side where the journalistic interpretive community should be viewed in a more racial lens. Vian Bakir's less "media-centric" approach to processes of propaganda-construction helps to explain how media function in a complex, secret, and elite program of information production and release.[38] Perhaps, then, journalists are best seen operating within an "inter-elite press community" of "shadow publics"—those who determine how news is selected, shaped, and applied that allows for the press to share *the interpretive community of the power elite* where what is interpreted today as the journalistic interpretive community is not separated to the degree scholars—and journalists—suggest based upon shared memories, language, processes, and socialization practices.[39]

What is needed in examining the role of the press in the United States falls along the lines of what Aeron Davis identifies in the UK media sphere as processes by which elite sources dominate news production through "public negotiation and conflict" that:

- "Block" particular audiences from influencing media construction (and that revolve around what, with my colleague Erica Salkin, I refer to as benefiting "perceived dominant news audiences," media users that specific media outlets identify as of "main priority or interest")[40]

- Develop "small elite communication networks which include top journalists" that form the pressures of how journalism maintains dominant power explanations of everyday life

- "Capture" reporters in and by "policy communities" upon which they report to reify dominant news explanations that benefit the power structure[41]

Examining influences of news myth that indoctrinate specific audiences, communities, and cultures to the same, dominant ideologies of imperialism, exceptionalism, and virtuous violence reveals the hegemonic function of journalistic storytelling. Complicating news practices becomes particularly important as "non-geographically based, participatory media messaging occurring through such venues as social media, blogs, and through mobile devices" expand in application and sophistication as means by which to tell stories "in terms of who media creators believe their primary audiences to be," Salkin and I write.[42]

This added knowledge, however, does not equate to "media literacy" or social action that we imagine it might; a "more educated" public does not equate to a changed media system that is operating as-designed. Discursive efforts that attack dominant articulations of news construction and meanings within journalism and scholarship might, however, over time, move us closer to a shared interpretation of the role of the power elite within and through media. Still, we each will have to measure the costs to our own comforts of knowledge and privilege to decide if moves to mass equal treatment and shared power is worth—and worthy—of the effort.

Discussion Questions

1. To what degree must alterations to formal education outside of journalism training be changed to address the socialization of journalists, and what would some of these changes look like?
2. How can journalists "relearn" their knowledge base to operate independent of cultural and social indoctrination inherent in formal education, and to what degree would these "new knowledges" influence mainstream media?

Notes

1   Art Silverblatt, *The Praeger Handbook of Media Literacy* (Santa Barbara, CA: Praeger, 2014), Introduction.

2   Deana A. Rohlinger, JoEllen Pederson and Giuseppina Valle, "Inclusive discourse? Local media coverage of the Terri Schiavo case," *Sociological Spectrum* 35 (2015): 1–25; Dominic Boyer, *The Life Informatic: Newsmaking in the Digital Age* (Ithaca, NY & London: Cornell University Press, 2013).

3   Ronald Wright, *A Short History of Progress* (New York: Carroll & Graf Publishers, 2004); Tom Standage, *Writing on the Wall: Social Media—the First 2,000 Years* (New York: Bloomsbury, 2014).

4   Stephen J. Heidt, "Presidential rhetoric, metaphor, and the emergence of the democracy promotion industry," *Southern Communication Journal* 78, no. 3 (2013): 233–255.

5   Ibid., 234.

6   Herbert J. Gans, "The American news media in an increasingly unequal society," *International Journal of Communication* 8 (2014): 2485.

7   Chris Welch, "Beam me up, Wolf!: CNN debuts election-night 'hologram,'" cnn.com, November 6, 2008, http://www.cnn.com/2008/TECH/11/06/hologram.yellin.

8   Mike Conway, "The origins of television's 'Anchor Man': Cronkite, Swayze, and journalism boundary work," *American Journalism* 31, no. 4 (2014): 445–467.

9   Gans, "The American news media in an increasingly unequal society," 2488–2489.

10 Kathleen Hall Jamieson, "The challenges facing civic education in the twenty-first century," *Dædalus* 142, no. 2 (2013): 65–83.

11 Rick Edmonds, "Capital flows like water to media companies (of a certain kind)," poynter.org, December 10, 2014.

12 http://www.medialit.org/reading-room/media-literacy-usa.

13 Robert W. McChesney, *Blowing the Roof off the Twenty-First Century: Media, Politics, and the Struggle for Post-Capitalist Democracy* (New York: Monthly Review Press, 2014).

14 Carl Patrick Burrowes, "Property, power and press freedom: Emergence of the Fourth Estate, 1640–1789," *Journalism & Communication Monographs* 13, no. 1 (2011): 1–66; Mark Hampton and Martin Conboy, "Journalism history—a debate," *Journalism Studies* 15, no. 2 (2014): 154–171; Carol Sue Humphrey, *The American Revolution and the Press: The Promise of Independence* (Evanston, IL: Northwestern University Press, 2013).

15 Paul Mihailidis, "Media literacy and mediatized communities: Emerging perspectives for digital culture," in *Mediatized Communities: Civic Voices, Empowerment and Media Literacy in the Digital Era*, edited by Moses Shumow (New York: Peter Lang, 2014), 19–20; See also, Kathleen Tyner,

Literacy in a Digital World: Teaching and Learning in the Age of Information (Mahwah, NJ & London: Lawrence Erlbaum Associates, 1998).

16 Mihailidis, 20.

17 Moses Shumow, "Epilogue," *Mediatized Communities: Civic Voices, Empowerment and Media Literacy in the Digital Era* (New York: Peter Lang, 2014), 195.

18 Robert Kubey, "Obstacles to the development of media education in the United States," *Journal of Communication* 48, no. 1 (1998): 58–69.

19 McChesney, *Blowing the Roof off the Twenty-First Century*, 106; For more on the marginalization of sources, see Kjersti Thorbjørnsrud and Ustad Figenschou, "Do marginalized sources matter?: A comparative analysis of irregular migrant voice in Western media," *Journalism Studies* (2014), doi: 10.1080/1461670X.2014.987549.

20 Dianne Lynch, *Above & Beyond: Looking at the Future of Journalism Education*, 2015, http://www.knightfoundation.org/features/journalism-education.

21 Eric Newton, *Searchlight & Sunglasses: Field Notes From the Digital Age of Journalism* (2013), http://searchlightsandsunglasses.org/index; Eric Newton, "How journalism education can, and should, blow up the system," May 23, 2012, http://www.pbs.org/mediashift/2012/05/how-journalism-education-can-and-should-blow-up-the-system144; In May 2015, Newton announced he was leaving Knight to join The Journalism School at Arizona State University..

22 Knight Foundation, "The 'teaching hospital'—a goal for journalism education, November 22, 2013, http://www.knightfoundation.org/press-room/speech/teaching-hospital-goal-journalism-education.

23 Michèle Lamont, *How Professors Think: Inside the Curious World of Academic Judgment* (Cambridge, MA & London: Harvard University Press, 2009).

24 Joby Warrick, "Florida politicians battle rhetoric as rising seas drive worries over climate change," *The Washington Post*, October 17, 2014; See also, Laura Parker, "Treading water," *National Geographic* February 2015, http://ngm.nationalgeographic.com/2015/02/climate-change-economics/parker-text.

25 Tristram Korten, "In Florida, officials ban term 'climate change,'" March 8, 2015, *Miami Herald*.

26 For more on the threats to university-related journalism, see Kate Golden, "Lawmakers' attempt to evict Center arouses national controversy," wisconsinwatch.org, June 6, 2013, http://wisconsinwatch.org/2013/06/lawmakers-attempt-to-evict-center-arouses-national-controversy.

27 Christine Evans, "Save the Wisconsin Idea," *The New York Times*, February 16, 2015, http://www.nytimes.com/2015/02/16/opinion/save-the-wisconsin-idea.html?_r=0.

28 Henry A. Giroux, "Beyond the swindle of the corporate university: Higher education in the service of democracy," truthout.org, January 18, 2013, http://www.truth-out.org/opinion/item/69:beyond-the-swindle-of-the-corporate-university-higher-education-in-the-service-of-democracy; See also, Henry A. Giroux, "Intellectuals as subjects and objects of violence," truthout.org, September 10, 2013, http://truth-out.org/opinion/item/18704-intellectuals-as-subjects-and-objects-of-violence.

29 Robert E. Gutsche, Jr. and Jim Malewitz, "Facing the future of online, nonprofit news," The Convergence Newsletter, September 2012, http://sc.edu/cmcis/archive/convergence/v9no7.html.

30 Nancy J. Evans, Deanna S. Forney, Florence M. Guido, Lori D. Patton, and Kristen A. Renn, *Student Development in College: Theory, Research, and Practice* (San Francisco: Jossey-Bass, 2010); See also, Robert E. Gutsche, Jr. and Erica R. Salkin, "News stories: An exploration of independence within post-secondary journalism," *Journalism Practice* 5, no. 2 (2011): 193–209; Robert E. Gutsche, Jr., "Missing the scoop: Exploring the cultural and sociological influences of news production upon college student journalists," in *Journalism Education, Training and Employment*, edited by Bob Franklin and Donica Mensing (New York & London: Routledge, 2011), 63–77.

31 Don Heider, *White News: Why Local News Programs Don't Cover People of Color* (Mahwah, NJ & London: Lawrence Erlbaum Associates, 2000), 43.

32 Sonya Alemán, "Locating whiteness in journalism pedagogy," *Critical Studies in Media Communication* 31 no. 1 (2014): 86; See also, Robin DiAngelo, "White fragility," *International Journal of Critical Pedagogy* 3, no. 3 (2011): 54–70.

33 Matt Carlson and Seth C. Lewis, *Boundaries of Journalism: Professionalism, Practices and Participation* (London & New York: Routledge, 2015), 4.

34 David Domingo and Florence Le Cam, "Journalism beyond the boundaries: The collective construction of news narratives," in *Boundaries of Journalism: Professionalism, Practices and Participation*, edited by Matt Carlson and Seth C. Lewis (London & New York: Routledge, 2015), 138.

35 Dan Berkowitz and James V. TerKeurst, "Community as interpretive community: Rethinking the journalist-source relationship," *Journal of Communication* 49, no. 3 (1999): 126.

36 Kristy Hess, "Making connections: 'Mediated' social capital and the small-town press," *Journalism Studies* (2014), doi: 10.1080/1461670X.2014.922293.

37 Kristy Hess, "*Tertius* tactics: 'Mediated social capital' as a resource of power for traditional commercial news media," *Communication Theory* no. 23 (2013): 122; Georg Simmel, *Inquiries into the Construction of Social Forms*, translated by Anthony J. Blasi, Anton K. Jacobs, Mathew Kanjirathinkal (Leiden, The Netherlands: Brill, 2009).

38 Vian Bakir, *Sousveillance, Media and Strategic Political Communication: Iraq, USA, UK* (New York & London: Continuum, 2010).

39 Debashish Munshi, Priya Kurian, Rebecca Fraser, and Verica Rupar, "'Shadow publics' in the news coverage of socio-political issues," *Journalism* 15, no. 1 (2013): 89–108.

40 Aeron Davis, "Whither mass media and power? Evidence for a critical elite theory alternative," *Media, Culture & Society* 25 (2003): 672.

41 Robert E. Gutsche, Jr. and Erica Salkin, "Who lost what? An analysis of myth, loss, and proximity in news coverage of the Steubenville rape," *Journalism* (2015): 4, doi: 10.1177/1464884914566195; See also, Robert E. Gutsche, Jr. and Erica Salkin, "'It's better than blaming a dead young man': Creating mythical archetypes in local coverage of the Mississippi River drownings," *Journalism* 14, no. 1 (2013): 61–77.

42 Gutsche, Jr. and Salkin, "Who lost what?," 13.

Glossary of Key Terms

Banishment: An act that precludes particular social groups from participating in community spaces, social roles, and storytelling. (See Chapter 3)

Collective Forgetting: The act by media and public voices that shape dominant interpretations of current-day events and issues in ways that maintain power structures for future remembrance. (See Chapter 4)

Conspiracy Theory: A term applied to articulations of power that reveal actions of the power elite and that subjugate alternative explanations through language and rhetoric embedded in policy, dominant ideology, and "common sense." (See Chapter 4)

Control: The process by which individuals and collectives are forced to conform to the demands and expectations of the powerful through psychological, ideological, and physical means of violence. (See Chapter 5)

Cultural Text: A source/symbol; a cultural manifestation that can be "read" for meaning. (See Chapter 2)

Cultural Trauma: Challenges associated with the failure of dominant journalistic articulations of values and identities to adequately explain disruptions to mediatized messages and meanings. (See Chapter 4)

Digital Distraction: Normative rhetoric that "digital media" technologies and ideologies hold inherent power to evoke social change, while ignoring issues of control, power, and subjugation inherent in the very rhetoric of technological development. (See Conclusion)

Ideology: Explanations of and meanings assigned to everyday life that serve the powerful and are evidenced by socially acceptable and unquestioned data. (See Introduction)

Incorporation: The process of adopting alternative, subordinate ideologies into dominant ideology as a means of pacification and normalization. (See Conclusion)

Information: Expressed knowledge shaped by cultural and social forces. (See Chapter 1)

Inverse Surveillance: The observation of behavior and ideologies of self and of and within a collective. (See Chapter 6)

Journalistic Boosterism: Everyday news that promotes mediatized notions of a community's dominant traditions, dominant identities, and potential for future prosperities. (See Chapter 3)

Journalistic Interpretive Community: A collective that shares dominant ideologies of their shared identities, purposes, and explanations of the world. (See Chapter 2)

Media Control: The common practices of news construction, institutions, and representations that occur across media outlets and mediums as a means to justify and enforce elements of social control. (See Introduction)

Media Shaming: The act of informally punishing through public displays of disapproval, including humiliation and immense unexpected exposure by the press. (See Chapter 5)

Media Sousveillance: A form of inverse surveillance enacted by media upon themselves and partners within the power elite; performed to identify ideological disjuncture and to perform paradigm maintenance. (See Chapter 6)

Media Waiting: The process of fear-construction related to what "might happen" in a pending news event. (See Chapter 5)

Media Watching: The process by which the press "watch" in a traditional sense of surveilling with the intention of employing moral overtones to what is otherwise "objective coverage." (See Chapter 5)

Mythical News Narrative: Long-standing cross-cultural storylines and characterizations of people, places, and events told by news media to apply dominant explanations approved and maintained through power. (See Chapter 2)

Neoliberalism: An economic and political ideology that supports increased private investment and operations in public institutions and responsibilities. (See Chapter 4)

Normalization: The application of dominant "common sense" principles to incorporate alternative or controversial explanations of social conditions into the mainstream. (See Chapter 4)

News Place-making: The ideological process by which journalists demarcate and characterize geography. (See Chapter 3)

Police Myth: An ideology that police are awarded as a natural right to "serve" the public through methods deemed effective and necessary. (See Chapter 6)

Power: A fluid and inherent ability to influence individuals and social situations through force, ideology, and/or information. (See Introduction)

The Power Elite: A collective of individuals and institutions that control a society's economy, political order, and military with interests of maintaining order. (See Chapter 1)

Press Pacification: Acts of indoctrination and socialization to normative ideologies that are pressed upon or that occur within the journalistic interpretive community that result in diminished antagonism between the press and fellow power institutions. (See Conclusion)

Propaganda: A pejorative representation of information used as a means by which to marginalize and distract from realities counter to dominant ideology. (See Chapter 1)

Virtuous War: The technical capability and ethical imperative to threaten and, if necessary, actualize violence from a distance—with no or minimal casualties. (See Chapter 6)

White Supremacy: Ideology perpetrated throughout culture that places the needs and interests of white and light-skinned members of society above those of a darker skin. (See Chapter 3)

Whiteness: Ideology of racial superiority by people considered to be white, which appears pervasive in dominant US cultural distinctions of class, language, race, and social norms. (See Chapter 1)

Index

Note: locators followed by "n" indicate the notes section.

Lightning Source UK Ltd.
Milton Keynes UK
UKOW05f0123300317
297880UK00006B/52/P

9 781501 320132